STUDIES PRESENTED TO
JOSHUA WHATMOUGH

Joshua Whatmough

STUDIES PRESENTED TO

JOSHUA WHATMOUGH

ON HIS SIXTIETH BIRTHDAY

EDITED BY

ERNST PULGRAM

MOUTON & CO · 1957 · 'S-GRAVENHAGE

PRINTED IN THE NETHERLANDS BY MOUTON & CO - PRINTERS - THE HAGUE

EDITOR'S NOTE

The existence of this volume in honor of Joshua Whatmough speaks for itself. I shall not attempt to add here words of my own to all the congratulations and good wishes that come from the authors of the articles and from those whose names are contained in the TABULA GRATULATORIA.

But it is my task, and my pleasure, to express thanks to all those who have been willing to support the publication of this book; without their help it could not have appeared. Yet since they accepted on promise and trust my offer to do all the secretarial and editorial chores, they are in no way responsible for whatever faults the completed work may show; that burden is mine alone.

I wish to say in particular that all the financial support needed came wholly from the persons listed in the TABULA GRATULATORIA; no funds were sought from or donated by any public or private institution (with the exception of one college library).

There are numerous friends of Joshua Whatmough, I am sure, who would also have liked to take part in honoring him but whom my solicitation did not reach. To them I apologize for the insufficiency of my efforts.

I also apologize to those who may have wanted to contribute articles to this volume but whom I did not invite or whose papers could not be printed. And I regret that some others could not accept the invitation. It would have been possible to fill a book several times the size of the present one. Instead I chose a restricted number of such contributions by his colleagues and former students as would reflect Whatmough's fields of work and research. The variety of subjects treated, from comparative Proto-Indo-European linguistics to mathematical linguistics, random though it may seem at first sight, merely testifies to the breadth and depth of Joshua Whatmough's interest and influence.

E. P.

TABLE OF CONTENTS

TABULA GRATULATORIA

F. E. ADCOCK	University of California
ROBERT M. ALBRIGHT	North Dakota Agricultural College
DONALD J. ALDERSON	Stanford University
D. A. AMYX	University of California
SAM F. ANDERSON	University of Kansas
SAMUEL DECOSTER ATKINS	Princeton University
CHARLES J. N. BAILEY (Rev.)	Lexington, Ky.
ERMINNIE H. BARTELMEZ	Western Reserve University
EDWARD LEWIS BASSETT	University of Chicago
S. V. BAUM	Temple University
THELMA MACKAY BAXTER	Rochdale, Lancs., England
MADISON S. BEELER	University of California
HREINN BENEDIKTSSON	University of Kiel
JULES EUGENE BERNARD	U.S. Department of State
CHARLES E. BIDWELL	U.S. Department of State
BERNARD BLOCH	Yale University
HERBERT BLOCH	Harvard University
JAMES HORACE BOOTHE	Nepean High School, Ottawa
CARL HJ. BORGSTRÖM	University of Oslo
FREDERICK P. BROOKS, Jr.	Clinton Corners, N.Y.
PAUL WILLIAM BROSMAN	New Orleans, La.
ROGER WILLIAM BROWN	Harvard University
RICHARD T. BRUÈRE	University of Chicago
NELLE M. BRUMELLE	Potsdam State Teachers College
MARGARET M. BRYANT	Brooklyn College
FREDERICK H. BUCK	Quincy, Mass.

Virginia W. Callahan	Howard University
Margaret D. Carlson	Chicago, Ill.
John B. Carroll	Harvard University
Frederic Gomes Cassidy	University of Wisconsin
Mortimer H. Chambers	University of Chicago
Kun Chang	University of Washington
Yuen Ren Chao	University of California
John H. Cheek	Cambridge, Mass.
Francis W. Cleaves	Harvard University
D. T. Cole	University of Witwatersrand
Eugenio Coseriu	University of Montevideo
J. Milton Cowan	Cornell University
Warren Crawford Cowgill	Yale University
Ella Nancy Cowles	Michigan State University
Albert Debrunner	University of Bern
Arthur S. Dewing	Cambridge, Mass.
Helga Doblin	North Tonawanda, N.Y.
Albert Lee Donnell	Wright Junior College
Léon Émile Dostert	Georgetown University
James E. Dunlap	University of Michigan
Gerald Dykstra	Columbia University
Ernst A. Ebbinghaus	University of Marburg
Samuel Hoyt Elbert	University of Hawaii
C. Douglas Ellis (Rev.)	Fort Albany, Ont., Canada
Elizabeth C. Evans	Connecticut College
Robert E. Evans	Brandeis University
DeCoursey Fales	New York, N.Y.
Charles A. Ferguson	Harvard University
James Overton Ferrell	University of Michigan
Peter Fishman	New York, N.Y.
Robert Allen Fowkes	New York University
Murray Fowler	University of Wisconsin
Francine Frank	Urbana, Ill.
Henri Frei	University of Genève
Helena M. Gamer	University of Chicago
Robert J. Getty	University of Toronto
Arthur E. Gordon	University of California
James Gough, Jr.	Watertown, Mass.
Eugene van Tassel Graves	New York, N.Y.
William C. Greene	Harvard University

MONROE Z. HAFTER	Williams College
E. ADELAIDE HAHN	Hunter College
MORRIS HALLE	Massachusetts Institute of Technology
ERIC P. HAMP	University of Chicago
ELSIE HANCOCK	Coventry, England
ROY W. HANNA, JR.	Litchfield, Conn.
JULIAN E. HARRIS	University of Wisconsin
WILLIAM HARRIS	Middlebury College
EINAR HAUGEN	University of Wisconsin
RAYMOND J. HEBERT	Georgetown University
ROE-MERRILL SECRIST HEFFNER	University of Wisconsin
GUSTAV HERDAN	University of Bristol
GEORGE HERZOG	Indiana University
DONALD C. HILDUM	Cleveland, Ohio
ARCHIBALD A. HILL	University of Texas
JOHN MAURICE HOHLFELD	Hartford Seminary Foundation
FRED WALTER HOUSEHOLDER	Indiana University
KARL K. HULLEY	University of Colorado
HERBERT IZZO	University of Michigan
CARY F. JACOB	University of Virginia
WILLIAM H. JACOBSEN, JR.	San Diego, Cal.
WERNER JAEGER	Harvard University
ROMAN JAKOBSON	Harvard University
ASSAR JANZÉN	University of California
WALTER CHARLES JASKIEVICZ (Rev.)	Fordham University
LAWRENCE GAYLORD JONES	Harvard University
MORGAN E. JONES	University of Michigan
THEODORE T. JONES	University of Kentucky
HARRY HIRSCH JOSSELSON	Wayne University
FREDERICK HENRY JUNGEMANN	Queens College
HAYWARD KENISTON	University of Pennsylvania
GEORGE ALEXANDER KENNEDY	Harvard University
MARY LEE HUNNICUTT KENNEDY	Cambridge, Mass.
J. ALEXANDER KERNS	New York University
JEAN GRIFFITH KERNS	Bronxville, N.Y.
HERMAN EUGENE KESSLER	U.S. Army
LAWRENCE B. KIDDLE	University of Michigan
JOHN S. KIEFFER	St. Johns College
ROBERT J. KISPERT	Harvard University
HAROLD L. KLAGSTAD, JR.	Indiana University

CLYDE KLUCKHOHN	Harvard University
EDGAR COLBY KNOWLTON	University of Hawaii
SELMA S. KÖNIG	University of Wisconsin
FRANKLIN BRUNELL KRAUSS	Pennsylvania State University
SYDNEY MACDONALD LAMB	University of California
GEORGE SHERMAN LANE	University of North Carolina
HENRY DEXTER LEARNED	Temple University
WINFRED PHILIPP LEHMANN	University of Texas
SAMUEL R. LEVIN	Philadelphia Textile Institute
SAUL LEVIN	Washington University
IRVING LINN	Yeshiva University
GEORG LUCK	Harvard University
HORACE G. LUNT	Harvard University
WILLIAM FRANCIS MACKEY	Université Laval
YAKOV MALKIEL	University of California
KEMP MALONE	Johns Hopkins University
DONALD STANLEY MARSHALL	Peabody Museum of Salem, Mass.
ANDRÉ MARTINET	École des Hautes Études, Paris
JOAQUIM MATTOSO CÂMARA, Jr.	University of Rio de Janeiro
MANFRED MAYRHOFER	University of Würzburg
ERNEST N. MCCARUS	University of Michigan
A. P. MCKINLAY	University of California
WALLACE E. MCLEOD	Harvard University
GAIL K. MEADOWS	Stanford University
GORDON MYRON MESSING	U.S. Embassy, Athens
CHRISTINE MOHRMANN	University of Nijmegen
WILLIAM IVERSON MOORE	U.S. Navy
GUSTAV MUST	Baldwin-Wallace College
LEONARD D. NEWMARK	Ohio State University
DINH-HOA NGUYEN	Washington, D.C.
ARTHUR D. NOCK	Harvard University
ANTHONY G. OETTINGER	Harvard University
EARNEST R. ONEY	Arlington, Va.
LEONARD E. OPDYCKE	Rochester, N.Y.
LEONARD R. PALMER	Oxford University
WESLEY C. PANUNZIO	Boston, Mass.
ARISTOBULO PARDO V.	Escuela Normal Rural Interamericana, Rubio, Táchira, Venezuela
ARTHUR S. PEASE	Harvard University
HERBERT PENZL	University of Michigan

THEODORE C. PETERSEN (Rev.)	St. Paul's College
GORDON E. PETERSON	University of Michigan
ROBERT H. PFEIFFER	Harvard University
ROBERT L. POLITZER	University of Michigan
EDGAR G. POLOMÉ	Université du Congo Belge
JAMES WILSON POULTNEY	Johns Hopkins University
JAAN PUHVEL	Harvard University
ERNST PULGRAM	University of Michigan
WALBURGA VON RAFFLER	Morris Harvey College
FRITJOF ANDERSEN RAVEN	University of Alabama
G. REDARD	University of Bern
J. F. C. RICHARDS	Columbia University
ROBERT HENRY ROBINS	University of London
DAVID M. ROBINSON	University of Mississippi
KIFFIN AYRES ROCKWELL	University of Tennessee
FRANCIS M. ROGERS	Harvard University
KARL M. D. ROSEN	Brighton, Mass.
THOMAS G. ROSENMEYER	University of Washington
DOROTHY ROUNDS	Cambridge, Mass.
ANTHONY SALYS	University of Pennsylvania
JESSE OTTO SAWYER	Oakland, Cal.
LAURISTON L. SCAIFE (Rt. Rev.)	Buffalo, N.Y.
PHILIP SCHERER	Brooklyn, N.Y.
EDWARD HENRY SEHRT	George Washington University
JUDITH SENIOR	Los Angeles, Cal.
G. P. SHIPP	University of Sydney
ADELAIDE D. SIMPSON	Hunter College
HILDA M. SIMPSON	Rochdale, Lancs., England
H. R. W. SMITH	University of California
FRIEDRICH H. R. SOLMSEN	Cornell University
ALF SOMMERFELT	University of Oslo
GEORGE PETER SPRINGER	New Haven, Conn.
ZEPH STEWART	Harvard University
ARTHUR F. STOCKER	University of Virginia
ARTHUR N. STOWE	Cambridge, Mass.
FRANCIS C. ST. JOHN	Harvard University
ST. VINCENT COLLEGE	
WALDO E. SWEET	University of Michigan
DOUGLAS MCR. TAYLOR	Magua, Dominica, British West Indies
PAUL TEDESCO	Yale University

Paul Thieme	Yale University
Graves H. Thompson	Hampden-Sydney College
Gaylord Herbert Todd	University of Michigan
Albert H. Travis	University of California,
W. Freeman Twaddell	Brown University
B. L. Ullman	University of North Carolina
Francis Lee Utley	Ohio State University
Jean-Paul Vinay	Université de Montréal
George B. Waldrop	Pittsburgh, Pa.
Edward G. Wasiniak	U.S. Air Force
Calvert Ward Watkins	Harvard University
Allen Leaming Weatherby	Drew University
T. B. L. Webster	University College, London
Ruth Hirsch Weir	Stanford University
B. J. Whiting	Harvard University
Cedric H. Whitman	Harvard University
Claude Merton Wise	Louisiana State University
Leonard Woodbury	University College, Toronto
Eric C. Woodcock	University of Durham
Isabella Yi-Yün Yen	University of Southern California
Arthur M. Young	University of Pittsburgh
Rudolf Zrimc	Hawaii Episcopal Academy

TABLE OF ABBREVIATIONS

JOURNALS

AAA	Annals for Archaeology and Anthropology
AfO	Archiv für Orientforschung
AGI	Archivio glottologico italiano
AHR	American Historical Review
AJPh	American Journal of Philology
ALMA	Archivium Latinitatis Medii Aevi
Arch Or	Archiv Orientalní
BSL	Bulletin de la Société de Linguistique de Paris
BSOS	Bulletin of the School of Oriental Studies
BzN	Beiträge zur Namenforschung
Bi Or	Bibliotheca Orientalis
CJ	Classical Journal
CP	Classical Philology
CQ	Classical Quarterly
CR	Classical Review
CW	Classical Weekly
DLZ	Deutsche Literatur-Zeitung
HSCP	Harvard Studies in Classical Philology
HTR	Harvard Theological Review
IF	Indogermanische Forschungen
JAOS	Journal of the American Oriental Society
JASA	Journal of the Acoustical Society of America
JCS	Journal of Cuneiform Studies
JEA	Journal of Egyptian Archaeology
JKF	Jahrbuch für kleinasiatische Forschungen
JKS	Journal of Keltic Studies
JRAI	Journal of the Royal Anthropological Institute
JRS	Journal of Roman Studies
Jb cl Ph	Jahrbuch für classische Philologie
KF	Kleinasiatische Forschungen
KZ	Kuhns Zeitschrift, Zeitschrift für vergleichende Sprachforschung
LN	Lingua Nostra
MDOG	Mitteilungen der Deutschen Orient-Gesellschaft
MLJ	Modern Language Journal
MSL	Mémoirs de la Société de Linguistique de Paris
Mod Phil	Modern Philology
NTS	Norsk Tidsskrift for Sprogvidenskap
OLZ	Orientalistische Literatur-Zeitung
PAPA	Proceedings of the American Philological Association
PBA	Proceedings of the British Association
PBB	Pauls und Braunes Beiträge, Beiträge zur Geschichte der deutschen Sprache und Literatur
PP	La parola del passato
Phil Quart	Philological Quarterly
RBPhH	Revue belge de philologie et d'histoire
REI	Revue des études indo-européennes
RHA	Revue hittite et asianique
RHR	Revue d'histoire des religions
RLiR	Revue de linguistique romane
RhM	Rheinisches Museum
Rev celt	Revue celtique
Rev ét anc	Revue des études anciennes
Rev ét lat	Revue des études latines
Rev phil	Revue de philologie

Rom Jb	Romanistisches Jahrbuch
Rom Phil	Romance Philology
St Etr	Studi Etruschi
St Rom	Studi Romanzi
TAPA	Transactions of the American Philological Association
TCLP	Travaux du Cercle linguistique de Prague
TPS	Transactions of the Philological Society
UCNW	University College of North Wales Magazine
WZKM	Wiener Zeitschrift für die Kunde des Morgenlandes
ZA	Zeitschrift für Assyriologie
ZES	Zeitschrift für Eingeborenen Sprachen
ZfcPh	Zeitschrift für celtische Philologie
ZfdA	Zeitschrift für deutsche Altertumsforschung
ZONF	Zeitschrift für Ortsnamenforschung
ZRPh	Zeitschrift für romanische Philologie

OTHERS

DEG	Emile Boisacq, *Dictionnaire étymologique de la langue grecque* (Heidelberg 1950).
DEL	A. Ernout — A. Meillet, *Dictionnaire étymologique de la langue latine*[3] (Paris 1951).
GEW	H. Frisk, *Griechisches etymologisches Wörterbuch* (Heidelberg 1954 ff.).
IEW	Julius Pokorny, *Indogermanisches etymologisches Wörterbuch* (Bern 1948 ff.).
KVG	Karl Brugmann, *Kurze vergleichende Grammatik der indogermanischen Sprachen* (Strassburg 1904)
LEW	A. Walde — J. B. Hofmann, *Lateinisches etymologisches Wörterbuch* (Heidelberg 1930-1956)
PID	R. S. Conway — E. Johnson — J. Whatmough, *The Prae-Italic Dialects of Italy* (Cambridge 1933)
REW	Wilhelm Meyer-Lübke, *Romanisches etymologisches Wörterbuch*[3] (Heidelberg 1935)
TLL	*Thesaurus Linguae Latinae*
Ve	Emil Vetter, *Handbuch der italischen Dialekte*, I (Heidelberg 1953)
WP	A. Walde — J. Pokorny, *Vergleichendes Wörterbuch der indogermanischen Sprachen* (Berlin — Leipzig 1927-32)

PUBLISHED WORKS OF JOSHUA WHATMOUGH

1916

1	On the Blackstone Edge Roman road	Rochdale (England) Observer, 13 Sept

1917

2	On the Blackstone Edge Roman road	Rochdale Observer, 23 June
3	Rev. of Walters and Conway, *Deigma*	The Serpent, March

1918

4	The Roman tradition	Rochdale Observer, 27 July
5	On the Blackstone Edge Roman road	Rochdale Observer, 24 Aug

1919

6	Rev. of Conway, *New Studies*	JRS 9.229–230

1920

7	*Key to exercises in Deigma*	115 pp. (John Murray: London)
8	Spicifera Virgo	CR 34.33–34
9	The people of ancient Rome	Discovery 1.340–346
10	The Antigone at Manchester	Rochdale Observer, 11 Dec
11	Herodotus in Bangor	UCNW Magazine

1921

12	Fordus and Fordicidia	CQ 15.108–109
13	On CIL 1.1538 (= 6.335)	CR 35.65–66
14	Rehtia, the Venetic goddess of healing	PBA, 442 and 466
15	On the Blackstone Edge Roman road	Rochdale Observer, 16 July

1922

16	Rehtia, the Venetic goddess of healing	JRAI 52.212–229
17	Rehtia, the Venetic goddess of healing	Nature 109.154
18	The Iouilae dedications	CQ 16.181–189
19	A new epithet of Juno	CQ 16.190
20	Le nominatif pluriel gaulois des thèmes en -o	Rev Celt 39.348–352
21	Plautus Curculio 192	CR 36.166
22	Version: To a Sycamore	UCNW Magazine
23	Raetic dialect	PBA, 386 and 409

1923

24	Inscriptions of Magrè and the Raetic dialect	CQ 18.61–72
25	Inscribed fragments of stagshorn from N. Italy	JRS 11.245–253
26	The Clermont-Ferrand MS of Lib. Gloss.	AJPh 44.158–161
27	The Vercelli MS of Lib. Gloss.	AJPh 44.161–163
28	A stray Welsh gloss?	Bull. Board Kelt. Stud. 1.309
29	Note to Festus p. 24.10 L	CQ 17.202–203
30	Vitulatio	CP 18.350–351
31	Rev. of della Seta, *Italia antica*	JRS 11.280–282

1924

32	The Rochdale Vellum Fragment (on Veritas)	Journ. Theol. Stud. 25.404–405
33	A Raetic fibula	CQ 18.168
34	Rev. of Orlando, *Spigolature glottologiche*	CR 38.88
35	— Cocchia, *Saggi glottologici*	CR 38.137–138

1925

36	Notes on Saliar Hymn; and other notes	A.B. Cook, *Zeuss* ii (see Index, Wh., J.)
37	The alphabet of Vaste	CQ 19.68–70
38	Etymology of *sororiare*	Mnemosyne 53.9
39	The Ligurians	PBA, 342 and 391

1926

40 *Liber Glossarum*, in collaboration with W. M. Lindsay and others — 604 pp. (Soc. an. Les belles lettres: Paris; for the Brit. Acad.)
41 Private life under the early empire — Al Qadim, 143–145 (Cairo)
42 New Messapic inscriptions — Proc. Camb. Philol. Soc. 130–132. 1–4
43 Latin *larix* — IF 44.153–154
44 Scholia Vallicelliana — ALMA 2.57–75, 134–169 (and separately)
45 Rev. of Cocchia, *Letteratura latina* — CR 40.35–36

1927

46 The phonology of Messapic — Language 3.226–231
47 The phonology of Messapic — PAPA 57. xxxiv
48 Oscan *deketasio-* — Language 3.105–108
49 Latin *hinnuleus* — CR 41.174–175
50 Rev. of Kent, *Textual criticism* — JRS 16.275
51 — Baudiš, *Gram. of Early Welsh* — Language 3.139–141

1928

52 The Lepontic inscriptions and the Ligurian dialect — HSCP 38.1–20
53 Latin *hinnuleus* again — CR 42.127
54 Rev. of Childe, *The Aryans* — Language 4.130–135

1929

55 A new fragment of Dorian farce — HSCP 39.1–6
56–58 Articles on Latin language, Oscan, Sabellic — Enc. Brit., ed. 14, 13.743–746, 16.947–948, 19.789–790, resp.
59 Rev. of Krahe, *Altillyr. Personennamen* — AJPh 50.205–208
60 — Jacobsohn, *Altital. Inschriften* — JRS 17.248

1931

61 The *Osi* of Tacitus — HSCP 42.139–155
62 The calendar in ancient Italy — HSCP 42.156–179
63 Rev. of Goldmann, *Beiträge* — Language 7.54–56

1933

64 The Raeti and their language — Glotta 22.27–31
65 Quemadmodum Pollio reprehendit in Liuio Patauinitatem — HSCP 44.95–130

66	New Keltic inscriptions of Gaul	HSCP 44.227–231
67	Rev. of Edmar, *Stud. Epp. ad Caes. Senem*	Language 9.218–220
68	— Lindholm, *Stilist. Stud.*	Language 9.218–220
69	— Lilliedahl, *Frage 'innerer' Wert d. Klauseln*	Language 9.323

1934

70	*The Prae-Italic dialects of Italy*, vols. II, III	xxxiii + 632 pp., viii + 163 pp. (Harvard University Press: Cambridge)
71	New Venetic inscriptions	CP 29.281–292
72	Editor	HSCP 43, 44, 45 (1932–1934)
73	Rev. of Buck, *Comp. Gram. Greek and Latin*	CP 29.261–263
74	— Kent, *Sounds of Latin*	CP 29.264–265

1935

75	Reply to Fraser	CR 49.45
76	Editor	Proc. and Trans. Am. Acad. of Arts and Sciences (1935–1936)
77	Rev. of Löfstedt, *Syntactica*	CP 30.276–278

1936

78	New Messapic inscriptions	CP 31.193–204
79	A new Raetic inscription	HSCP 47.205–208
80	Indo-European labiovelars	Rés. Communic., 4th Int. Cong. of Linguists 116–117
81	M. Parry (obituary)	Language 12.151
82	R. S. Conway (obituary)	Proc. Am. Acad. 70.514–515
83	Report, 4th Int. Cong. of Linguists (with W. F. Twaddell)	Language 12.310–311
84	Rev. of Purdie, *Latin verse inscc.*	AJPh 57.487–489
85	— Marouzeau, *Traité de stylistique*	AJPh 57.207–210
86	— Moore, *Comp. syntax*	CP 31.364–367

1937

87	*The foundations of Roman Italy*	xx + 420 pp. (Methuen: London)
88	Indo-European labiovelars	Pedersen Festschrift 45–56
89	Id genus	CP 32.267–268
90	Tusca origo Raetis	HSCP 48.181–202

91 Rev. of Liddell and Scott, *Lexicon*, pt. 8	CP 32.168–170
92 — Pasquali, *Preistoria, poesia romana*	AJPh 58.483–488
93 — Rosenzweig, *Iguuium*	CR 51.193–194
94 — Bottiglioni, *Atlante Corsica*	Language 13.319–321

1938

95 Indo-European labiovelars	Actes, 4th Int. Cong. of Ling., 267
96 Eine neue raetische Inschrift der Sondrio Gruppe	Anzeig. f. Schweizer. Altertumskunde 40. 121–123
97 Rev. of Rosenzweig, *Iguuium*	AJPh 59.250–253
98 — Liddell and Scott, *Lexicon*, pt. 9	CP 33.233–236
99 — Löfstedt, *Verm. Stud.*	CP 33.322–324
100 — Hofmann, *Lat. Umgangssprache*	CP 33.320–322
101 — Svennung, *Kl. Beitr. z. lat. Lautlehre*	CP 33.429–430
102 — Svennung, *Palladius*	CP 33.109–112

1939

103 A new Umbrian inscription	HSCP 50.89–93
104–106 (Various items)	Réponses au Quest., 5th Int. Cong. of Linguists 9, 48, 88–89
107 The neutral basis of language and the problem of the 'root'	Rés. Communic., 5th Int. Cong. of Ling. 52
108 Robert Seymour Conway	Biographisches Jahrbuch (Bursian) 266. 21–40
109 Rev. of Blomgren, *De serm. Am. Marc.*	CP 34.74–75
110 — Friedmann, *Ion. und att. Wörter im Altlatein.*	CW 32.172–173
111 — Altheim, *History of Roman religion*	CP 34.255–266
112 — Elg, *In Faustum Reiensem studia*	CP 34.398–399
113 — Kent, *Varro de L. L.* I	CP 34.379–383

1940

114 A note on Raetic	CP 35.188–190
115 An inscribed situla at Providence	Bull. Museum of Art, Rhode Island School of Design, 28.1.32–33

116	Co-editor (with Arntz)	Berichte zur Runenforschung 1
117	Rev. of Olzscha, *Agramer Mumienbinde*	AHR 45.447
118	— Kent, *Varro de L.L.* II	CP 35.82–86
119	— Zmigryder Konopka, *Guerrier de Capestrano*	AJPh 61.245–246
120	— *LEW*, pt. 11	CP 35.95–97
121	— Kent, *Varro de L.L.* II	CJ 35.368–369
122	— Erikson, *Sancti Epiphanii interpretatio*	CP 35.318–321
123	— Erikson, *Sprachliche Bemerkungen*	CP 35.318–321
124	— Schrijnen, *Collectanea*	CP 35.343–344
125	— Merkx, *Syntax Kasus und Tempora in Hl. Cyprian*	CP 35.442–443

1941

126	The neural basis of language and the problem of the root	HSCP 52.125–137
127	Editor	HSCP 52–59 (1941–1948)
128	Rev. of Siegert, *Syntax Tempora und Modi d. ältesten lat. Inschriften*	CP 36.95–96
129	— Devoto, *Storia della lingua di Roma*	AJPh 62.387–388
130	— Lejeune, *Observations sur les actes d'affranchissement delphiques*	CP 36.311–312
131	— Olzscha, *Agramer Mumienbinde*	AJPh 62.505–507
132	— Sturtevant, *Pronunc. of Gk. and Lat.*[2]	CP 36.409–411
133	— Björck, *Periphrast. Konstr.*	CP 36.416–417

1942

134	Quid expediuit psittaco? or The soul of grammar	Bull. New. Eng. Class. Assn., 1942 meeting (summary pp. 13–14)
135	Two Etruscan inscriptions (at S. Hadley)	CP 37.431
136	(Class. Assn. of New Eng., 1942 meeting, S. Hadley, Mass.)	CW 35, opp. p. 159

137	Rev. of Liddell and Scott, *Lexicon*, pt. 10	CP 37.96–98
138	— Norden, *Aus altrömischen Priesterbüchern*	AJPh 63.225–230
139	— Warmington, *Remains of Old Latin*	CP 37.337–339

1943

140	A last word on *patauinitas*	CP 38.205
141	Quid expediuit psittaco? or The soul of grammar	CJ 39.105–113 (cf. 37.441)
142	'Root' and base in Indo-European	HSCP 54.1–23
143	"*Hoti's* business: let it be."	39th Annual Bull., Class. Assn. of New Eng. 10–11
144	Rev. of Wistrand, *Instrumentalis als Kasus der Anschauung im Lat.*	CP 38.66–67
145	— Bloch and Trager, *Outline of linguistic analysis*	CP 38.210–211

1944

146	Κελτικά	HSCP 55.1–85
147	Up from Gilgal	CP 39.218–222
148	Note on ὀργεῶνες	HTR 37.83, 132
149	Rev. of Henry, *The late Greek optative*	CP 39.200–201

1945

150	On 'speaking with tongues'	CW 38.123–125
151	In reply to Sturtevant	MLJ 29.163–164
152	Report of the Sub-Committee on Languages and International Affairs	Harvard Faculty, 12 Nov

1946

153	Information given	CW 40.67–68
154	Emendations in Servius	apud Rand, The Harvard Servius II, pp. 10, 170, 211, 271, 295, 299, 360, 495
155	Rev. of Powers, *Commercial vocab. of early Latin*	CP 41.125–126
156	— Norberg, *Beitr. z. spätlat. Syntax*	CP 41.238–239

157	— Hendriksen, *Untersuch. über d. Bedeutung d. Heth. für d. Laryngaltheorie*	CP 41.248
158	— Grenier, *Les Gaulois*	AJA 50.323–324

1947

159	Editor	CP 40–42 (1945–1947)
160	Rev. of Bonfante, *Los elementos populares en la lengua de Horacio*	CP 42.67–68
161	— Strömberg, *Fischnamen*	CP 42.134
162	— Strömberg, *Wortstudien*	CP 42.134
163	— Chantraine, *Morphologie*	CP 42.134
164	— *Löfstedt Festschrift*	CP 42.203–204

1948

165	Grammatica quaedam	Phoenix 2(3).65–72
166	ΩΣΠΕΡ ΟΜΗΡΟΣ ΦΗΣΙ	AJA 52.45–50
167	Italic religion	Oxf. Class. Dict., s.v.
168	Iguvine Tables	Oxf. Class. Dict., s.v.
169–171	Rapports	Actes, 6th Int. Cong. of Linguists 25, 44, 89
172	Rev. of Jensen, *Det latinske perfekt system*	CP 43.140–141
173	— Marmorale, *Cena Trimalchionis*	CP 43.204–205
174	— Svennung, *Compositiones Lucenses*	AJPh 69.453–354
175	— Handford, *Latin subjunctive*	CP 43.270–271
176	— Kent, *Forms of Latin*	CP 43.275–276
177	— Bloch, *Origines de Rome*	CP 43.278–279
178	— Meyer, *Die Indogermanenfrage*	German Books 1.5 (Dec.), Chicago, 294–295
179	— Ernout, *Philologica*	CP 43.208–210

1949

180	The Lower Rhine – language and archaeology	Archaeology 2.91–94
181	On gerund grinding	CW 43.19–22
182	CVR, QVOR, QVR	CP 44.253
183	Πάρεργα	Die Sprache 1.123–129 (Havers Festschrift)

184 Gentes uariae linguis	Word 5.106–115
185 auot, ieurus, tuθθus	JKS 1.7–10
186 Gaulish *Vimpi*	Language 25.388–391
187–192 (Various items)	Actes, 6th Int. Cong. of Linguists, 89, 214, 260, 301, 347, 375 [25, 44, 421, 497, 602]
193 Rev. of Bolling, *Iliad*	CW 42.158–159
194 — Wagenvoort, *Roman dynamism*	CP 44.42–46
195 — Lejeune, *Traité de phonétique grecque*	CP 44.59–60
196 — Dressler, *Usage of ἀσκέω*	CP 44.60–62
197 — Koppers, *Indogermanen- u. Germanenfrage*	Language 25.195–196
198 — Wistrand, *Nach innen oder nach aussen?*	CP 44.138–139
199 — Saint-Denis, *Vocab. des animaux marins en latin classique*	CP 44.209–211
200 — Thompson, *Glossary of Greek fishes*	CP 44.209–211
201 — Keller, *Iste deiktikon*	CP 44.214
202 — Brandenstein (ed.), *Frühgeschichte und Sprachwissenschaft*	Language 25.283–285
203 — *IEW*, pts. 1, 2	Language 25.285–290
204 — Fournier, *Verbes 'dire' en grec ancien*	CP 44.271–272
205 — Wilson, *Miraculous birth of language*	CP 44.272–273
206 — Marmorale, *Questione petroniana*	CP 44.273–274

1950

207 *Dialects of ancient Gaul*	
1: Alpine regions 2: Narbonensis	238 pp. (University Microfilms: Ann Arbor, Michigan) See Microfilm Abstracts 10.1, 1950, 141–142, no. 1571
3: Aquitania	pp. 238–480. See Microfilm Abstracts 10.2, 1950, 175–176, no. 1733
4: Lugdunensis	pp. 481–661. See Microfilm Abstracts 10.3, 1950, 265–266, no. 1911
5: Belgica 6: Germania Inferior	pp. 662–843 and 844–984. See Microfilm Abstracts 11.1, 1951, 207–208, no. 2319

	7: Germania Superior 8: Agri Decumates with the Upper Rhine and Danube 9: Appendices	pp. 985–1153, 1154–1317, and 1318–1376. See Microfilm Abstracts 11.3, 1951, 797–798, no. 2495
208	Etruria	Chamber's Encyclopedia, s.v.
209	On improving the Shining Hour	CJ 45.355–359
210	Associate Editor	Word 3–6 (1947–1950)
211	Rev. of Waszink, *Tertulliani de Anima*	CP 45.61–62
212	— *Mana*	CP 45.62–63
213	— Hammerich, *Laryngeal before sonant*	CP 45.67–68
214	— Gries, *Constancy in Livy's Latinity*	CP 45.125–126
215	— Gallavotti, *Lingua degli poeti eolici*	CP 45.138
216	— Adrados, *Sistema gentilicio decimal de los Indoeuropeos*	AJPh 71.219–220
217	— Albenque, *Études d'histoire, d'archéologie et de toponymie gauloises*	AJA 54.155–156
218	— Hubschmid, *Praeromanica*	Language 26.298–299
219	— *IEW*. pt. 3	Language 26.299–302
220	— Beeler, *Venetic language*	Language 26.302–304
221	— *LEW*, pts. 12, 13, 14	CP 45.201–202
222	— *Lexis* 1	CP 45.252–253

1951

223	On an inscription of Nimes	KZ 69.207–208
224	Alpes populique inalpini	HSCP 60.175–185
225	Selective variation	Newsweek, 30 July, p. 62
226	Religio grammatici	Presidential Address, Linguistic Soc. of America, 29 Dec 51, New York
227	On 'rules' in grammar	CJ 47.42
228	Indo-European and Semitic	Wisconsin Centennial
229	Rev. of Buck, *Synonyms in IE languages*	CP 46.42–45
230	— Magnien, *Gram. comparée*	CW 44.223
231	— *Beiträge zur Namenforschung*	Word 6.239–242
232	— *IEW*, pt. 4	Language 27.80–81
233	— Sherlock, *Syntax in St. Hilary*	CP 46.127–129

234	— Lejeune (trl. by March), *Posición del latín*	Language 27.81–82
235	— *DEL*, A-L	CP 46.196–197
236	— Krahe, *Venetisch*	Language 27.375–376
237	— *LEW*, pt. 15	CP 46.247–248
238	— Bolling, *Ilias Atheniensium*	CW 45.41–42
239	— *IEW*, pt. 5	Language 27.570–571
240	— Tovar, *Prim. lenguas hispanicas*	Language 27.571–575

1952

241	'Triballic' in Aristophanes	CP 47.26
242	Selective variation	Scientific American, April, 82–86
243	Selective variation	Scientific American, June, 4–5
244	On teaching languages	N Y Times, 3 April, p. 34
245–248	(Various items)	Prelim. Rep., 7th Int. Cong. of Linguists, 136–141, 16–17, 26, 145
249	On an underestimated feature of language	Norwood Essays 248–254
250	Hi omnes lingua inter se differunt	Orbis 1.428–441
251	Rev. of Odelstierna, *Inuidia*	CW 45.188
252	— Schwyzer, *Griech. Gram.*	CP 47.41–43
253	— Nencioni, *Anatolia*	CW 45.261
254	— Herbig, *Etr.* fler	AJA 56.99
255	— *LEW*, pt. 16	CP 47.110–112
256	— Ernout, *Adjectifs en* -osus *et* -ulentus	CP 47.126–127
257	— Redard, *Noms grecs en* -της	CP 47.127–128
258	— *IEW*, pt. 6	Language 28.265–267
259	— Hubschmid, *Alpenwörter*	Language 28.268–269
260	— Penti, *Gerundiuum*	CP 47.182–183
261	— Laroche, *Racine* -nem	CP 47.183–184
262	— Labey, *Particules grecques*	CP 47.185
263	— *Beiträge zur Namenforschung*	Word 8.169–170
264	— Krahe, *Sprachverwandtschaft*	Word 8.170–171
265	— Bertoldi, *Colonizzazioni*	Language 28.525–526

1953

266	A. E. Housman	Word Study 28.4.1–4
267	New ideas on how language began	Amer. Mercury, June, 120–124
268	Report on 7th Int. Cong. of Linguists	Language 29.105

269	Some lexical variants in the dialects of ancient Gaul	Robinson Essays II.477–482
270	Epigraphica	Language 29.297–301
271	Joseph Wright	Word Study 29.1.1–4
272	Genius Cucullatus	Ogam 5.4.65–66
273	Rev. of Ernout and Thomas, *Syntaxe latine*	CP 48.51–52
274	— Hakamies, *Diminutive Latin*	CP 48.66–67
275	— Sturtevant, *Hittite Gram.* I	CP 48.122–123
276	— Robins, *Gram. theory*	CP 48.123–124
277	— Ullmann, *Words and their uses*	CP 48.124–125
278	— *DEL*, M–Z	CP 48.125–127
279	— Löfstedt, *Coniectanea*	CP 48.127
280	— Diringer, *The alphabet*	CP 48.128–129
281	— Whatmough, *Dialects of ancient Gaul*	ZfcPh 24.154–156
282	— Delebecque, *Le cheval*	Language 29.189–190
283	— Devoto, *Antichi Italici*[2]	Language 29.190–192
284	— Pisani, *Lingue d'Italia*	Language 29.192–193
285	— Snell, *Aufbau der Sprache*	AJPh 74.329–331
286	— *LEW*, pts. 17,18	CP 48.254–255
287	— Gelb, *Study of writing*	CP 48.252–254
288	— *LEW*, pt. 19	CP 48.202
289	— Onions, *Origins*	CP 48.256–258
290	— *IEW*, pt. 7	Language 29.481–483

1954

291	Interlingual communication	N Y Times, Sunday 28 Feb
292	On modern linguistics	Confluence 3.2.240–242
293	Peter Giles	Word Study 30.1–3
294	One use of language: literature	New World Writing, no. 6, October, 288–302
295	Statistics and semantics	Debrunner Festschrift 441–446
296–321	A, B, C ... X, Y, Z (Twenty-six articles on the letters of the alphabet)	Encyclopedia Americana, 1951–55
322	Editor, *Bibliographie critique de la statistique linguistique*	xii + 152 pp. (Utrecht and Bruxelles)
323	Rev's of Hatcher, Gode, Newmark	CP 49.63
324	Rev. of Johannesson, *Gesture origin of language*	CP 49.63–64

325	— Banta, *Abweichende Perfektbildungen*	CP 49.64–65
326	— Georgakas, *Griech, Gram.* III: Register	CP 49.70–71
327	— Mette, *Krates of Pergamum*	CW 47.87–88
328	— Vetter, *Hdb. ital. Dial.*	Language 30.108–110
329	— Jakobson, Fant, and Halle, *Prelim. to speech analysis*	CP 49.136–137
330	— Vetter, *Hdb. ital. Dial.*	CP 49.138
331	— Hahn, Subjunctive and optative	CW 47.155
332	— Aalto, *Infinitiv*	Language 30.282
333	— Frei, *Deux mille phrases*	Language 30.282–283
334	— Gonda, *ōjas*	CP 49.204–205
335	— *LEW*, pt. 20	CP 49.206–207
336	— Erkell, *Augustus*	CP 49.207–209
337	— Brogan, *Roman Gaul*	CP 49.209–210
338	— Chantraine, *Gram. homérique*	CP 49.210–212
339	— Enk, *Truculentus*	Erasmus 7.546–550
340	— Entwistle, *Aspects of language*	Mod. Phil. 52.57–58
341	— Bardon, *Lit. lat. inconnue*	Erasmus 7.229–233
342	— *IEW*, pt. 8	Language 30.399–401
343	— Gonda, *one/two*	CP 49.205–206

1955

344	Letter to the Editor	America, 29 Jan., p. 464
345	Letter to Harvard Crimson	Harvard Crimson, 17 May
346	R. S. Conway	Word Study 31.1–5
347	Gaulish *f*?	Zeuss Memorial Volume 249–255
348	Interview on Interlingua	Harvard Crimson, 3 Dec
349	Symbols and society	14th Conf. Sci., Phil., and Religion, pp. 69–70, 227–228, 425–426
350	Rev. of Debrunner, *Geschichte der griech. Sprache*	CP 50.65–66
351	— Flew, ed., *Logic and language*	CP 50.67–70
352	— Gode, *Interlingua*	CP 50.70
353	— Amman, -IKOS	CW 48.53–54
354	— Aalto, *Infinitiv*	CP 50.151
355	— Redard, χρή	CP 50.148–149
356	— Humbert, *Syntaxe grecque*	CP 50.150–151

357 — Ernout, *Vocabulaire latin*	CP 50.192
358 — Bottiglioni, *Manuale dialetti italici*	CP 50.149–150
359 – Pallottino, *Testimonia linguae etruscae*	CP 50.148
360 – Ronnet, *Demosthenes*	Erasmus 8.298–299
361 — *GEW*, pt. 1	CP 50.282–283
362 — *LEW*, pt. 21	CP 50.284
363 — van Windekens, *Onomastique pélasgique*	CP 50.284–285
364 — Palmer, *Latin language*	CP 50.293–294

1956

365 *Language*	x + 270 pp. (London and New York)
365a (Translation of above into Japanese by Toshio Hirunuma)	(Tokyo, 1957)
366 *Poetic, scientific, and other forms of discourse*	x + 285 pp. (Univ. of California Press)
367 Lugdunum and Lugdunensis	Ogam 7.353–356
368 Quadrimester	N Y Times, 27 Sept
369 How many this? How many that?	Word Study 32.1–5
370 Homeric ἐπὶ ἦρα φέρειν	For Roman Jakobson 668–669
371–418 Articles on African languages, Alphabet, Australian languages, Balts, Baltic languages, Basic English, Boustrophedon, Brahui language, Caucasian languages, R.S. Conway, Dialect, Etruscan, Peter Giles, Gloss and Glossary, Grammar, Greek (ancient), Gustav Herbig, Hottentots: language, A. E. Housman, Indo-Europeans, Italic dialects, Kanarese, Karen, R. G. Kent, Kharosthi and Brahui, Language, Latin language, Letter, Linguistics, Max Müller, Onomatopoeia, Oscan, Palaeo-Asiatic languages, Punctuation, Rasmus Rask, Vilhelm Thomsen, Runes, Sabellic, Semantics and Significs,	Encyclopaedia Britannica, 1956 revision, s.vv.

No.	Title	Publication
	Herbert Weir Smyth, Translation, Transliteration, Umbrian, Universal language, Volapük, Benjamin Ide Wheeler, Joseph Wright	
419–428	(Various items)	Actes, 7th Int. Cong. of Linguists li, lxii–lxiv, 16–17, 26, 137–141, 145, 201–202, 211–212, 463, 485.
429	Italic (for 'Dictionary of Languages')	Orbis 4.323–348
430	Adviser on Linguistics to Encycl. Brit.	
431–436	Six Radio Talks 'About the way you talk' 1. What do *you* think talking is? 2. What *I* think talking is. 3. The puzzle of meaning. 4. Meaning is our destination. 5. The vulgar mob. 6. Language and life.	Lowell Institute FM Broadcast, January–February 1956
437	On 'Language'	Times Literary Supplement, 23 November 1956, p. 697
438	Rev. of Cles-Reden, *The buried people*	Lowell Institute (Television)
439	— Bloch, *Les Étrusques*	CP 51.49
440	— *IEW*, pt. 9	Language 31.554–556
441	— Georgiev, *Kreto-Mycenean inscriptions*	CP 51.130–131
442	— Collart, *Varron*	CP 51.131–132
443	— Thesleff, *Intensification in early and classical Greek*	CP 51.132–133
444	— Hubschmid, *Sardische Studien*	Rom. Phil. 9.350–353
445	— Hubschmid, *Alpenwörter*	Rom. Phil. 9.398
446	— Buck, *Greek dialects*	CP 51.209–211
447	— Niedermann, *Recueil*	CP 51.211–212
448	— Moulinier, *Le pur et l'impur dans la pensée des Grecs*	Erasmus 8.617–619
449	— Debrunner, *Gesch. d. griech. Sprache* II	CP 51.266–267
450	— Vossler, ed. Schmeck, *Vulgärlatein*	CP 51.267–268
451	— *GEW*, pt. 2	CP 51.268–271
452	— Schlisman, *Mensch und Wort*	Word 12.293-298
453	— *IEW*, pt. 10	Language 32.716–718

454	— Carnoy, *Lyciens, Étrusques et Indo-Européens*	Language 32.718–719
455	— Dörries, *Das Selbstzeugnis Kaiser Konstantins*	Erasmus 9.500–502
456	Note on Heiermeier, *Indogermanische Etymologien des Keltischen*	Language 32.244
457	Language the measure of man	Institute Lecture (in press) Lowell

1957

458–464	Articles on Article, Aryans, Coptic, Hamatic, Karl K. F. Lachmann, Philology, Michael Ventris	Encyclopaedia Brittannica, 1957 revision, s.vv.
465	Report on Mathematical Linguistics	8th Int. Cong. of Linguists (in press)
466	Rev. of *GEW*, pt. 3	CP 52.118–119
467	— Gonda, *Indo-European moods*	CP 52.121
468	— Lejeune, *Phonétique grecque*[2]	CP 52.120

(This bibliography runs to 28 February 1957)

MADISON S. BEELER

NORTH VENETIC *KATUS*

THE STUDY of the Venetic language was one of the first subjects to which Professor Whatmough directed his attention, and his contributions to this study many years ago aided materially the notable advances in our knowledge of this pre-Roman language of ancient Italy that have been made in the course of the last generation. I would like to think that this discussion of a problem in the reading and interpretation of some Venetic inscriptions will be welcome to one who has long been interested in and devoted to this discipline, the importance of which for comparative Indo-European studies can hardly be measured by the meager amount of linguistic material still known to us.

The Venetic inscriptions may be classified geographically into two groups, those found in various sites on the north Italian plain and those discovered at several points in the mountainous regions to the north and northeast. Until recent years the southern or plains group afforded us the most plentiful evidence for the language; excavations at the site called Làgole (near Pieve in the Cadore region along the upper Piave), however, have, since 1949, considerably increased our knowledge of Northern Venetic. The Làgole finds constitute the largest number of inscriptions recovered from any one site, excepting that of Este; and they, when added to the few from this area previously known, yield a number quite as large as that found to the south.

In one of the northern inscriptions long known (PID 159, from Monte Pore) there are two occurrences of a symbol >, both of which are preceded by I . Pauli[1] read the complex > I as *k*, although there are on the same stone two ꓘ's also taken as *k*; and this interpretation could be corroborated by the observation that in many

[1] C. Pauli, *Die Veneter und ihre Schriftdenkmäler*, in: *Altitalische Forschungen* 3. 60–61, 93–95 (Leipzig 1891).

other alphabets of ancient Italy[2] what is obviously *k* is written with the lateral bars not in contact with the vertical stroke. Conway *ad loc.* did not wish to admit the occurrence of variant forms of the same letter in the same inscription, and his transliteration of 159 gives *nicokal̠ro.s* and *vońaico* in place of Pauli's *nkokalro.s.* and *vonako*.

There may be two or three additional occurrences of this symbol in the northern material known before 1949; but the Làgole inscription contain more than twenty examples of >I and about twenty five of ꓘ ; >, not preceeded by I, appears two or three times. Pellegrini,[3] the first editor, follows Conway and transcribes consistently as *ic*; and Vetter and Pisani[4] do likewise. Lejeune,[5] on the other hand, proposes a new reading, and transliterates everywhere as *ií*, which he takes as an alternative group of symbols for the common *ii*; and the phonetic value [y] is assigned. His argument is based on the identification of the *trumus.iiat* in which *-ii-* is written II, of P. 11, with the frequent *trumuskatei* (P. 2, 32, 33 etc.), where >I appears. But in P. 11 *trumus.iiat* is associated with another divine name, to wit *śa.i.nat*, which is not the case in the other occurrences referred to. And hence an obvious explanation is that, as in P. 11, we also have in these other occurrences an abbreviated form. The second argument adduced by Lejeune, the equation of P. 7 *tribu.s.iiati.n.* (with *-ii-* written II) with the *...ribusiatin* of P. 13, in the Latin alphabet, is of course without relevance for the question of the reading of >I.

Lejeune's critique of the interpretation as *ic* is to the point: the weightiest argument against it is that the supposed *c*, with but two or three dubious exceptions, occurs only after *i*. He, however, has presented no convincing statement of how, graphically, the supposed *ic* (= *ii*, [y]) can have been developed from the *ii*, known at Este and elsewhere, as well as at Làgole. A difficulty with his reading, as with that of Pellegrini *et al.*, as *ic*, is the pointing in P. 7: *na.i.son.*I<*o.s.*; the point after the *-n-* makes sense only by reading *k*, which is what Lejeune does.

The French scholar speaks in one passage[6] of "l'impossibilité phonétique, dans plus d'un cas, de voir dans I< un *k* disjoint." Whatever interpretation of this symbol

[2] I.e. those of Sondrio, Lepontic, Gallic, Etruscan, Umbrian, East Italic and Messapic. See the tables facing p. 502 of PID II.

[3] The inscriptions from this site are cited according to the number assigned to them in the following publications of G. B. Pellegrini: (1) Iscrizioni Paleovenete da Làgole di Calalzo (Cadore), *Accademia Nazionale dei Lincei, Rendiconti della Classe di Scienze morali, storiche e filologiche*, ser. 8, vol. 5. 307–329 (1950); (2) Nuove iscrizioni etc., *ibid.* vol. 7. 58–74 (1952); (3) Iscrizioni Paleovenete da Làgole, III Ser., *ibid*, vol. 8 (1953); (4) Iscrizioni Paleovenete, IV Ser., *Atti del II convegno internazionale di Linguisti* (Sodalizio Glottologico Milanese), 1–12 (n.d.).

[4] E. Vetter, Die neuen venetischen Inschriften von Làgole, *Beiträge zur älteren europäischen Kulturgeschichte, Festschrift für R. Egger*, 2.123–136 (Klagenfurt 1953). V. Pisani, *Le lingue dell' Italia antica oltre il latino* 253 ff. (Torino 1953).

[5] *Rev. phil.* 25. 224–229 (1951).

[6] La consonne yod en vénète, *Word* 8. 51 (1952).

is adopted there is going to remain a residue of forms which that reading is ill suited to account for; a thoroughgoing attempt to read *k* everywhere has not yet been published. Let us see whether there are so many cases of 'phonetic impossibility'.

In P. 4 the first editor, followed by Vetter, reads the first word as *turiconei.* (Lej. *turiíonei*) . An interpretation *turkonei.* is strikingly supported by *tu.r.k- na*, PID 136, from Este. The lack of puncts accompanying the *r* cannot be adduced against this; for there are other obvious deviations from the strict system of punctation in this inscription. What then follows, if read *okkai.* (P. and V. *okicai.*, Lej. *okiíai.o.i.*), may be compared with *Occus*, from Helenenburg in Carinthia (CIL 3.4987), *Occo*..., Werfen (CIL 3.5529), *Ucconis*, St. Leonhard (CIL 3.5084), etc. Complete consistency, however, requires us to adopt the reading *okkako.i.*, in which we may isolate the well known Keltic suffix *-āco-*. Keltic elements in the Venetic nomenclature of the Cadore region are, as Lejeune has well pointed out, present in large number.

P. 7 contains the *na.i.son.* K*o.s.* mentioned above, which offers least difficulty if read *na.i.son.ko.s.*. Similarly, in P. 41, we have *resun.* K*o.s.*, taken by all previous editors as *resun.ko.s.* because of the punct after *n*, although the symbol in question is clearly a '*k* disjoint'. And in P. 51 we find ...*n.* K*a*, which all read as ...*n.ka*, although a second occurrence of an identically shaped symbol at the end of the same inscription is read variously as *ic* or *ií*. On the other hand, to interpret *letkako.s.* in P. 10 is admittedly less attractive than Lejeune's *letiíako.s.* or Pisani's *leticako.s.*, though by no means impossible. And in P. 15 a reading *ku.k.uta* (P. *kuhcuta*, V. *ku.i.cuta*, Lej. *ku.i.íuta*), although phonetically quite acceptable, and supported by Latin parallels, would constitute as serious an infraction of the punctation system as *na.i.son.ico.s.*. The same objection may legitimately be raised against a *bro.k.oko.s.*, P. *φrohcoko.s.*, V. *φro.i.coko.s.*, Lej. *Bro.i.íko.s.*) in P. 48 (and P. 11, ?), but again there is no phonetic difficulty. Parallel to *letkako.s.*, in that it appears after *t*, is the *butkakos.* (P. and V. *φuticakos.*, Lej. *butiíakos.*) of P. 33. The second word in P. 50 is as plausibly read *eneko.s.* as *eneico.s.* or *eneiío.s.*.

We now come to the discussion of one of the most frequent environments of the symbol in question, I<*ate.i.*. As is well known, Pellegrini, Vetter and Pisani read *icatei* (although the initial 'vowel' is nowhere pointed) and interpret it as a loanword from Gk. Ἑκάτῃ. (We might rather expect in Venetic a **hekata.i.*.) In all occurrences except one this segment is preceded by *trumus*[.]; Lejeune therefore takes the complex *trumus*I<*atei* as a single word and, transliterating *trumusiíatei*, places it in relationship with the word (or words) written in the Venetic alphabet as *tribus.iiati.n.* (and *trumus.iiat.*) and in the Latin as ...*RIBUSIATIN.* Crucial to the proper interpretation, however, is the one occurrence (P. 1) of the recipient of the dedication, simply as I<*atei.*; and with this we must associate *trumuskate.i.*, so transcribed by Pellegrini in P. 70. Should we then take the obvious step and isolate a divine name *katei*, we must take the *trumus* appearing before *ka* and *katei* as an abbreviation of an epithet **trumusiiati-* (meaning?), which in P. 11 accompanies *śa.i.nat.*, a different *nomen sacrum*.

I propose to interpret *kate.i.* as the dative singular of a u-stem noun, associating with it the *katu.s.iaio.s.* of PID 152 from Vicenza, in which I see a theophoric name. As for its form, I have elsewhere[7] given my reasons for thinking that the dative singular of i-stems in Venetic ended in *-ei*; and the interaction of u-stems and i-stem inflection in Indo-European nouns is well known, e.g. in Sanskrit and Germanic. In *kate.i.* we would then have the i-stem ending which had replaced the old u-stem termination, whatever this might have been. I then connect the Venetic stem *katu-* with the well known Indo-European root (WP 1.339, IEW 534), appearing in Keltic and Germanic as a u-stem: Gallic *catu-* in the divine name *Caturix* 'king of battle', Irish *cath* 'battle, fight', OEng. *heaðu-* and OHG *hadu-* 'battle, fight'. The Germanic stem **haþu-* itself appears as a divine name in the ONorse *Hǫðr*.

Was the deity worshipped in the sanctuary of Làgole a god of battle? Among the archeological discoveries at the site are a number of statuettes[8] representing nude warriors, wearing helmets and variously equipped with sword, scabbard, and lance. Should we assume that these figures were intended to portray the martial divinity **Katus*, we could combine this hypothesis with the fact that the most numerous among the Latin dedications found at Làgole are those (e.g., P. 39, 40, 47, 62, 68) to Apollo, of which there are some half dozen. Apollo was a god of war and of battle, among the many other forms in which he was worshipped (Pauly-Wissowa, Real-Encyclopedie, *s.v.*). In the process of Romanization, of which there are so many evidences at this site, may we not suppose that our **Katus* was syncretistically identified with the Latin deity? It has, of course, been suggested that the cult here was devoted to a female divinity;[9] but this guess rested upon the assumption that the **trumusiiatis*, or the **tribusiiatis*, or the **icata* was in some way to be connected with the *loudera.i. kane.i.* of the well known inscription (PID 162) discovered some forty years ago at a site about three miles distant. But I know of no really convincing argument in favor of this assumption.

The word Cadore, the modern name of the region along the upper valley of the Piave, has been derived by Pellegrini[10] from the medieval Catubrium or Catubria; and this in turn, according to him, comes from a Keltic **Catu-briga*. *-briga* is the well known element in Keltic place-names with the meaning of 'mountain, fortress, elevation'; and the compound is interpreted as 'Battle Mountain' or simply 'The

[7] *The Venetic Language*, 16 and 24, (Univ. of California Pubs. in Linguistics, vol. 4, 1949).
[8] See e.g. E. de Lotto and G. Frescura, *Le iscrizioni veneto-euganee scoperte a Làgole di Calalzo Cadore*, 19ff. (Feltre 1950); and G. Pellegrini, *Rendiconti . . . Lincei* 7.58ff. (1952).
[9] Lejeune, *Rev. phil.* 25. 229–234 (1951).
[10] *Archivio Storico di Belluno, Feltre e Cadore* 21 (1950).

Stronghold.' But according to Dottin[11] there are theophoric Keltic place names, and he cites for example a *Divodurum*, which he thinks may mean "la forteresse des dieux." Accordingly I should suggest that **Catu-briga* may rather contain the name of the deity which I have tried to recover from the inscriptions and that the region may have been named for a 'Stronghold of Katus' or 'Mountain of Katus'.

The hypothesis that >I or I< is *k* requires that we admit the use of two different forms of that letter in the North Venetic writing system. Lejeune on the other hand is forced to allow the presence of two divergent symbols for [y], i.e., I I and I<; of the two assumptions, I think that the one defended in this article is no less plausible than that presented by the French scholar. And I cannot see that any phonetic impossibility is encountered; after all, what we know of Venetic phonology is strictly limited by the nature and amount of linguistic material available to us.

UNIVERSITY OF CALIFORNIA, BERKELEY

[11] *La langue gauloise* 88 (Paris 1918).

WILHELM BRANDENSTEIN

ETYMOLOGICA

DER FORMENKREIS von idg. **ĝhesr̥-* ‘Hand’ wurde von A. Heubeck, *BzN* 7.275–279 (1956), der sich wiederum auf V. Pisani stützte, so weitgehend geklärt, daß nur noch einige weitere kleine Schritte nötig sind. Der Stamm lautete **ĝhesr̥-* (vgl. die heth. Weiterbildung *kessara-* ‘Hand’), der Nominativ hätte als Nominativzeichen, weil geschlechtig, eine Dehnung aufweisen und daher eigentlich im Griechischen *χέᾱρ heißen müssen (vgl. μάκᾱρ). Aber es entstand ein Ausgleich, da das Wort ja im Gen. χειρός und im Nom. Pl. χεῖρες usw. regelrecht ein (unechtes) ει hat. Die Grundform für den Gen. ist **ĝhesrós* > jon. χειρός; für den Dativ **ĝhesrí* > χειρί = heth. *kisri*. Vom erschlossenen Nominativ *χέᾱρ aus ist der Beiname der Artemis ἰοχέαιρα ‘die den Pfeil in der Hand hält’ abgeleitet.

Der Dat. Pl. **ĝhesr-si* wurde schon in vorhistorischer Zeit (das ist vor dem Verlust des Wurzel-*s*) durch Dissimilation zu **ĝhersi* > χερσί. Es ist also nicht notwendig, wie man in älteren Handbüchern findet, eine zweite Wurzel **ĝher-* anzunehmen; dafür wird als Beleg der armenische Nom. Pl. *jeṙ-kʿ* angeführt; aber das armenische Wort besitzt ein *-ṙ-*, was übersehen wurde, da dieses *-ṙ-* aus *-sr-* (oder auch *-rs-*) entstanden ist.

Denselben dissimilatorischen Schwund des ersten *-s-* (wie bei χερσί) zeigt auch χέρνιψ ‘Waschwasser für die Hand’, welches Wort aus **ĝhesr-snib-* entstanden ist. Ebenso ist das Wort χερνῆτις ‘Handarbeiterin, Spinnerin’ gebildet, welches aus *χεσρ- und *σνηjειν ‘spinnen’ zusammengesetzt ist.

2. In meinen beiden Arbeiten *Die erste indogermanische Wanderung* (Wien 1936) und ‘Die Lebensformen der Indogermanen’ in dem Sammelband *Die Indogermanen- und Germanenfrage* (Wiener Beiträge zur Kulturgeschichte und Linguistik IV, Salzburg 1936), habe ich das Mittel des irreversiblen Bedeutungswandels benützt, um eine chronologische Schichtung der idg. Grundsprache zu erweisen. Zur Erläuterung meiner Methode sei ein ganz einfaches Beispiel für den irreversiblen Bedeutungswandel

gebracht. Wenn germ. **fehu* 'Vieh' (= lat. *pecu* 'Vieh') im got. *faíhu* die Bedeutung 'Geld' hat, so ist der hier vorliegende Bedeutungswandel 'Vieh > Viehbesitz > Besitz > Geldbesitz > Geld nur in dieser Richtung möglich, so wie ja auch lat. *pecunia* zunächst den Viehbestand meint und dann erst Besitz und Geld. Die umgekehrte Bedeutungsentwicklung ist nicht gut möglich, oder, wie ich jetzt vorsichtshalber hinzufüge, höchstens auf einem Umweg, bezw. auf dem Weg der Entlehnung anzunehmen. Jedenfalls liegt das onus probandi bei dem, der die umgekehrte Richtung behauptet. Dasselbe gilt für die Bedeutungsentwicklung Gott > Teufel; z.B. wurde der Hauptgott der Perser *Ōramazdā* zu einem Dämon, so in einem Pamirdialekt *Alamastẹ* 'einäugiger Dämon' (W. Lentz, *Pamir-Dialekte*, 153 [Göttingen 1933]).

Ebenso zeigt mp. *Indar* 'Erzteufel', daß der Entwicklungsverlauf von Gott > Teufel nur in dieser Richtung möglich ist. Der Begriff ap. *daiva* m. 'Götze', später 'Teufel', ist sekundär gegenüber der ursprünglich allgemeinen idg. Bedeutung **dei̯u̯os* 'Gott'. Trotzdem sind im iranischen Bereich Verehrer der alten Götter (die sonst durch Ōramazdā verdrängt worden sind) übrig geblieben. Wenn dann in späterer Zeit diese religiöse Sekte von den umliegenden Stämmen als Teufelsanbeter bezeichnet wurden, so ist diese Benennung vom Standpunkt der Namensgeber zu verstehen. In den Augen der genannten Sekte waren die alten Götter natürlich nicht zu Teufeln geworden. Auf ein anderes Beispiel eines irreversiblen Bedeutungswandels hat Porzig, *Die Gliederung des indogermanischen Sprachgebietes* 100–103 (Heidelberg, 1954), hingewiesen, indem er zeigte, daß die Verwendung eines Wortes als Kenning jünger sein müsse als die ursprüngliche Verwendung.

Zu den Beispielen, die ich a.a.O. verwendet habe, gehört auch die Verbalwurzel **sēi-*, deren Bedeutung im arischen Bereich ausschließlich 'werfen' ist, und im außerarischen Bereich ausschließlich 'säen'. Die Konsequenzen dieser Feststellung sind weittragend: zu jener Zeit, als die Vorläufer des Arischen sich noch im Bereich der idg. Grundsprache befanden, hat **sēi-* im Indogermanischen die Bedeutung 'werfen' und nur diese. Dann müssen sich die Vorläufer des Arischen aus dem Bereich der idg. Grundsprache losgelöst haben und dabei die alte Bedeutung in unveränderter Weise bewahrt haben, während der außerarische Bereich als geschlossenes Ganzes den Bedeutungswandel zu 'säen' vollzogen hat, wobei jede Spur der alten Bedeutung verloren gegangen ist. Daraus geht hervor, daß sich der erste Zerfall der idg. Grundsprache in einem arischen und in einem außerarischen Bereich vollzog (von den kulturgeschichtlichen Folgen, die gerade unser Beispiel zeigt, sei hier abgesehen).

Ungefähr gleichzeitig mit mir hat Nehring (Studien zur indogermanischen Kultur und Urheimat, in: *Die Indogermanen- und Germanenfrage* [Salzburg 1936]) das Argument der geographischen Verteilung der Bedeutungen dieser Verbalwurzel für seine Betrachtungen verwendet. Gegen beide Auffassungen hat Specht in der *KZ* 66. 1ff. (1939) polemisiert, indem er auf eine gewisse lautliche Differenz hinwies. Im außerarischen Bereich erscheint nämlich die Wurzel **sēi-* als **sē-*. Das berechtigt aber noch nicht dazu, die beiden Wurzeln zu trennen, weil im Indogermanischen lange *i*-Diphthonge das *i* häufig verlieren (vgl. etwa H. Krahe, *Indogermanische Sprachwissenschaft* § 16 [Göschen no. 59]). Einen ernsteren Einwand bilden die Ausführungen von Bloch (*BSOS* 8. 411ff. [1935]), der versucht, die Bedeutung 'säen' auch für den arischen Bereich zu erweisen. Zwar versucht Bloch dies nicht beim vorauszusetzenden Verbum ai. **sāi-* (vgl. *sāyaka-* 'zum Schleudern bestimmt') selbst darzutun, das ist nämlich unmöglich; aber Bloch wendet sich dafür gewissen Ableitungen zu. Nach seiner Auffassung bedeutet ai. *sī́ram* 'Säpflug' und *sī́tā* 'die (besäte) Furche', wodurch die Bedeutung 'säen' auch für die ai. Fortsetzung von **sēi-* erwiesen sei. Diese Auffassung Blochs wurde von Kronasser (*Handbuch der Semasiologie* 129 [Heidelberg 1952]) gegen meine dargelegte These verwendet (ohne Bloch zu zitieren und mit einem Druckfehler im ai. Wort). Es läßt sich aber leicht zeigen, daß der Gedankengang Blochs einen Zirkelschluß enthält, der dadurch nicht besser wird, daß er von anderen wiederholt wird: *sī́ram* kann nur dann 'Säpflug' heißen, wenn ai. **sāi-* 'säen' bedeutet. Diese Bedeutung soll aber durch die Deutung *sī́ram* 'Säpflug' erschlossen werden. Das *x* wird also durch das *y* bewiesen, das *y* durch das *x*. Zudem hat Bloch auch noch einen methodischen Fehler begangen. Er hätte zuerst, etwa durch ein Lichtbild, beweisen müssen, daß *sī́ram* wirklich jenes Gerät bezeichnet. Richtig ist, daß es im alten Orient Säpflüge gegeben hat, d.h. Pflüge, die mit dem Kasten für das Saatgut versehen waren, aus welchem Kasten, meist durch eine Röhre, die Saatkörner einzeln herausrutschen konnten. Aber ein solches Gerät ist für das vedische Indien nicht erwiesen; zudem ist es recht unwahrscheinlich, daß der Säpflug, der doch in erster Linie zum Pflügen dient, als 'Säer' benannt worden sei. Aus dem ganzen Sachverhalt ergibt sich also, daß *sī́ram* eine schwundstufige Ableitung von ai. **sāi-* 'werfen, schleudern' ist und daher den '(Erdschollen-)Werfer' bezeichnet, was eine gute bildhafte Benennung für den Pflug ist. Zur Bildung vgl. ai. *dhī́ra-* 'sehend': *dīdheti* 'nimmt wahr.'

Analog sind die Einwände gegen die Auffassung gegen ai. *sī́tā* 'Furche'. Das Wort kann nicht die '(besäte) Furche' bedeuten, weil auch hier der oben erwähnte Zirkelschluß zugrunde liegt. Außerdem wäre die Bedeutungsentwicklung recht unwahrscheinlich; denn eine Furche ist ja zunächst nicht besät (außer bei Benützung des ominösen Säpfluges); zudem kann man auch säen, ohne eine Furche zu ziehen. Da *sī́tā* eine Ableitung von ai. **sāi-* 'werfen' ist, bedeutet es offenkundig 'die aufgeworfene (Erde)'. Den von der partizipialen Bildung abweichenden Akzent hat Bloch a.a.O. aufgeklärt. – Zur Bedeutungsentwicklung vgl. d. *Furche*, das ursprünglich die 'Aufwühlung' bedeutet hat, vgl. *IEW* 821/3 mit der wichtigen Erweiterung durch F. R. Schröder, *Festgabe für Karl Helm* 25ff. (1951).

Es bleibt also dabei, daß *sī́ram* 'der Pflug' und *sī́tā* 'die Furche' mit dem Säen nichts zu tun haben, sondern zu der im Indischen allein erweisbaren Deutung von **sāi-* 'wirft (Erde) auf' gehören.

3. *Abracadabra* wird zuerst von Q. Serenus Sammonicus (Anfang des 3. Jh. n. Chr.) erwähnt als Zauberwort bei magischen Beschwörungen gegen Krankheiten. In späterer Zeit hat es auch die Bedeutung 'sinnloser Wortschwall'. Die Serenusstelle ist im *TLL* zitiert. Die weiteren Formen dieses Wortes behandelt ausführlich A. Nelson in *Eranos* 44. 326ff. (1946), während das Wort im *LEW* fehlt und im *DEL* 6 mit den dürren Worten "mot magique" und dem Verweis auf "Axel Nelson, Eranos Rudbergianus, 326 et s." abgetan wird. Hinter diesem schlechten Zitat steckt der oben erwähnte Aufsatz von Nelson. Die verschiedenen Erklärungen hat A. Jacoby in seinem großen Artikel im *Handwörterbuch des deutschen Aberglaubens* verzeichnet. Nelson versucht gegenüber diesen Deutungen eine neue Erklärung. Er liest ἄβρα κατ' ἄβρα und glaubt, daß darin das spätgriechische Wort ἄβρα 'Dienerin' stecke; der Sinn der Formel sei, daß die 'Dienerin' die Wiederherstellung der Gesundheit zuwege bringen solle, indem sie sich selbst vernichtet. Dabei weist Nelson darauf hin, daß die Lesung *-cat-* gelegentlich in den Codices vorkomme. Vielleicht sei auch, so vermutet Nelson, ein Zusammenhang mit der orientalischen spätantiken Gottheit Abraxas oder Abrasax anzunehmen, wogegen aber die völlige Verschiedenheit im zweiten Teil dieses magischen Wortes spricht. Er hält auch die bei Jacoby verzeichnete Erklärung für möglich, daß ein hebräischer, aber zur Gänze erfundener Satz **abar-dak-dabar* dahinter stecke, der die Bedeutung hätte 'er (= der Fieberdämon) geht weg wie das Wort'. Diese Deutung scheint mir schon deswegen sehr bedenklich zu sein, weil 'Wort' (*dabar*) eine sakrale Bedeutung gehabt hat und daher nicht als flatus vocis aufgefaßt werden kann.

W. Deonna geht in der Zeitschrift *Genava* 22. 116ff. (1944) von einem mittelalterlichen kreuzförmigen Anhänger aus, auf dem ein Teil unseres magischen Wortes vielfach wiederholt vorkommt, und zwar in den Formen *abraca*, *abrac*, *abra*, also mit ständiger Verminderung, ein Verfahren das in solchen Zauberformeln häufig der Fall ist; die Wiederholung bewirkt eine Verstärkung der bannenden Wirkung. Deonna behandelt dann analoge Zauberwörter; auch unser Abracadabra empfiehlt Q. Serenus in dieser Weise (in ständigem Abbau) zu verwenden. Aus dieser Tatsache ergibt sich, daß unser Wort bereits ein unverständlicher Ausdruck geworden ist. Weiters behandelt Deonna Fälle von Palindromen. Daß unser Wort kein solches ist, geht m.E. daraus hervor, daß es durch eine leichte Umstellung zu einem geworden wäre und daß man dies unterlassen hat. Daher handelt es sich vielmehr um zwei Reimwörter, nämlich *abra* und *dabra*, die durch *-ca-* verbunden sind. Dieses verbindende Wörtchen erinnert an idg. *$q^{w}e$, wobei zu bemerken ist, daß es, wie seine Stellung zeigt, invers verwendet wurde; das ist eine Verwendung, die man gelegentlich findet, z.B. im Awestischen. Der abweichende Vokalismus ist entweder lautgesetzlich (s.u.) oder als eine Vokalassimilation zu erklären. Das Wort *abra* fasse ich als Entsprechung des griech. ἄφρος 'Schaum' auf. Es könnte demnach aus dem Thrakischen stammen, in dem das *bh* > *b* wurde und nicht zu φ wie im Griechischen, also aus **m̥bhros*; vgl. den thrakischen Nymphenmamen Ἄβα (< **m̥bha*, s. Detschew,

Charakteristik der thrakischen Sprache 101 unten [Sofia 1952]). Der Plural auf *-a* ist als Kollektiv zum Singular auf *-os* aufzufassen, vgl. τὰ σίτα als Plural von ὁ σίτος usw. Man könnte ferner an den thrakischen Pflanzennamen ἀβρότονον denken, der auch als femininer Eigenname verwendet wird. Besonders, wenn das Wort wirklich, wie vermutet wird, das 'Wiesen*schaum*kraut' bezeichnet. Der Name ἀβρότονον wird allerdings von O. Hoffmann, *Die Makedonen* 40f. (Göttingen 1906) als echt griechisch aufgefaßt, wobei das ἀβρο- mit dem deutschen Pflanzennamen *Ampfer* gleichgesetzt wird. Der Auffassung Hoffmanns schließt sich Detschew, *Die thrakischen Sprachreste* 3 (Wien 1957) an. Diese Auffassung ist schon deswegen unsicher, weil das Element ἀβρο- in thrakischen Personennamen sehr häufig ist und im Griechischen nicht verankert ist. Daher hat auch J. B. Hofmann im *Etymologischen Wörterbuch des Griechischen* (München 1949) den Pflanzennamen als thrakisch aufgefaßt, ohne jedoch auf die Deutung von O. Hoffmann einzugehen. Als thrakisch betrachtet den Namen auch das *GEW*, *s. v.*

Das Reimwort *dabra* hat eine Entsprechung im griech. τέφρα fem. 'Asche' (< **dheg*^{w}*hra*), so daß wir also für unseren Zauberspruch eine ursprüngliche Bedeutung von 'Schaum und Asche' hätten (eventuell auch 'Nebel und Rauch'). Unsere magische Formel würde demnach aus dem thrakischen Bereich stammen, der dem Griechischen sehr viel Mystisch-Magisches geliefert hat. Durch die Formel würde daher die Krankheit zu einer Nichtigkeit reduziert. Der Vokalismus kann wohl lautgesetzlich sein, weil im Thrakischen häufig aus *e* ein *a* wird; aber in unserem Fall kann natürlich auch der Reimzwang wirksam gewesen sein. Die einzige Schwierigkeit bietet die Labiovelare, da wir nach den thrakischen Lautgesetzen eine Entwicklung **dagrā* erwarten. Hier muß aber der Reimzwang umformend gewirkt haben, vgl. d. *Hokuspokus.*

GRAZ

GIACOMO DEVOTO

VOFIONO 'TRIBUNO' E VOFIONO 'SCUOTITORE'

È STATO più volte osservato come una indagine etimologica richiami l'imagine di un processo indiziario.[1] Ma, a differenza del diritto processuale, che distingue accuratamente tra possibilità astratte, prive di qualsiasi rilevanza giudiziaria, e probabilità concrete, che servono da fondamento a una sentenza, gli etimologisti confondono spesso i due termini e su una mera possibilità costituiscono etimologie. Per fortuna, queste a differenza delle sentenze sbagliate non hanno ripercussioni spiacevoli sugli individui.

D'altra parte se si volesse etimologizzare solo su prove evidenti, si uscirebbe dall' etimologia. Una etimologia troppo evidente appartiene ancora al mondo della derivazione vivente delle parole, e cioè alla morfologia. L'etimologia si volge invece per definizione solo alla restituzione dei legami disseccati, morti.

Affine nella definizione della 'prova', essa si differenzia perciò dal diritto processuale nel fine: aspirando la prima, anzichè alla certezza, a una disinteressata e sportiva correttezza di procedimenti; volta la seconda tutta quanta a stabilire una certezza, con mezzi più o meno ortodossi.

La disinteressata correttezza del procedere fa sì che non si debba allora discutere tra una etimologia vera e molte errate, ma solo graduare fra più etimologie concorrenti, il diverso *costo* di costruzione: anche se risulta, nella maggioranza dei casi, proibitivo.

Il dio umbro Vofiono è stato definito un tempo come il 'consacratore' in base a una connessione etimologica con il latino *uoueo*. In tempi più vicini a noi, dal Pisani[2] dal Benveniste[3] dal Polomé[4] è stato derivato da **leudho*- 'popolo', intendendolo

[1] V. il mio scritto, Di la dalla grammatica, *Riv. it. per le scienze giuridiche* 85.414 sgg. (1948).
[2] *REI* 1.230 sgg (1938); e poi nelle *Lingue dell'Italia antica* 157 (Torino 1953).
[3] *RHR* 129.7–9 (1945).
[4] In *Hommages... Niedermann* 274–285 (Bruxelles 1956)

naturisticamente come il 'fruttificatore', o giuridicamente come il 'tribuno'.

La forza di questa etimologia non sta nella regolarità fonetica per cui **leudho-* indeuropeo deve diventare *vof-* in umbro: ché altrettanto regolare è il passaggio da una base indeuropea *$*weug^wh$-* a *vof-*. I confronti del Benveniste con *uocu* 'bosco sacro' che deriva da **louko-* (*v-* da *l-*); con *tota* 'città' che deriva da **teuta* (*o* da *eu*); con *rofu* 'rosso' che deriva da **reudho-* (*f* da *dh*) sono dei paralleli, non delle 'prove'.[5]

La forza di questa etimologia sta nell'avere sostituito all'indizio di una assonanza fonetica, pura e semplice, l'assonanza fonetica confortata da una analogia culturale.

Vofiono si trova infatti compreso in una triade, in cui gli altri due componenti sono Giove e Marte. Giove e Marte si ritrovano come primi componenti di una triade romana il cui terzo elemento è Quirino.[6] E poichè Quirino ha una 'etimologia'[7] che richiama una collettività di uomini, il suo membro corrispondente umbro, a parità di evidenza fonetica, dovrà discendere da una nozione letterale o simbolica parallela di 'collettività umana' quale è quella insita precisamente in **leudho-*.

L'etimologia di Vofiono (come 'tribuno' o 'fruttificatore') non discende dunque né da una osservazione evidente né da un fatto certo. È la conseguenza ragionevole e verosimile di un parallelismo[8] tra due triadi, accettato in partenza. Il costo della interpretazione del dio Vofiono, come 'tribuno' o come 'fruttificatore' derivato da **leudho-*, è rappresentato da questo parallelismo che i tre autori citati trovano conveniente e quasi ovvio da accettare.

Al di là delle sue apparenze esso può però essere sottoposto a controllo. Di fronte alla triade romana, la cui compattezza si misura piuttosto attraverso i tre flamini, il *Dialis*, il *Martialis*, il *Quirinalis*,[9] la triade iguvina non solo manca di sacerdozî caratteristici, ma si rivela tutt'altro che chiusa in se stessa. Vofiono pone problemi che suggeriscono una interpretazione dei suoi antefatti alquanto diversa. Da questa diversità di interpretazione derivano conseguenze etimologiche non indifferenti.

L'omogeneità della triade umbra consiste inanzi tutto nel nome 'Grabovio', proprio, oltre che di Vofiono, anche di Giove e di Marte.

Per il Benveniste, la compattezza preesistente a questo battesimo consiste nella coesistenza dei tre principî di sovranità, forza e fecondità, che G. Dumézil[10] ammette come caratteristica della società indeuropea. L'accettazione dell'evidenza della triade si sposta dal parallelismo romano a un antefatto ereditario. Ma questi principî sono il risultato di una elaborazione complessa e più o meno convincente, per definire in modo concreto quella società nei suoi tratti fondamentali, quali a noi è dato di

[5] E. Benveniste, *RHR* cit., 15.
[6] G. Wissowa, *Religion und Kultus der Römer* 153 sgg. (2 ed., München 1912).
[7] *LEW*: Quirinus da **ko-wiris*.
[8] A. von Blumenthal, *Die iguvinischen Tafeln* 61 (Stuttgart 1931), e sopratutto G. Dumézil, *L'héritage indo-européen à Rome* 223 sgg. (Paris 1947).
[9] Wissowa, *op. cit.* 504 sg.
[10] Dumézil, *op. cit.* 187 sg.

delineare. Non sono una chiave che si possa poi adoperare in senso inverso per discendere dalla antichità indeuropea a chiarire situazioni oscure delle singole comunità nazionali, senza cadere in un circolo vizioso.

L'omogeneità della triade è data dal comune attributo 'Grabovio', che non si addice in modo particolare piuttosto a sovranità che a forza o a fecondità. Esso è suscettibile della interpretazione di 'quercia', se davvero *vogliamo*, col Kretschmer,[11] andare alla ricerca di un legame transadriatico. Obiettivamente, non ha altre connessioni se non con un culto locale, superstite in età romana, quello di Giove *Apenino*.[12] Poichè Pennino richiama la nozione di vetta montana, e *krapa/graba* è un relitto di un termine mediterraneo significante 'sasso',[13] ecco che l'unità della triade viene ricondotta agevolmente a un battesimo concreto e locale anzichè a una tradizione comune, rispettabile ma generica.

Non è solo il contrasto tra un battesimo mediterraneo e uno indeuropeo, che il termine *Grabovio* presenta. Anche in Roma potremmo avere avuto nella organizzazione della triade un contributo locale sia pure innominato, e quindi Quirino potrebbe irradiar luce su Vofiono, per una via indiretta, che non siamo in grado di escludere.

La vera difficoltà per il parallelismo nasce, quando si consideri che, al di fuori del battesimo dei tre componenti della Triade, una assoluta omogeneità tra i tre dèi non appare. Il fatto di ricevere grani (*arvia*) e la innominata bevanda (*poni*)[14] è comune alle tre divinità della triade, ma anche a quasi tutti i sacrifici umbri. Il fatto di vedersi presentate le offerte su un tavolato o palco (*ferine*)[15] è comune, oltre che alla triade grabovia, anche alle due divinità che seguono nello stesso sacrificio e che, come appare dai loro attributi, *Marte Hodio*[16] e *Hondo Çerfio*,[17] non hanno nulla di comune con la triade grabovia.

Al di fuori di queste comunanze 'sovrabbondanti', compaiono poi all'interno della triade le differenze seguenti: (1) che Vofiono riceve la libazione anche col vino, come Giove Grabovio ma *non* come Marte Grabovio, cui si liba con la sola Bevanda; (2) che Vofiono riceve dei bovi *calersos* 'callidi' e cioè con una macchia bianca in fronte e quindi scuri nel resto del mantello, mentre Giove e Marte Grabovio ricevono bovi con la fronte non differenziata nel colore né con altri accenni al colore e perciò presumibilmente bianchi; (3) che mentre a Giove e a Marte si prega *gutef* (secondo me 'a voce alta'[18]) "davanti" alle porte Trebulana e Tessenaca "come" alle divinità

[11] P. Kretschmer, *Festschrift... Bezzenberger* 89–96 (Göttingen 1921).
[12] CIL 11.5803; cfr. i miei *Antichi Italici* 222 sg. (2 ed., Firenze 1951).
[13] G. Alessio, *St. Etr.* 10.186 sg. (1936).
[14] V. le mie *Tabulae Iguvinae* (2 ed. Roma 1940): per *arvis* p. 200 sg; per *poni* p. 204 sg.
[15] *Ibid.* 377 sgg. (per *ferine*).
[16] *Ibid.* 257.
[17] *Ibid.* 257.
[18] *Ibid.* 202 sg.

che gli corrispondono "dietro" alle porte stesse, a Vofiono si prega *gutef*, a differenza della divinità corrispondente dietro la porta Veia, cui ci si rivolge *taçez*, in silenzio.[19]

L'omogeneità dell'attributo sembra dunque piuttosto una etichetta recente che armonizza vecchie divinità individuali piuttosto che un resto superstite di una unità, che nell'interno sia in procinto di disfarsi.

Il rito italiano del vino aggiunto a quello indeuropeo, o comunque pre-italiano, della bevanda, non rivela, associato com'è a Giove, una particolare natura. È questa presumibilmente una impronta italiana data a qualcosa che italiano nelle origini non era: per questo il fatto del vino, preso da solo, non favorisce l'una piuttosto che l'altra etimologia indeuropea.

Viceversa la macchia bianca sulla fronte e il conseguente colore scuro del mantello investono, come ha fatto correttamente osservare Silvio Ferri, la natura del dio.[20]

Il colore scuro non è unico e non significa automaticamente le qualità ctonie e infere. Dal Sacrificio della lustrazione apprendiamo che vittime rosse o nere (*rofas ote peias*) erano offerte alle due divinità Çerfo Martio e Prestota Çerfia Çerfer Martier: queste divinità sono ctonie in senso largo, collegate alla nozione della Terra e della sua Fecondità e insieme anche infere.[21]

Le divinità ctonie in senso stretto, alle quali si offrono vittime da seppellire (*pelsanas*), sono Dicamno, Hondo Giovio, Pomono, e, caso particolarmente interessante, Tefro Giovio, la divinità cui si sacrifia "dietro la porta Veia", davanti alla quale si sacrifica invece a Vofiono.[22] Davanti e dietro alle porte Trebulana e Tessenaca si sacrifica a divinità supere; davanti e dietro alla porta Veia si sacrifica a una divinità infera e rispettivamente a una ctonia. L'ipotesi del Ferri è, fino a questo punto, perfettamente corretta: Vofiono *non* è confrontabile con Quirino.

Fatto questo, non bisogna lasciarsi prendere dal desiderio di dare a Quirino un successore romano a qualsiasi prezzo. Se si ammette questo postulato, ecco che la somiglianza fonetica di *Ved*-(iovis) tenta di imporsi sulla morfologia, escludendo la analisi tradizionale *Ve-diovis*,[23] e alla semantica, definendo l'attività infera, non attraverso una associazione evidente, ma attraverso una possibilità simbolica: quella che, ricorrendo alla complessa famiglia lessicale di *wedh-* 'legare' permette di vedere nel dio infero, il lanciatore di un laccio, l'accalappiatore.[24]

Ma la natura infera così definita è solida fino a tanto che ci si muove sul suo terreno e le si attribuiscano attività specificatamente infere. Perde qualsiasi capacità di illuminazione e persuasione non appena le si vogliano associare dei simboli attraverso collegamenti non automatici. L'unica evidenza fonetica che aderisca a

[19] *Ibid.* 202 sg.
[20] *PP* 16.65–67 (1951).
[21] *Tab. Ig.* 289.
[22] *Ibid.* 267.
[23] V. *DEL* 1266.
[24] *PP* cit. alla nota 20. Cf. *LEW* 1.256.

questo gruppo di significato è quella di *Vof-* – derivato da **wodh-* (gr. ὠθέω) –, cui io ho attribuito altra volta il significato di 'scuotitore'.[25]

Il valore primitivo della radice **wedh-*, cui così si ricorre, è stato precisato da E. Polomé[26] come 'portare un colpo distruttore'. Ma qui non si tratta di risalire a preistorie lontanissime. Qui si tratta di valersi di associazioni esistenti; non occorre andar molto lontano per trovare, proprio in Grecia, l'imagine tratta dalla stessa famiglia lessicale di ὠθέω, quella di *Posidone ennosigaîos*.[27]

Il Polomé rappresentante, in questo, della vecchia etimologia induttiva, ora ipercritica, ora brancolante, ebbe a dire che "nessun appoggio sussiste nel rituale umbro"[28] per un dio scuotitore. Io non dirò che "tutto" lo appoggia.

Ma una volta che (a) sia riconosciuta negativamente la singolarità di Vofiono nella sua triade e nel pantheon umbro in generale, e (b) questa si precisi positivamente attraverso il colore come di natura infera, la attività di scuotitrice, si presenta in una forma che alla moderna etimologia deduttiva sarà lecito dire armoniosa, e al lettore non prevenuto deve apparire 'poco costosa'.

UNIVERSITÀ DI FIRENZE

[25] *St. Etr.* 22.175 (1923); Devoto, *Antichi Italici* 222 sgg.

[26] E. Polomé, *Mélanges... Grenier* 2.545 (Bruxelles 1940).

[27] F. Schachermeyr, *Poseidon* (Bern 1950).

[28] *Hommages... Niedermann* 284.

ALFRED ERNOUT

SUR QUELQUES NOMS DE DIEUX SABINS

ALORS que certains parlers voisins du latin de Rome nous sont connus par un petit nombre d'inscriptions anciennes qui nous permettent par des témoignages authentiques d'en connaître quelques traits – c'est le cas notamment pour le falisque et le parler de Préneste[1] – cette bonne fortune nous manque pour le sabin. Il est inutile de rappeler longuement les raisons historiques qui expliquent cette absence: dès le début de la tradition, à l'origine même de Rome, nous voyons les Sabins intimement mêlés à l'histoire de la ville, et l'on a pu soutenir à juste titre que Rome était née du synoecisme entre les différentes tribus romaines et sabines qui occupaient et se disputaient les sept collines et leurs alentours. Selon Tite-Live, dépositaire de la légende, de même que les femmes sabines ont assuré à leurs ravisseurs les enfants qui leur manquaient pour perpétuer leur puissance, des 'rois' sabins, dont le plus illustre est Numa, ont contribué à donner à la ville naissante ses institutions politiques et religieuses, et l'on sait que, tout au moins dans l'esprit des Romains, les *Quirites* sont inséparables du nom de la ville de *Cures*, comme aussi la tribu *Quirina*,[2] et la *Iuno Curis* ainsi appelée parce qu'elle portait une lance, *curis* en sabin. Mais il y a dans l'onomastique et la toponymie romaines des traces sabines: je crois avoir montré que la forme *Marmar* du nom du dieu Mars, qui figure dans le *Carmen fratrum Arualium*, est d'origine sabine, comme le nom de la rivière *Fabaris* est le doublet latin du sabin *Farfarus*.[3] Des fouilles récentes ont permis de situer avec

[1] Cf. en dernier lieu Vetter, *Handbuch* (Ve): *Faliskische Inschriften*, 277–327, nos. 241–355; Latium, Praeneste, 333–356, nos. 365–510; Vittore Pisani, *Le lingue dell' Italia antica oltre il latino*: Il falisco e altri dialetti latini 316–334 (Torino, 1953) – (moins complet que Vetter).

[2] Cf. entre autres Ovide, *Fast.* 2.475 et s., qui s'inspire sans doute d'un passage des *Res Diuinae* de Varron (cf. Macrobe *Sat.* 1.19.16). La correspondance sabin *Cu-* = lat. *Qui-* s'explique sans doute par la difficulté pour les Latins de noter la prononciation de l'*u* sabin (comparable à l'*u* français?). Sur *Iuno Curis* (plutôt que *Curitis*) voir Paul. Fest. 43.5, 55.6, 56.21 (Lindsay).

[3] Cf. l'article "Farfarus et Marmar," *St. Etr.* 24.311 sqq. (1955).

exactitude sur le territoire capénate, à Scorano, l'emplacement du *Lūcus Fērōniae*, déesse dont le caractère sabin, indiqué entre autres par Varron, *L.L.* 5.74, se trouve ainsi confirmé.[4] Et si Mars est un dieu sabin, il est naturel d'attribuer la même origine à sa parèdre *Neria*[5] ou plutôt *Neriō*, dont la flexion singulière avec alternance *ō/ē*, *Neriō*, *-ēnis* ne se retrouve que dans le nom, dialectal lui aussi, de la rivière *Aniō*, *-ēnis*.[6] On sait du reste que, dans le même chapitre 23 du livre XIII des *Nuits Attiques* où Aulu-Gelle cite le couple *Nerienem Martis*, et rappelle le vers 510 du *Truculentus* de Plaute

Mars peregre adueniens salutat Nerienem uxorem suam,

il rappelle que le surnom de *Nero* 'fortis' a été introduit à Rome par la gens Claudia, qui est elle-même originaire de la Sabine: "Id autem, siue 'Nerio', siue 'Nerienes' est, Sabinum uerbum est, eoque significatur uirtus et fortitudo. Itaque ex Claudiis, quos a Sabinis oriundos accepimus, qui erat egregia atque praestanti fortitudine, 'Nero' appellatus est ... Nerio igitur Martis uis et potentia et maiestas quaedam esse Martis demonstratur." La parèdre et l'épouse de Mars incarne la qualité essentielle du dieu, comme *Mōlēs* dans le groupe *Mōlēs Mārtis* ou *Heriēs* dans *Heriem Iūnōnis*, de la racine **gher-* qu'on retrouve dans le nom osque de Vénus, *Herentas*, et dans **heria-*, que l'on traduit par *uis* (Buck) ou *delectus* (Vetter). Par *Nero*, *Neriō* le sabin se rattache à l'osco-ombrien, où la racine **ner-* est bien représentée, tandis qu'elle n'existe pas en latin, où c'est le groupe de *uir* qui a pris sa place.

Parmi les divinités sabines se range encore *Vacūna* qui avait un temple et un bois sacré près de Réate, et dont le culte remontait, d'après Ovide, à une haute antiquité.[7] Mais sous l'Empire, le temple était tombé en ruines, *fanum putre Vacunae*, dit Horace, *Epist.* 1.10.49, et la figure de la déesse, tellement effacée qu'on avait oublié sa fonction, les uns l'assimilant à Bellone, ou à Minerve, ou à Diane, d'autres à la Victoire, rapprochant son nom de *uacare* et l'expliquant par "deam uacationis, quod faciat uacare a curis", ou en faisant une Minerve "quod ea maxime hi gaudent qui sapientiae uacant",[8] comme on rapprochait *Fērōnia* de *fĕrō*.[9]

[4] Cf. R. Bloch et G. Foti ,"Nouvelles dédicaces archaïques à la déesse Feronia," *Rev. Phil.* 27.65–77 (1953). Le culte de *Fērōnia* n'est du reste pas exclusivement sabin; la déesse était honorée en divers lieux, mais c'est de la Sabine qu'il semble s'être répandu. Sur la possibilité d'une origine étrusque, voir W. Schulze, *Lat. Eigennamen*, 165.

[5] *Neria* qui n'est attesté que dans les fragments des Annales de Cn. Gellius cité par Aulu-Celle est sans doute une forme récente, latinisée de *Neriō*.

[6] La forme du vocatif *Neriēnes* qu'Aulu-Gelle attribue à Varron dans une de ses Ménippées est déconcertante; elle supposerait une flexion *Neriēnes*, gén. *Neriēnis* – peut-être d'après *Mōlēs Mārtis*? Mais le texte est peu sûr, et Bücheler a proposé de lire *Neriēnis*; on pourrait songer à *Neriēnis* <Mars>.

[7] *Fast.* 6.305 sqq: Ante focos olim scamnis considere longis
Mos erat mensae credere adesse deos.
Nunc quoque, cum fiunt antiquae sacra Vacunae,
Ante Vacunales stantque sedentque focos.

Est également donné comme sabin le dieu *Sancus*, associé à *Semo*, et identifié à *Dius Fidius*. Mais ce dieu ne nous est pas mieux connu que *Vacuna*, et son nom même est mal fixé: à côté d'une forme *Sancus,-ī* existe un doublet *Sancus,-cūs* ou *Sangus*, sans compter un neutre Σάγκος qui d'après Lydus, *Mens.* 4.58, serait le nom du ciel dans la langue sabine.[10] L'identification avec *Dius Fidius* repose sur l'étymologie qui rattachait *Sancus* à *sancio, sacer*, mais ce n'est peut-être là qu'une construction de grammairien, comme aussi la traduction de *Dius Fidius* par Ζεύς πίστιος. Ce n'est pas du reste la seule explication proposée: selon Varron, *L.L.* 5.66, Aelius Stilo "Dium Fidium dicebat Diouis filium, ut Graece Διόσκορον Castorem, et putabat hunc esse Sancum ab Sabina lingua". On entrevoit ici une histoire compliquée et obscure, des rapprochements fondés sur des étymologies douteuses ou fausses: il est possible que la parenté de *Fidius* et de *fido, fidēs* ne soit qu'apparente, et que *Fidius* soit à rapprocher du nom de dieu ombrien *Fiso-*, datif singulier *Fise* dont l'adjectif dérivé **fisio-* revient souvent dans les Tables Eugubines, et qui est accompagné de l'épithète *sansio-* qui qualifie également *Fisovius, Jupiter* et *Vesticius*: cf. Tab. Eug. Ia 14 et 15: *pus veres tesenakes tref sif feliu fetu/fise saçi ukriper fisiu tutaper ikuvina* 'post portam Tessinacam tres sues lactentes facito / Fiso (ou *Fidio*) Sancio pro arce Fisia, pro ciuitate Iguuina'. Le groupe ombrien *Fiso- Sansio-* aurait son correspondant exact dans le sabin *Fidius Sancus*.

La forme ombrienne *fiso-* peut être issue de **fidyo-* avec passage du groupe *-dy-* à *s*, sans doute sonore, comme dans le sabin *Clausus* en face de *Claudius*, et le pélignien *Musesa*=*Mussedia* (Ve, no. 204); à ce traitement du groupe *-dy-* correspond en osque le passage de *-ty-* à *-s-*: *Bansa* est issu de **Bantia*, comme le prouve le dérivé *Bantinus*. Ce phénomène réapparaît dans des inscriptions de basse époque, où l'on trouve les graphies *zebus*=*diebus*, *oze*=*hodie*, *Zodorus*=*Diodorus*, etc.

Quant à *Sēmō*, il est vraisemblable d'y voir le doublet masculin du neutre *sēmen*, comme le grec a τέρμων à côté de τέρμα: ce serait le 'dieu des semailles' invoqué dans le *Carmen fratrum Arualium*, sous la forme du pluriel *Simunis* (*Semunis*)=*Sēmōnēs*. On notera que l'autre dieu qui figure dans le *Carmen* est *Marmar*, c'est-à-dire la forme sabine de *Mars*, imploré comme divinité agraire: la présence de *Marmar* et de *Semones* dans le *Carmen* révèle une influence sabine dans le rituel agraire romain. Quel sens faut-il donner à *Sancus* dans le couple *Semo Sancus*? Je n'en sais rien, mais le

[8] "Vacuna in Sabinis dea quae sub incerta specie est formata. Hanc quidem Bellonam, alii Mineruam, alii Dianam; sed Varro in I rerum diuinarum Victoriam ait, quod ea maxime hi gaudent qui sapientiae uacant", *Schol. Hor. ad* 1.

[9] L'*e* long de *Fēronia* est bien attesté par la scansion, cf. Virgile *Aen.* 7.800 et 8.964; Horace, *Sat.* 1.5.24. La graphie φερωνία est 'étymologisante'.

[10] Voir les témoignages recueillis par R. S. Conway, *The Italic dialects* 1.357 (Cambridge, 1897). La forme *Sangus* est donnée par les mss. de Tite-Live 8.20.3 où on lit *Semoni Sango;* 32.1.10 *Sangus aedes;* ce peuvent être des doublets dialectaux; ils proviennent, le premier de Privernum, le second de Veliternum.

rapprochement de *sancio* ne paraît fournir rien de raisonnable. *Marmar*, sous cette forme ou sous une autre, *Mamers*, *Mauors*, *Maurs*, *Mars* est sans étymologie; *Iuno Curis* n'est pas plus sûre; *Fērōnia*, *Vacūna* non plus; il n'est pas téméraire d'en dire autant de *Sancus*. Seuls s'expliquent *Neriō*, dont l'antiquité est attestée par la persistance de la flexion à alternance, et *Sēmō*; il est possible que la flexion *Sēmō*, *Sēmōnis* soit le résultat d'une normalisation d'un ancien **sēmō*, *-ēnes*: le lituanien oriental a en effet des formes de pluriel en *-e-*: nom. masc. *semenes*, gén. *semenu*, comme *akmuõ*, gr. ἄκμων, gén. *akmeñs*. Ces brèves remarques n'ont d'autre objet que de souligner nos incertitudes en ce qui concerne la préhistoire de l'Italie, et il faut être reconnaissant à M. J. Whatmough de s'y être consacré:

> Illi robur et aes triplex
> Circa pectus erat...[11]

ÉCOLE DES HAUTES ÉTUDES, PARIS

[11] Horace, *Carm.* 1.3.9.

ROBERT A. FOWKES

GENDER REDISTRIBUTION IN KELTIC – A PRELIMINARY STUDY

THE FIRST drastic redistribution of gender in Keltic occurred with the accomplishment of the elimination of neuters in Brythonic, for, as is well known, no Brythonic dialect exhibits the neuter gender of the noun at any period, while even pronominal retentions are merely vestigial and scarcely recognizable as such. It is uncertain when this disappearance of the neuter gender took place, although some authorities[1] believe that there is evidence for the persistence of the neuter gender in Brythonic until at least after the date of the earliest borrowings from Latin. Support for this assumption is allegedly found in those Latin words transmitted by Old British (pre-Welsh, possibly) to Irish, a process which supposedly occurred early enough for such Latin neuters to retain their gender in Old Irish. A favorite example is Old Irish *ór* n. 'gold' (from a pre-Welsh equivalent of modern Welsh *aur* [now masculine], itself from Latin *aurum*; in modern Irish the gender is masculine). This sort of evidence is, however, far from conclusive. It is not inconceivable that the Latin loanwords had lost their neuter gender in Brythonic, becoming masculine or feminine, and their subsequent re-assignment to the neuter gender in Irish may well have been the result of other factors, such as partial paradigmatic resemblance to Irish neuters. It is, at any rate, certainly true that borrowings from modern English are assigned to masculine or feminine gender in Welsh and Irish, but this obviously does not constitute evidence for the existence of those genders in English.

By now the neuter has disappeared from Goidelic too, so that it remains nowhere in Keltic. Shifts in gender distribution might superficially be regarded as induced by the need to accommodate former neuters, some becoming masculine, the rest feminine, as has been seen in many languages, for example Romance, where old neuters have largely become masculine, although many have also become feminine for various

[1] Cf. H. Pedersen, *Vergleichende Grammatik der keltischen Sprachen* 2.66–67 (Göttingen, 1909–13).

reasons (resemblance of neuter plurals to feminine singulars, etc.). This constitutes only a partial explanation of the phenomenon, however, as is clearly shown by the situation in German,[2] which has retained all three genders but which shows, nevertheless, transfer from masculine to feminine, from feminine to masculine, in fact from any gender to any other. Here, too, plausible explanations have been given, historical and otherwise, but none, of course, on the basis of gender loss, since that has not occurred.

Despite repeated fluctuation in gender in all periods of Keltic (with not too much evidence, admittedly, for Gaulish), there seems to be a specific direction of change in which all Keltic languages have participated and are still participating: the reduction in number of nouns of feminine gender. It is not necessary to invoke teleological terminology to state this. The process is going on, as is easy to ascertain. Later studies may conceivably avail themselves of recent techniques based on refinements in statistical methodology and may even be able to provide some reasonable prognosis.

In the course of preparatory work on a proposed etymological dictionary of the Welsh language, the writer noticed an apparent shrinkage in the proportion of feminines to masculines as between medieval and modern Welsh. Rather laborious counting has confirmed the impression. The task of determining the number of nouns of each gender in Middle Welsh is not simple, since lexicographical tools are incomplete. But the four 'branches' of the *Mabinogi* provide a fairly extensive body of Middle Welsh prose, particularly in Mühlhausen's edition,[3] with its convenient glossary. And, although the glossary has over one hundred nouns of unspecified or dubious gender, it has proved possible on the basis of internal and external evidence (syntactic sandhi, occurrence in other works, etc.) to reduce these to fourteen, so that the proportion obtained is not materially affected by these nouns of doubtful gender. The *Mabinogi* shows, then, 412 masculine nouns and 263 feminines, which means that there are 1.56 times as many masculines as feminines. But the picture in Modern Welsh changes significantly. There, with a greater lexicon to draw upon, we find the proportion of 7,892 masculines to 3,815 feminines, which is to say that there are 2.17 times as many masculines as feminines. This count is based upon the twelfth edition of Spurrell,[4] which has the advantage of being more reliable than most other Welsh dictionaries in the validity of its entries. A number of competent scholars succeeded in ridding it of most of the 'ghost-words' that have beset so many Keltic lexicons, and there is a careful designation of those words which are now archaic and obsolete. None of these were included in the above count. In one point of procedure a choice had to be made among various possibilities, and it is to be hoped that the decision of the writer has not been too faulty. A number of words have both masculine and

[2] Hermann Paul, *Deutsche Grammatik*[2] 91–124 (Halle, 1917).

[3] Ludwig Mühlhausen, *Die vier Zweige des Mabinogi* (Halle, 1925).

[4] J. Bodvan Anwyl, ed., *Spurrell's Welsh-English Dictionary* (12th ed., Carmarthen, 1924).

feminine gender. Although this is sometimes determined by geographic and dialectal considerations, in most instances this is not so. Most of these words with fluctuating gender are treated now as masculine and now as feminine, even by the same author. A word like *munud* 'minute' occurs as masculine on page 126 of a recent Welsh novel[5] (the sandhi of *mor anhapus ag yr ydw' i'r munud 'ma* 'as unhappy as I am this minute', with retention of the radical, non-lenited initial of *munud*, points unequivocally to masculine gender), whereas the same word occurs as a feminine two pages earlier (*y funud nesaf* 'the next minute', with lenition of *m-* after the article, a situation that marks the word as a feminine noun). Such words have been counted twice in the above figures, as if there were in each instance two separate words, one of each gender.

It then occurred to the writer that a bare lexical count of the words of each gender might be of dubious, or partial validity. If, for example, a high percentage of masculine nouns rarely occurred in writing or speech, whereas the lexically outnumbered feminines were to prove of greater frequency, the entire count might very easily be vitiated. A textual count was therefore made of all the nouns occurring in the novel *Diwrnod yw ein Bywyd* (see fn. 5 above). Here, including duplicates, there are 3,398 masculine nouns and 1,482 feminines. Hence there are 2.29 times as many masculines as feminines in this body of contemporary Welsh prose, a proportion which does not differ greatly from that yielded by the lexical count. There is always the chance that any statistical conclusions drawn from one work or one author may be atypical for the language as a whole, even though the work in question combines literary Welsh with a representative selection of colloquial language. Therefore a similar count was made of all the articles in the Welsh weekly *Y Cymro* for November 15, 1956. This issue contained in its 24 pages actually far more nouns than the novel mentioned. The scope of subjects treated included politics, poetry, sports, automobiles, editorial comment, history, archeology, music, and news. The count of nouns by gender was: 4,436 masculines and 2,205 feminines, or slightly more than twice as many masculines as feminines. There seemed to be no great diversity among various writers, and the subject matter seemed to have no bearing on the distribution of genders. Before any absolutely final statement can be made regarding the relative frequency of masculines and feminines it will be necessary to provide statistics based on a greater number of works in all genres, but it seems safe to predict, for Welsh at least, that the masculines will outnumber the feminines about two to one. (The writer is aware of the difficulties encountered by anyone attempting to determine vocabulary frequency, but the objections raised in various quarters on that score seem not to apply very directly to the question of gender, which seems to depend on factors cutting across all lines of genre, occupation, social strata, etc.)

But, in addition to lexical and textual counts there is still another type of statistical

[5] Jane Ann Jones, *Diwrnod yw ein Bywyd* (Cardiff, 1954).

observation that may be more significant than either, especially for Keltic, and more so for Brythonic than Goidelic: a count of those nouns whose gender is unambiguously recognizable from their contextual occurrence alone. For what is the meaning of gender in languages which have lost their old nominal inflectional endings, where very few suffixes are unequivocally masculine or feminine and where the gender of virtually no noun can be identified in isolation? It means, essentially, that the gender of a noun (in Welsh or Breton, say) is marked only in context, that the initial consonants of masculine nouns are treated differently from those of feminines in the operation of mutation, that a few numerals have specific masculine and feminine forms or cause different types of mutation, that adjectives undergo a characteristic mutation after feminine nouns, that certain adjectives have specifically masculine and feminine forms, and that special forms of the demonstrative pronoun refer to specific genders. (In the plural of Welsh nouns the feminine and masculine genders behave exactly the same syntactically, hence gender is, in effect, neutralized in the plural. Therefore a bare contextual count of all occurrences of masculines and feminines is misleading, in that a statistical recording of a plural as belonging to a specific gender implies a distinction not actually present.) When the nouns in *Diwrnod yw ein Bywyd* were re-examined and recounted from this point of view, the striking result was that out of 3,398 masculine nouns only 830 were clearly marked as such in context, and out of 1,482 feminines only 380 were recognizably so. The remaining 3,680 nouns were, as far as their actual occurrence in the text was concerned, undifferentiated as to gender, even though the attribute of grammatical gender is theoretically attached to them in the lexicon and most speakers of Welsh would know their gender, or would treat them as masculine or feminine in a syntactic situation calling for specific marking. But there must be something significant in the fact that such a situation was avoided in the case of over three quarters of the nouns occurring in the novel examined. It is obviously necessary to have a similar count for other works and other authors.

For Breton the lexical count of genders[6] reveals 6,779 masculines to 3,850 feminines. This represents 1.74 times as many masculines as feminines, which is not so striking a discrepancy as that seen in Welsh but which is still a fairly high preponderance of masculines over feminines. And, although no extensive count of textual occurrences could be made, the masculines in Breton promise to outnumber the feminines at an even higher proportion than in Welsh. (For some short stories the proportion was as high as seven to one, but this was based on random sampling that may not be reliable, hence it is not the intention of the writer to record the actual figures here.) Since Middle Breton lexicons shy away from designating gender, a count of gender distribution there must wait until the time is available for a gender analysis of texts. Needless to say, no gender can be ascertained unless the word occurs in a context that

[6] Roparz Hemon, *Dictionnaire Breton-Français* (Brest, 1943).

reveals whether it is masculine or feminine. From the analysis of the Welsh text given above, it can be seen that a small minority of genders can be identified on the basis of one work alone.

For Old Irish a count based on sampling reveals that the feminine gender was apparently the most numerous and the neuter least. The selections from the *Táin* edited by Strachan[7] show 41.5 per cent feminines, 36.6 per cent masculines, and 21.9 per cent neuters, while the brief selections from the Old Irish glosses[8] show 40.5 per cent feminines, 33.5 per cent masculines, and 26.0 per cent neuters. These figures must, once again, be regarded as tentative and await subsequent confirmation or correction, but their essential agreement in two such different types of language may be more than accidental. In modern Irish, a lexical count[9] shows that masculines now outnumber feminines in the proportion of 1.56 to one (10,252 masculines to 6,569 feminines), which is the same figure as was ascertained for Middle Welsh, although it is perhaps prudent to refrain from drawing any conclusion from this. Random sampling in the sparse amount of Manx literature available indicates that there too the masculines considerably outnumber the feminines (almost two to one). Figures for Scots Gaelic and Cornish remain to be compiled.

It seems clear that all Keltic dialects are undergoing a diminution of their feminine nouns. One area in which the process is plainly seen is that of loanwords. A word borrowed into Welsh at present has a very slight chance of being assigned to the feminine gender. The same applies to coinages. Recent lists[10] of technical terms in that language in the fields of chemistry, philosophy, music, etc. show that the feminines in these lists are outnumbered by the masculines almost ten to one. This was not always the case. In those loanwords which entered Welsh from Old English there were only 9 nouns of feminine gender in the originals, but there were 18 feminines among the Welsh borrowings. Although one or two of these came from OE neuters, there were several OE masculines that became feminines in Welsh (including *camp*, *ffald*, *crefft*, *ffordd*, etc.[11]). In these early borrowings the critical factor in gender transfer was, apart from nouns designating animate beings, phonic resemblance to native words of a specific gender. The same was true of still earlier borrowings from Latin, as Joseph Loth[12] showed. Any Welsh word of Latin origin that had the ending *-ell* in its Welsh form became feminine, regardless of its Latin gender. Thus *cangell* f. 'chancel' is from a Latin masculine *cancellus*. The reason for this was that *-ell* had practically become a sign of the feminine, since in inherited words of Keltic origin it

[7] John Strachan, ed., *Stories from the Táin*, 2nd ed., rev. O. Bergin (Dublin, 1928).

[8] Ibid., *Old-Irish paradigms and selections from the Old-Irish glosses*, 3rd ed., rev. O. Bergin (Dublin, 1929).

[9] Patrick S. Dineen, *An Irish-English Dictionary* (London, 1904).

[10] E.g., *Termau Technegol* (Cardiff, University of Wales Press, 1950).

[11] Cf. R. A. Fowkes, "Gender of early English loanwords in Welsh," *Word* 10.60–70 (1954).

[12] Joseph Loth, *Les mots latins dans les langues brittoniques* (Paris, 1892).

represented *-*illā*. Such considerations seem not to operate in late borrowings where a feminine gender seems to be avoided whenever possible.

The cause of this reduction in feminines seems to lie in linguistic economy. Ernst Pulgram suggests (by correspondence) that this may be part of a wider move away from gender distinctions which are, as he points out, apart from sex distinctions, a burden on any language. This may be so. It may very well be that the disappearance of the neuters was the first stage in a move which will ultimately result in a system of one gender (which virtually equals no gender), provided that the Keltic languages survive long enough to achieve that state. It is not too clear why the neuter gender was the most vulnerable in Keltic (as in English and Romance), although some reasons suggest themselves.

But the specific reason for the peculiar vulnerability of the feminines seems to be slightly different for Keltic. It is connected with the phenomenon of initial mutation (lenition and aspiration). Feminine nouns induce a far greater frequency of initial mutation than masculines. They require, for example, lenition of their initial sounds (if susceptible) when preceded by the definite article, and they cause lenition of the initial sound of a following adjective. Masculines undergo and cause no such change in those situations. Such processes call for greater expenditure of effort on a speaker's part. It was not clear to the writer how much difficulty the mutations cause even to native speakers until he had been to Wales. There he discovered that Welsh speakers (and the same holds true, in all essential respects, for other Keltic speakers) do find the mutations a strain. They do not use them 'instinctively' or automatically by any means. And how could such changes be automatic, when their original causes vanished centuries ago? Speakers are constantly worried about making errors; worry leads to hyperurbanisms. Apparent facility or surety in the use of lenition evokes expressions of admiration, even in the press. But the complete loss of all such mutations, insofar as they relate to grammatical gender, would not constitute a disadvantage, except possibly to a poet looking for variety in alliteration. For the 'functional yield' of mutations is, as far as genders are concerned, extremely low. All they succeed in doing is marking the feminine gender (which is what brought them about in the first place!). There are other situations, in Brythonic and Goidelic alike, where mutation is a positive economy, resulting in reduction of effort coupled with greater precision of expression. But this is not so with the feminine gender. There the only result is inconvenience and difficulty. In fact, in some instances, a reduction of fifty per cent in the number of feminine nouns would mean a two-hundred per cent increase in facility and economy.

Since initial vowels are not subject to mutation (with one or two minimal exceptions), it might be expected that there would be less opposition to feminine nouns which had vocalic initials. This does not prove to be true for Welsh or Irish, so that we can simply conclude that the entire category of feminine nouns has become vulnerable, whether the specific noun itself would cause any difficulty or not. On the other hand, masculine nouns with initial *p-* in Welsh outnumber the feminines by almost three to one (617 : 208). The reason for this is not hard to find. Apart from those nouns whose initial *p-* represents Indo-European q^{u} (and they are not excessively numerous), any Brythonic noun beginning with *p* must be a loanword. Here the chance to reject feminine gender was most opportune.

It might well be queried whether the statistics arrived at could be nullified by disproportionate occurrence of endings confined (or largely confined) to one gender, cf., e.g., the vast number of nomina agentis in *-wr*, which are masculines. (This ending *-wr* represents a merger, in some cases, of a Welsh word for 'man', [*g*]*wr*, with Latin *-or*, E. *-or*, *er* and possibly one or two other elements.) But there are other terminations, no less numerous in occurrence, which are feminine. Thus, monopoly is perhaps effectively eliminated. There are numerous feminines with the termination *-fa* (an old word *ma*, **magos* 'place'); another termination that is largely restricted to the feminine gender is (*i*)*aeth* (**i̯aktā?*). But the sanctity of its femininity has now been invaded as a result of the pressure to reduce the number of feminines. This is clearly seen in the case of *anghyflogaeth* 'unemployment', which is masculine. A relative neologism, first attested in 1931, it is a coinage of depression days. It is formed from the negative prefix *an-* plus *cyflogaeth*, a feminine noun. In early Modern Welsh the ending would have almost been a guarantee that such a formation was feminine, but that is no longer so.

Since every language loses a percentage of its vocabulary in the course of time, it might be objected that the procedure of counting the words of masculine and feminine gender in Middle Welsh, Modern Welsh, etc. and comparing the statistics thus arrived at is invalid, since we are not actually comparing two stages of the same vocabulary so much as two different vocabularies that happen to overlap to some extent. Those very words that were lost might accidentally have belonged primarily to one gender, and the percentage balance would then be tipped by what was a cultural or historical accident – for example, the loss of chivalric and feudal vocabulary. And we might be told by hypothetical critics that it would be more significant to compare only those words existing in both Middle and Modern Welsh (or Breton) and to note their treatment with reference to retention or alteration of gender. This would have a point, but it would be precisely the point that this paper is not intended to make, for it would concentrate on the specific to the neglect of the overall picture. For we would not only ignore those words which have been lost but also the mass of later acquisitions by loan or coinage. And it is highly pertinent to ascertain what happens to gender when a new word is incorporated into a language as well as to attempt to determine why a certain word or group is lost or transferred to another gender. We are concerned more with the total system of gender distribution; therefore it is not pertinent to observe what individual words are lost or retained except insofar as they illuminate the general process of gender distribution. It has been shown that the reduction in the number of feminine nouns in Keltic languages is, in all probability, linked to factors of linguistic economy. But this does not preclude the likelihood that it is, beyond this, one phase of a wider move. Whether general linguistic or 'panchronic' conclusions can be deduced is a matter into which the present writer is not prepared to go.

NEW YORK UNIVERSITY

MURRAY FOWLER

HERDAN'S STATISTICAL PARAMETER AND THE FREQUENCY OF ENGLISH PHONEMES

WHEN applied to samples having large numbers of distinctly different units, Herdan's formula for deriving "The coefficient of variation for the sampling distribution of means" (v_m)[1] appears to have an advantage over Yule's derivation of characteristic K. When the morpheme is the unit, the number of units (N) is changeable, the mean ($\bar{x}$) cannot be predicted, and the usefulness of v_m as a characteristic is clear. When the phoneme is the unit, the value of N remains constant, $\bar{x}$ is predictable, and the advantage of Herdan's formula is negligible.

Nevertheless, there is presumably a certain value, even if only a negative, or precautionary, one, in the application of the same method in all stages of a uni-directional investigation; the present study, therefore, uses Herdan's statistical parameter to characterize the frequency-distribution of English phonemes.

2. The tables below represent the initial results of an attempt to discover whether a distinction between langue and parole can be exhibited in the terms of a distinctly variant distribution about a mean of the members of one of the three sets of elements which can be isolated on the phonemic, morphemic, and syntactic levels. In this instance the distribution of phonemes only has been considered. The results tentatively show that the distributional arrangements of phonemes is a part of the structure of the langue which is not significantly disturbed by any individual difference either in author or in subject.

[1] The formula is introduced and explained in G. Herdan, *Language as choice and chance* 23–34 (Groningen, 1956). I have found it convenient to use the following notation, wherein σ = the standard deviation, N = the number of units, and $\bar{x}$ = the mean:

$$v_m = \frac{\dfrac{\sigma}{\sqrt{N}}}{\bar{x}}$$

The four samples examined have all been chosen from modern English prose.[2] Each sample has been transcribed into a phonemic alphabet of twenty-four consonants and six vowels.[3] Spelling has been normalized.[4] Three of the samples consist of 5000 consecutive phonemes each; the fourth, a story for children, is complete in 501 phonemes. The occurrences of each phoneme in each 1000 units of each sample have been tabulated and v_m calculated; a similar study has been made for each total of 5000. N has been maintained at a constant 30, a zero occurrence of /ʒ/ always being recorded. In the tabulation, errors of counting are reflected in the numbers given for exact counts, which represent a re-totaling of the units actually recorded.

The tabulation of the results is intended to be self-explanatory, but it should perhaps be added that experiments with smaller samples chosen from the same texts (i.e. sequences of 100, 200, and 500 phonemes) seem to show that the statistical norm of v_m is not reached until about 1000 phonemes have been counted. For this reason samples of 1000 units have been used. For the same reason the Beatrix Potter sample is possibly not statistically valid; but it may be, on the other hand, that the extreme simplicity of the language is concomitant with an abnormally high value for v_m. No test has been made of the latter hypothesis.

UNIVERSITY OF WISCONSIN

[2] The first sample (Table I) is from Graham Greene's short story *A Drive in the Country*; the second (Table II) from the same author's essay entitled *Fielding and Sterne*; the third (Table III) is from the opening of Chapter II, "Conceptions in Antiquity", of *The Concepts of the Calculus* by Carl B. Boyer (Hafner, 1949); the fourth (Table IV) is the complete *Story of a Fierce Bad Rabbit* by Beatrix Potter.

[3] The six vowels are i, e, a, o, u, ə. The following are typical examples of my phonemic transcription: *bit*/bit/; *beat*/biyt/; *put*/put/; *boot*/buwt/; *cut*/kət/; *fur*/fr/; *furry*/frri/; *surrey*/səri/; *surly*/srli/; *sorry* /sori/; *sorely*/sohrli/; *ferry*/feri/; *fairly*/fehrli/; *cot*/kot/; *caught*/koht/; *court*/kort/.

[4] E.g., *The* is always /ðə/, never /ðiy/; *a* is always /ə/, never /ey/; *and* is always /and/.

TABLE I

A Drive in the Country by Graham Greene

	1st 1000 phonemes	2nd 1000 phonemes	3rd 1000 phonemes	4th 1000 phonemes	5th 1000 phonemes	1st 5000 phonemes
Exact Number Counted	997	996	999	1005	993	4990
i	83	89	78	78	87	415
ə	69	76	79	81	55	360
y	58	72	58	69	79	336
t	52	53	75	73	80	333
r	61	74	75	60	56	326
a	56	60	54	62	65	297
n	51	65	46	53	64	279
d	43	52	47	53	54	249
w	55	40	51	42	54	242
e	45	43	39	40	42	209
o	41	26	53	46	39	205
l	50	34	35	39	33	191
s	37	38	36	33	40	184
h	40	30	45	25	29	169
ð	30	34	35	34	25	158
z	39	27	20	32	19	137
k	36	25	22	29	22	134
u	19	21	24	14	28	106
m	20	20	20	15	18	93
f	19	25	14	22	12	92
v	15	23	17	17	19	91
p	13	23	25	14	9	84
b	15	11	17	11	17	71
ŋ	17	10	7	14	15	63
ʃ	7	7	13	19	10	56
g	8	6	4	11	8	37
c	7	3	5	9	3	27
θ	10	4	4	5	2	25
j	2	5	1	3	9	20
ʒ	0	0	0	2	0	2
Mean	33.2	33.2	33.3	33.5	33.1	166.367
Standard Deviation	21.688	23.6	23.91	23.216	24.77	114.04127
Coefficient of variation of sampling distribution of means (V_m)	.1191	.1297	.1311	.1295	.1396	.125139

TABLE II

Fielding and Sterne by Graham Greene

	1st 1000 phonemes	2nd 1000 phonemes	3rd 1000 phonemes	4th 1000 phonemes	5th 1000 phonemes	1st 5000 phonemes
Exact Number Counted	998	995	994	1001	996	4984
ə	99	101	86	78	89	453
i	69	80	87	84	104	424
n	72	70	80	72	62	356
t	78	69	70	52	67	336
r	64	63	49	67	58	301
y	57	58	63	51	56	275
w	48	49	50	55	45	247
a	46	42	49	54	43	234
o	39	43	44	54	42	222
l	38	46	31	36	49	200
e	36	46	39	37	39	197
d	38	31	43	53	31	196
s	46	44	36	30	37	193
z	30	17	32	30	37	146
k	24	26	26	39	24	139
ð	35	34	24	21	20	134
m	23	28	21	29	30	131
h	19	22	22	28	31	122
v	25	22	20	18	28	113
u	21	23	21	18	23	106
f	18	18	27	19	14	96
p	12	16	26	28	8	90
b	20	10	14	7	22	73
ʃ	12	8	11	15	13	59
j	5	11	7	7	5	35
g	5	3	9	5	9	31
ŋ	10	3	7	4	5	29
c	4	5	5	6	2	22
θ	5	6	5	3	3	22
ʒ	0	1	0	1	0	2
Mean	33.266	33.166	33.133	33.366	33.2	166.133
Standard Deviation	24.56	25.117	23.803	23.56	25.133	120.704
Coefficient of variation of sampling distribution of means (V_m)	.1348	.1382	.1311	.1289	.1381	.13265

TABLE III

Concepts of the Calculus by Carl B. Boyer

	1st 1000 phonemes	2nd 1000 phonemes	3rd 1000 phonemes	4th 1000 phonemes	5th 1000 phonemes	1st 5000 phonemes
Exact Number Counted	1000	995	991	995	989	4970
ə	97	103	94	92	110	496
i	96	96	91	105	105	493
n	76	62	70	64	53	325
r	64	81	64	60	55	324
t	55	60	69	63	58	305
y	59	45	61	58	46	269
a	45	42	55	49	47	238
s	52	36	43	47	58	236
e	47	39	37	43	33	199
l	45	39	39	32	34	189
k	30	37	38	32	40	177
m	30	33	34	31	38	166
w	33	29	37	37	28	164
d	33	33	25	34	37	162
ð	28	34	34	32	27	155
o	31	39	30	25	27	152
z	26	27	22	33	28	136
v	20	26	20	22	24	112
u	11	16	26	22	24	99
p	20	23	15	14	21	93
b	14	13	19	16	21	83
h	24	16	6	14	19	79
f	17	20	16	15	8	76
ʃ	15	16	10	10	11	62
θ	9	5	7	15	15	51
ŋ	7	7	9	11	6	40
g	6	4	12	6	10	38
j	5	9	6	8	5	33
c	4	5	1	5	1	16
ʒ	1	0	1	0	0	2
Mean	33.333	33.166	33.03	33.166	32.966	165.6666
Standard Deviation	25.439	25.49	25.25	27.484	25.855	124.86509
Coefficient of variation of sampling distribution of means (V_m)	.1393	.1403	.1395	.1483	.1432	.137534

TABLE IV

The Story of a Fierce Bad Rabbit by Beatrix Potter

501 phonemes									
i	67	y	28	ð	15	o	8	v	5
a	37	n	25	c	14	n	7	f	4
ə	36	r	25	w	14	g	6	c	3
z	31	d	22	k	13	u	6	j	2
t	30	s	21	l	12	θ	5	ʃ	2
h	29	b	19	p	10	m	5	ʒ	0

Mean	16.7
Standard Deviation	14.297
Coefficient of variation of sampling distribution of means (V_m)	.1563

E. ADELAIDE HAHN

A LINGUISTIC FALLACY

(BASED ON A STUDY OF VERGIL[1])

IN LANGUAGE, certain types of departure from strict logic may result in the achievement of variety, of suggestiveness, or of effectiveness in a way that considerably enriches the piece of literature concerned, especially if this be of a class that depends for value in part on esthetic or imaginative appeal. Such forms of expression are to be expected and desired particularly in poetry or poetic prose. We shall not find them to a great extent in *straightforward prose* like that of Caesar, who resorts to practically no embellishments; or even in *rhetorical prose* like that of Cicero, who does assuredly resort to embellishments, but of a more mechanical or superficial type, so to speak, embellishments primarily of outer form such as anaphora or antithesis. We shall not find them in *prosaic poetry* like that of Plautus or Terence, who, as Horace realized well,[2] are giving us merely the commonplace language of conversation in metrical form – language abounding in departures from logic but of a less subtle type. We shall find them to some extent in *poetic prose*, prose which breaks away from the prose norm: prose which is rich in overtones like that of Livy, who shows so often the influence of his contemporary Vergil; or prose which is, so to speak, rich in undertones, like that of Tacitus, who says so much more to the mind[3] than meets the eye or the ear. But above all we shall find them in *genuine poetry*, particularly that of so supremely sensitive and suggestive a poet as Vergil, to whom and in whom variety and imaginative appeal count so much more than precise logic.

On the basis of a study of Vergil, I have come to the conclusion that many instances

[1] In citing Vergil, I designate passages from the Eclogues and the Georgics by E and G respectively; all passages not specifically designated are from the Aeneid. I quote enough to show the sense and the syntax, with no indication of omitted words.

[2] Cf. Serm. 1.4.45–62.

[3] I believe it is beginning once more to be respectable to talk about the mind.

of supposed confusion of expression[4] are due to the application of one of two formulas. One is the formula, rarely true in mathematics, frequently but not always true in logic, that if *a* bears a certain relation to *b*, *b* will bear the same relation to *a*. The other is the formula, almost always true in mathematics, frequently untrue in logic, that if $a = b$ and $b = c$, then *a* also $= c$. With the first of these misconceptions, the misconception that leads us to say that the harbor approaches the boat or the land recedes from it[5] when actually the boat nears or leaves the harbor or the land, or that a boat is shaken away from its pilot[6] when actually the pilot is shaken away from the boat, or that the fire is put under spits[7] when actually the spits are put over the fire, or that a living creature leaves life[8] when actually life leaves the creature,[9] I have dealt elsewhere.[10] The second misconception, based on the notion that things equal to the same thing are always equal to each other, has so many ramifications and applications that it cannot be treated in a single paper. Examples of it are numerous. A person may be confused with some fundamental part of himself, such as his body,[11] or his soul,[12] or his name;[13] or with some representation of himself, such as the image,[14] or the lot,[15] that stands for him. The confusion of the *ego* with the *nomen* or with the *effigies* or with parts of the *corpus* accounts for many practices in contagious or sympathetic magic as well as for certain linguistic phenomena. From the fact that the *ego* is used interchangeably now with the body, now with the soul, it results that these two really opposed entities come to be used interchangeably too, in English as well as in Latin: it does not seem to make the least difference whether an old woman is called a poor old body or a poor old soul, whether we say that in a shipwreck everybody[16] perished or every soul perished.[17] This is a form of what we call metonymy. And it is by a form of metonymy too that we so often

[4] I am using the word *confusion* as a convenient cover-term. I wish to stress the fact that it should not be understood as conveying derogatory implications; cf. my opening paragraph.

[5] 3.430–1 portus patescit iam propior, 3.72 prouehimur portu terraeque urbesque recedunt.

[6] 6.353 excussa magistro, with which contrast 1.115 excutitur magister.

[7] 5.103 subiciunt ueribus prunas, with which contrast Homer, Il. 2.426 σπλάγχνα δ'ἄρ' ἀμπείραντες ὑπείρεχον Ἡφαίστοιο.

[8] G 3.547 uitam relinquunt and 5.517 uitam reliquit, with which contrast 6.735 uita reliquit and 10.819–20 uita corpus reliquit.

[9] At least according to Vergil's conception of the *uita* as a tangible thing that departs or flees at death: cf. 4.705, 10.819–20, 11.831 = 12.952.

[10] *TAPA* 87(1956) – in press.

[11] E.g. 6.362 nunc me fluctus habet (said by the ghost of Palinurus in Hades).

[12] E.g. 11.829 exsoluit se corpore.

[13] E.g. 1.286–8 nascetur Iulius, a magno demissum nomen Iulo.

[14] E.g. E 8.73–5 terna tibi licia circumdo, terque haec altaria circum effigiem duco.

[15] 5.498 extremus galeaque ima subsedit Acestes.

[16] The phrase *every body* has even become a single word, *everybody*, as we show by our manner of pronouncing it as well as by our manner of writing it.

[17] Obviously a complete inaccuracy when used by those who believe the soul to be immortal.

confuse a group of persons with the place wherein they are to be found. This is the particular type of confusion that I am dealing with in the present paper.

The confusion between the name of a place and the name of a people may be due in part to the fact that occasionally they actually do coïncide, as *Delphi*, *Locri*, perhaps *Argi*.[18] While such perfect coincidence in form seems rare, the name of the place and the name of the people at least show an identical root in the vast majority of cases, as *Oenotria* : *Oenotrii*, *Lydia* : *Lydii*, etc. But the confusion of use is due far more, I think, to the fact that in so many instances place-names and people-names may be employed as practically equivalent.

The place and the people may each keep its own identity and be used in its own proper sense, as is probably the case in 8.635-7 Romam et raptas Sabinas addiderat, where the meaning seems to be that Vulcan has represented both the place, Rome, and the actors, the Sabine women (although they are not the only actors, and *Romanos* is probably implied in *Romam*,[19] whether the two are actually identical or not).

But more often the two types of entities are used indiscriminately and interchangeably, either one in its own right being appropriate enough. Thus in 4.40–3 hinc Gaetulae urbes et Numidae infreni cingunt et inhospita Syrtis, hinc deserta siti regio lateque furentes Barcaei, Anna talks with equal appropriateness about the Gaetulian *cities* and the Numidian *people*, as well as a *body of water*, and then of a barren *region* and another *people*, the Barcaeans, as surrounding Dido's settlement. In 1.338–9 Punica regna uides, Tyrios et Agenoris urbem, sed fines Libyci, Venus tells Aeneas with equal truth that he sees Punic *realms* and the *city* of Agenor, and also the *people*, the Tyrians. In 1.223–5 Iuppiter despiciens mare terrasque litoraque et latos[20] populos, and again in 10.3–4 terras omnis castraque Dardanidum adspectat populosque Latinos, Jupiter from on high beholds both *countries* and *peoples*.[21] In 6.891 Laurentis docet populos urbemque Latini, Anchises is suitably represented as instructing his son concerning both the *peoples*[22] and the *city* that he will come

[18] On *Locri*, cf. Conington's note on 3.18. On *Argi*, cf. Plautus, Amph. 98 Amphitruo, natus Argis ex Argo patre. On the basis of *Argo* in this line, it might be possible to interpret *Argis* in 1.23–4 belli, quod pro caris gesserat Argis as referring to the people rather than to the place, though I would not advocate it, since the passage deals primarily with Juno's concern for *places*: note *Karthago* (13) and *Samo* (16).

[19] Exactly so, just below in 8.638 Romulidis Tatioque seni Curibusque seueris, *Curibus* stands for *Sabinis*; as Conington says ad loc., *Romulidis* represents Romulus and his nation, *Tatio Curibusque* represents Tatius and his.

[20] However, the adjective here would seem to apply rather to the countries than to the peoples. On this see below, fn. 48.

[21] We may compare a not dissimilar collocation of words denoting both *locality* (*campum* and *urbem*) and *persons* (*acies*) in the description of Juno looking down from a mountain-top, 12.136–7 campum adspectabat et ambas Laurentum Troumque acies urbemque Latini.

[22] Conington ad loc. explains *Laurentis populos* as "the *towns* [italics mine] of the Laurentian territory", but I do not see the necessity for this.

to know in the following book. In 11.420 auxilioque urbes Italae populique supersunt, and in its parallel just below, 11.428 non erit auxilio nobis Aetolus et Arpi, the collocation of nouns, whether common or proper, for *people* and *place*, is suitable, since both people and place might be a source of help, the former as allies and reinforcements, the latter as refuges and bases of supplies. Above all in 1.6–7 genus unde Latinum Albanique patres atque altae moenia Romae, *genus* and *moenia*[23] are alike of cardinal importance; the Roman gloried alike in his *race* and in his *city*.[24]

This sort of collocation is particularly likely to occur in rather lengthy enumerations such as the lists that enter naturally into the didactic material of the Georgics, or that belong to the account in the Aeneid of the gathering first of the Italian clans and then of the Etruscan ones. Vergil, doubtless in order to add life and charm to catalogues that might tend to become monotonous and tedious, makes use to a great degree of variety. Thus it is natural that he should place side by side elements really disparate. Elsewhere, the feeling that a list is imposingly long, that it is composed of an impressively large number of members, is perhaps enhanced if these members are made as diverse as possible. I select a few instances of this general type for special comment.

(1) G 2.114–7

adspice et extremis domitum cultoribus orbem
Eoasque domos Arabum pictosque Gelonos:
diuisae arboribus patriae. sola India nigrum
fert hebenum, solis est turea uirga Sabaeis.

(2) G 2.136–9

sed neque Medorum siluae, ditissima terra,
nec pulcher Ganges atque auro turbidus Hermus
laudibus Italiae certent, non Bactra neque Indi
totaque turiferis Panchaia pinguis harenis.

(3) G 1.56–9

nonne uides, croceos ut Tmolus odores,

[23] The common use of *moenia* in the sense of *urbs* throws light on 7.409–10 audacis Rutuli ad muros, quam dicitur urbem Danae fundasse, where at first sight the reference of *quam urbem* to *muros* seems rather odd. By once more introducing our 'things equal to the same thing' axiom, we may put *moenia* in one sense in the place of *muros*, and in another in the place of *urbem*.

[24] Thus T. R. Glover, perceptive and sensitive though he is, seems to me for once to err when he says reproachfully (*Virgil*³ 206): "Dido's anguish seems to suggest that the gods think more of seven hills beside a river than of human woe or of right and wrong." As for right and wrong, surely right was on Rome's side, wrong on Dido's: she knew of Aeneas's divine mission, even of the *regia coniunx* (2.783) that was destined for him in Italy. As for human woes, these were not just *any* seven hills beside *any* river: the river was the Tiber, *caeruleus Thybris, caelo gratissimus amnis* (8.64), *corniger Hesperidum fluuius, regnator aquarum* (8.77); and the seven hills, like the walls in 1.7, represent *Rome*, the end and aim that justifies any amount of personal sorrow and suffering (whether of Dido, Turnus, Laocoon, Aeneas himself) – *tantae molis erat Romanam condere gentem* (1.33).

India mittit ebur, molles sua tura Sabaei,
at Chalybes nudi ferrum, uirosaque Pontus
castorea, Eliadum palmas Epirus equarum?

(4) G 4.210–2
praeterea regem non sic Aegyptus et ingens
Lydia nec populi Parthorum aut Medus Hydaspes
obseruant.

(5) 8.705–6
omnis eo terrore Aegyptus et Indi,
omnis Arabs, omnes uertebant terga Sabaei.

(6) 7.794–802
agmina densentur campis, Argiuaque pubes
Auruncaeque manus, Rutuli ueteresque Sicani,
et Sacranae acies et picti scuta Labici;
qui saltus, Tiberine, tuos sacrumque Numici
litus arant Rutulosque exercent uomere collis
Circaeumque iugum, quis Iuppiter Anxurus aruis
praesidet et uiridi gaudens Feronia luco;
qua Saturae iacet atra palus gelidusque per imas
quaerit iter uallis atque in mare conditur Vfens.

(7) 10.183–4
qui Caerete domo, qui sunt Minionis in aruis,
et Pyrgi ueteres intempestaeque Grauiscae.

(8) G 4.461–3
flerunt Rhodopeiae arces
altaque Pangaea et Rhesi Mauortia tellus
atque Getae atque Hebrus et Actias Orithyia.

(9) G 3.30–1
addam urbes Asiae domitas pulsumque Niphaten
fidentemque fuga Parthum uersisque sagittis.

(10) 8.724–8
hic Nomadum genus et distinctos Mulciber Afros,
hic Lelegas Carasque sagittiferosque Gelonos
finxerat; Euphrates ibat iam mollior undis,
extremique hominum Morini, Rhenusque bicornis,
indomitique Dahae, et pontem indignatus Araxes.

In No. 1 (G 2.114–7) Vergil bids his readers behold with their mind's eye *places*, the whole *universe*, the *dwellings* of the Arabs, and also a *people*, the Geloni; and he adds that trees are distributed among different *countries*, for instance India bears ebony, but a *people*, the Sabaeans, possess frankincense. From an example like this one, it is but a step in one direction to No. 2 (G 2.136–9), where we are told with perfect logic that *countries*, Bactra and Panchaea, cannot vie with the *country* of Italy; with less perfect logic that *rivers*, the Ganges and the Hermus, cannot; and with practically no logic that *people*, the Indians, cannot.[25] And it is but a step in the other direction to No. 3 (G 1.56–9), where we are told logically that *peoples*, the Sabaeans and the Chalybes, export certain objects; and not quite so logically, or at least metaphorically, that *places*, India, Pontus, Epirus, and even a *mountain*, Tmolus, export certain others.

Examples of the type of No. 3 are commoner than those of the type of No. 2; that is, it seems to be particularly natural to use the name of the *country* for that of the *people*. We can talk just as readily, as in 7.799–80 quis Iuppiter Anxurus aruis praesidet,[26] of presiding over *fields*[27] as of presiding over *peoples*, or, as in G 3.30 urbes Asiae domitas,[28] of conquering *cities* as of conquering *peoples*. And so it is very easy in No. 4 (G 4.210–2) to say that *peoples* (the Parthians), *countries* (Egypt and Lydia), and even a *river* (the Hydaspes) guard their king; and in No. 5 (8.705–6) to have Egypt[29] flee along with the Indians, the Arabs, and the Sabaeans. In No. 6 (7.794–802) Vergil makes parallel with the phrases (*Argiua pubes* etc.) and nouns (*Rutuli* etc.) describing *tribes*, the *qui* clause, likewise describing *tribes*, and then the *quis* clause and the *qua* clause, describing districts. In No. 7 (10.183–4) the *qui* clauses referring to *peoples* are made coordinate with the two proper nouns referring to *towns*. In No. 8 (G 4.461–3) not only a *people*, the Getae, weep, but also the *land* of Mars, that is, Thrace, not to mention *mountains* (the citadels of Rhodopeia and lofty Pangaea) and a *river* (the Hebrus). These last, of course, are personifications suitable to a mythological passage. They do not stand for dwellers in the vicinity, but themselves represent distinct personalities,[30] just as the nymph Orithyia does. Again in No. 9 (G 3.30–1), the reference to the routed Niphates (whether a *river* or a *mountain* is meant) as a parallel on the one hand to the conquered *cities* of Asia and on the other to a *people*, the fleeing[31] Parthian(s), is rendered

[25] Also – an additional inconcinnity – the forests of the Medes. For this see below, fn. 55.
[26] Quoted above as part of No. 6.
[27] Cf. too the coordination of *peoples* and *fields* in 7.738 Sarrastis populos et quae rigat aequora Sarnus, and perhaps just above (provided *iuxta* is an adverb) in 7.725–8 mille rapit populos, uertunt Massica qui rastris, et quos Aurunci misere patres Sidicinaque iuxta aequora.
[28] Quoted above as part of No. 9.
[29] Shakespeare even makes Egypt stand for a single person, its *queen*, in the famous apostrophe "I am dying, Egypt, dying". (Ant. and Cleo., Act 4, Scene 13).
[30] In E 8.44–6 (of the ancestry of Amor) duris in cotibus illum aut Tmarus, aut Rhodope, aut extremi Garamantes puerum edunt, Conington holds that *extremi Garamantes* "seems to show" that Vergil "was thinking less of the rocks than of their inhabitants". That may be; yet I find more effective the suggestion that the rocky mountains themselves, as well as the extremely remote and savage Garamantes, might have engendered the monster (cf. in a very different setting Horace's *parturient montes*).
[31] Flight (feigned) and arrows directed backward usually meant successful trickery for the Parthians,

easier by the fact that in Roman triumphs the representations of mountains and rivers frequently figured along with the representatives of conquered nations,[32] so that again a sort of personification is involved. This applies too to the references in No. 10 (8.724–8) to *rivers* as well as to *peoples.* But there is less personification in Nos. 2 (G 2.136–9) and 4 (G 4.210–2), where *rivers* are listed along with *places* and *peoples*, and in No. 3 (G 1.56–9), where a *mountain* is similarly dealt with. In such cases it is neither important nor even possible to determine whether the reference is primarily to the *people* who dwell on the mountain or by the river, or to the *place* where the mountain stands or the river runs.

But we have a quite different situation in G 2.224–5 talem arat Capua et uicina Veseuo ora iugo et Clanius non aequus Acerris, where the river plays a two-fold rôle:[33] it is thought of specifically as a *river*, as is proved by the reference to its floods in *non aequus Acerris*; and at the same time it is put for the *country* through which it flows, and is thus made parallel to *Capua* and *ora*.[34] But there is a certain additional confusion here in that all three alike – *Capua* and *ora* and *Clanius* – ultimately do not stand for places at all, but for people, since *arat Capua* certainly means *arant Capuani*, like *Numici litus arant* in 7.797–8 (quoted as part of No. 6 above).[35] In the same way in G 1.509 hinc mouet Euphrates, illinc Germania bellum, the name of the *river* is made parallel to the name of the *country*, but actually *both* names stand for the *people* involved.[36]

More frequently, we have the collocation of the name of the *country* representing the *people*, and the actual name of the people. In E 1.62 aut Ararim Parthus bibet, aut Germania Tigrim, Germany, that is the Germans, will drink from the Tigris as the Parthian will from the Arar. In 10.8 abnueram bello Italiam concurrere

but here Vergil seems to be envisaging their future defeat (which he actually lived to see, since their surrender of the captured Roman standards took place a year before his death), so their trust in flight is probably ironic, and perhaps *uersis sagittis* suggests a military reverse.

32 Cf. Conington on G 3.28 and 30 and on 8.722 and 726.

33 Cf. the double presentation, both as geographical entity and as tutelary genius, of the Tiber in 8.62–7, the Nile in 8.711–3, and Mt. Atlas in 4.246–51; also of the Tiber in Horace, Carm. 1.2.13–20.

34 Similarly in 5.797–8 liceat Laurentem attingere Thybrim, si dant ea moenia Parcae, the river is put for the city that was ultimately to be erected upon its banks.

35 Cf. the attribution to cities of an act really carried on by their inhabitants in 7.629–31 urbes tela nouant, Atina Tiburque, Ardea Crustumerique et Antemnae. There is an additional inconcinnity here if one of the five names, *Crustumeri*, applies rather to the *inhabitants* than to the *town*; but this seems doubtful. Vergil seems to have coined the term, the usual names for both the people (*Crustŭmīni*) and the town (*Crustŭmĕrĭa* or *Crustŭmĕrĭum*) being alike impossible in dactylic meter; but whether he meant the people or the town is impossible to say with certainty. However, if he wanted to denote the people, it seems odd that he did not say *Crustumii*, a form which he employs as an adjective in G 2.88, and which would have fitted perfectly into his verse. Conington suggests that he might have called the town *Crustumium*, which would also have fitted the verse; but this does not seem to have occurred before Silius (8.366), who perhaps invented this name for the sake of the meter as I believe Vergil did *Crustumeri*.

36 Cf. Juvenal's maliciously vivid line 3.62 Syrus in Tiberim defluxit Orontes.

Teucris Italy contends with the Trojans, Italy representing the Italians. In 10.364–5 Arcades uidit Latio dare terga the Arcadians flee before Latium, Latium representing the Latins. These are all quite understandable, and we would accept without question the figurative use of a geographical term[37] were the figure preserved throughout – that is, if we had *Parthia* as well as *Germany* drinking, *Italy* contending with *Troy*, *Arcadia* fleeing before *Latium*. The salient irregularity lies in the combination of the literal and the metaphorical, and it is just this irregularity that constitutes the unexpectedness and consequently the pleasingness of the passages. It is to be noted, too, that in introducing this agreeable variety, Vergil chooses well when to use literal and when to use figurative language. Since his scene is actually laid in Italy, in Latium, in the two passages from Aeneid 10 just quoted, it is far more appropriate to personify these regions than it would be to introduce the notions of distant Troy or Arcadia – it is far more effective to speak of *Italy* and the *Trojans*, of *Latium* and the *Arcadians*, than it would be to reverse the situation.

But there can be no question about the incongruity of 12.567–9 urbem hodie, causam belli, regna ipsa Latini, ni frenum accipere et uicti parere fatentur, eruam; here the *city* and the *kingdoms* are first spoken of as localities to be destroyed, and then are said to do what their inhabitants really do, that is, confess[38] – unless we prefer to say that *fatentur* has an indefinite subject like our English *they* in the sense of German *man* or French *on*,[39] designating the persons who live in the city and the kingdoms. We have a double example of this sort of inconcinnity in 3.104–10

> Creta Iouis magni medio iacet insula ponto,
> mons Idaeus ubi et gentis cunabula nostrae.
> centum urbes habitant magnas, uberrima regna,
> maximus unde pater, si rite audita recordor,
> Teucrus Rhoeteas primum est aduectus in oras,
> optauitque locum regno. nondum Ilium et arces
> Pergameae steterant; habitabant uallibus imis.

The logical subject of *habitant* in 106 would certainly be *Cretenses*, implied by *Creta* in 104; and of *habitabant* in 110 would be *Troiani*, implied by *Ilium* and *Pergameae* in 109–10 (or possibly *Teucri*, implied by *Teucrus* in 108). We have a similar problem in 7.601–3

[37] Indeed, this is particularly easy for us since we are quite as ready to say that Italy fights as to say that the Italians fight. Since the Romans in prose did not customarily do so, their substitution of Italy for the Italians has a distinct poetic value, perhaps more evident to them than to us.
[38] It is this double usage that makes the inconcinnity so much more striking than that, for instance, in 7.629–30 urbes tela nouant, cited in fn. 35.
[39] Cf. G 3.158 notas et nomina inurunt, and perhaps G 3.311–2 barbas incanaque menta Cinyphii tondent hirci (on the latter passage see Conington's discussion ad loc.).

> mos erat Hesperio in Latio, quem protinus urbes
> Albanae coluere sacrum, nunc maxima rerum
> Roma colit, cum prima mouent in proelia Martem.

Here the implied subject of *mouent*, *Romani*, has to be supplied from *Roma*; *Roma mouet* would have been acceptable by metonymy as is *Roma colit*, just preceding, but the number of *mouent* complicates matters.[40]

A particularly striking example of incongruity is found in 4.106 quo regnum Italiae Libycas auerteret oras. Of course it is really the kingdom of the *Trojans*, not the kingdom of *Italy*, that is to be turned aside to Libyan shores.[41] But the two geographical terms in juxtaposition are far more effective than would be the logical form of expression, including *both* place name and people name.[42]

On the other hand, logic demands *only* geographical terms, but rhetoric prefers the inclusion of a reference to *both cities* and *peoples*, in 3.502–5

> cognatas urbes olim populosque propinquos,
> Epiro Hesperia[43] (quibus idem Dardanus auctor
> atque idem casus), unam faciemus utramque
> Troiam animis.

Strictly speaking, it is only the two *cities*, the one in Epirus and the other in Italy, that are to be made a single Troy, *not* the two *peoples*; but the personal touch that enters with the reference to the peoples and to their common ancestor and their common *casus*[44] is highly desirable, and is carried out by the final word *animis*,[45] which is of course suitable in relation rather to *populos* than to *urbes*.

[40] Is it possible that the plural *urbes Albanae* (in 601–2), subject of *coluere*, had some influence on the number of *mouent* in 603, and also of *parant* in 605, though the reference here is clearly to contemporary Roman events?

[41] Wakefield actually reads *Italia*, as in 1.38 nec posse Italia Teucrorum auertere regem; but Conington is surely right in defending the reading of the MSS as more forcible. Force and logic are by no means inseparable!

[42] Thus this example differs from most of the instances here under consideration, in which the inconcinnity regularly lies in the combination of two *unlike* terms.

[43] There is another MS reading *Hesperiam*, which Hirtzel adopts in the Oxford text. This would involve a still further – though less illogical – confusion of the country and the city, as in 11.245 Ilia tellus, of the *city* of Ilium (the same phrase in 9.285 may refer to the surrounding *country*). But the combination *Epiro Hesperiam* (presumably in the sense of *Epiro cognatam propinquamque Hesperiam*, with *Hesperiam* in apposition with *cognatas urbes populosque propinquos*) appears to me extremely harsh.

[44] A remarkable word in that it says so much! How shall we translate it – fortunes, misfortunes, vicissitudes, calamities, history, destiny?

[45] The editors disagree as to whether *animis* is to be combined with *faciemus* or with *unam*. I think surely with the latter: the point is not what we are to do in spirit, but what the cities are to become in spirit. Furthermore, *unam animis* suggests *unanimam*, though here the use of *unam* as a separate word is far more effective.

Geographical terms only are again called for by logic in 6.59–60 tot maria intraui penitusque repostas Massylum gentis praetentaque Syrtibus arua[46] and 11.324 alios fines aliamque capessere gentem;[47] one does not enter (*intrare*) *nations* as one does *seas*, and one does not precisely betake oneself (*capessere*) to *nations* as one does to *countries*. (Exactly the reverse phenomenon occurs in 6.92 quas gentis Italum aut quas non oraueris urbes; literally, one appeals to *nations* rather than to *cities*.)

In 1.224–5 despiciens mare ueliuolum terrasque iacentis litoraque et latos populos, Jupiter may with perfect propriety be said to look down on both *countries* and *peoples* alike; but the word for 'peoples' has an epithet (*latos*) that in sense applies rather to 'countries'.[48] In 1.21 populum late regem, where *populum* definitely refers to a *people* and not a *country*, the epithet used seems much more appropriate.

Again a *people* is said to receive a name belonging to a *place* in 1.532–3 = 3.165–6 nunc fama minores Italiam dixisse ducis de nomine gentem (the *gens* is called *Italia*); in 8.321–3 genus composuit Latiumque uocari maluit (the *genus* is called *Latium*); probably in 1.247–9 sedesque locauit Teucrorum et genti nomen dedit armaque fixit Troia (most likely the name said to have been bestowed by Antenor upon the *gens* is *Troia*, to be supplied from the adjective *Troia* in the following line[49]). Conversely, a *city* (*moenia*) is said to receive a name belonging to a *people* in 3.17–8 moenia prima loco Aeneadasque meo nomen de nomine fingo (the *city* is given as a name the patronymic *Aeneadae*), and in 1.276–7 Romulus excipiet gentem et Mauortia condet moenia Romanosque suo de nomine dicet (probably the entity receiving the ethnic name *Romani* is designated by the nearer noun, *moenia*, rather than by the more remote – and more logical – one *gentem*[50]).

The *city* and the *people* are again treated as interchangeable in 7.670–1 fratres

[46] One is reminded of Catullus 101.1 multas per gentes et multa per aequora uectus, where, however, the common participle *uectus* applies equally to both the *per* phrases.

[47] Cf. 4.346 Italiam capessere.

[48] This has already been pointed out in fn. 20.

[49] According to tradition, the first *place* Antenor came to was named *Troia*, but the *gens* (consisting of a conglomeration of Romans and Eneti or Heneti) was named *Veneti*. (Cf. Livy 1.1.3 et in quem primum egressi sunt locum, Troia uocatur, pagoque inde Troiano nomen est; gens uniuersa Veneti appellati.) Some editors hold that the name which Vergil has in mind is the one really given to the *gens*, *Veneti*; but there does not seem to be very much point in his saying (or making Venus say) that Antenor gave the *gens* a name if there is no indication what the name was.

[50] I am assuming that *Romanos* here, like *Aeneadas* in the preceding example, is a predicate accusative, even though the direct object is not present (it is, as indicated above, implied by *moenia*). We might of course take *Romanos* as the direct object, the meaning being 'he will name the Romans after his own name', in which case there is no confusion at all. The same ambiguity exists even in passages in which two accusatives are present, such as 8.330–2 Thybris, a quo post Itali fluuium cognomine Thybrim diximus; is the direct object *fluuium Thybrim* 'the Tiber River', or is it merely *fluuium*, with *Thybrim* the predicate accusative? But in our own passage it seems more impressive in emphasizing Romulus' achievements to treat *Romanos* as a predicate accusative, in other terms as an accusative of effect, as is *moenia* before it: the city was not there till Romulus founded it, and the Romans were not so called till Romulus named them.

Tiburtia moenia linquunt, fratris Tiburti dictam cognomine gentem, where *moenia* and *gentem* are in apposition with each other. The following instances, too, exhibit the use as appositives of pairs of words which designate respectively a *place* and a *people*. A particularly interesting passage is 1.339 sed fines Libyci, genus intractabile bello, because here the ambiguous form of *Libyci* may be a factor: either *fines Libyci* alone, with *Libyci* an adjective, 'Libyan territory', or *Libyci, genus intractabile bello*, with *Libyci* a substantive, 'the Libyans, a race invincible in war', is perfectly possible; and Vergil's words might perhaps be viewed as a fusion of the two expressions rather than as simply a substitute for *fines Libycorum, generis intractabilis bello*. Except that it contains no such ambiguous term, 4.40 Gaetulae urbes, genus insuperabile bello, is precisely parallel, the *cities* here, like the *territory* in 1.339, being called a *race*; and 12.232 fatalisque manus, infensa Etruria Turno, is similar, the *country* being called a *band*.[51]

Much the same sort of apposition is to be found in 3.86–7 serua altera Troiae Pergama, reliquias Danaum atque inmitis Achilli, where *Troiae Pergama* refers to the city, but *reliquias Danaum* refers not to the new city of *Troy* but to the *Trojans* who sought it when driven out of the old city. The new city, never seen by the Greeks, could scarcely be called their *reliquiae*. In 1.30–1 Troas, reliquias Danaum atque inmitis Achilli, arcebat longe Latio, the same phrase, *reliquias Danaum* etc., is logically used in apposition with *Troas* – the *people*, not the *city*. On the other hand we have *reliquias Troiae* used in just the reverse way in 5.785–8

non media de gente Phrygum exedisse nefandis
urbem odiis satis est nec poenam traxe per omnem
reliquias Troiae: cineres atque ossa peremptae
insequitur.

Here logic would demand *reliquias Troum*,[52] the remains of the Trojans, whether the phrase is the object of *traxe* (in accordance with the punctuation here given) or of *insequitur* (in accordance with the punctuation preferred by many editors, who place the semicolon or colon before instead of after *reliquias Troiae*); in the latter case *cineres atque ossa* must be in apposition with *reliquias*, and though *cineres* could apply as well to the city as to the people, *ossa* cannot. But to interpret in such a literal way is to take all the poetry out of this impassioned passage: the city is personified from start to finish (note *exedisse*, used as if Juno in bringing about the destruction of Troy was eating the very heart out of the midst of the race of the

[51] Or a collection of bands, if with most editors we prefer the reading *fatales*. But the singular *manŭs* before the caesura is not metrically impossible; cf. *domŭs* in 2.563.

[52] Of course *Troum* is a different type of genitive from *Danaum* in the two previous passages. It might be classified, by those who insist on classifying all genitives, as partitive or appositional or even, if we stress the relationship of *reliquias* with the verb *relinquo*, objective, whereas *Danaum* would have to be called subjective.

Phrygians;[53] and also *poenam traxe per omnem*, if that too has *urbem* as its object); 'the remains of Troy', the city abandoned by its friends and burned by its foes, is even more poignant a picture than 'the remains of the Trojans' would have been.

Finally, there remains to be noted one more example of illogical apposition: G 2.136 Medorum siluae, ditissima terra.[54] This at first sight may look logical, since *siluae* and *terra*, the terms in apposition with each other, both refer to geographical entities. But there is really a double confusion here, since strict logic would demand: (1) that *terra* be in apposition not with *siluae* but with *Medorum*, and (2) that if a word meaning 'country' is to be placed in apposition with the genitive, the latter should be not *Medorum* but *Mediae*,[55] i.e., should refer to the *country*, not to the *people*. Thus this passage is exactly the opposite of such passages as 1.339, 4.40, and 12.232.[56]

I believe I have provided a sufficient number of examples to illustrate amply the fact that Vergil uses geographical and ethnological terms interchangeably. In certain cases he may be influenced by metrical convenience: a cretic such as *Mēdĭae*,[57] or a tribrach such as that contained in *Crustŭmĕrĭum*,[58] he of course cannot use. But apart from these limitations, Vergil is the master and not the slave of his meter; if he really wanted to use a particular term or a particular form, he generally could have managed to do so. And I believe rather that his main purpose in mixing his terminology as he has done was to suggest *at once* the place and the people, thus enriching the word picture that he was painting, or – to change the metaphor – providing with exquisite overtones the music of his stately measure.

HUNTER COLLEGE

[53] Here again we may note a lack of logic: the *city* is eaten rather *de Phrygia* than *de gente Phrygum*. But once again I cite the logical form only to illustrate its inferiority.

[54] I think this is surely the best punctuation, as denoting the best interpretation. Editors differ. Reiske took *siluae* as the genitive with *ditissima*, which would involve pointing *Medorum, siluae ditissima, terra*; probably the editors of the Teubner texts, Ribbeck and Ianell, who use no commas at all, also follow this analysis. But Conington, though only "after much hesitation", restored the older punctuation *Medorum siluae, ditissima terra*; and most editors (e.g. Hirtzel, the editor of the Oxford text) follow him. I think Conington's view gives a much more smoothly-flowing verse; if we follow Reiske, *terra* seems to me to come in very weakly at the end of the line after its two modifiers, genitive and adjective, nor is such a heaping up of modifiers in accord with Vergil's usual style.

[55] *Mēdĭae* is of course metrically impossible, but it would not be desirable even were it possible: *Medorum* provides pleasing variety in combination with the following proper nouns. Note the interlocking order in the succession of names in the passage (already quoted p. 56): *Medorum* (people); interpolation of *Ganges* and *Hermus* (rivers); *Bactra* (country); *Indi* (people); *Panchaia* (country). Cf. above, fn. 25.

[56] Quoted two paragraphs back.

[57] Cf. fn. 55.

[58] Cf. fn. 35.

MORRIS HALLE

IN DEFENSE OF THE NUMBER TWO*

THE SUBJECT of this essay is the Jakobsonian distinctive feature system, in particular its most controversial proposition concerning the binary structure of all features.[1] The distinctive feature system is a framework for the description of the phonetic facts of language. In the history of phonetics other such frameworks have been known: e.g. Alexander Melville Bell's Visible Speech and its direct descendant, the well-known phonetic alphabet of the International Phonetic Association, Jespersen's antalphabetic notation, or Pike's phonetic system.

These frameworks are fundamentally questionnaires. In using a particular phonetic system, just as in using a particular questionnaire, certain information will be obtained and this information will have a certain structure. And as in the case of a questionnaire, the choice of one system over another is determined by the investigator's belief that the particular set of questions and the manner in which they are phrased are the most appropriate to the research he is interested in. Thus, for example, in the phonetic frameworks just mentioned the position of the epiglottis in the articulation of the different sounds is not considered, in sharp contrast to the position of the major tongue constriction which is of primary concern in all frameworks. The disregard of the epiglottis and the great attention paid to the position of the tongue constriction would normally be justified on the grounds that the former information does not seem to do much for our systematization of the facts of speech, whereas the latter does. If one wanted to force a change one would have to show that this change actually was

* This work was supported in part by the U.S. Army (Signal Corps), the U.S. Air Force (Office of Scientific Research, Air Research and Development Command), and the U.S. Navy (Office of Naval Research); and by the National Science Foundation.

1 For a detailed presentation of the distinctive feature system see R. Jakobson, M. Halle, C. G. M. Fant, *Preliminaries to speech analysis, M.I.T. Acoustics Laboratory Technical Report 13* (1st printing: January 1952; 2nd printing with additions and corrections: May 1952; 3rd printing: June 1955), and R. Jakobson and M. Halle, *Fundamentals of language I. Phonology and phonetics* (The Hague, 1956).

helpful, in that it deepened our insight into the phenomena under investigation. One would thus justify this change exactly in the same manner as one would justify replacing one set of questions in a questionnaire by another, namely by showing that the new questions lead to a better understanding of the problem involved.

The questions that a scientist poses are, of course, always influenced by his hunches regarding the properties of the phenomenon he is studying. A physicist who believed that matter consists of atoms would ask different questions – i.e. perform different experiments – than one who believed that matter is infinitely subdivisible. The scientist cannot avoid posing questions that are 'loaded' in the sense that they reflect the scientist's picture of the phenomenon prior to the investigation. The scientist is under an obligation to show that these questions are fruitful, but he can show this only after performing his experiments, after asking his questions, not before.

In using the distinctive feature system one commits oneself to the view that all features are of a simple, binary type: i.e., one restricts oneself to asking about the phonetic features of a language only questions that can be answered by 'yes' or 'no.' It is impossible to know a priori whether this is a wise decision or not. But then it is also impossible to know before investigating a particular language whether the decision to represent all utterances as sequences of discrete segments, or any of the many other a priori decisions inherent in a particular phonetic system is wise or not.

If I understand the argument correctly, it is precisely this unsatisfiable condition which some would require the distinctive feature system to meet. In a recent book we read: "Pour avoir le droit d'affirmer que toutes les oppositions phonologiques sont binaires, il faudrait ou bien avoir constaté, après examen exhaustif, que tel était le cas, ou bien être arrivé à prouver que, l'homme étant ce qu'il est, il ne peut faire autrement qu'organiser ses unités distinctives selon le mode binaire. Mais qui pourrait se vanter d'avoir fait un examen exhaustif de toutes les langues existantes ou attestées? Et que dire des langues disparues sans laisser de traces et de celles qui apparaîtront demain sur la terre?"[2] Even if we omit from consideration the tendentious last question, which demands knowledge not ordinarily considered accessible to mere mortals, the author in effect limits the admissible statements of phonetics to those that have in fact been completely verified. In other words, he would allow us to pose questions only if we knew the answer, which seems somewhat pointless outside of an examination or quiz program. It is also to be noted that the condition given in the first sentence of the quoted passage would rule out not only scientific hypotheses – e.g. the binary nature of the features – but also statements containing the universal quantifier 'all', in other words, all generalizations. It is unlikely that any scientific description could be carried out under such severe restrictions. In the past no such restriction has ever been accepted by science, and I can find no justification for this move in the cited work or elsewhere.

[2] A. Martinet, *Economie des changements phonétiques* 73–74 (Berne, 1955).

While it is impossible to show that all features *are* binary, in advance of introducing this hypothesis into phonetics, the proposition can be confirmed in much the same manner as can other scientific hypotheses – i.e., by exhibiting its scope, its degree of factual confirmation, and the formal simplicity of the resultant description.[3] I shall attempt to show (1) that accepting the limitation of using only binary features in the description does not impair in any way the ability of the framework to handle data as compared with that of other frameworks not containing this limitation; (2) that in a number of instances it leads to a simplification both of the framework and of the description; and (3) that it admits certain developments in phonetic theory, in particular the formulation of an evaluation procedure for alternative descriptions, that could not be achieved with the more conventional frameworks. The discussion here will deal almost exclusively with the articulatory correlates of the distinctive features. The same arguments hold, of course, for the acoustical side of the problem since acoustic properties of speech are a consequence of the articulatory processes.

In the discussion concerning the binary feature system the fact seems to have been obscured that in many respects the distinctive feature system is substantially identical with such traditional frameworks as that of the IPA. Thus the distinctive features *voiced-unvoiced* and *nasal-nonnasal* are, of course, identical with the same features in all other frameworks. The distinctive features *sharp-plain* and *checked-unchecked* are identical except in name with the traditional distinctions palatalized-nonpalatalized and glottalized-nonglottalized.

In a number of instances the distinctive feature framework contains a single feature where the traditional systems have several binary features. This collapsing of the framework was done in cases where it could be demonstrated either that no single language possesses both features or that one of the traditional features applies to one class of phonemes – e.g. the vowels – and the other to a totally different class of phonemes – e.g. the consonants – and furthermore that these different traditional features possess common physical (i.e. articulatory and acoustical) properties. This unification under a single heading is thus only an extension of the well-known principle of complementary distribution.

The distinctive feature *flat-plain* includes the traditional features of pharyngalization, velarization, retroflection, labialization, and rounding. In the phonetic literature rounding and labialization are used to refer to the same articulatory process: the former term is restricted to the vowels and the latter is used only in reference to phonemes other than vowels.[4] There is thus no need for two separate terms.

The features of pharyngalization, velarization, retroflection, and labialization never

[3] Cf. C. G. Hempel, "Fundamentals of concept formation in empirical science," *International Encyclopedia of Unified Science* 2.7.39–50 (Chicago, 1952).

[4] Cf. R.-M. S. Heffner, *General phonetics* 98 and 133, (Madison, 1950). Earlier phoneticians like Sweet and Sievers used a single term; cf. E. Sievers, *Grundzüge der Phonetik* 75 and 144 (Leipzig, 1881).

function distinctively in the same phonemic context. We find either that one process – e.g. pharyngalization – is used in one language, while another process – e.g. labialization – is used in another language, or that one process is used only with certain classes of phonemes and another process is used with other classes of phonemes; facts that can be accounted for by the great similarity of the acoustical correlates of these articulatory processes.[5] Elementary considerations of economy dictate that these features be unified under a single heading.[6]

For essentially the same reasons the traditional features of tense–lax, aspirated–unaspirated and fortis–lenis are included in the single distinctive feature *tense–lax*.[7]

The above reduction in the number of features in no way affects the ability of the framework to describe the phonetic facts, since up to this point we have eliminated only features that never function independently. The reduction has the added advantage of requiring fewer independent variables in the framework. We therefore feel justified in claiming that a real gain in simplicity has been realized without any loss in scope.

More substantial differences between various traditional frameworks and the distinctive feature system are found in the treatment of the liquids and glides, of the affricates, and of the so-called point of articulation feature. Here the insistence upon a binary framework leads to a picture that is not simply related to that found in almost every textbook on phonetics.

In the treatment of the vowel-consonant distinction various traditional systems differ from one another. On the one hand, we have systems, like that of the IPA, where the glides and liquids are included among the 'consonants', which are sharply distinguished from the vowels. In these frameworks the 'vowel' – 'consonant' distinction is binary by definition. On the other hand, in a system like that of Pāṇini the liquids occupy an intermediate position between vowels and consonants. The distinction between the classes: vowel, consonant, liquid, and glide, must be maintained because of various grammatical and distributional statements which always have to be made in describing a language. The solution that is, therefore, adopted in the distinctive feature system is the following: Two binary features *vocalic-nonvocalic* and *consonantal-nonconsonantal* are defined: the first distinguishes the vowels and liquids from the consonants proper and from the glides; the second distinguishes the consonants and liquids from the vowels and glides.

In adopting this solution the descriptive scope of the framework is in no way affected. Whatever can be described in the traditional terms can be described in the distinctive feature framework. The binary framework gains in addition the

[5] For details see *Preliminaries*, secs. 2.4222 and 2.4236.

[6] This was evidently the reason why in the IPA system a single diacritic mark is used for both pharyngalized and velarized consonants.

[7] Cf. *Preliminaries*, secs. 2.43–2.434.

following advantages: (1) In separating the liquids and glides from the consonants it eliminates much unnecessary machinery which is represented on the IPA chart by the many empty boxes for the rows labelled 'Lateral Fricative', 'Lateral Non-fricative', 'Rolled', and 'Flapped'. The distinctive feature framework employs a smaller number of independent variables in the description, thereby realizing a definite economy. (2) Another kind of economy is realized by maintaining the same binary feature structure as in other parts of the description.

The standard phonetic frameworks treat the affricates as special sequences of stops and continuants. In some cases this treatment shows up gaps in the framework which are compensated for only at the price of abandoning the motivating principle of the entire scheme, the principle of phonetic realism. Thus, for example, the affricate represented in the IPA system by [p͡f] does not ordinarily have bilabial occlusion, as the presence of the symbol [p] would make it appear, but since the IPA does not possess a special symbol for a labiodental stop, the symbol for a bilabial stop is made to do double duty. In other cases the treatment of affricates as sequences reveals an excess of descriptive means. For instance, phonemes like */pφ/ and */*tθ*/, for which symbols are implicit in the IPA system, are not found in any language.

These disadvantages are avoided in the distinctive feature scheme by considering the affricates as special kinds of interrupted phonemes. The feature *continuant-interrupted*, which distinguishes between phonemes produced with a constriction and those produced with total occlusion, opposes all types of continuant to affricates and stops, which are classed together. The stops are distinguished from the affricates by means of the feature *strident-mellow*, which separates phonemes with strongly marked noisiness from phonemes where noisiness is slight or totally absent. Our confidence in this solution is further increased by the fact that the *strident-mellow* feature, which we set up to handle distinctions among interrupted phonemes – i.e., to separate affricates from stops – turns out to function distinctively also among the continuants. Thus, in Ewe in addition to the strident /p͡f/ and the mellow /p/, both of which are interrupted phonemes, there are also two kinds of continuants, a strident /f/ and a mellow /φ/.[8] Or in Gilyak there are four velar consonants, of which two are mellow, /k/ and /x/, and two strident, /q/ and /χ/.[9] Similarly in certain Slovene dialects

[8] D. Westermann, *A study of the Ewe language* (London, 1930).

[9] In speaking of the latter two phonemes, Zinder and Matusevič note: "It might not be superfluous to remark that these sounds cannot be called extreme post-linguals, for it is not a matter of the point of articulation being more or less far back, but of the active organ: /k/ is produced by contact between the back of the tongue with either the hard or the soft palate, depending on which, it will be either more or less front (without, however, being necessarily soft [palatized – M. H.]) or further or even very far back (without becoming /q/). On the other hand, sounds of the type of /q/, which are called velars or uvulars, are produced by contact between the edge of the soft palate (velum) and the back of the tongue either somewhat in front of or behind the former and consequently can themselves be 'back 'in varying degree. The /k/ series and the /q/ series thus represent two completely different series having essential qualitative differences." L. R. Zinder and M. T. Matusevič, "Èksperimental'noe

there are four dental consonants exhibiting the same paired structure: mellow /t/ and /θ/; strident /t͡s/ and /s/.[10] In Sutherlandshire Gaelic there are four palatal consonants, which are again paired in the same fashion: mellow /c/ and /ç/; strident /t͡ʃ/ and /ʃ/.[11] The differences in the points of articulation in all these cases are secondary effects of the primary differences between *strident* and *mellow* consonants, while the difference between affricates and fricatives is simply characterized by the feature *continuant-interrupted.*[12]

The introduction of the feature *strident-mellow* provides exactly the right amount of descriptive machinery, since it makes allowance neither for nonextant phonemes like */pφ/, nor forces upon us what are basically incorrect symbolizations like [p͡f]. It has the further advantage of providing a convenient description for the strident liquids like /ř/ in Czech and /σɫ/ in Zuñi. Finally it reduces to four the number of different points of articulation that need to be considered separately. This reduction is achieved without loss of descriptive power: all actually occurring phonemic patterns can be adequately described with the available machinery. It is also to be noted that the insistence on binary features does not impose any additional limitations on this framework as compared with those in general use.

The most marked deviations from the prevailing phonetic schemes will be found in the treatment of the so-called point of articulation parameter for the consonants and the dimensions of the so-called vowel triangle. It is a characteristic of many of the phonetic schemes now in use, and particularly of that of the IPA, that the vowels and consonants are described in terms that have nothing in common. It is evident that if one were concerned with descriptive economy one would inquire into the possibility of using the same set of dimensions for the vowels and for the consonants. The distinctive feature scheme obtains this in the following manner:

The distinction between open and close vowels is based on two fundamentally different vocal tract configurations. Open vowels are produced with a vocal tract that approximates a horn; in producing close vowels the vocal tract approximates a Helmholtz resonator, a large cavity with a small aperture to which a neck may be attached. This distinction, however, applies also to the configuration for the articulation of consonants. Thus, the velar [k] and palatal [c] stops have a horn-shaped vocal tract; while the labial and dental consonants have cavities that differ from those of the close vowels [u] and [i] only in that the aperture is greatly narrowed or totally occluded.

issledovanie fonem nivxskogo jazyka," in E. A. Krejnovič, *Fonetika nivxskogo (giljackogo) jazyka* 115 fn. 2 (Moscow-Leningrad, 1937).

[10] N. S. Troubetzkoy, *Principes de phonologie* 172 (Paris, 1949).

[11] Eric Hamp, "Unstressed and minimally stressed vowels in Sutherlandshire Gaelic" (Paper read at the Thirty-First Annual Meeting of the Linguistic Society of America, December, 1956).

[12] This point was first made by R. Jakobson in his "Observations sur le classement phonologique des consonnes," *Proceedings of the Third International Congress of Phonetic Sciences* 39–40 (Ghent, 1938).

These two extremes of vocal tract shape, the horn and the Helmholtz resonator, are taken as the defining characteristics of the features *compact-noncompact* (horn shape or not) and *diffuse-nondiffuse* (Helmholtz resonator shape or not). In terms of these features the close vowels are characterized as *diffuse* and *noncompact*; the open vowels like [a] and [æ] are classified as *compact* and *nondiffuse*; and vowels of intermediate degree of openness – e.g. [e] [ø] and [o] – are both *noncompact* and *nondiffuse*. Since all *compact* consonants are *nondiffuse* and all *diffuse* consonants, *noncompact*, only one of the two features functions distinctively in the consonants. We therefore describe labials and dentals as *noncompact*; and palatals, velars, gutturals, etc., as *compact*, and omit reference to feature *diffuse-nondiffuse*.

To complete the description we need a feature which would separate front from back vowels as well as labial and postpalatal consonants from dentals and palatals; i.e., [u] and [ɯ] from [y] and [i] as well as [p] and [k] from [t] and [c]. This is achieved by redefining the front-back distinction in vowels as a distinction between phonemes produced with a major constriction in a peripheral region of the oral cavity (i.e., at the lips or at the velum and further back) and those produced with a constriction in a central region (somewhere along the hard palate). This feature, which is known as *grave-acute*, permits us to characterize the distinctions mentioned at the beginning of this paragraph.

In the preceding section I have tried to show that the distinctive feature framework is capable of describing all facts that other phonetic systems can handle, but that by an extension of the principle of complementary distribution and the judicious redefinition of several features commonly used in phonetics, these results can be achieved with much less machinery than is usually employed.

Only in the case of the feature *diffuse-nondiffuse* has the insistence upon binary features led us to introduce a parameter which has an extremely restricted applicability and therefore may be said not to be optimal. It is for this reason that in previous formulations of the distinctive feature framework the feature *compact-noncompact* was defined as a ternary feature. In recent months we have been led to accept the more consistent solution of postulating two binary features in place of the ternary one, because, in connection with our work on evaluation procedures for alternative phonemic solutions, we found that the consistently binary system fitted our requirements better than the mixed system previously used.

Almost since the very beginning of modern phonology, linguists have realized that the criteria at their disposal admitted of several descriptions for the same set of facts.[13] As in other sciences the choice among alternative solutions was said to be decided by considerations of descriptive economy or simplicity. Attempts to characterize this

[13] Y. R. Chao, "The Non-uniqueness of phonemic solutions of phonetic systems," *Bulletin of the Institute of History and Philology, Academia Sinica*, 4, part 4, 363–397 (1934).

notion have been few and cannot be said to have been altogether successful. It seems intuitively correct that, all other things being equal, a reduction in the number of phonemes is a definite gain in economy. But how is one to decide between two descriptions having the same number of phonemes?

The difficulties experienced are no doubt due in part to the absence of a uniform system for presenting phonemic data. It is impossible to compare solutions in which prosodic features like accent and intonation are considered phonemes, with solutions in which they are considered features of vowels. But even if this difficulty could be overcome by an agreement to adopt a single system, it is unlikely that an answer could be suggested since, as we have seen, in the traditional frameworks considerations of economy play no rôle in the presentation of data. No attempt is made to minimize the number of features used, nor is there any obvious way in which equivalences can be set up among different features.

In the distinctive feature system a consistent attempt is made to minimize the number of features used in the description. An obvious extension of this would suggest that the simplicity of a description be measured by the average number of feature-questions per phoneme. We could then consider as best the description which on the average has the lowest number of feature-questions per phoneme. The presence of a ternary feature, however, again raises the problem of equivalence of features. Since there is no obvious way for setting an 'exchange rate' between binary and ternary features without simultaneously complicating the framework, postulating such an equivalence function would at best be an arbitrary step. If, however, we eliminated ternary features from our framework altogether – a move that is strongly suggested by the structure of the rest of the framework – the above difficulty would disappear. In our recent work on an evaluation procedure we have therefore replaced the ternary feature compact-diffuse by the two binary features *compact-noncompact* and *diffuse-nondiffuse*.[14]

MASSACHUSETTS INSTITUTE OF TECHNOLOGY

[14] The evaluation procedure is the joint work of N. Chomsky and myself. A preliminary report on this work was presented in our paper, "On the logic of phonemic descriptions," at the M.I.T. Conference on Problems of Speech Communications in June, 1956.

ERIC P. HAMP

ALBANIAN AND MESSAPIC

THE PROBLEM of the linguistic antecedents of Albanian has always been a vexed one. For nearly a century a few stock lexical comparisons have been known which the standard handbooks claim, explicitly or by implication, as evidence for the genetic connexion of Albanian and Illyro-Messapic. But these really promising clues are few, and not without their difficulties; furthermore, really deep-cutting structural comparisons have been disappointingly absent. Perforce, in varying degrees much of the discussion has been an argument from ignorance to ignorance. Despite the truly tremendous achievement of Meyer in establishing the basic IE correspondences for Albanian, it was not until the work of Pedersen, at the turn of the century, and of Jokl, in the second and third decades of this century, that our knowledge of the internal development and chronology of Albanian was refined enough to permit of really sensitive judgments on this score at all. As a summation of this stage of scholarship, Jokl's painstaking and exhaustive sifting of the evidence in *Eberts Reallexikon*[1] took things about as far as they could go for that time; since Jokl's strength lay in his talent for minute and erudite etymology rather than in structural synthesis, it is understandable that his conclusions, while being compact, solidly based on carefully marshalled data, and admirably reasoned, are somewhat complex and lack the incisiveness that we might desire. It should be said in Jokl's defense, however, that he was not a man to find simple, monolithic solutions where the internal complexities of the evidence dictated otherwise; on the other hand, he had the virtue of saying explicitly which way he thought the evidence, however tortuous, was pointing.

But, having taken account of the slow, yet gratifying, growth in our mastery of Albanian historical grammar and of the complexities of Jokl's scholarly personality, our impediments to a clear understanding of the place of Albanian are not at an end.

[1] N. Jokl, in *Eberts Reallexikon der Vorgeschichte*, articles Albaner (1924), Illyrier (1926), Thraker, Phryger (1927–8).

A thorough sifting and accounting of the elusive corpus of Illyrian (sensu stricto) and of Thracian was yet to be done. Though Jokl (*ZONF* 2. 238–45 [1927]) hailed enthusiastically the agreement with his own recent studies shown by the independent maiden voyage of Krahe, it is clear from the long parade of later studies by Krahe and the somewhat speculative work of Dečev[2] that finality was and is far from having been reached. More than that, the attested corpus of Illyrian comes almost exclusively through channels of other linguistic systems, and, like any onomastic corpus, is in effect a fragmentary text with no bilingual, with almost no sure semantics, limited practically to a single major form-class (singular substantives) and utterly asyntactic – brutally put, a set of dim hypotheses linked with some hopeful distant cognates. Indeed, by comparison our descriptive knowledge of Etruscan and Lycian is almost encyclopaedic! Were this our only base, the position would be frankly desperate.

We are rescued from almost total embarrassment by one priceless batch of really direct, solid data – the Messapic inscriptions, supported in turn by the ancillary gloss and onomastic materials. There can be no doubt that Messapic and Illyrian are sister languages, though separated by perhaps a half a millennium of divergence, and that in a general way what we say for Messapic probably applied equally to Illyrian. Two qualifications are at this point necessary: (1) To invest our statements with useful meaning, we must understand 'Illyrian' as applying only to the East Adriatic and Dardanian areas perhaps as far north at most as the Danube, and not in the wide sense adopted by such workers as Pokorny and criticized rightly and trenchantly by Whatmough[3]. Until the problem dealt with glibly and speculatively by Georgiev and van Windekens, and which may be labelled 'Pelasgic', has been resolved, I consider it dangerous, though not quite so damaging, to use items from the historical Greek area in a consideration of the Illyrian problem. Thus the first qualification is an insistance on the use of Illyrian in the most limited sense practicable; consequently, apart from the rigour hereby induced for the pursuit of the Albanian-Illyrian problem, pertinent data are then left free and uncommitted for unprejudiced attack on the continuing problems subsumed under the labels Pelasgic, Thracian, Macedonian, Keltic and Lepontic (in relation to Illyrian), 'Alteuropäisch'[4], etc. (2) To exclude Venetic, long included in Messapic-Illyrian discussion. Recent reanalysis[5] has shown Venetic to belong unquestionably to the Italic family, and, in this writer's opinion, almost as surely to the Latin-Faliscan subgroup.

Yet even taking into account the then state of Albanian historical grammar, and

[2] *Xarakteristika na trakyskija ezik* (Sofia 1952); see also W. Brandenstein, in *Pauly-Wissowa* (2. Reihe) 6 (1937), *s.v.* Thraker, Sprache.

[3] *Word* 6.242 (1950).

[4] H. Krahe, *Sprache und Vorzeit* (Heidelberg 1954).

[5] See Hamp, The relationship of Venetic within Italic, *AJPh* 75. 183–186 (1954), and the literature there cited; the corpus is in process of reedition by Lejeune; see *Latomus* 13.117–28 (1954) and preceding articles.

had the above qualifications, by elegant hindsight, been possible at that time, Jokl's synthesis lacked one important tool: the Messapic inscriptions and corpus were in bad need of thorough reedition, and their yield needed a modern and inclusive analysis and codification. Since that time details, chiefly lexical, of the ancestorship of Albanian have been elaborated, but no additional fundamental correspondences with Illyrian or Thracian have been advanced, and activity has been heaviest on the post-Roman '*linguistique balcanique*' side of the ledger.

With this background behind us, we may now move to the substance of this brief note, whose purpose, it may here be said, is not the thorough and exhaustive reorganization and statement of the genetic relationship of Albanian and (Illyro-) Messapic! Not only would such a claim be presumptuous and preposterous in so brief a space; but on the contrary, what is needed at present, in this writer's opinion, is not a turgid tome of increasing minutiae, but a run-down of the crucial, decisive questions, as they may now be seen and disengaged from the mass of scattered hypotheses. Indeed, in such a subject as this it is likely that in the millennial definitive work the broad lines of recoverable crucial points should be compactly passed in review (not that the present modest note is for a moment being arrogated to the status of such a grand quintessential preamble) before the reader is steeped in the total flood of evidential particulars.

The important happenings of the past quarter-century that have made possible the present survey of the cruxes are the following: Following the somewhat uneven, though valuable, work of Ribezzo in the preceding decade, yet enhanced by an independence for the most part from Ribezzo's studies, the long-needed grounding and codification of Messapic philology was furnished in the relevant sections of Whatmough's PID and succeeding articles[6]. This was a monumental step forward and, quite apart from the rest of his prodigious production, would of itself have assured a lasting place in Indo-European scholarship to the man to whom I am honoured to join in paying tribute. In short, we have an ever more dependable Messapic corpus. Secondly, the firm establishment of the laryngeal theory and contemporary improvements in the general theory and technique of exact description and reconstruction commonly recognized today under the label of 'structural linguistics' have together combined to give us tools of a decisively new level of sensitivity for the handling of our data. Thirdly, our understanding of the phenomena of Albanian (despite the interrruption of the war) has continued to be deepened and further codified, largely through the efforts of Jokl and Tagliavini, and more recently through the work of Cimochowski on North Geg[7]; to these men and to the earlier work of Pedersen, as well as to my own field

[6] For a convenient listing of Ribezzo's and Whatmough's fundamental work on this subject, see Krahe, *Die Sprache der Illyrier, I. Die Quellen* 13 (Wiesbaden 1955).

[7] See Hamp, review of Cimochowski, *Le dialecte de Dushmani* (Poznań 1951), *Language* 29.500–512 (1953).

work on the Italian and Greek enclaves, I owe the impetus for what advances I have been able to make within the study of historical Albanian grammar. Fourthly, the recent appearance of Porzig's survey (see fn. 10) relieves me of the necessity of rehearsing much scattered and involved detail; though it leaves the Illyrian question so far as Albanian is concerned much as Jokl left it, it conveniently summarizes the present state of published knowledge. Fifthly, the appearance of Krahe's new book (see fn. 6) brings together in most welcome fashion a wealth of hitherto scattered scholarship in which he has been the main participant, and thus relieves present workers of an almost insuperably onerous task of preparatory presentation.

On this basis, we may proceed to a consideration of the main points.

1. It has been alleged that the Illyrians and the Thracians were either closely kindred linguistic groups or that they were merely different socio-political names for the same linguistic unit. This view has been held by Vasmer, Jokl, Barić, Ribezzo, and Tagliavini[8]. This is an imposing array of names, but the theory does not explain why we seem to find the dichotomy in the onomastics that appears to be there. This question is left completely open for the time being; the relationship between Albanian and Illyrian, it can now be said, is not such as to preclude a further kinship between Illyrian and Thracian, if that should be conclusively demonstrated. On the other hand, regarding the conceivable genetic chain Albanian-Illyrian-Thracian-Phrygian-Armenian which we might try to construct, I have been able to find little positive evidence from the two end members beyond the tenuous threads tentatively suggested by Pedersen (*KZ* 36.340–341 [1900]). Meantime, the suggestion of a Phrygian-Armenian kinship rests on little more than the gossipy mention of antiquity[9], and the recent excavations at Gordion have brought to light no new raw material of note; the picture at the moment is not encouraging. Yet we may profitably proceed by restricting our focus.

2. The relevant key arguments presented by Porzig[10] may be summarized as follows. Illyrian is held (p. 131) to have a close kinship with his West Indo-European; it is further claimed (p. 151) to be more closely related to this unit than to Greek. Amongst vocabulary, Albanian *burrë*: OHG *gibur(o)* is said (p. 139) to belong to the "Illyrian component of Albanian". But Porzig finds two important features that seem to divorce Illyrian and Albanian. Says he (p. 138, referring to 67), Albanian shares with Keltic the development of IE *$\text{*}\mathring{r}$ > *ri*, whereas Illyrian has a "dark vowel-colouring" as its reflex; this receives further mention on p. 149. On that same page, it is asserted that since Albanian is satem, in so far as Illyrian is accepted as showing centum features it cannot be the ancestor of Albanian.

[8] *Rivista d'Albania* 2.188 (1941).

[9] See J. Friedrich, *Pauly-Wissowa* 20 (1941), *s.v.* Phrygia: Sprache; cf. also G. Bonfante, Armenians and Phrygians, *Armenian Quarterly* 1.82–97 (1946).

[10] *Die Gliederung des indogermanischen Sprachgebiets* (Heidelberg 1954).

These points may be commented on briefly: the lack of a particularly close relationship to Greek agrees with what we know of Albanian. In so far as Porzig's groupings exclude Balto-Slavic from his West-IE, his finding for Illyrian is at variance with what Jokl found for Albanian and Balto-Slavic; my research continues to turn up ever more cogent and numerous connexions between these last two. Perhaps there are simply too few recoverable features known for Illyrian to make Porzig's dialect-geographical argument on this point stick; we may simply be victims of statistics. While it is certainly true that *one* reflex of IE **r̥* in Albanian is *ri*, the picture is more complex than that, and the reflex in some environments may well be *ur*; the development for other syllabic sonants is even more obscure. The satem-centum argument is dealt with specifically below. In short, while Porzig's synthesis conveniently summarizes for us a vast mass of scattered and heterogeneous material, the arguments adduced against pairing Illyrian and Albanian are not at all strong. His conclusions (pp. 213–217), moreover, leave us straddling the fence.

3. Having thus discouraged a pairing of Illyrian and Albanian, Porzig remarks (p. 149) "Es bliebe also nur der Wortschatz." This leads him to observe very soundly that regardless of the genetic origin of Albanian, because of its geographical position we may expect to turn up Illyrian elements in the lexicon, if only as loans. This ties in with the remarks of Pulgram (*For Roman Jakobson* 414 [1956]), as well as his cautions, regarding the bases for linguistic expansion and the classification of the resulting data. Whatever the origins of an individual lexical item, we must treat lexical correspondences separately from structural items, even though some etyma may turn out also to be our sole, and therefore perhaps imperfectly recognized, example for a given feature. It is convenient here to offer some brief comments on lexical items that have been discussed comparatively by others, as well as to offer some comparisons that are believed to be new.

3.1. Mess. *aran* 'land' seems a likely cognate to Alb. *arë* 'field'. I find that Pisani[11] has anticipated me with this identification, but then he goes on (p. 234) with the impossible suggestion that perhaps the *r* is from earlier **gr*. On the Albanian word, see a note of mine to appear shortly in *KZ*.

3.2. Mess. *argorian* is claimed by Whatmough (PID 3.6) and by Porzig (p. 150), following Krahe, to be cognate to and not a loan from Greek. Krahe has argued that it should be inherited because the element occurs in Illyrian place-names; but I do not see how this proves that it is not borrowed. It is noteworthy that Albanian has borrowed (*ë*)*rgjënt* from Latin, though that of course does not prove of itself that they had no native word for 'silver'.

3.3 Mess. *balakrahiaihi* may well contain as first element a cognate of Alb. *ballë* 'forehead'; I cannot seem to locate the source for this correspondence, but I am sure

[11] *Le lingue dell'Italia antica oltre il latino* 230 (Torino 1953).

it is not original with me. While the Baltic correspondence found in OPruss. *ballo* /balō/ 'forehead'[12] is worth noting, the presence of a cognate with (in part) the same meaning in Sanskrit and of a form with closely similar meaning in Welsh[13] shows that we do not have here a diagnostic innovation.

3.4. Mess. *bili(v)a* has been much discussed.[14] Of itself the comparison with Alb. *bilë* 'daughter' is quite unobjectionable. Tagliavini[15] objects that, apart from whether the lexical meanings actually fit, this still leaves Alb. *bir* 'son' unexplained. Jokl has attempted to explain *bilë* as a diminutive in *-l-* on the base *bir-*; while it is possible to devise such an *ad hoc* sequence to take care of the observed result, in the absence of convincing support this solution looks contrived. But all these arguments fail to account for a crucial feature: the plural of *bir* in the conservative Italo- and Greek-Albanian dialects is *bil.* Thus, whether or not the Messapic forms are cognate with the Albanian *-l-* forms, the suppletive masculine forms still require explanation within Albanian. Now suppletion is well attested in several common Albanian nouns; therefore *bir/bil* could easily go back as far as we can trace to a suppletive relationship. If *bir* really is related to Goth. *baur*, perhaps an old consonant stem gave a homophonous singular and plural; the plural could then have been filled out with the bigeneric *bil-*. If that is so, then Lat. *fīl-* may well not be from a base **dhēi-*. In brief, I do not see that, within Albanian, *bir* stands in the way of a possible cognateship in *bil-* (of the other three forms) with Messapic.

3.5. The well attested base *daz-*, etc., has not yet received a satisfactory explanation; the following is at present only a tentative suggestion. It is noteworthy that Illyr. *Dalmasius*, Mess. *dalmaθoa*, which may be considered cognate with Alb. *djalë* 'boy', pl. *djelm*, *djem*, show *da-*. With this in mind, we may perhaps compare *daz-/das-* with Alb. 'right, dexter', which in Greek-Alb. is *djathë* and *djathëtë*. The semantics make a likely candidate for personal names, and it should be noted that formations in *-t-* are well attested. Some of the numerous formations may well be deverbal, and in some cases an original *-o-* vocalism would not be excluded.

3.6. Instead of δαζουν, Pisani[16] takes αζουν and tries to compare it to Alb. *unë* 'I'. This would be one of his slender supports for a claimed satem character in Messapic; in principle, we must remain prepared to find satem-like reflexes in Messapic (see below), and I have just suggested as much in 3.5, but Pisani's evidence will simply not do. It would be hard to invent a more unacceptable comparison: if the first syllable had the accent, we should get something like **adh* or **ath* (or, depending on the length of the

[12] Trautmann, *Baltisch-Slavisches Wörterbuch* 30.

[13] *S.v. bal*[1] 'having a blaze on the forehead (esp. a horse)', *Geiriadur Prifysgol Cymru* 250 (1952).

[14] It may here be conveniently noted that the reading of PID 2. 494 has received more recent study and revision (see Krahe, *op. cit.* 26), but that the word in question still seems assured.

[15] *Atti dell'Istituto Veneto di Scienze Lettere ed Arti* 106.211 (1948), where a good summary of the competing proposed solutions is to be found.

[16] *Op. cit.* 223–224.

imagined original vocalism, even **vodh* or **vedh*; true enough, this might have been reduced in unstressed position to *u*, but then anything could happen!). If the second had the accent, we should have Geg **d(h)û(n)*. In any case, if Geg kept *n*, Tosk should show *r*; but that would be if the **-n-* were originally intervocalic. If we had a proximate final **-n* we should have a nasal vowel in Geg and a long vowel in Tosk. Actually, because of Italo- and Greek-Albanian *u* 'I', it is clear that the standard form includes a suffixed element *-në*. I have located such an optional suffix, found occasionally with pronominal forms, in the Greek dialects, but it seems normally to combine with oblique cases. In the dialect of Dara (Arcadia), however, *-në* actually occurs freely with *all* subject pronouns. As for the length of the Tosk vowel, Sophikó (Corinthia) has /ú/, Barile (Potenza) has /ǘ/ (not /ú/), and Variboba writes *u* (but *uu* for 'hunger'). The etymology remains as obscure as ever.

3.7. Pisani[17] would have *denθavan* a complex of *denθ(i)-* (:εὐ-θένεια, **g^when-*) and *avan* (:αϝιναμι), and thus an example of a labio-velar before a palatal vowel. That is all very ingenious, but it may equally well be pure imagination.

3.8. In σιππα Pisani[18] would have the *s*, which according to him usually becomes *h*, preserved by onomatopoeia. This is scarcely rigourous reasoning, especially with so small a corpus.

3.9. Because he thinks *θ* an affricate (a questionable opinion), Pisani[19] derives the enclitic *θi* from **-k^we*, with **e* reduced to *i*, and compares Alb. *pesë* 'five'. Yet on p. 227 he accounts for *penkeos* as a genitive of **penkēu-*. We must continue to regard Whatmough's account (PID 3.45) as the best thus far advanced.

3.10. The Sallentini divine name *Menzanas* has a stock comparison in Alb. *mëz*, Rum. *mînz*.[20] That this comparison is less than specific because of the widespread geographical distribution and uncertain origin of the term has been pointed out by E. Çabej[21].

3.11. Çabej has also compared[22] Albanian forms to the Messapic etyma supposed to underlie the south Italian Greek and Italian dialect forms which are reconstructed as *kárparo* and **gríno*. For the first of these, Ribezzo and Vasmer have maintained the purely Illyrian character which we should require to make the comparison significant, but Tagliavini[23] argues that its distribution is more widespread than that. Circumspection is clearly called for here.

3.12. If any etymology is generally conceded, it is that which links Mess. βρενδον and Alb. *brî*. Because of Tosk /bríi/, def. /bríri/, the proto-form for Albanian is surely

[17] *Ibid.* 231.
[18] *Ibid.* 235.
[19] *Ibid.* 230.
[20] See Krahe, *op. cit.* 84; Porzig (p. 150) uses it as an isogloss criterion.
[21] *Glotta* 25.51–52 (1936).
[22] *Glotta* 25.54–5, 57 (1936).
[23] *Rivista d'Albania* 2.188 (1941).

**brínV-*, with no dental extension. It is strange that Krahe (*op. cit.* 39–40) does not seem even to entertain the argument put forth by Skok[24], whereby the Messapic dental would have been *d*. Even if his ingenious argument to the effect that this *d* was a diminutive suffix cognate with the Alb. feminine *-zë* < *-di̯ā* is not accepted, his discussion of the evidence for the voiced dental and of the vocalism are valuable and stimulating. If Skok's accounting for the suffix is right, one immediately wonders whether the Albanian masculine diminutive *-th* is not after all this same suffix, devoiced in final position. Even the solidest cognates are not yet completely solved.

3.13. Porzig[25] calls the correspondence ῥινός·ἀχλύς Hes. : Geg *rê*, Tosk /rée/ (Bogdan wrote *ren*) 'cloud(s)' "weniger kennzeichnend". I do not know what he means by this. To be sure, Albanian may here simply have borrowed from some Balkan stock, but nevertheless, in the present state of our knowledge, I consider this correspondence the most specific and diagnostic that we have in the lexical category.

Porzig further remarks that by this feature Albanian and Illyrian mark themselves off from both his 'East' and 'West'. Elsewhere (p. 169–70) he points out Gk. ὀμίχλη, Lith. *miglà*, OCS *mьgla* as a shared feature. He credits the **-lā* convincingly enough to **nebhelā*, and concludes that since Balto-Slavic does not show the latter the innovation must be a diffusion from Hellenic. But Balto-Slavic does have **nebhos*, and **nebhelā* could easily have been present earlier; silence is a poor witness. Further, Porzig overlooks the fact that Albanian has *mjegullë*. There is no direct descendent of **nebhelā* extant in Albanian; I find an alternant *njegull* in the *Fjalor i gjuhës shqipe* (Tiranë 1954: Instituti i Shkencavet), but I know no such form at first hand and feel sure it has an internal explanation. Yet we must assume for *mjegullë* 'fog' contamination from a descendent of **nebhelā*, since otherwise the aberrant vocalism of the first syllable cannot be explained. It seems likely that the distribution of the *-lā* suffix was simply not originally quite so circumscribed as Porzig imagines.

The following comparisons are thought to be new, and will be mentioned very briefly at this time.

3.14. Mess. *anda*. Bogdan uses *endë* 'also'. Common Alb. *ndë* 'if' may also be related. In light of Krahe's discussion (*op.cit.* 31), Alb. *ndë* 'in' may be related to at least part of the occurrences.

3.15. Mess. *atabulus*. For discussion, see Krahe, *op. cit.* 41. Alb. *ávull* (Sophikó has /*ávuu*/, where **ll* > /w/ merges with the preceding /u/) means 'steam, vapour', and has no good etymology. We must presume that the *v* arose in hiatus (other such instances are known), in this case as a glide before *u*, and therefore there can be no direct connexion between it and the Mess. *b*, since an intervocalic voiced obstruent would in any event be lost in Albanian. Thus **á(u̯)ul-* is a good match for *-abulus*. But what in turn is that? We have spoken above of the interference of **nebhelā*; our present word

[24] *ZONF* 1.81–90, esp. 87–9 (1926).
[25] *Op. cit.* 150; see also Krahe, *op. cit.* 38 for literature.

belongs to the same semantic knot. On the other hand, Gk. ἀχλύς has a good cognate in OPruss *aglo* 'rain';[26] a similar form could well have existed too in Proto-Illyro-Albanian. Thus we posit **miglā*, **aglā*, and **nebelā*. Through contamination with the last, we emerge with **meglā* and **abelā*, or **abulā*; the gender history of the last is not obvious or sure.

3.16. Mess *atavetes*. While accepting Torp's explanation 'αὐτόετες', perhaps we may see in the first element a cognate with Albanian *a-tá* 'that', wherein the first element, which would be lost in unstressed position, has been restored from other forms. The compound as a whole matches exactly, so far as its parts are concerned, Alb. *sivjet* 'this year'. From the vocalism of the final syllable of *atavetes*, a locative seems more probable than an accusative; if the case is accusative, then the first element could be inflected, showing a neuter *ata-* < **-tod* with loss of the final stop already accomplished. But if we have a locative, then a strict compound is more likely, and the form would reflect simply **-o-*. Pedersen has perceptively remarked[27] that *si-vjet* 'this year', *sot* 'today' (*ditë* 'day') and *sonde* 'tonight' (*natë* 'night') match the demonstrative ablative singular masc. *a-sí* and fem. *a-só*; elsewhere[28] he has derived *-si* from **tojéi*, *-so* from **tojā́* or **tojā́i*, the ablative pl. masc. *-sish* from **tojéisu*, and fem. *-sosh* from **tojā́su*, with **-toj-* > **-t(V)j-* > **-tj-* > *-s-*. Of course, not all these forms necessarily had the *-j-*; once the consonantism had affricated, it could have spread to related forms. Presumably the *-j-* started in the feminine; cf. Vedic instrum. sg. masc. *téna*, fem. *táyā*. Baltic shows instrum. sg. masc. **t'ṓ*, fem. **t'ā́n*, after the nouns, but locative sg. fem. **tāj'e*. Slavic shows what must be an intermediate stage between the Indic and the levelled-out Baltic with an expansion in the **-j-* forms, thereby furnishing a revealing morphological correspondence with Albanian: instrum. sg. masc. *cěmь* < **kʷoi-mi* 'whom', *čîmь* < **kʷei-mi* 'what', *tě̑mь* < **toi-mi* 'that', fem. *tojǫ́* < **toi-āN*, dat.-loc. fem. *toi* < **toji*[29]. Once the **-j-* forms were set up in the feminine, the syllabic **ei* came to mark the Albanian masculine. Thus we may well do better to reconstruct for the 'ablative' a sg. masc. **t(j)éi*, fem. **tVjā́*, pl. **t(j)éisu*, **t(j)ā́su*. Thus *sonde* reflects something like **(a)t(V)jā́-na(k)t(V)jā(s)* (the precise case-endings are somewhat in doubt and schematic); *sivjet* gives **(a)t(j)éi-uetes-*. The Greek enclaves generally attest

[26] See Hamp, *KZ* 74.127 (1956) on further ramifications.

[27] *Festskrift til Vilh. Thomsen* 248–249 (1894).

[28] *KZ* 36.314 (1900).

[29] The pertinent support for the Slavic shapes is as follows: OCS *cěmь*, with accent shown by Serb. *k'ìjem*: OCS *čimь*, with accent shown by Serb. *čîm* (*č'ìjem* is analogical). OCS and ORuss. *těmь*, Serb. *t'ìjem* (*tîm* is analogical) point to *tě̑mь*; but OCz. *tiem* > *tím* points to *tě́mь*, and I am unable to explain this divergence. Spoken Czech *čim* could be a continuation of the old form, and, contrary to Vey (*Morphologie du tchèque parlé* 5 [1946]) *tim* may be not a shortening but an analogical formation. OCS *toją*, Russ. *toj*(*u*); OCz. *mezi-tojú*, *-tojí* shows the old long rising accent by its length. Polish *tą*, Kashub *tǫ* show contraction, against the accusative Pol. *tę*, Kashub *tą*. Little can be said for OCS *toi*, Serb. *tôj* with compensatory circumflex, Pol. and Upper Sorb. *tej* modelled on *jej*, and OCz. *téj* with length from loss of *-i*.

sívjet and *sívje*, but from Vaccarizzo Albanese (Cosenza) I have *símbjit*; the dictionaries also cite *simjet*, *simvjet*. These latter point to a (by-)form with nasal on the first element. The case structure makes a frozen accusative nasal unlikely within the Albanian; is it possible that we have here a trace of the instrumental suffix? If so, is it the nasal of Vedic *téna*, or, more likely, that of Slavic *tě̑mь*, Lithuanian *sūnumì*, *tuomì̃*?

3.17. Mess. *maberan*. If this verb means 'conferant', perhaps it is related to Alb. *mba* 'hold'.

3.18. Mess. *pido* 'gave'. Besides the shape *pi-* here attested, Illyrian also had *epi-*, as is shown by *Epicadus*, etc. (see Krahe, *op. cit.* 54). While the aorist and the participle of 'give' in Albanian clearly come from IE **doX-/dX-*, the present stem, 1 sg. *jap*. 2, 3 sg. *jep*, has never been explained. Perhaps it represents a compound **epid-*, with loss amongst the suffixal material of the **-d-*.

3.19. Mess. *porvaides*. Perhaps the first part is the equivalent of Alb. *parë* 'first' < **prXuo-* (i.e. **pr̥̄u̯o-*). In any case, Kretschmer's suggestion that *Asso-paris* contained this element (Krahe, *op. cit.* 52) is unlikely, since we expect to see *-v-*.

3.20. Mess. *solan*. The *o*, instead of an *a*, has bothered scholars (see PID 3.42). But if we assume this to be **ō*, we may see here an exact cognate in form to Alb. *gjellë* 'life', as contrasted with *gjallë* 'alive'. This would also be a correspondence in the noteworthy predilection of Albanian for Dehnstufe formations. On the other hand the absence of *-v-* is puzzling; if this paragraph is correct, then the last one may be wrong.

3.21. Mess. *tan*. On the morphology, ignoring the question of possible sandhi with a following *n-*, it is worth pointing out that Albanian has kept distinct to the present day the masc. **tan* > *-të* and the neuter **ta(d)* > *-ta*. Albanian also shows that the demonstrative was used both before the noun, as a demonstrative pure and simple and as a marker of 'inherently possessed' items such as kin, and after the noun as a noun-phrase link with following modifiers; the Rumanian 'article' is of course a continuation in Latin substance of this same structural pattern so far as the postnominal position goes. This point should be borne in mind for the exploration of Messapic syntax.

3.22. Illyrian (?) Καν-δάων. If this is in fact Illyrian (see Krahe *op. cit.* 56), and if the first element is 'dog', perhaps the Albanian *qen* does not have a simple Latin loan origin, as has been thought.

3.23. Illyr. *Avitus*, *Avittius*, *Apl-avita*[30]. This base is supposed to be related to Lat. *avēre*. The *DEL* shows no cognates outside Italo-Keltic; the *IEW* (77) gives some more data. Tagliavini[31], *s.v.* *ę̨t* 'thirst', says the etymology of this Albanian word is dubious. An internal *-i-* would umlaut a preceding *a* and then be lost: *emtë* 'aunt' < Lat. *amita*, *qelq* 'glass' < Lat. *calice(m)*; an intervocalic *-v-* would vanish. I do not find the Sophikó cognate available amongst my notes at present to be able to check the

[30] See Krahe *op. cit.* 51; cf. also Krahe, *Lexicon altillyrischer Personennamen* 13–14.

[31] *L'albanese di Dalmazia* 114.

vowel-length[31a]; Variboba writes *ett*, but on at least one parallel form, *de(e)t* 'sea', he is inconsistent. Therefore Illyr. *avit-* and *et* may well be cognate. I do not find a likely Hittite cognate in *ḫ-* to bear upon the initial laryngeal.

3.24. Mess. (?) ἄνδινος · περίπατος. Perhaps to Alb. *ëndem* 'I wander, graze'.

3.25. Illyr.-Mess. *Odruntum, Hydruntum, Otranto*[32]. According to K. Finsterwalder, "Venetic-Illyrian" *udria* is supposed to have given Tyrol. *Itter*. Attempts have been made to etymologize Alb. *ujë* 'water' without great success; Pedersen suggested a 'hiatus' *-j-*, and derived the base from a consonant-stem **ud*. The basis for the disappearance of the dental stop and the development of the hiatus is hard to see. A perfectly acceptable series would be **udrjā* (a neuter plural-collective) > **urjë* > *ujë*.

The above lexical remarks must suffice for the present. A detailed inspection of the total onomatological corpus would take one too far afield and would plunge us immediately into a welter of uncertain detail which requires the most elaborate sort of control to yield anything at all.

Considering the fragmentary and difficult nature of the corpus, it is believed that the above represents (eliminating the doubtful items) a tidy set of significant correspondences of a specific sort. Whether a number of them are really just common loans we will probably never know. But so far as a careful use of our methodology permits us to arrive at genetic statements, the above items include a significant body of ancillary evidence on which we may hope to build a firm demonstration of the close kinship of Illyro-Messapic and Albanian. We may now raise briefly the structural points relevant to this supposed kinship.

4.1. The IE *u*-diphthongs. Pisani (*op. cit.* 234) compares the supposed Messapic development with Albanian *e* < **eu, *ou*, but *a* < **au*. There are just two flaws in this comparison. We are not at all certain yet that *e* really is the fate of **eu, *ou*. Sure examples in Albanian are few, and then the ablaut grade is far from assured; it is possible that **eu* gave *u*, while **ou* > **au* gave *a*. Secondly, while we do indeed observe a monophthongization within the recorded history of Messapic, the earliest monuments show the diphthongs pretty much intact; and for our purposes the status at the presumed prehistoric time of divergence is what matters, since no one supposes the Albanians to be transplanted descendents of Iapygians.

4.2. Treatment of C plus yod. As *Θeotoridda* and other forms abundantly show, Messapic developed geminates from original clusters with nonsyllabic *i̯*. While **l* in Albanian develops in several clusters (including yod and geminate **l*) in the same way, and while **n* and **s* palatalize in a way that could be argued to conceal their intermediate stages, the dentals fuse with yod to produce the affricates that have ended

[31a] The cognate, I now find, is /éetjë/. Though the suffix shows signs of reshaping (-jë perhaps analogical on 'hunger'), the vocalism is clearly "long" /ée-/. This is what I have come to expect for old intervocalic loss of *-C-.

[32] See Krahe *op. cit.* 100.

up as *s* and *z*, **r* is lost in **rj*, and otherwise, at least in the case of a following **ā*, the yod fuses with the following vowel. This treatment contrasts with the Messapic, so that we must regard at least these features, so characteristic in each language, as resting on developments dating from periods after their divergence. This fact alone should be instructive in deterring us from expecting to recover much in the way of shared *allophonic* traits; the time-depth is simply too great and the intermediate interferences too many.

4.3. IE **sw*. One treatment in Albanian, supposedly when the accent immediately followed[33], is highly distinctive, even surprising, but seems clearly so. Something like **suél-* gave *diell* 'sun', and **suídrVtiā* > *dirsë* 'sweat', and the later-layer derived verb with displaced stress *dërsínj*, from which, no doubt, the analogically 'restored' vocalism in *djersë* was extracted. It is difficult to say exactly what the intermediate stages in this development were, and I see no way as yet for so much as searching for candidate cognates in Messapic.

But Albanian has another treatment whereby the **s* is simply lost; thus **suek̑urós* > **suesurós* > *vjehër*.[34] The Albanian for 'self' and 'alone', *vete* and *vetë*, have been traced to **sweti*[35]; but that would lead us to expect a diphthongization of the **e*. It seems we must start from a form **suoit-*, with an *i*-diphthong; this is reminiscent of Balto-Slavic and Germanic in vocalism.[36] When we consider Mess. *veinan*, we find a three-way correspondence. The initial matches Albanian; the vocalism is cognate to those found in Albanian, Balto-Slavic, and Germanic, if we except some probably unconnected forms in Iranian; the *-n-* suffix, as Whatmough points out (PID 3.49), is matched in Germanic, and we find further cognates in Baltic. It is just possible that the same derivative suffix in *-n-* is to be seen in the third person plural (demonstrative) genitive-dative Geg *tyne*, Tosk *tyre*.

4.4. Masculine genitive sg. in *ī*. In this respect, Messapic seems to agree with Italo-Keltic (see Porzig *op. cit.* 89 and 106), yet on pure *a*-stems the Messapic formation (*-aihi*) is not exactly equivalent. Pedersen[37] has expressed the opinion that the Albanian masc. gen.-dat. sg. *-i* (which alternates with *-u* after velars) may well be an accidental match with Latin *-ī*; Tagliavini has expressed similar doubts[38]. From what we know of the attrition of final syllables in Albanian, and of the difference in their treatment from that of internal syllables, it is almost inconceivable that there can be a direct connexion; this, apart from the consideration of the parallel allomorphic alternations in the nominative definite and the 3 sg. aorist of the verb. Whatever

[33] See Pedersen, *KZ* 36.288 (1900).
[34] See Jokl, *Linguistisch-kulturhistorische Untersuchungen aus dem Bereiche des Albanischen* 49 (Berlin–Leipzig 1923).
[35] Tagliavini, *L'albanese di Dalmazia* 280.
[36] Trautmann, *Balt.-Slav. Wtb.* 294–295.
[37] *Le groupement des dialectes indo-européens* 11 fn. 2 (1925).
[38] *Rivista d'Albania* 2. 187 (1941).

underlies the Albanian and Messapic formations, now that Venetic has found its place within Italic, only Keltic clearly shares this Italic phenomenon.

4.5. Noun plural suffixal **-b(h)-*. It is well known that Baltic, Slavic and Germanic share *-m-* in these situations. Perhaps, as seems reasonable on other grounds, this represents an innovation marking the last cohesive grouping of IE after all the other groups had filtered off bit by bit before these dialects in turn became mutually distinct and independent. If that is so, and if on the other hand we seem to see a close genetic connexion between Illyro-Albanian and Balto-Slavic, we may then date the departure of the former from close proximity with the latter. For Messapic clearly has *-b-* (*laidehiabas*). Whether the Albanian gen.-dat. pl. *-ve* reflects **-b-* is hard to say. Pedersen regarded the *-v-* as a hiatus filler, and the ending as derived from a circumflected genitive plural. But that is so *ad hoc* as to admit of no honest criticism one way or the other. We now know (witness the sandhi in Sanskrit) that these endings had a juncture phoneme before the **bh* in IE; this again is so unique for what we have attested of Albanian that we could equally well posit the development as regularly producing *-v-* here. We must be content to reserve judgment for the time being.

4.6. Centum-satem. What needs to be said here is important, but can be said quickly. In a fundamental article Whatmough has shown in masterly fashion that the internal evidence of Messapic gives us no basis for calling it a satem-speech;[39] there is simply no evidence either that it labialized the velars or that it sibilized the palatals. Working from the evidence Whatmough had at his disposal, no other conclusion could reasonably be reached, and Messapic and Albanian had to be kept apart.

Now the general handbooks usually characterize Albanian as satem, and let the matter go at that. But in reality the situation is much more complicated, and, incidentally, carries as a corollary the clear implication of the futility in trying to divide all IE into two mutually exclusive dialects of satem and centum. As early as 1900, Pedersen[40] adduced powerful evidence to show that in position before front vowels Albanian preserved distinct reflexes of all three IE orders, palatals, labio-velars, and "pure" velars. In 1937, Jokl[41] refined and enlarged on Pedersen's theory; in 1954, the present writer[42] added one more item of evidence. Clearly, Albanian is not simply a 'satem' dialect.

In the case of the labio-velars, Messapic is understandably slim on evidence. If it had been a mirror-image of early Albanian, the labio-velars may have already ceased to be distinctive before all but palatal vowels; as it is, *penk-* is the only sure base we have yet identified, and it tells us nothing. We may be sure that *z* (whatever it sounded like) does not reflect **g*^{w} (/z/ is the distinctive Albanian reflex), since we find it before *a*.

39 *Language* 3.226–231 (1927).
40 *KZ* 36. 277–340 (1900).
41 *Mélanges Pedersen* 127–161 (1937).
42 *AJPh* 75.186–9 (1954).

Jokl attached importance to fluctuating spellings where velars seem to alternate orthographically with labials, but the evidence is slender and the precise interpretation difficult. We must simply wait to see what closer analysis brings up.

However, we may reasonably hope to see some clear reflexes of the palatals. The sole really clear example is *klaohizis*, but as Whatmough remarks, both Albanian and Balto-Slavic show *k* in their cognates. However, I have recently been able to show[43] that it is probable that in Albanian the palatals depalatalized regularly before *l*. Jokl has shown (*op. cit.*) that in combination with a following *u* the palatals fell together with the labio-velars. At the very least, Messapic speakers may well have had a roster of phonemes and distributions quite different from the languages that first furnished them with writing. They might have had three orders of phonemes something after the fashion of /k/, /ḱ/, /$k^{\ddot{u}}$/, with a limited distribution for the last. We know that Mongolian failed to distinguish orthographically its voicing correlation; a similar situation may have arisen with the Messapians.

After observing the fate of the palatals before **l*, we might profitably consider their treatment before **r*. Geg *krye* pl. *krêna*, Tosk (Sophikó) *kríe* pl. *krérë* 'head'[44] still remains without a convincing etymology[45]. Because of its phonological shape and its archaic status as the only neuter noun left in Albanian without a collective meaning (the predominant semantic correlate of the Albanian neuter), it is hard to believe that it is not IE, and related to Skt. *çīrṣán-*. Porzig (*op. cit.* 175) thinks *ka* ' ox', pl. *qe*, a loan (**k̂ₑroṷo-*) from his 'West', but there are two things wrong with his hypothesis. While Balto-Slavic seems clearly to have borrowed *some* items from centum dialects, unlike Albanian it shows satem remains in the same positions: beside Russ. *koróva*, Lith. *kárvė* 'cow', OPruss. *kurwan* (acc.) 'ox', we find Russ. CS. *srъna*, Lett. *sirna*, OPruss. *sirwis* 'Reh'. Secondly, the Balto-Slavic acute accent and the vocalism of Welsh *carw*, Corn. *carow*, Bret. *karo* < **krXu-* (**kr̥̄ṷ-*) point clearly to a laryngeal; thus, **korXuā*, **krXuo-*. In different Edgerton-Sievers syllabifications, the last form would give in Albanian **kar*(*ë*) (cf. *parë* 'first' < **prXuo-*) or **krā*. Without even invoking other possible ablaut forms that may earlier have coexisted and without assuming with Jokl[46] a difficult loss of final *-r* (which was *not* lost e.g. in *duar* 'hands'), a cross of these two normal forms gives *ka*, Sophikó /káa/. Again we find **k* immediately followed by **r*. A further illustration comes from *mjekrë* 'chin, beard', and the similarity to the Baltic words which Porzig points out (*op. cit.* 181) would be accidental. The evidence seems to point to an early depalatalization in position before **r* as well. Therefore, we find just what we should expect in *Balacros*, *balakrahiaihi*, *kriθonas*,

[43] *KZ* 74.127–8 (1956).

[44] For the vocalism, cf. *derë* pl. *dýer* 'door' < **d*(*h*)(*ṷ*)*ōrā* pl. (or dual?) **d*(*h*)(*ṷ*)*ōre*(*s*). Hence **krōn-*, pl. **krōnā*, perhaps < **ḱroA*(*s*)*n-*.

[45] See Tagliavini, *L'albanese di Dalmazia* 160.

[46] *Wörter und Sachen* 13.68.

kritaboa, *kraθeihi*, *kraapati*, *kordomaos*, *gronehias*, perhaps *korah[*, and the forms in *gor*(*r*)-. Because Albanian has long used the bases **lei*- and **leudh*-[47] for the notions 'be born, originate, family', **bher*- for 'bear, pregnant', and **pe*(*X*)l- for 'plant, bear (of animals)'[48], we may suspect that the second element of *oroagenas* may be borrowed. Scholars have already suspected the possible loan status of *trigonoxoa* and *argorian*, also seen in *argora-pandes*.

With these forms thus removed as apparent major obstacles to a reconciliation of the attested Messapic corpus with the satem features of Albanian, we find that there is little else in the way of certain or convincing etymologies proposed by earlier scholars that we may test for Albanian cognates.

One pertinent known Albanian environment remains to be mentioned: palatals before (nonliquid) obstruents. Alb. *dritë* 'light' < **dŕḱtā*, *tetë* 'eight' < (*o*)*ḱtő-tV*- show that as in *natë* 'night' < **nok*^{w}*t*-, at least before dentals (and we have no other sure examples), the stop, of whatever order, was lost. That this had occurred in pre-Roman times is shown by the different treatment in Latin loans: *luftë* 'war' < *lucta*, *troftë* 'trout' < *tructa* (or dialect *trokta*?), *ftua* 'quince' < *k*(*o*)*toniu*(*m*). The sole piece of evidence for position before nasal is *njeh* 'he knows', and here we cannot be sure of the exact status of the stop before it palatalized the nasal; the situation may well have been the same as that obtaining for Proto-Romance.[49]

Let us now summarize the present position. Albanian had clear reflexes of the labiovelars in a limited number of environments, but to date no crucial cognates *in these environments* have been identified in Messapic. Because of early neutralizations of the palatals in Albanian, perhaps before all phonemes except pure vowels[50], either by conversion to pure velars or by loss, the distribution of these phonemes must have been rather limited for a time; this explains the highly complex history of all these sounds in Albanian, and these faulty distributions are, quite apart from the great time-span involved, clearly what has made Albanian so unyielding to scholars in this respect. For the environments where we may expect to find distinctiveness, we still lack good cognates in the Messapic corpus. Finally, Messapic may have had in this fashion a roster of distinctive, but skewly distributed, *k*-like (or '*z*-like') phonemes which met difficulties of representation in the orthography and graphic system which they found available. On these lines, the insurmountable satem-centum difficulties in uniting Albanian and Messapic referred to by Porzig (*op. cit.* 149) are removed.

4.7. Laryngeals in Messapic. Having set aside the difficulties which have seemed to

[47] See Hamp, *JKF* 3.93–95 (1955), and Tagliavini, *L'albanese di Dalmazia* 284, *s.v. vlọ* 'brother'.

[48] See Hamp, *Bulletin of the Board of Celtic Studies* 16.280–281 (1956).

[49] Geg *thni*, Tosk *th*(*ë*)*ri* (Sophikó /*θríi*/) 'nit', and cognate with the Germanic word, shows by the Tosk -*r*- that the *-*n*- was intervocalic; hence **ḱVnid*-. This causes us seriously to wonder whether, rather than being a Latin loan as has been assumed ever since Miklosich, Alb. *qind* 'hundred' is not a native depalatalized **ḱmtóm* > **kmt*- > **kétan*, conflated with Lat. *centum*.

[50] If so, *gjashtë* 'six' is < **sés-tV* < **s*(*u*)*eḱs*-.

keep Albanian and Messapic apart, we now turn to the feature that in my opinion is the firmest trait linking Albanian and Messapic that I have been able to observe.

It has already been pointed out elsewhere[51] that Albanian alone among the subgroups of IE preserves a unit-reflex in initial position of the 'fourth' laryngeal, that is, the *a*-colouring **X* that does *not* show up in Hittite, but that has been heretofore posited on the basis of patterning. The full evidence for this observation will be presented at a later date; suffice it to say that the other three laryngeals do *not* show unit-reflexes subsisting in Albanian. This particular pattern of laryngeal retention is a striking feature that characterizes Albanian in contrast with all other known subgroups. Among the clearest examples are: (Geg forms are quoted) *hyp* 'mount' : Hittite *upzi* 'rises'; *hap* 'open' : Gk. ἀπό; *hî* 'ashes' : Gk. αἴθω. I posit as the proto-shape for the last **hídh(V)no-*. It is worth while pointing out that these conclusions were reached some time ago before it had occurred to me to consider the Messapic evidence at all; in fact, at that time, I was persuaded, along lines of Jokl's argument, that there was no way of choosing between a Thracian and an Illyrian descent for Albanian, if indeed its ancestor were really known. Thus the present argument, quite the reverse of being sought deliberately, has been forced on me by the data.

The starting point is the prefix *hipa-*, whose *h-* has always given trouble (see PID 3. 23). When we connect Alb. *hyp* and consider what has just been said above, we have a striking correspondence. After framing this hypothesis, I found that Bugge had made the same comparison[52], reconstructing *(*h*)*ūpo-*; but the very point that he could not account for was the all-important *h-*! He further claimed, wrongly, that the *i* <**ū* agreed with southern Albanian; the south Tosk feature of *i* in such forms is a recent and secondary development from common Albanian *y*. The second element of *hipakaθi* has been compared to Alb. *kam* 'I have'. Krahe (*op. cit.* 26) takes exception to this, but, as we have seen above, a **p* before **t* would have been lost in Albanian before Roman times (e.g. *shta-të* '7'). Therefore, **hŭpo-kapti* is here quite acceptable as a possible anterior verb form. Besides *hipades* and *hipavales*, we now have *hipakabl̦a* (Krahe, *op. cit.* 25) to add to the attestations.

The next form to consider is *hi* 'here(?)', probably to be seen in *hi-beran* (PID 3 .23). This fits very well with Alb. *hŷj* 'enter', which I have already linked with Hitt. *u-* 'hither'[53], Lat. *au-*, etc. We may now note the gratifying fit of the vocalisms of all these forms. In each case we have Alb. *y*; therefore, the Mess. *i* (graphic, at any rate) must reflect **ū*, perhaps **uX*.

Mess. *hadive*(*s*) may tentatively be put alongside Alb. *hodha* 'I threw', and compared to Lat. *ad*, etc.; on the possible relationship of *ad* to *sed-* see Hoeningswald, *Language*

[51] *Modern Language Notes* (January 1954) 41; Proceedings of the VII International Congress of Linguists, London 1952, 472 (1956).

[52] *Bezzenbergers Beiträge* 18.195 (1892).

[53] See E. H. Sturtevant, *Hitt. Grammar*² 53, on the Hittite cognates.

28.183 (1952). Tagliavini cites (*L'albanese di Dalmazia, ss. vv.*) etymologies purporting to link Alb. *mbet* and *jes*, both meaning in different dialects notions and nuances such as 'remain, stand', to **sodeįō*, but this is not at all sure. If Alb. *hodha* really belongs here, the present tense variant *hjedh* would have an analogical *j-* following the common modern ablaut pattern in Albanian, while *hedh* would show umlaut to *e* of the earlier **a* provoked by the suffix **-(e)į*$^{e}/_{o}$, which perhaps we see reflected in the Messapic *-i-*. Thus *hodha* morphologically and in vocalism would match *mora* 'I took' and *dolla* 'I went out' (: *marr* 'I take', *dal* 'I go out', these two, however, being old **-n-* presents).

We may speculate that *haidavoa* is related to Alb. *hî*, Gk. αἴθω, Hitt. *a-a-an* 'hot'. If *haivahias* really is related to Gk. οἶ(ϝ)ος, then the Balto-Slavic vocalisms that point to an *e*-colouring laryngeal in this base must be later and analogical. I can suggest nothing at present for *hazavaθi*; Pisani's[54] guess at a cognate with Lett. *sa-* is impossible.

On a more general patterning basis, the frequency of Mess. *h* adjacent to *a*, and the near-absence of an adjacent *e*, is significant. The lone item *hennai* may well be from some linguistic neighbour in Italy.

One converse item is highly useful in tending to confirm these conclusions. Mess. *ana*[55], which is also attested in our one Illyrian inscription, 'queen, lady' has been connected (see Krahe *op. cit.* 80) with Lat. *anus* 'old woman'. Now the Latin word and its cognates have been connected in turn with Hitt. /ḫanas/ 'grandmother' (see Sturtevant *Hitt. Gram.* 42). It is thus quite in accord with the Albanian picture that we find no trace of this other *a*-colouring laryngeal, that yields Anatolian *ḫ*(*ḫ*), in the Messapic and Illyrian form.

While admittedly this feature of agreement between Albanian and Messapic *h-* is an item of retention, and not of shared innovation, to the extent that we can recover the picture from the fragmentary data, the general treatment of the laryngeals that we see is a unique syndrome not shared by any other known IE subgroup. We appear to have here the strongest structural feature yet adduced in support of the specific kinship of Albanian and Illyro-Messapic.

Addendum to 4.3:

Kretschmer thought Raetic was Italic. Apart from *estum* 'istorum', if *-sna* of *udisna* is comparable to Umbr. *snāta*, this plus *šnušur* (contrast Alb. *nuse* 'bride') point to preservation of **sn*. If Modern Albanian and the behaviour of **sw* are relevant, this points away from a Raetic-Illyrian relationship of any proximity. On the other hand, the Raetic *-š-* and the problematical Alb. *-s-* of *nuse* look interesting.

UNIVERSITY OF CHICAGO

[54] *Op. cit.* 232, No. 87; CIM 147.
[55] PID 3.4; Krahe, *op. cit.* 80; see also the new inscription, Krahe *op. cit.* 24, fn. 46.

GUSTAV HERDAN

THE NUMERICAL EXPRESSION OF SELECTIVE VARIATION IN THE VOWEL-CONSONANT SEQUENCE IN ENGLISH AND RUSSIAN

A CHARACTERISTIC feature of true language statistics, capable of providing linguistically relevant information, is that they do not stop at collecting figures about language units, but always aim at the comparison with a standard. This enables us to ascertain the presence and the degree of selective variation, as distinct from all possible, or the most probable, occurrences of the linguistic event in question. The type of standard differs according to the material. Thus, it is not enough to have ascertained the relative frequencies of the different phonemes in a language, but we ought to make such information the basis for linguistically relevant comparisons; for instance, the comparison of the frequency of a given phoneme in phonetically relevant position with its global frequency, or the number of different vocabulary items in which the phoneme has distinctive function with the total number of vocabulary items containing that phoneme. In short, we could utilise the global frequency as a basis for deriving information about the functional burdening of phonemes.(1)* Here the standard is provided by the *global* frequency of a given phoneme. In other cases, the standard may be the number of *possible* occurrences of a phoneme in a certain position of the word, against which to judge the actual or observed number of words having the phoneme in that position. A third type of standard – which we shall use in this investigation – is the *probable* range of variability of a certain language feature, that is its variation according to a law of chance, with which to compare the actual or observed variation of that language feature; according to the outcome of the comparison, we may conclude

(a) that the feature in question varied no more than could be accounted for by chance only, and thus that its occurrence is purely random;

(b) that there is an assignable cause at work which made it vary in excess of what was possible by chance only; and

* These numbers refer to items in the bibliography at the end.

(c) that there existed a linkage between certain linguistic features which significantly reduced the variation due to chance.

I

The investigation has a double purpose:

(a) to find a numerical expression for selective variation in the vowel-consonant sequence in a given language, and to account for it in terms of the particular transition probabilities between vowels and consonants, and their combinations in pairs, triplets etc., and

(b) to compare selective variation in vowel-consonant sequences in English and Russian.

The method employed is that of the Markoff chain, so-called after the Russian mathematician, A. A. Markoff, whose exposition of his theory in the Bulletin of the Imperial Acadamy of Sciences of St. Petersburg in 1913 (2),[1] may be regarded as one of the classical papers of mathematical linguistics, though few linguists will have a first-hand knowledge of it. Markoff's purpose, however, was not to contribute to the science of linguistics, but to give an application of his statistical theory of chains. Consequently, although faultless as a piece of applied mathematics, his paper is open to certain criticism fiom the linguistic point of view. Apart from dealing with letters and not with phonemes, the method requires a continuous sequence of linguistic elements disregarding the empty spaces between words, with the consequence that what is, for instance, called 'vowel sequence' does not only refer to the vowel sequence within words, but comprises also that between the end and beginning of words. However, I have followed his method closely, for these reasons. Statistical linguistics in their present state suffers from one disadvantage which was already stressed by Trubetzkoy (1) in 1939, and that is its lack of uniformity which prevents valid comparisons. A typology of languages requiring statistical methods is impossible as long as results are not comparable. It is readily admitted that very often the discrepancies arise from the desire on the part of the investigator to correct or improve upon methods previously used, but it should be made an important methodological point to weigh the advantage of a change in experimental design against that of uniformity. In the present case I thought it best to design the experiment in accordance with that carried out by Markoff, and thus ensure the possibility of valid comparisons between results, being fully aware of the limits imposed by Markoff's particular design, viz. that the comparison is restricted to one of *printed English and Russian* and that the vowel-consonant sequences referred to are not only those within words, but those within and between words. Within

[1] The mathematical theory of the Markoff process was developed in two earlier papers by Markoff (3), (4).

those limits, however, the procedure is not only unobjectionable, but may serve as a model for other typological investigations.

Markoff's material were the 20,000 letters comprised in the first chapter and the first 16 Sonnets of the second chapter of Pushkin's novel in verse *Evgeny Onegin.* In order to make the comparison between English and Russian letter sequences a truly valid one, and to forestall criticism on account of difference in subject matter and style, the first 10,000 letters, representing the first 29 sonnets and the first 4 lines of the 30th, of the English translation of Pushkin's poem by Oliver Elton (5) were chosen as the material of the present investigation. This gives a sequence of 10,000 connected observations, each of which is either a vowel or a consonant. From this material, it is possible to obtain an estimate of the basic probability of a vowel, or a consonant, in continuous pieces of the English language; we shall denote these probabilities by p and $q = 1 - p$, respectively. Moreover, we can obtain the estimates of the probability of a vowel following a vowel – p_1, of a vowel following a consonant – p_0, of a vowel following two vowels – $p_{1,1}$, of a vowel following a consonant which is preceded by a vowel – $p_{1,0}$, of a vowel following a vowel which is preceded by a consonant – $p_{0,1}$, and a vowel following two consonants – $p_{0,0}$. The complementary probabilities are denoted respectively by q_1, q_0, etc.

II

The total sequence of 10,000 letters is divided into 100 groups of 100 letters each, as following each other in the text. With a view to combining the observations in two ways, which is necessary for our purpose, we arrange every group of 100 successive letters in a square as follows:

1	2	3	4	5	6	7	8	9	10
11	12	13	14	15	16	17	18	19	20
...	...	...	...	...	...	...	...	...	...
91	92	93	94	95	96	97	98	99	100

and count in each column the number of vowels. We then combine the counts in columns

1st & 6th, 2nd & 7th, 3rd & 8th, 4th & 9th, 5th & 10th

and denote these sums by the symbols

$$(1,6),\ (2,7),\ (3,8),\ (4,9),\ (5,10).$$

This gives five figures for each text sample of 100 whose sum

$$(1,6) + (2,7) + (3,8) + (4,9) + (5,10)$$

is the total number of vowels in a sequence of 100 letters. In this way we obtain 100 figures for the vowel number in successive samples of 100 letters.

If now, instead of summing over the different column-pairs belonging to one sample of 100 consecutive letters, the double-column counts each representing the number of vowels per 20 letters are combined for 5 samples of 100 letters each by summing over the *same* column-pairs in the 5 samples, we get a new distribution of the 10,000 letters in groups of 100, and the quantities

$$\Sigma(1,6),\ \Sigma(2,7),\ \Sigma(3,8),\ \Sigma(4,9),\ \Sigma(5,10)$$ [2]

represent new figures for the number of vowels in samples of 100 letters, viz. the vowel number in disconnected but corresponding column-pairs.

Thus, whereas the first summation gives the vowel numbers in successive or connected parts of the text, the second gives the vowel numbers in disconnected parts of the sequence of 10,000 letters. From a difference between the two results, certain inferences may be drawn about the amount of selective variation present.

Table 1 exhibits the results of our vowel count in 20 blocks, each of which gives in the first line five figures for the (1,6) count and their sum, in the second five figures for the (2,7) count, etc., and, consequently, in the last line the vowel numbers for the first 100 letters of text, for the second 100 letters, etc., and, ultimately, the total vowel number in five groups of 100 consecutive letters. The last column gives the sums $\Sigma(1,6)$, $\Sigma(2,7)$ etc.

We concentrate first on the numbers in the last line of each square of Table 1 being the vowel frequencies per 100 consecutive letters of text, from which we get the frequency distribution as shown in col. 2, Table 2.

The arithmetic mean results as

$$a = 39.07 \backsim 39.1$$

The total number of vowels in the sample of 10.000 letters is 3907, and the total number of consonants 6093. Since a represents the average vowel number per 100 letters, the probability of a letter being a vowel is

$$39.1/100 = .391$$

which we shall denote by p. The complementary probability $1 - p = .609$ must be that of a letter being a consonant, and we shall denote it by q.

The square of the standard deviation, as a measure of dispersion, is calculated as the average square deviation from the mean, and results as

$$s^2 = 6.73.$$

[2] Σ is the symbol for summation.

7	8	8	12	11	46	13	9	7	7	10	46	12	12	9	9	10	52	8	12	10	7	7	44
8	4	12	2	9	35	7	8	9	7	8	39	6	5	9	8	7	35	7	6	7	7	8	35
4	11	3	7	7	32	8	7	11	7	8	41	7	7	9	8	9	40	13	7	6	10	7	43
10	8	9	9	5	41	8	12	4	10	12	46	4	10	7	7	8	36	7	8	10	10	10	45
8	9	6	7	8	38	5	6	10	8	6	35	6	7	5	4	9	38	5	3	5	9	10	32
37	40	38	37	40	192	41	42	41	39	44	207	35	41	39	36	43	194	40	36	38	43	42	199
8	12	8	6	5	39	9	9	6	6	12	42	8	9	7	3	11	43	6	10	9	7	7	39
8	5	5	8	10	37	6	8	8	6	9	37	6	7	7	11	7	38	7	6	6	11	9	39
7	9	11	8	7	42	9	10	6	8	5	38	7	8	9	3	5	32	7	10	8	4	6	35
8	7	7	10	3	40	2	9	11	8	13	43	12	10	5	8	11	46	7	9	9	9	9	43
10	6	10	11	7	44	9	8	7	10	7	41	9	4	11	6	7	37	10	5	6	6	12	39
41	39	41	43	38	207	35	44	38	38	46	201	42	38	39	36	41	196	37	40	38	37	43	195
6	8	7	6	5	32	6	8	7	9	9	39	9	7	12	12	6	46	10	12	11	8	6	47
7	6	9	10	11	43	6	8	7	3	3	27	7	10	3	8	4	32	5	6	10	10	10	41
7	10	5	9	6	37	12	8	7	8	10	45	8	8	11	6	11	44	8	7	6	7	9	37
9	8	9	8	8	42	6	7	12	7	6	38	7	10	13	9	10	49	10	12	9	9	6	46
7	9	8	7	8	39	8	10	5	9	7	39	4	8	5	4	7	28	9	6	9	9	7	40
36	41	38	40	38	193	38	41	38	36	35	188	35	43	44	39	38	199	42	43	45	43	38	211
10	6	8	7	6	37	9	6	9	6	7	37	6	6	9	7	10	38	8	7	7	5	5	32
9	6	7	4	9	35	10	8	8	6	7	39	9	5	6	7	3	30	7	6	10	8	5	36
6	8	5	6	7	32	3	11	6	7	5	32	8	11	6	10	11	46	8	6	4	7	11	36
7	8	9	9	7	40	10	5	4	8	9	36	3	7	12	6	7	35	8	6	9	9	4	36
4	8	9	8	9	38	3	7	12	10	9	41	10	8	9	10	7	44	11	9	4	10	10	44
36	36	38	34	38	182	35	37	39	37	37	185	36	37	42	40	38	193	42	34	34	39	35	184
9	10	7	8	7	41	5	10	11	2	10	38	7	9	7	6	7	36	10	12	10	12	8	52
6	5	8	12	7	38	11	5	7	8	7	38	5	6	6	8	10	35	11	2	9	13	8	43
12	14	9	5	8	48	9	11	9	7	7	43	9	8	7	5	8	37	4	10	13	6	9	42
7	7	5	8	10	37	5	9	9	8	9	40	4	6	6	7	7	30	10	12	7	5	9	43
9	6	8	7	5	35	9	8	7	10	5	39	8	9	9	7	6	39	7	5	7	7	6	32
43	42	37	40	37	199	39	43	43	35	38	198	33	38	35	33	38	177	42	41	46	43	40	212

TABLE 2

Vowel number per 100 letters	Frequency of connected counts	Frequency of disconnected counts
27		1
28		1
29		
30		2
31		1
32		9
33	2	
34	3	
35	8	9
36	8	6
37	10	9
38	19	9
39	8	11
40	9	5
41	8	6
42	8	4
43	11	8
44	3	5
45	1	2
46	2	7
47		1
48		1
49		1
50		
51		
52		2
	100	100
Average	39.1	39.1
(Standard deviation)^2	6.73	29.11

However, the standard deviation may be calculated in yet another way, namely under the assumption of a pure random or chance distribution of the vowel frequencies in groups of 100 letters. We then obtain for it, according to the so-called Bernoullian law

$$\sigma^2 = npq = 23.81$$

What we are interested in is whether there is a linkage, in the sense of selective affinity, between vowels and consonants, between vowels and vowels or consonants and consonants. The answer is obtained by comparing the observed standard deviation with the value that would arise on pure chance, that is without linkage. The ratio of the two standard deviations is known as Lexis' *Q*. (6) If the fluctuations of the vowel frequencies in samples of 100 letters were completely random, there would be no significant difference between the observed and the theoretical measure of dispersion, and consequently the expectation of Q under this condition is unity.

On the other hand, if the fluctuations of the vowel numbers cannot be regarded as random variations in a Bernoullian or normal statistical population of such numbers, then we should expect the ratio of the two standard deviations to differ significantly from unity. In the first case, we speak of a 'normal' dispersion, and in the second of either a 'super-normal' or a 'sub-normal' dispersion, according to whether Q is greater or smaller than unity. A mass event with a constant probability leads to a Q indicative of normal dispersion, and a mass event with a variable probability to a Q indicative of super-normal dispersion, and since another possibility of unconnected chance events is unthinkable, it follows that a Q which is significantly less than unity does no longer refer to pure chance events, but must be indicative of a linkage or correlation between the individual events. (7)

As every statistic obtained from a sample, Q has an error. This error is calculated as $2/(k-1)$, where k is the number of degrees of freedom or categories. We regard a value of Q as significantly different from unity, if it lies outside the range of twice or three times that error.

The ratio: observed/theoretical squared standard deviation, in symbols

$$Q = s^2/\sigma^2$$

results for our data as

$$Q = 6.73/23.81 = .282$$

with a standard error of

$$2/14 - 1 = .153.$$

Since Q is less than $1 - (3 \times .153) = .541$, it must be regarded as highly significant of a tie or linkage between the observations, that is between vowels and consonants.

III

In order to ascertain the type of linkage between vowels and consonants, we use the Markoff chain method. That is, we shall calculate a coefficient comparable to Lexis' Q, but on the basis of the actually observed numbers of joint occurrence of vowels and consonants. Agreement between the two coefficients, obtained independently, admits the conclusion that it is the peculiar mechanism of the Markoff chain which provides the explanation of the linkage ascertained in a global manner by the sub-normality of Lexis' Q.

Scanning the sequence of 10,000 letters for

vowel vowel

sequences, we find 696, which divided by the total number of vowels, 3907, gives

$$p_1 = 696/3907 = .178.$$

In a similar manner, we could calculate the probability of

consonant consonant

sequences. However, it is possible to save ourselves the tedious counting labour by the following considerations. Substracting 696 from 3907 we get 3211 as the number of consonants following a vowel, which is also the number of vowels following a consonant,[3] and thus briefly, the number of joint vowel-consonant occurrences. Since now every consonant, except the first, follows either a vowel or a consonant, the difference between the total consonant number and the number of joint vowel-consonant occurrences

$$6093 - 3211 = 2882$$

must be the number of

consonant consonant

occurrences.

We then get for the probability of a joint vowel-consonant occurrence

$$p_0 = 3211/6093 = .526.$$

It should be observed that we use as the denominator for p_0, not the total vowel number, but the total consonant number. Since there are more consonants than vowels in our sample, we must expect, if the distribution were random, the joint vowel-consonant occurrences to exceed in number the vowel-vowel occurrences, and the comparison of the two numbers would tell us nothing about the linkage in which we are interested.

The difference $p_1 - p_0$, which is an index of the preference of joint vowel-consonant occurrence, we obtain as

$$\delta = .178 - .526 = - .348.$$

On the assumption that our sequence of 10,000 letters represents a '*simple Markoff chain*', the theoretical value of the coefficient of dispersion with which to compare the empirical value of Q is calculated as the quantity (3)

$$\frac{1 + \delta}{1 - \delta} = \frac{.652}{1.348} = .483$$

The difference of this value from unity is indicative, just like a sub-normal Q, of a bond or linkage between the events.

[3] Ref. (4), p. 173.

But although pointing in the same direction, the two values do not approximate to one another too closely. The reason may be that, so far, we have only considered a simple chain, or a chain of the first order, that is one of letter pairs. From an examination of the letter sequences, it is evident that not only double, but triple etc. combinations occur which must be considered if the sub-normality was to be accounted for more fully. Consequently, if we wish to achieve by the chain method a closer approximation to Q, we must consider the letter sequences in the light of what Markoff has called a '*complex chain*', i.e. a chain of the second or higher order (4).

We first scan the sequence of 10,000 letters for the triple combinations

vowel vowel vowel

and

consonant consonant consonant,

and obtain the first as 85, and the second as 969. Dividing these numbers by the vowel-vowel and consonant-consonant numbers, respectively, we get the probabilities

$$p_{1,1} = 85/696 = .122$$

and

$$q_{0,0} = 969/2882 = .336.$$

Considering that a vowel-vowel combination (vv) may be preceded by either a vowel (v) or a consonant (c), and that, therefore, the vv occurrences may form part of either a vvv or a cvv (vvc) occurrence, the difference vv/v — vvv/vv must represent the probability of a v occurrence to form part of a cvv (vvc) occurrence. Similarly, the difference cc/c — ccc/cc represents the probability of a c occurrence to form part of a vcc (ccv) occurrence. Dividing each result by the corresponding probability of simple joint occurrences cv (vc), we get

$$\frac{\text{cvv/v}}{\text{cv/v}} = \text{cvv/cv},$$

being the probability of a simple joint occurrence cv to belong to the triple combination cvv, and

$$\frac{\text{vcc/c}}{\text{vc/c}} = \text{vcc/vc},$$

being the probability of a simple joint occurrence vc to belong to the triple combination vcc.

These quantities are quite analogous to cv/v and vc/c, respectively.

Combining the probabilities obtained before,

$$\begin{aligned} p &= .391, & q &= .609 \\ p_1 &= .178, & q_1 &= .822 \\ p_0 &= .526, & q_0 &= .474 \\ p_{1,1} &= .122, & q_{0,0} &= .336 \end{aligned}$$

as indicated above, we calculate the triple transition probabilities between vowels and consonants as follows:

$$\varepsilon = \frac{\text{vvv/vv} - \text{vv/v}}{\text{cv/v}} = \frac{p_{1,1} - p_1}{q_1} = \frac{.122 - .178}{.822} = -\frac{.056}{.822} = -.068$$

$$\eta = \frac{\text{ccc/cc} - \text{cc/c}}{\text{cv/c}} = \frac{q_{0,0} - q_0}{p_0} = \frac{.336 - .474}{.526} = -\frac{.138}{.526} = -.262$$

We then calculate the coefficient of dispersion under the assumption of a complex Markoff chain as (3), (4)

$$\frac{1+\delta}{1-\delta}\left\{\frac{1+\varepsilon}{2(1-\varepsilon)} + \frac{1+\eta}{2(1-\eta)}\right\} + \frac{(q-p)(\eta-\varepsilon)}{(1-\varepsilon)(1-\eta)}$$

Substituting in the above formula the values for δ, ε, η, p, q, we get

$$.483\left\{\frac{.466}{1.068} + \frac{.369}{1.262}\right\} + \frac{(.609 - .391)(-.262 + .068)}{.932 \times .738} = .319$$

which approximates the value for Q (.282) satisfactorily. We could, of course, get a still closer approximation by considering fourfold, fivefold, etc. letter combinations.

The coefficient of dispersion which we calculated from the quantities

$$p,\ q,\ \delta,\ \varepsilon,\ \eta$$

under the assumption of a complex Markoff chain thus agrees satisfactorily with that obtained empirically by the method of Lexis' Q. We are therefoıe justified in regarding the particular selective affinities between vowels and consonants, which we call a complex Markoff chain, as the explanation of the sub-normal Lexis' Q. The results are collected in Table 3, together with the corresponding ones for the Russian letter count. In order to write the transition probabilities as positive quantities, the table lists the values $-\delta$, $-\varepsilon$, $-\eta$.

IV

We now turn to the second summation according to column-pairs of the same denomination, and thus to the vowel count in disconnected samples of 100 letters

TABLE 3

Letters (v = vowel, c = consonant)	English (10,000 letters)	Russian (20,000 letters)
	Numbers	
v	3907	8638
c	6093	11361
vv	696	1104
cc	2882	3827
cv (vc)	3211	7534
vvv	85	115
ccc	969	505
	Probabilities	
v/v + c . . . . p	.391	.432
c/v + c . . . . q	.609	.568
vv/v. . . . . p_1	.178	.128
cv/v . . . . q_1	.822	.872
cv/c (vc/c) . . . . . . p_0	.526	.663
cc/c . . . . q_0	.474	.337
vvv/vv. . . . . $p_{1,1}$	.122	.104
ccc/cc . . . . $q_{0,0}$	.336	.132
cv/c–vv/v. . . . . . . $p_0 - p_1 = -\delta$	.348	.535
cvv/cv . . . . $\frac{p_1 - p_{1,1}}{q_1} = -\varepsilon$	.068	.027
vcc/vc . . . . $\frac{q_0 - q_{0,0}}{p_0} = -\eta$	.262	.309
Markoff simple chain coefficient	.483	.300
Markoff complex chain coefficient	.319	.195
Lexis' Q	.282	.208

each. The frequency distribution of these numbers, which we denoted by $\Sigma(1,6)$, $\Sigma(2,7)$, etc. and listed as the last column of each block in Table 1, is given in Table 2, col. 3.

The arithmetic mean is, of course, the same as for the distribution of consecutive letters, viz.

$$a = 39.1.$$

The standard deviation (squared) results as

$$s^2 = 29.11.$$

From this we obtain Lexis' Q as

$$Q = 29.11/23.81 = 1.222.$$

Since the error of Q is $2/(20–1) = .10$, the difference of Q from unity is still within three times its error, and thus need not be regarded as significant, which implies that the vowel-consonant sequence in disconnected parts of text is not essentially different from a random sequence. On the other hand, the difference between the squared standard deviations obtained from connected pieces of text, 6.73, and from disconnected parts, 29.11, is sufficiently great to convince us of the presence of bonds or affinities between the individual events in the former.

V

Discussion and Conclusions.

(a) Compaiing the vowel-consonant sequences in printed English and Russian, we find it non-random in both languages, but subject to selective variation, due to selective affinities between vowels and consonants. The resulting structure corresponds to what mathematicians call the Markoff chain.

The implied bond or correlation between the types of letters, which is significant in both languages, is measured by the deviation of Lexis' Q from unity. That this difference is slightly greater for Russian, does not necessarily mean that the bond between the types of letters is stronger there, since a sub-normal Q decreases with sample size until a stable value is reached. Other things being equal, we should, therefore, expect it to be smaller for the Russian count of 20,000 letters, than for the English one of 10,000. In any case, it is not so much the difference between the values for Q which interests us, as the differences between the particular probabilities and transition probabilities by which to account for the deviation of Q from unity.

(b) Turning now to these probabilities, and the differences between corresponding ones in English and Russian, it should be noted that, unlike Q, they are not affected by the difference in size of the English and Russian samples. The count of English letters was stopped at 10,000, because it was found that this was a sufficient sample size for the different probabilities to approach their true values closely enough to be regarded as valid estimates of the true values (in the sense of the Law of Great Numbers).

The probability, q, of English consonants is greater than that of Russian consonants; consequently, that of English vowels, p, is smaller. On the other hand, both vowel and consonant pairs (vv and cc) have a greater probability in English. The reverse is true for the vc (cv) combination which has a greater probability in Russian. These results would seem to point to English preferring letter clusters of the same type (vv and cc), and Russian those of the mixed type (vc ∽ cv).[4]

This is confirmed by the higher probabilities of the vvv and ccc combinations

[4] This shows the difference between Q for English and Russian to be, to some extent at least, systematic, and indicative of a stronger linkage between vowels and consonants in Russian.

in English, and the higher probability of the vcc combination in Russian; the cvv combination, on the other hand, has a greater probability in English.

(c) The difference between Q and the coefficient of dispersion obtained from δ is an indication that the chain is not a simple or first order one, i.e., one in which the bond does not extend beyond the immediate neighbour.

This is confirmed by the fact that the complex chain coefficient, which takes triple combinations into account, is a much better approximation to Q. This is true for both, English and Russian, and shows the assumption of a complex Markoff chain structure to be correct for both languages. To be a little more explicit, it means that the selectivity of letters does not lead to mere repetition of either v or c, nor only to simple alternation of vowels and consonants, but that the selection extends to letters other than the immediate neighbour, resulting in a complex pattern of the vowel-consonant sequence.

(d) The value of Lexis' Q for the distribution of vowel frequency per 100 letters in disconnected parts of the sequence of 10,000 letters, namely in 5 column-pairs of the same denomination, is not significantly different, by the three-standard-error criterion, from the theoretical value according to the Bernoullian law. The dispersion is, therefore, not significantly different from normal, which implies a random sequence of vowels and consonants. This is what might have been expected, since by the method of summing over disconnected parts of the text, the ties between types of letters were severed. It also confirms the conclusion that the sub-normality of the distribution obtained by the first summation is due to the presence of ties between the types of letters.

(e) Apart from providing information for a typology of languages (Russian and English, in our case), as regards the vowel-consonant sequence, our investigation reveals in a rather striking way the inadequacy of the English alphabet as a written code for the English phonemic system.

Attention is first drawn to the fact that English uses more consonant letters than Russian, which as a Slav language is much richer in consonant phonemes. The same applies to consonant pairs which have a greater probability in English, and still more to consonant triplets, whose probability in English is almost three times that in Russian. That a language like English, which is rich in vowel phonemes and very economical in the use of consonant phonemes should, in the written language, be excessively burdened by consonant letters and their double and triple combinations, and more so than Russian, which is rather poor in vowel phonemes, but very rich in consonant phonemes, shows how badly suited is our alphabet to the phonemic structure of the language.

Summary

1. The material for the investigation is a sequence of 10,000 letters representing the first 30 sonnets of the English translation by O. Elton of Pushkin's novel in verse *Evgeny Onegin*. The object of the investigation was to express numerically the selective variation in the sequence of vowels and consonants in a continuous text, and to compare the results with those obtained by A. A. Markoff from a count of the first 20,000 letters of the Russian original.

2. The vowel-consonant sequence in English is shown to be in accordance with the stochastic mechanism known as a complex Markoff chain. The numerical expression of selectivity so obtained is not only a yes-no answer (selectivity or randomness), nor is it restricted to giving only a global measure (in terms of the ratio Q, or rather its deviation from unity), but it analyses that empirical, global measure into its constituent elements in terms of the transition probabilities between vowels and consonants, each occurring singly, in pairs, triplets etc.

3. On the basis of these results, English and Russian are compared with a view to arriving at a typology for the vowel-consonant sequence in these languages.

4. The comparison shows English, which as a spoken language is rich in vowel phonemes and very economical in consonant phonemes, as using more consonants and consonant clusters in alphabetic writing than Russian, which as a Slav language is notoriously rich in consonant phonemes and their combinations. This paradoxical result may be of interest to advocates of a spelling and alphabet reform for English, such as envisaged in G. B. Shaw's Will.

UNIVERSITY OF BRISTOL

Bibliography

(1) N. S. Trubetzkoy, *Grundzüge der Phonologie*, *TCLP* 7 (1939).

(2) A. A. Markoff, Примерь статистическаго изследованія надь текстомь "Евгенія Онегина" иллюстр. связь испытаніи вь цепь, *Bulletin de l'Académie Imperiale des Sciences de St. Pétersbourg*, 1913.
The mathematical theory of the Markoff chain is more fully developed in the following publications, also published in the *Bulletin* of 1907 and 1911, respectively:

(3) A.A. Markoff, Изследованіе замечательнаго случая зависимыхь испытаній.

(4) A. A. Markoff, Объ одномъ случае испытаній связанныхь вь сложную цепь.

(5) A. S. Pushkin, *Evgeny Onegin*, translated by Oliver Elton (London, 1937).

(6) G. Herdan, *Language as choice and chance* 95, 109, 341 (Groningen, 1956).

(7) E. Czuber, *Wahrscheinlichkeitsrechnung* 321 (Leipzig, 1903).

ROMAN JAKOBSON

MUFAXXAMA

THE 'EMPHATIC' PHONEMES IN ARABIC

1. COMPONENTIAL ANALYSIS OF ARABIC NONSYLLABIC PHONEMES

THE DIALECT of the North Palestinian Druzes is used here to exemplify the dissolution of such phonemes into distinctive features. (See Table 1.) The phonemes of this dialect have been carefully inventorized by H.Blanc, and his inquiry, particularly the discussion of the role of the so-called 'emphatic' consonants, is indeed one "of the clearest and best descriptions in all Arabic dialectology" (s. Ferguson, 1955).

TABLE 1

	ɔ	^{c}	h	ḥ	d	t	ṭ	δ	δ̣	θ	z	s	ṣ	b	ḅ	f	(g)	k	q	ž	Γ	š	x	n	m	ṃ	r	l	ḷ	y	w
vocalic *vs.* non-voc.	−	−	−	−	−	−	−	−	−	−	−	−	−	−	−	−	−	−	−	−	−	−	−	−	−	−	+	+	+	+	+
cons. *vs.* non.cons.	−	−	−	−	+	+	+	+	+	+	+	+	+	+	+	+	+	+	+	+	+	+	+	+	+	+	+	+	+	−	−
flat *vs.* plain	−	+	−	+	−	−	+	−	+	−	−	−	+	−	+	−	−	−	+	−	+	−	+	−	−	+	−	−	+	O	O
nasal *vs.* oral	O	O	O	O	−	−	−	−	−	−	−	−	−	−	−	−	−	−	−	−	−	−	−	+	+	+	O	O	O	O	O
compact *vs.* diffuse	O	O	O	O	−	−	−	−	−	−	−	−	−	−	−	−	+	+	+	+	+	+	+	O	O	O	O	O	O	O	O
grave *vs.* acute	O	O	O	O	−	−	−	−	−	−	−	−	−	+	+	+	O	O	O	O	O	O	O	−	+	+	O	O	O	−	+
fortis *vs.* lenis	−	−	+	+	−	+	+	−	−	+	−	+	+	−	−	+	−	+	+	−	−	+	+	O	O	O	O	O	O	O	O
continuant *vs.* abrupt	O	O	O	O	−	−	−	+	+	+	+	+	+	O	O	O	O	−	−	O	O	+	+	O	O	O	−	+	+	O	O
strident *vs.* mellow	O	O	O	O	−	O	O	−	−	−	+	+	+	O	O	O	−	O	O	+	+	O	O	O	O	O	O	O	O	O	O

For terms and definitions consult *Preliminaries to speech analysis* by R. Jakobson, C. G. M. Fant, and M. Halle (third printing: Cambridge, Mass., 1955), a concise restatement in *Fundamentals of language*, Part I, by R. Jakobson and M. Halle (The Hague, 1956), or a shortened and revised version of the latter study in the *Handbook of phonetics* (Amsterdam, 1957).

The following sketch is dedicated to Professor Joshua Whatmough, who was one of the first to recognize "the gain in theoretical simplicity and scientific objectivity" obtainable through applying the "principle of binary choices" to the study of phonemes (*Class. Phil.* 49. 137 [1954]).[1]

[1] My thanks for valuable suggestions are due to the Harvard Arabists – Ch. A. Ferguson and R. C. Harrell, and to the astute phonetician of Jerusalem University, Irene Garbell.

2. PHARYNGEALIZED DENTALS

An acute phoneme is opposed to its grave counterpart, for instance a dental to the corresponding labial, perceptually by a higher pitch and acoustically by the concentration of energy in the upper frequencies of the spectrum. On the motor level, the difference between the acuteness and gravity of oral phonemes lies in the size and shape of the mouth resonator. A stricture in a medial – dental or palatal – region of the mouth builds a smaller and more divided cavity, whereas a stricture in a peripheral – labial or velar – region forms an ampler and less comparted resonator.

The pitch of a phoneme depends not only on the volume and the shape of the resonating cavity, but also on the size of its front or back orifice: a decreased orifice shifts downwards or weakens, and an increased orifice shifts upwards or strengthens certain uper frequency components of the spectrum. The difference in pitch between velar and palatal vowels is reinforced when the former are produced with a contraction and the latter with a dilation of the front orifice (rounded *vs.* unrounded). The emission of grave vowels and consonants is usually accompanied by a contraction and the emission of acute phonemes by a dilation of the back orifice: in comparison with the rest-position of the pharynx, it is narrowed when labials or velars are uttered, and widened when producing dentals or palatals.

The changes in the size of the orifice may assume an autonomous phonemic role. The French /u/ is produced with a wide mouth resonator and narrowed front orifice, and /i/ with a reduced and divided resonator and widened front orifice, whereas /ü/ is uttered with an /i/-like resonator and /u/-like orifice. The Arabic /f/ is produced with a wide mouth resonator and narrowed back orifice, and /s/ with a reduced and divided resonator and widened back orifice, whereas the 'emphatic' /ṣ/ requires a resonator slightly modifying that of /s/ and a pharyngeal tract approximating that of /f/.

The characteristic articulatory feature of all the 'emphatic' phonemes is the contraction of the upper pharynx. Native informants usually point to their throat to elucidate the 'emphatic' articulation (cf. Marçais, p. 19).[2] The first X-ray pictures of these Arabic and Somali articulations brought Panconcelli-Calzia (1920–21) to the conclusion: "Die differenzierende Hauptursache in dem Klange dieser Laute liegt – wie Meinhof schon lange mit Recht vermutet hat – im Kehlkopf und im Rachen". This finding was confirmed by the detailed roentgenographic study of Marçais. The X-rays reveal the projection of the root of the tongue toward the back wall of the pharynx and the resulting reduction of the pharyngeal aperture: "Si l'on prend comme point de repère la partie de la langue qui se trouve à 2 cm. au dessus de l'épiglotte on

[2] As Irene Garbell notes in a letter, Yemenites, Iraqi, and other native speakers of Arabic, when asked to describe the production of their 'emphatic' (vs. un-emphatic) consonants will invariably reply that "something is happening in their throat". Cf. M. v. Tiling, p. 26.

relève 3.5 cm. d'aperture pour /s/, et 2.5 cm. pour /ṣ/;" 4 cm. for /t/ and 3 cm. for /ṭ/; 5 cm. for /d/ and 3.5 cm. for /ḍ/.

Often labialized consonants are substituted for the corresponding pharyngealized phonemes of Arabic words by Bantus and Uzbeks, unfamiliar with such 'emphatic' articulations: ṭ > t^w, ṣ > s^w, etc. (s. Polivanov, p. 109f.). Instead of the back orifice, the front orifice is contracted.[3]

The lowered pitch is a striking perceptual mark of pharyngealized phonemes which is synaesthetically expressed by native grammarians in such terms as 'dark, fat, thick, corpulent, heavy'. According to the 'subjective impression' attested by Jušmanov, "les timbres des emphatiques et des non-emphatiques ont pour intervalle une duodécime". Spectrograms confirm that the pharyngealized consonant displays energy in a lower frequency region and affects the second formant of the following vowel in a downward direction (see *Preliminaries*, p. 50).

When the narrowing of the back or front orifice of the mouth cavity and the resulting lower pitch is utilized as an autonomous phonemic device, we may use the musical term 'flat' (*bémol*) and label this distinctive feature as an opposition 'flat *vs.* plain' (pharyngealized *vs.* non-pharyngealized, or rounded *vs.* unrounded). The label 'sharp (*dièse*) *vs.* plain' is correspondingly applied to the autonomous phonemic use of the dilated pharyngeal passage and the resulting rise of pitch. Traditionally this device is called 'palatalization', because of a concomitant tongue activity restricting and comparting the mouth resonator.

While a flat phoneme, for example /ṣ/, displays a noticeably lower pitch than the English /s/, the Arabic plain /s/ is, as Harrell notes, "of higher pitch than most allophones of English /s/." *Mutatis mutandis*, in a similar way a velarizing and pharyngealizing shift of /s/ or other plain consonants serves in Russian to separate more distinctly the sharp (palatalized) and plain (non-palatalized) phonemes. The sharp Russian /s,/, has a much higher pitch and correspondingly the plain /s/ a perceptibly lower pitch than the English /s/. Of the two Arabic phonemes /s/ and /ṣ/, it is /ṣ/ that the Russian observer is inclined to identify with his own plain, unpalatalized /s/.

3. VELARIZATION AND LABIALIZATION

Usually the production of pharyngealized buccal phonemes is accompanied by a velarization: "L'emphase vue à l'écran radioscopique comporte une extension de la langue de l'avant vers l'arrière, avec affaissement du milieu du dos, donc l'élargissement de la cavité palatovélaire. Et cette disposition typique de la langue... accompagne (et peut-être résulte) des mouvements postérieurs, pharyngiens et laryngiens..." (Marçais, p. 27). Thus the opposition grave *vs.* acute, primarily due to the increase

[3] On the equivalence of pharyngealization and labialization cf. the stimulating remarks by H. Rosén.

and decrease in the volume of the mouth resonator, involves a concomitant decrease and increase of its back orifice, and the opposition flat *vs.* plain, primarily due to the decrease and increase of the orifice, is supported by a subsidiary increase and decrease in the volume of the resonator itself. Furthermore, a tendency must be noted to emit the pharyngealized phonemes with a lip protrusion and slight rounding; on the other hand, the rounded phonemes occur with a slight narrowing of the pharynx to reinforce the acoustic effect of labialization. Whatever orifice is contracted, there appears a concomitant velarization: it pertains not only to the pharyngealized, but also to the labialized phonemes.

4. PHARYNGEALIZED LABIALS

These phonemes, unknown in Classical Arabic, play but a marginal role in modern Arabic dialects. Their distinctive function is confined to solitary instances. Blanc cites two minimal pairs with /b/-/ḅ/, /ba:ba/ 'its (f.) door' – /ḅa:ḅa/ 'father!', /kalbak/ 'your dog' – /kalḅak/ 'astrakhan hat', and one dubious example with /m/-/ṃ/, /yamma/ 'or' – /yaṃṃa/ 'mother!'. The scarcity of pharyngealized labials in comparison with dentals is easily explainable. The narrowing of a wide orifice separating a pharyngealized dental from its plain counterpart is much more contrastive than the narrow orifice with an additional narrowing which distinguishes the pharyngealized from the non-pharyngealized labials (cf. Ferguson, 1956).

5. PHARYNGEALIZED NASALS

The phoneme /ṇ/ is an even rarer occurrence than /ṃ/: it appears only in a few Arabic dialects, e.g. in Damascus, where Ferguson (1954) notes such a pair as /na:yek/ 'having sexual intercourse' – /ṇa:yek/ 'your (f.) flute'. The presence of /ṇ/ in an Arabic dialect implies the presence of /ṃ/ in the phonemic pattern, whereas /ṃ/ may occur without /ṇ/. This relation too is easily interpretable.

The phoneme /n/, opposed to the labial /m/, is described by Harrell, with reference to Egyptian Arabic, as a "non-labial nasal": when not followed by consonants, it is implemented as dental; otherwise it is variable in place of articulation according to the articulation of the following consonant. In North Palestinian Arabic, according to Blanc, the phoneme /n/ "is post-dental or alveolar before vowels, but tends toward a post-palatal [ŋ] before most consonants," especially before velars and palatals.

The nasal consonants have in common with the oral stops a complete closure followed by opening, but they differ from the oral stops by a nasal murmur produced throughout their closure period. In some languages nasal consonants like the corresponding oral stops are opposed to each other on the basis of the resonance audible at the release of their oral occlusion. Thus in Gilyak, /m/ like /p/ is grave diffuse, /n/

like /t/ acute diffuse, /ŋ/ like /k/ grave compact, and /ɲ/ like the palatal oral stop /c/ acute compact. In Russian, there are no compact nasals, and the labials both oral and nasal are grave, while the oral and nasal dentals are acute. In French, the two diffuse nasals, the grave /m/ and the acute /n/, find their compact counterpart in a phoneme usually implemented as [ɲ] with a subvariant [ŋ]. In these cases, high pitch (acuteness) originates in a mouth resonator with a medial (dental or palatal) stricture, and low pitch (gravity) in an ample resonator with a peripheral (labial or velar) stricture. There are other languages, however, where the coaction of both components, murmur and release, underlies the phonemic patterning of the nasal consonants. The resonator responsible for the murmur is the invariable nasal cavity plus the adjacent portion of the buccal cavity from the velic to the oral stricture. Thus the resonator is smaller and the pitch of the murmur higher when the stricture is effected in the posterior (velar or palatal) part of the mouth cavity; the resonator is vaster and the pitch lower when the occlusion is made in the anterior (labial or dental) part. Each nasal consonant presents a different distribution of the two resonances.

	murmur	release
[m]	low pitch	low pitch
[n]	low pitch	high pitch
[ŋ]	high pitch	low pitch
[ɲ]	high pitch	high pitch

In Arabic /m/, the twofold low pitch is opposed as grave to the other nasal phoneme, which is acute either in its nasal murmur or in its oral release. Basically the same, but more complex patterning may be exemplified by the three Czech nasal phonemes: /m/, /ɲ/, and /n/ implemented as [ŋ] before a velar and as [n] elsewhere. The opposition grave *vs.* acute is split into two oppositions: grave *vs.* non-grave, and acute *vs.* non-acute. The phoneme /m/ is grave as in Arabic; /ɲ/ with its twofold high pitch is acute; /n/ with its two varieties of high and low pitch joint is non-grave and non-acute.

It is clear that the Arabic /m/, homogeneous in its implementations and built always with a narrow pharynx, is more adopted for a phonemic pharyngealization than /n/, which varies the pharyngeal orifice – wide in the allophone [n], and narrow in [ŋ].

6. PHARYNGEALIZED VELARS

The Arabic grammarian tradition has assigned /q/, /x/, and /Γ/ to the 'emphatic' (*mufaxxama*) series (cf. Bravmann, p. 30; Gairdner, p. 107). These consonants are produced with a distinctly contracted pharynx. Trubetzkoy correctly classed them among the 'emphatic' consonants and recognized that the pair /q/ *vs.* /k/ carries the same opposition as the pairs /ṭ/ *vs.* /t/ and the like (p. 125). In Cantineau's (1947) opinion, "c'est une erreur: le /q/ a bien un point d'articulation vélaire et même uvulaire... mais il n'en a pas d'autre, il est vélaire et non vélarisé, il lui manque pour cela un point d'articulation principal plus en avant, par rapport auquel l'articulation vélaire jouerait le rôle de 'travail accessoire'... Ce qui le confirme, c'est qu'en général une autre consonne ne devient pas emphatique au contact de /q/, alors que cela arrive au contact des emphatiques: *iqtabara*, mais *iṣṭabara*" (p. 113f.). In a similar way, Cantineau (1950) rejects Harris's interpretation of the Moroccan Arabic /q/ as the emphatic counterpart to /k/: "Cela n'est pas certain du tout et devrait être démontré d'une façon objective: il faudrait voir si /q/ emphatise les consonnes voisines, et notamment /t/, /s/ et /r/... D'après M. L. Brunot... le /q/ n'emphatiserait jamais /t/; il n'emphatiserait pas non plus /s/, en règle générale; mais il emphatiserait très souvent /r/..."

A phonemic feature, however, cannot be defined on the basis of the degree of its assimilatory power upon the adjacent phonemes. Thus no one will question the phonemic identity of the palatalization feature in such Russian pairs as /t,/-/t/, /s,/-/s/, /p,/-/p/, /f,/-/f/, /r,/-/r/, /l,/-/l/, and nonetheless each series acts differently both in its palatalizing effect upon the preceding consonant and in its capacity of being affected by the following palatalized phoneme, e.g. [z,d,és,] but [zr,ét,] and [bd,ét,]; cf. for example S. C. Boyanus, *Russian pronunciation*, chapt. V (Harvard University Press, 1955). Furthermore the Arabic /q/ is velar and at the same time pharyngealized, just as /ṭ/ is postdental and pharyngealized. Precisely this pharyngeal constriction is the 'accessory work' common to /ṭ/ and /q/; in his early descriptive studies, the most rich in phonetic data, Cantineau stressed the insufficiency of those definitions which are confined to the velarization of the phonemes /ṣ/, /ḍ/, /ṭ/, and /ð̣/ and pay no attention to the glottal contraction. In this connection he referred to the old and new Arabic grammarians, for whom the velarized (*muṭbaqa*) dentals and the velars /q/, /x/, /Γ/ were mere subclasses of the vaster category of 'emphatic' (*mufaxxama* 'heavy') speech sounds (1935, p. 38). The stronger pressure of the articulators, and in particular of the laryngo-pharyngeal tract strikes the listener, not only in the *muṭbaqa*, but also in all other *mufaxxama*: "ce serait une emphase un peu plus faible" (1946, p. 85f.). Strangely enough, this common denominator of all the *mufaxxama*, clearly viewed in Cantineau's early studies, is totally ignored in his later essays.

In the dialect of the North Palestinian Druzes, /k/ is postpalatal before /a/, palatal before palatal vowels, and velar before velar vowels. The constrictive counterpart of this plosive phoneme is /š/, "a prepalatal or mediopalatal voiceless spirant" (Blanc). In Trubetzkoy's table of Arabic phonemes (p. 125) both compact (forward-flanged) continuants of the 'non-emphatic' series, the fortis /š/ and the corresponding lenis /ž/, found no 'emphatic' opposites; on the other hand, in the 'emphatic' series of Trubetzkoy's table, the compact fortis /x/ remained without a non-emphatic opposite, and the corresponding lenis /Γ/ was mistaken for the 'emphatic' partner of the stop /g/. Similarly the scheme of the 'consonantal system' in Hassan El-Hajjé's description of

Tripoli Arabic severs the 'non-emphatic' pair /š/-/ž/ from the 'emphatic' pair /x/-/Γ/. As a matter of fact, the prepalatal continuants /š/ and /ž/ *vs.* uvular continuants/x/ and /Γ/ present an equivalent relation as /k/ *vs.* /q/. The 'emphatic' phonemes /q/, /x/, and /Γ/ are characterized by a contraction of the pharynx and by a retraction of the tongue and a raising of its back toward the soft extremity of the velum. It is true that the interval between the points of articulation is considerably wider for /x/ and /š/ than for /ṣ/ and /s/. The phonemes /x/ and /š/ differ substantially not only in the size of the pharyngeal orifice but also in the volume and shape of the mouth resonator: thus the two tonality features – flat *vs.* plain, and grave *vs.* acute – merge.

There are two reasons, however, to consider the first of these two features distinctive and the second redundant in respect to the compact consonants. It is primarily the pivotal role played in the total pattern of Arabic nonsyllabics by the feature flat *vs.* plain (or in native terms, *tafxîm* 'heaviness' *vs. tarqîq* 'lightness'), and I shall return to this item after having discussed the extra-buccal phonemes. Furthermore the character of the phonemes /k/ in the North Palestinian and many other Arabic dialects is to be taken into account: like in English /k/, the scope of contextual variation extends from a palatal to a velar stricture, and correspondingly the concentration of energy wavers between the upper and lower frequencies of the spectrum. What primarily opposes this phoneme to the postvelar /q/ is not the contour of the mouth cavity, but the size of the pharyngeal orifice and its acoustic effect. The same relation extends to the corresponding constrictives.

Self-evidently there is no identity between the point of articulation of /k/ and /š/, /ž/, or the dental stops /t/, /d/ and the alveolar /s/, /z/, or the bilabial stop /b/ and the labio-dental constrictive /f/. Plosives tend toward a maximum reduction of energy, while constrictives tend toward an intensive noise. Hence the optimal constrictives are strident, or in motor terms, rough-edged: they require a supplementary obstruction creating edge effects at the point of articulation. The optimal plosives are, on the contrary, mellow, or in motor terms, smooth-edged, with a less complex impediment. Therefore in the labial pair of plosive and constrictive, the optimal stop is bilabial and the optimal constrictive labio-dental, the latter involving and the former annulling the role of the teeth in the barrier. The relevant question asked by the French phonetician about the pair /t/ and /s/, "pourquoi une contrepartie fricative tendue de /t/ devrait s'articuler avec la pointe de la langue oisive et appliquée contre les dents d'en bas et non, comme l'occlusive, avec cette pointe active et dirigée vers les dents supérieures" (A. Martinet, *Economie des changements phonétiques*, Berne, 1955, p. 77) receives a similar answer: the lower teeth are the additional obstacle, utilized by the optimal strident constrictive /s/ (and likewise by the strident plosive – the hissing affricate) but cut off by /t/, the optimal mellow plosive (and equally by the mellow constrictive /θ/). For the same reason the optimal constrictive counterpart of the postpalatal /k/ automatically tends toward a hushing articulation: here too the lower teeth offer supplementary resistance to the air stream and thus achieve the strident effect, whereas the retracted velar stop finds its strident constrictive counterpart in the uvular with its characteristic scratchy sound. Thus the Arabic equivalence /q/:/k/ = /x/:/š/ = /Γ/:/ž/ is well grounded.

The mutually opposed strident constrictives and mellow stops possess free variants omitting one of the two joined properties: for the fortes the constant opposition is constrictive *vs.* plosive (while mellowness is omissible: /t/ and /q/ may be implemented as affricates); for the lenes the constant opposition is strident *vs.* mellow (while the difference constrictive *vs.* plosive may be suppressed: /b/ tends toward spirantization and /ž/ toward affrication).

In the Horan dialect the class of compact plosives is represented by the two prepalatal affricates /č/, /ǯ/ and by two postpalatal stops /k/, /g/. Despite a noticeable difference between the shape and size of the mouth cavity, the strong pharyngealization of the second pair remains the distinctive mark: /k/ and /g/ in this dialect are "*mufaxxama* par nature", and they, like all 'emphatic' buccals, prevent the so-called *imâla*, an otherwise compulsory change of the following final /a/ into /e/ (s. Cantineau, 1946, p. 124f.).

7. PHARYNGEALS

Phoneticians, in particular Worrel, Panconcelli-Calzia (1916), Gairdner and Vilenčik, offered instructive data about the extra-buccal phonemes of Arabic. Students endeavoring to master /ḥ/ are advised by Gairdner to pronounce an ordinary glottal /h/ "and try to tighten the pharynx during its production" (p. 27). In other words, /ḥ/ is essentially a pharyngealized laryngeal. Of the two phonemes of this type, /ḥ/ is usually produced without voice and /ᶜ/ with voice. Since a considerable part of the air used by /ᶜ/ is consumed by the voicing alone, this phoneme is a lenis, in contradistinction to the fortis /ḥ/. Thanks to the pharyngeal contraction, the voice-pitch in /ᶜ/ and the whisper-pitch in /ḥ/ are very low: "In passing to /ᶜ/ from a preceding vowel the voice has to descend rapidly, often through more than an octave, and is cut off at its lowest pitch. If a vowel *follows*, the pitch begins at its lowest and rises quickly, through a similar interval, to normal vowel pitch. When /ᶜ/ is final and preceded by another consonant (as in /manᶜ/ 'prevention') a hardly audible grunt is all that is produced, being merely a momentary touch below the lowest note the voice is capable of producing" (p. 28).

Of the two non-pharyngealized laryngeal phonemes, /h/ is opposed to /ʾ/ as spiritus asper *vs.* spiritus lenis, which is implemented either as a glottal catch (e.g. in the dialect described by El-Hajjé) or as # – absence of a nonsyllabic (cf. Cantineau, 1951), or finally as a glottal catch "in free variation with zero"(Blanc). This spiritus lenis, or *hamza* of the Arabic grammarians, is adequately classed by them among the *majhûra*. The distinction of *mahmûsa* and *majhûra* is often erroneously interpreted as voiceless *vs.* voiced, while actually it means, as Meinhof had clearly seen (p. 83f.), fortes *vs.* lenes (cf. Bravmann's quotations from Arabic phonetic tradition, pp. 23, 27). Hence /h/:/ʾ/ = /ḥ/:/ᶜ/ (or /ˀ̣/ in Meinhof's ingenious transcription). The phonetic affinity of the two lenes /ʾ/ and /ᶜ/ is reinforced by the glottal closure which in dialects accompanies the production of /ᶜ/ or at least its anlaut variant (s. especially Bergsträsser, p. 40f., and Vilenčik, p. 104f.).

Both Trubetzkoy's (p. 125) separation of /ʾ/ from /ᶜ/ and the far-fetched attempts to rank the phoneme /ʾ/ with the 'emphatics' (s. Cantineau, 1952, p. 94, and El-Hajjé, p. 20) are invalid.

The extra-buccal phonemes are obviously deprived of any features generated in the mouth resonator, and in particular of the features grave *vs.* acute and compact *vs.* diffuse. They are both non-vocalic and non-consonantal phonemes (glides). *Hamza* /ʾ/ is entirely unmarked: neither fortis nor flat; /h/ is not flat but fortis; *ayn* /ᶜ/ is not fortis but flat; /ḥ/ is doubly marked: both flat and fortis. *Ayn* is the mere flat, while the pharyngealized buccals, sometimes labeled the 'ayned' phonemes, superimpose flatness upon a bundle of other features.[4] When these features are lost, the phoneme becomes a mere pharyngeal; thus "das emphatische /ṣ/ wird im Aramäischen ziemlich regelmässig durch /ᶜ/ ersetzt. Die orale Artikulation ist aufgegeben und lediglich die Pressung übrig geblieben" (Panconcelli, 1916: Meinhof's remark, p. 53).

The opposition of flat *vs.* plain is a feature involving not only all the types of consonants but also the glides, and mostly the continuant and/or the abrupt liquids; in some dialects even the pair of semivowels /y/ and /w/ may enter into the same opposition, as Charles A. Ferguson brought to my attention.

Cantineau objects to the interpretation of pharyngealization as a feature common to buccals and extra-buccals: "L'aspiration sourde qu'on transcrit souvent *ḥ* est bien prononcée avec contraction du larynx, mais elle n'est pas emphatique et ne produit pas (sauf dans certains parlers determinés) les effets que produisent sur les voyelles les emphatiques et les consonnes assimilées comme les vélaires" (*BSL* 48–2. 17 [1952]. He distinguishes dialects where /ḥ/ and /ᶜ/ are "*mufaxxama* par nature", always produced with a strong contraction of the pharyngeal muscles, from other dialects where the strength and depth of this contraction depend on the phonemic environment of the pharyngeals. But whatever degree of contraction is attained by /ḥ/ and /ᶜ/, it concerns "la même région arrière de la langue que la constriction d'emphase" (Marçais, p. 20).

As to the influence upon the adjacent vowels, the componential analysis of a phoneme cannot proceed from the contextual variants of the neighboring phonemes: often the variation is due not to a single feature but to a combination of concurrent

[4] A similar relation between the pharyngeals and the pharyngealized dentals and velars was observed in Somali by Maria v. Tiling.

features. Furthermore, in many instances the pharyngeals modify the adjacent vowels in the same direction as the pharyngealized buccals. In colloquial Egyptian both the pharyngealized buccals and the pharyngeals appear to exert a modifying retracting influence on preceding and following a-vowels (Gairdner, p. 46f.). In the dialect of El-Hamma, Cantineau observes that the /a:/ is pronounced "entre *a* et *o* ouvert" in contact with pharyngealized dentals, in contact with the pharyngeals as "*a* moyen français", in contact with velars it oscillates between the two positions mentioned, and in other contexts it is a front vowel. In the same dialect the phoneme /u:/ is shifted towards the closed *o* in the neighborhood of pharyngealized dentals, velars, and pharyngeals (1951, p. 78f.).

8. SOME CONCLUSIONS

The nine features underlying the nonsyllabic pattern of the North Palestinian dialect and equally of Classical Arabic are, despite all the differences in their distribution and concurrence, common to the great majority of Arabic dialects. Yet some dialects, e.g. Egyptian Arabic, have lost the autonomous feature strident *vs.* mellow which elsewhere keeps its distinctiveness in the pairs of hissing and interdental continuants; for instance Tripoli /faẓẓ/ 'rough' – /faδ̣δ̣/ 'he dismissed' (El-Hajjé, p. 13). In Classical Arabic this feature seems to have been used in laterals as well: the mellow /l/ probably had a strident counterpart – in Jušmanov's view, a "voiced lateral spirant" surviving in Yemenite (p. 56).

By combining these features a mechanical synthesizer may obtain a discriminable and identifiable approximation of all the nonsyllabic phonemes present in Arabic. According to Cantineau's figures, based on his phonemic description of Classical Arabic, "les 26 phonèmes du système consonantique arabe fournissent $\frac{26 \times 25}{2} = 325$ oppositions" (1947, p. 110). A componential analysis applied to the 28 or 29 nonsyllabic phonemes of Classical Arabic (with addition of the two semivowels and of the conjectural /ḷ/) or to the 31 phonemes of the North Palestinian dialect gives altogether nine binary oppositions. The contrast of these two numbers – 325 (or even 465 in the case of North Palestinian) and 9 – exemplifies the economy of the componential analysis and enables us to assume that the members of the Arabic speech community, speakers and listeners, in their everyday encoding and decoding operations lighten their emissive and perceptive task by resorting to the informative cues of the distinctive features, which always present them advantageous two-choice situations.

HARVARD UNIVERSITY

REFERENCES

G. Bergsträsser, *Zum arabischen Dialekt von Damaskus* (Hannover, 1924).

H. Blanc, *Studies in North Palestinian Arabic* (Jerusalem, 1953).

M. Bravmann, *Materialen und Untersuchungen zu den phonetischen Lehren der Araber* (Göttingen, 1934).

J. Cantineau, *Le dialecte arabe de Palmyre*, I (Beirut, 1935).

J. Cantineau, *Les parlers arabes du Horan* (Paris, 1946).

J. Cantineau, Esquisse d'une phonologie de l'arabe classique, *BSL* 43 (1947).

J. Cantineau, Réflexions sur la phonologie de l'arabe marocain, *Hespéris* (1950).

J. Cantineau, Analyse phonologique du parler arabe d'El-Hâmma de Gabès, *BSL* 47 (1951).

J. Cantineau, Le consonantisme du sémitique, *Semitica* 4 (1952).

H. El-Hajjé, *Le parler arabe de Tripoli* (Paris, 1954).

Ch. A. Ferguson, review of *Manuel élémentaire d'arabe oriental.* By J. Cantineau and Y. Helbaoui, *Language* 30 (1954).

Ch. A. Ferguson, review of *Studies in North Palestinian Arabic.* By H. Blanc, *Word* 11 (1955).

Ch. A. Ferguson, Arabic baby talk, *For Roman Jakobson* (The Hague, 1956).

W. H. T. Gairdner, *Phonetics of Arabic* (Oxford University Press, 1925).

R. S. Harrell, *The phonology of Colloquial Egyptian Arabic*, Ph. D. Dissertation, Harvard University (1956).

Z. S. Harris, The phonemes of Moroccan Arabic, *JAOS* 62 (1942).

N. Jušmanov, Théorie des consonnes emphatiques sémitiques, *Comptes Rendus de l'Académie des Sciences de Russie* (1925).

Ph. Marçais, L'articulation de l'emphase dans un parler arabe maghrébin, *Annales de l'Institut d'Études Orientales*, Faculté des lettres de l'Université d'Alger, 7 (1948).

C. Meinhof, Was sind emphatische Laute, und wie sind sie entstanden?, *ZES* 11 (1920–21).

G. Panconcelli-Calzia, Experimentelle Untersuchungen des ᶜ im Arabischen von Yemen und Aleppo, *Vox* 26 (1916).

G. Panconcelli-Calzia, Experimental-phonetische Untersuchungen, *ZES* 11 (1920–21).

E. D. Polivanov, *Vvedenie v jaszykoznanie dlja vostokovednyx vuzov* (Leningrad, 1928).

H. B. Rosén, The stele of Lemnos, its text and alphabetic system, *Scripta Hierosolymitana*, I (Jerusalem, 1954).

Maria v. Tiling, *Somali-Texte und Untersuchungen zur Somali-Lautlehre = Beiheft zur ZES* 8 (1925).

N. Trubetzkoy, *Grundzüge der Phonologie = TCLP* 7 (1939).

Ja. S. Vilenčik, Arabskie gortannye, *Zapiski Kollegii Vostokovedov*, 5 (1931).

W. H. Worrel, Zur Aussprache des arabischen ḥ und h, *Vox* 24 (1914).

LAWRENCE GAYLORD JONES

PRELIMINARY PHONETIC SEGMENTATION

THE PHONETIC analysis which precedes phonematic analysis of a language must divide sets of speech continua into segments which can be compared one with another to determine relevant differences and similarities in the resulting units. It is usually agreed that such segmentation is made in an 'arbitrary' manner, i.e., without any preconceived notions about the distribution or distinctive qualities along the continua. Unless one holds an 'algebraic' view of phonematics which "aims at the maximal estrangement between phoneme and sound or, correspondingly, between phonemics and phonetics",[1] this process amounts to recognizing differences of a physical nature (articulatory or acoustic) along the duration of a continuum. Probably the most arbitrary, and at the same time, the least fruitful preliminary segmentation would divide a continuum into equal time units. (The practical disadvantages of such a system are obvious.)

The following paragraphs suggest a simple method with which to begin such segmentation and which can be adapted to phonematic techniques. It is designed for use wherever a detailed mechanical recording of the data is available. That is not to say that the method is inapplicable in the case of 'impressionistic' phonetics wherein the recording is in the form of a series of phonetic symbols written by the linguist and representing what he hears. In such a case, any method proposed is in a sense irrelevant since the data have already been segmented and await only the regrouping and elimination of symbols in the original transcription.

Briefly, this method consists of applying the feature vocalic/non-vocalic as defined by Jakobson and Halle as:

acoustically – presence *vs.* absence of a sharply defined formant structure;

[1] R. Jakobson and M. Halle, *Fundamentals of language* 15 (The Hague 1956). (The authors, of course, do not endorse this view.)

genetically – primary or only excitation at the glottis together with a free passage through the vocal tract.[2]

The difference between successive intervals of these two types of sound structure is easily detectable on spectrograms or oscillograms. To go from one type to the other necessitates a "turning on and off of the exciting source or sources" and "sudden severe drops in over-all level,"[3] postulated by Halle for segmentation into phonematic units.

Each utterance is thus divided into alternations of vocalic stretches (W) and non-vocalic stretches (K). For instance, the English word 'scrounged' as well as the word 'pit' are divided into the same pattern of alternations:

/ skrawnǯd /   /pɪt/
K W K   KWK

The data in the corpus can be immediately classified into a relatively small number of such patterns of alternation to which a number of tests can be applied. This ability to organize the data on the basis of only one binary choice is perhaps the greatest advantage of the method. In a negative way it also leads toward the organization of the data into minimal pairs. For instance, if two samples have the same number of alternations but in reverse order, there will be no word in one group which bears only a minimal phonematic difference to a word in the other group. Thus 'bay' /bɛj/ (KW) need not be compared with 'wet' /wet/ (WK). This is not true where the number of alternations is different. For instance, 'bill' and 'mill' are minimal pairs but represent two different patterns: (KW) and (W) respectively.

Before proceeding any further it should be made clear that this segmentation does not group the data into syllables since a syllabic boundary may occur within either a K or W segment. It might also seem at first that there should be at least one syllable for each W segment. Whereas this is true for English, it is not so for Russian where, e.g. *rtu* /rt′u/ 'mouth' (dative), is a monosyllabic form and has a WKW pattern.

Another advantage of this method of segmentation appears in the comparison of several occurrences of the same utterance. Such comparisons occur early in the phonological methods outlined by Harris. At this stage we have reached a rather crucial point in the phonematic analysis, because in comparing several samples of what we know to represent the same linguistic form, we are attempting to adduce from the data the phonetic invariants in the speech in order to set up the relation of identity between various segments within the system of this particular language. Harris states that "if an utterance represented by segments A′B′C′ is a repetition of the utterance recorded as ABC (where A′ is the first n % – e.g. the first third – of

[2] Jakobson and Halle, *op. cit.* 29.
[3] M. Halle, The strategy of phonemics, *Word* 10.202.

the length of A'B'C' and A is the first n % of the length ABC, etc.) then A′ = A, B = B′, C = C′ ".[4] His justification for the use of percentages is that the two utterances may vary in length. But this is a rather dangerous procedure unless it can be shown that all components change uniformly when the utterance is spoken at varying speeds. The danger is particularly acute when it is applied to the stop consonants.

In the method under discussion, the corresponding K and W stretches can be compared without running this risk. We can then say that wherever K and K′ differ in physical quality, the differences are not distinctive.[5]

The only uses to which this system of preliminary segmentation can be put are given above. Beyond this point one must admit finer shades of phonetic (articulatory or acoustic) difference in order to accomplish further segmentation leading to the stage at which each segment represents only one phoneme. This point is arrived at when the transcription system which represents the segments, can transcribe uniquely and unambiguously all non-homophonic utterances in the language.

HARVARD UNIVERSITY

[4] Z. S. Harris, *Methods in structural linguistics* 29–30 (Chicago, 1951).

[5] Theoretically, at least, it would be possible that the K and W segments in several samples of the same utterance might differ in number or order or both. In such a case the percentage system breaks down completely and the method presented herewith can do no more at this stage of the analysis than catalogue this fact to be brought up again later in the analysis.

HEINZ KRONASSER

GUTTURALE UND DENTALE ERWEITERUNGEN BEIM HETHITISCHEN VERBUM

DIE NICHT gerade sehr häufigen gutturalen Erweiterungen sind besonders aus dem Griechischen bekannt: τμήγω neben τέμνω 'ich schneide', ἐρύκω neben ἐρύω 'ich ziehe, νήχω 'ich schwimme' neben νάω 'ich wasche', τρύχω neben τρύω 'ich quäle' u.a., Lit. bei Schwyzer I. 702. Außergriechische Beispiele bei Hirt III. 253ff. Für das Armenische hat Meillet BSL 26.3ff. (1925) (mit weiterer Lit.) *-k-* nachgewiesen in *lsem* 'ich höre' aus **k'lu-ke-* zu κλύω, *har-k-anem* 'ich schlage' neben *hari* 'ich schlug' (**-g-* wie air. *org-* 'töten, verwüsten').

In einigen Fällen wurden unter der Voraussetzung gutturaler Erweiterungen, wobei zwischen *k*(*h*) *k*'(*h*) *g*(*h*) und *g*'(*h*) nicht geschieden werden kann, auch für das Hethitische schlagende Etymologien gefunden:

mark- 'zerlegen' (Opfertier), ohne Erweiterung *marr-iya-* 'zerstückeln' nach Benveniste, *BSL* 33.140 (1932), zu μέρος 'Teil'.

dug- bzw. *duk-*: die von Friedrich, *JCS* 1.298f. (1947), beigebrachten Belege ergeben eine Bedeutung '(an)sehen; beachten', daher nicht mit Mudge, *Language* 7.253 (1931), zu τυγχάνει 'wird zuteil', got. *daug* 'es ist zuträglich' u.a. Vielmehr mit Čop, *Zbornik* 2.402f. (1955) zu alb. *dukem* 'ich leuchte hervor; erscheine', d.i. (nach Jokl, *Mél. Pedersen*, 157 Fn. [1937]) erweitertes **dheu-* (IEW 261), wie es für toch. A *cok-* B *cauk-* 'aufleuchten' von Lane, *Language* 14.27 (1932), angenommen worden ist. Semantisch wurde natürlich λεύσσω 'ich (er-)blicke' neben λευκός 'leuchtend' verglichen.

malk- mit Goetze, *Tunnawi* 93f. 'verwirren, zusammendrehen' (Wollsachen; 'entangle'), somit wohl zu toch. AB *mälk-* 'zusammenlegen, zusammenfügen, vereinigen', das Van Windekens, *Lexique* 64 m.E. richtig zu μέλος 'Glied', kymr. *cymmal* 'Verbindung(sglied)' stellt; also *malk-* zu μέλος wie *mark-* zu μέρος.

Weniger eindeutig heth. *hark-* 'umkommen, zugrundegehen': entweder mit Cuny, *RHA* 14.205 (1934) zu air. *org-* und arm. *hark-* (s.o.), die aber ebenso gut bei **per-g-*

'schlagen' (aksl. *perǫ* 'ich schlage' usw., IEW 818f.) belassen werden können, oder mit jüngerer *k*-Erweiterung zu heth. *harra-* 'zerstoßen, zermalmen; beschädigen', vgl. auch *harga-* 'Untergang'; dann wohl mit Machek, *Arch. Or.* 17.132f. (1949) zu aksl. *oriti* 'auflösen; zerstören' u.a.

Unter derselben Voraussetzung gutturaler Erweiterungen möchte ich auch folgende Fälle als sicher bzw. einigermaßen sicher betrachten:

**hurk-* 'drehen' in *hurki-* 'Rad', d.i. alte Erweiterung **u̯er-g'(h)-/urg'(h)-* in lit. *veržỹs* 'Strick', ai. *vr̥-ṇakti* 'er dreht', kaus. *var-j-ayati*, part. *vr̥kta-* u.a. Die Vollstufe heth. *wark-* hat schon Otten *ZA* 50.235 (1952) in *wa-wark-ima-* 'Türflügel' erkannt. Über heth. *h* äußere ich mich hier nicht mehr; soweit die hier vorkommenden Wörter in Betracht kommen, schreibe ich ihm keinen etymologischen Wert bei.

istalk- 'glätten, ebnen' für **stal-k-* mit dem bekannten anlautenden *i-* vor *s*-Gruppen und dem häufigen *a* für *e*, aus **stel-k-* zu **stel-* 'flach, hinbreiten' (WP II. 643) in aksl. *steljǫ* 'ich breite aus', lat. *lātus* 'breit' aus **stl-ātus* u.a.

istark- 'erkranken' (zur genauen Verwendung Friedrich, *Vertr.* I, 31). Gegenüber *irmaliya-* ds. ist *istark-* der Oberbegriff, etwa 'in einen schlimmen Zustand geraten', vgl. auch Goetze, *Hatt.* 72. Wie so oft ist auch hier im Heth. die Grundbedeutung nicht recht faßbar. Sicherheit läßt sich im einzelnen nicht gewinnen, weil mehrere semantisch sehr verzweigte **ster-* zur Verfügung stehen: am ehesten zu **ster-* 'hinbreiten' (WP II. 638), dessen Reflexe verschiedentlich auch 'niederstrecken' oder 'in eine trostlose Lage versetzen' bedeuten (*istark-* auch transitiv! Vgl. Friedrich, *loc. cit.*); das Subjekt bzw. die Ursache können Tod, Krankheit, Zorn der Götter u.a. sein, vgl. etwa lat. *stratus morte* (Petron 121.11), *wulgus stratum* (durch die Pest, Ovid, *Met.* 7.585), *sternitque a culmine Troiam* (der Zorn der Götter, Vergil, *Aen.* 2.603) u.a. Vgl. heth. 'wenn ein Gott einem Menschen zürnt und es diesen *istarktsi*' (*iš-tar-ak-zi*); da paßt wohl als Grundbedeutung 'und es (*sic*) diesen niederwirft'.

markist- nur im gen. sg. des Verbalsubstantivs *markisd-uwas*, das Goetze, AM 239 als 'des Dahinschwindens' (?) deutet; wenn richtig, wie ich meine, dann zu heth. *mer-/mir-* 'verschwinden; absterben', das Sturtevant schon längst zu lat. *morior* usw. gestellt hat. In *mar-k-* kann **mer-* **mor-* oder **mr̥-* stecken. Bei *-ist-* kann *i* Stummvokal sein; *-st-* ist m.W. als verbale Erweiterung singulär (*sesd-/sisd-* und *kist-* sind anders zu beurteilen): entweder ist es ein Rest oder stammt aus einer verwandten Sprache, vgl. bildhethitisch (bh.) *a-i-(a-)s-tu-na* inf. 'machen' neben *a-i-a-ha* 'ich machte' (*aya-* = kh. [keilhethitisch] *iya-* 'machen'). Die Gleichsetzung von bh. *-st-* mit kh. *-ss-* (z.B. *waressa-* neben *warra-* 'helfen') bei Bossert, *JKF* 2.310 (1953) entbehrt der lautlichen Grundlage. Erwähnt sei auch lyk. *qastti* 'er läßt zahlen, bestraft', das V. Thomsen (bei Pedersen, *Lyk.* 26f.) zu lyk. *qanuweti*, *qã̃nti* bzw. *qãti* stellte (alle drei 3. sg. und mit *qastti* semantisch identisch oder verwandt). Man kann *qastti* als **qan-st-ti* auffassen (*qan-* nach Pedersen, *loc. cit.* zu kh. *hanna-* 'richten, urteilen'). Wir wissen jedoch über die lyk. Lautentwicklung und Orthographie zu wenig Bescheid, als daß dies sicher wäre. Pedersen hält das *-s-* für altes *-sk-*, muß aber dann auch mit Synkope rechnen: **qan-ske-ti* im Hinblick auf den thematischen Charakter der *sk*-Verba. Hingegen tritt beim kh. und bh. Beispiel die Endung unmittelbar an *st* an, vgl. bh. *a-ru-na* 'zu essen' für **at-una* neben *a-ta-tu-u* = *atatu* 'sie sollen essen'.

Auch im Tocharischen finden sich Reste dieses *-st-*, vgl. A *pyaṣt-* 'wachsen' zu *(*s*)*pē*(*i*)- in ai. *sphāy-ati* 'er nimmt zu', Van Windekens, *Lexique* 104; ferner AB *kärṣt-* 'abschneiden' zu *(*s*)*ker-* in aisl. *skera* 'schneiden', κερῶ 'ich werde abschneiden', u.a., Van Windekens 27, wo *-ṣt-* als Kontamination von *-s-* (κορσόω, heth. *kars-* 'abschneiden') und *-t-* (lit. *ker-t-ù* 'ich haue um') aufgefaßt wird; dieses *-ṣt-* sei dann auf das bedeutungsverwandte A *koṣt-* 'schlagen, treffen' (zu lit. *káu-ti* 'schlagen', ahd. *houwan* 'hauen' usw.) übertragen worden (Van Windekens 44). Dennoch bleibt aber *-st-* als Erweiterung bei *pyaṣt-* bestehen. Etymologisch unklar A *päṣt-* 'heranziehen' (??).

Als sicher galt bisher die *st*-Erweiterung nur für die baltischen Sprachen, Endzelin, *Lett. Gramm.* 580ff., über Möglichkeiten im Griechischen Schwyzer I. 704 mit Fn. 9. Es fällt nun auf, daß einerseits die balt. Sprachen bei einer Fülle von *st*-Verben nur Spuren von solchen mit *sk* aufweisen (Endzelin 589), während anderseits das Hethitische und Tocharische bei einer Fülle von *sk*-Verben solche mit *st* nur in Resten zeigen. So scheinen die beiden Erweiterungen ursprünglich eine (pän)-identische Funktion gehabt zu haben. Da es nun in allen idg. Sprachen (mit Ausnahme der balt.) einen großen Bestand an *sk*-Verben gibt, erklärt sich damit das Absterben von *st*.

sark- im Iterativum *šar-kiš-k-* wohl = *sarksk-* 'steigen, sich erheben', *sark-aliya-* 'sich überheben' (?), *sarg-aniya-* 'sich erheben' (?) neben *sarku-* 'erhaben; hervorragend; Held' auch mit Stammform *sargaw-*, wozu *sargaw-atar* 'Erhabenheit, Hoheit'; *sark-* aus **ser-k-* unmittelbar zu heth. *ser* 'oben', zu *sark-* trat *sarku-* nach dem Muster von *parku-* 'hoch' = arm. *barjr* 'hoch' aus **bhr̥g'hu-*. Zu verbalen Ableitungen unmittelbar von Adverbien (eine ausführliche Untersuchung wäre der Mühe wert) vgl. heth. *u-up-zi* = *up-tsi* 'geht auf' (Gestirn), das Sturtevant, *Language* 9.10 (1933) richtig zu **upo* 'von unten hinauf', ὑπό, ai. *upa* u.a. gestellt hat. An sich erwartet man **upa-tsi*, das nach *luk-tsi* 'es wird hell, es wird Tag' umgebildet ist. Zur Bildung vgl. dt. *sich empören* zu *empor* (O. Haas mündl.), wofür umgangssprachlich auch *hochgehen*. Auch *handaye-* 'ordnen, fügen' (wie es sich gehört) beurteile ich so: zu *handa* 'gemäß, entsprechend'. Vgl. auch *appa-* oder *appaye-* und *appiya-* 'fertig sein, zu Ende sein' neben *appa* 'darnach, später, hinter'. Schließlich kann auch heth. *pask-* 'aufrichten, aufpflanzen' unmittelbar als *pas-k-* zu **pos* 'unmittelbar bei, hinter, nach' gehören, lit. *pàs* 'an, bei', aksl. *po* 'hinter, nach', aber *poz-dь* Adj. 'spät' u.a. (IEW 841f.). Lat. *pōnō* 'ich setze, stelle' (**po-znō*) bleibt jedoch fern. Und schließlich sei auch noch heth. *wak-/wag-* 'abbeißen' mit pal. *waq-* 'beißen' genannt (zweifelnd von Friedrich, *Wtb.* 241 zusammengebracht; vgl. Otten, *ZA* 48.131 mit Fn. 21). Man könnte es wohl unmittelbar zu **ue̯-* 'weg' stellen, heth. *u-/wi-/wa-* verschiedentlich verbaut mit Zielpunktänderung (vgl. *ta-* 'nehmen' zu **dō-* 'geben') 'hierher' bzw. 'her-'.

urk-* 'aufspüren' in *urki-* 'Spur' und *urkiya-* 'aufspüren' zu **u̯er-/ur-* 'finden' in arm. *gerem* 'ich nehme (gefangen)', εὗρον 'ich fand' (*ε-Ϝρ-), air. *fuar* ds. (u̯e-u̯r-a*).

Für wahrscheinlich möchte ich folgende Fälle halten:

ark-/arg- ist in Gesetzestexten ein schwieriger Terminus, s. Sommer, *HAB* 126f. mit Fn. 5, Goetze, *NB* 58 mit Fn. 1. Doch scheinen mir die Bedeutungen 'zuteilen' (Landparzellen) und 'an sich nehmen' (Diebsgut) gesichert. Die von Friedrich angenommene weitere Bedeutung (bei Sommer, *loc. cit.*, und *Wtb.* 30) 'zerlegen' (Opfertiere) ließe sich als Sinnstreckung damit vereinigen, doch kann es sich auch um ein Homonymon handeln. Jedenfalls ist die semantische und formale Übereinstimmung mit **ar-* 'zuteilen' und med. 'an sich bringen' gegeben, vgl. ἄρ-νυμαι 'ich erwerbe, empfange', aw. *ar-* 'gewähren, zuteil werden lassen' (IEW 61). Im Hinblick etwa auf lat. *tribuere* 'zuteilen' mit *tributum* 'Abgabe, Tribut' kann wohl auch heth. *ark-amma(n)-* 'Tribut' samt Zubehör angeschlossen werden.

Als immerhin möglich seien folgende Fälle gennant:

ha-aš-ši-ik- bzw. *ha-še-ek-* 'sich sättigen'. Der Imperativ *hassik* 2. sg. weicht von der üblichen Bildung der *sk*-Verba ab, vgl. *pi-eš-ki* 'gib!', *uš-ki* 'sieh!', *ak-ku-uš-ki* 'trink!', *me-mi-iš-ki* 'sprich!' u.a. = βάσκε, ai. *gaccha* 'geh!', lat. *ignosce.* Es ist vielmehr eine *k*-Erweiterung zu dem von Otten, *AfO* 15.81 (1945–51) gedeuteten und verglichenen pal. *haš-* 'sich satt trinken'. Auffallend ist bei heth. *hask-*, daß es sich auf Essen und Trinken beziehen kann, wie Ehelolf *KF* 1.140f. (1927) gezeigt und wofür er Parallelen aus semitischen Sprachen und dem Ewe beigebracht hat, vgl. auch πατέομαι 'ich genieße, nehme zu mir', ebensowohl bei Fleisch, Brot und Wein gesagt. Vor allem sticht aber das in letzter Zeit mehrfach behandelte ai. *aś-nāti* in die Augen (Lit. bei Winter, *KZ* 72.161 [1955]), das ähnlich wie πατέομαι bei festen Speisen und Getränken verwendet wird ('genießen, zu sich nehmen'); es bezieht sich auch wie heth. *has-k-* oft auf kultisches Essen und Trinken (*aś-nā-* nur in den Formen des Präsensstammes, sonst *aś-*). So ist vielleicht an eine dünne ai. Lehnwortschicht auch außerhalb der Kikkuli-Texte zu denken, zu der ich z.B. auch heth. *hissa-* 'Deichsel' von ai. *īṣā* 'Deichsel' rechnen möchte (trotz Sommer, *Die Sprache* 1.161 [1949], mit Mayrhofer, *Studien zur idg. Grundsprache* 48 [Wien 1952]), ebenso heth. *turiya-* 'anschirren' von ai. *dhur-* 'Anspannwerk' (= Deichsel + Joch; Sommer, *loc. cit.* 161f., Mayrhofer 48). Für diese Auffassung der drei Gleichungen spricht der Umstand, daß sie ausschließlich sind, d.h. sonst ohne Anknüpfung: so ist m.E. Entlehnung wahrscheinlicher als drei neue grundsprachliche Ansätze. Auffallend ist auch die Übereinstimmung von heth. *westara-* (*tar*-Stämme generis communis gibt es nicht) und aw. (!) *vāstar* 'Hirt' (gleichzeitiger Hinweis bei Hrozný, *Code hittite* 158 [1922], und Sommer, *Bogh. Stud.* 7.62 [1922]).

hatk- 'schließen' (Tür), viell. als urspr. '*verriegeln' oder '*einzäunen' zu **edh-/odh-*

'Zaun(stecken)' in ae. *eodor* 'Hecke, Zaun', čech. *odr* 'Pfahl', aksl. *odrъ* 'Lager, Bett', aber auch 'Zaun' u.a., vgl. IEW 290. Anders Sturtevant, *CG.*[2] 132f.

igaye- bezieht sich auf eine Art des Zugrundegehens, aber m.E. ist es nicht prägnant das Bersten oder Zerspringen des heißen Steines, der in das Wasser geworfen wird. Von diesem Stein ist auch gesagt, daß er 'aufschreit' und 'verstummt', Ehelolf, *KF* 1.400 (1930). Die Bedeutung kann einfach '*perire*' gewesen sein (die Schwierigkeiten der Rektion können hier nicht erörtert werden). So kann an **ei-/i-* + *-gh-* gedacht werden, vgl. formal toch. B *yku* 'gegangen', lit. *eigà* 'Gang' und semantisch οἴχεσθαι, das oft (auch ohne κατὰ χθονός u.a.) 'zugrundegehen, sterben' bedeutet. Vgl. auch heth. *ig-za* = *ig-t-s* n.sg. (ein Teil des Fußes, 'Sohle' ??), das als urspr. Verbalnomen mit *-t-* (wie *ku-ut-ti* d.sg. = *kutt-i* 'Wand, Mauer', d.i. '*Schüttung' zu **g'heu-* 'gießen', χῶμα 'Erdwall') zu **ig-* aufgefaßt werden kann, vgl. ἴχνος 'Fußspur', aber auch 'Fuß' und 'Sohle', ἰχνο-βλαβής 'fuß-verletzt', ἰχνο-πέδη eine Art Fußfessel oder Fußfalle.

isg- bzw. *isk-* bzw. *iskiya-* mit Iterativum *iskisk-* 'salben, bestreichen' (z.B. ein Opfertier mit Öl). Möglicherweise ist von 'ausschütten, begießen' auszugehen, dann viell. zu **eis-* 'heftig bewegen' (IEW 299f.), vgl. die Flußnamen *Isar*, *Oise* u.a.; ved. *iṣ-* 'in schnelle Bewegung setzen', als Objekt auch Flüssigkeiten.

putkiya- wird vom Teig gesagt, wohl 'aufgehen, zunehmen, dick werden' (im Sinne von 'gären' ?), dann zu mehrfach belegten **put-* in lit. *putà* 'Schaum' (bei Seife oder Bier), *puntù*, *pùsti* 'anschwellen' u.a., IEW 847ff. Die Bedeutungsbrücke kann auch 'faulen' sein (Gärung ist Fäulnis), lit. *pū́stu*, *pū̃sti* 'faulen', lat. *pūtidus* 'faul', vgl. auch verwandtes norw. *føysa* 'anschwellen' und 'aufgären'.

sa-li-k/g- 'anstoßen, sich nähern; gegen jemanden vorgehen; sich vergreifen; Unzucht treiben mit jem.' wurde seit Sturtevant, *CG.*[1] 89 mehrmals als **sm̥-legh-* 'sich dazulegen' aufgefaßt, unter Hinweis auf ἄ-λοχος 'Gattin'. Doch wird diese Etymologie nur der letzten Bedeutung gerecht. Als Grundbedeutung läßt sich annehmen etwa 'sich in feindlicher oder unlauterer Absicht nähern'; dann kann bei **sel-* 'schleichen, kriechen' angeknüpft werden. Vgl. ai. *t-sar-ati* 'er schleicht, beschleicht', vor allem aber air. *int-led* (**-sleth*) 'Fallstrick' und *sleith* (**-sl̥-tā*) 'das Beschleichen einer schlafenden Frau' mit ganz ähnlicher Bedeutungsentwicklung. Weiteres IEW 900. Was die Schreibung *sa-li-k/g-* für *salk-* betrifft, so ist mit distinktiver Absicht gegenüber *salk/g-* 'hineinkneten' (?) zu rechnen (letzteres geschr. *šal-k-*), das möglicherweise zu heth. *salwina-* 'Mörtel aus Lehm und Häcksel' ('*Verknetetes'?) in Beziehung steht; doch kommt ein Suffix *-wina-* sonst nicht vor.

Semantisch unsicher oder etymologisch unklar sind:

hamink-/hamank-/hamenk- 'binden', *galank-* 'besänftigen' (?) oder 'erfrischen' (?), *nink-* 'den Durst löschen; sich betrinken'; *damenk-* 'sich anschmiegen' oder 'an etwas anwachsen' (?) unklar trotz Bossert, *JKF* 2.329 (1953), der von einer nicht erwiesenen Bedeutung 'wachsen, gedeihen' ausgeht; noch mit irriger Bedeutung

Benveniste, *BSL* 33.143 (1932). Indogermanisches Gepräge zeigen *kunk-* 'wiegen, schaukeln' (?), auch 'hängen lassen' (?), und *kurk-* 'aufbewahren, zurückbehalten'. Bei *da-a-ak-ki* bzw. *ta-ak-ki* 3. sg. 'entspricht, ist äquivalent' (Ehelolf, *OLZ* 328 [1929] Fn. 1, Sommer, *HAB* 219) möchte ich fast an *ta-* bzw. *da-* 'zwei' denken (*t/da-a-an* 'zweiter, zweitens', *ta-a-i-u-ga* = *ta-yuga-* 'zweijährig'), obgleich ich eine genaue semantische Parallele nicht anführen kann. Doch gibt es Fügungen, welche die Beziehung zwischen Zweizahl und Gleichheit augenfällig machen: *Verres alter Orcus* = 'Verres wie der Orkus'(Cic.) usw. Ehelolfs Zusammenstellung von *d/takki* mit *d/ta-* erfolgte a.O. noch vor Kenntnis des verbalen Charakters von *d/takki.*

Die m.E. richtigen Etymologien verzeichnet Friedrich, *Wtb. s.vv.* bei folgenden mit wurzelhaftem *-k-/-g-*: *hark-* 'halten', *luk-* 'hell werden', *huek-* = *hwek-/huk-* 'beschwören', *mugaye-* 'beten, bitten', *park-* 'sich erheben' (*s.v. parku-*), *sarnink-* 'ersetzen', *wek-* 'wünschen' (wo jedoch 'usw.' fehl am Platze ist); *lenk-* (geschr. meist *link-*) 'schwören' jedoch eher mit Sturtevant *CG.*[2] 58 zu ἔλεγχος 'Beweismittel'. Ferner *ak-* bzw. sekundär(?) *ek-* 'sterben' m.E. doch mit Sturtevant, *Language* 3.164f. (1927) (und öfter) zu lat. *agere* 'führen' usw. Sturtevant hat diese Etymologie dann selbst mehrfach in Zweifel gestellt (vgl. *CG.*[1] 75 mit Fn. 79). Im Hinblick auf intransitives ἄγει, bret. *a* 'er geht' halte ich dies jedoch für richtig, vgl. *ŠA 1-EN* GAL-*ya Ú-UL pa-it* etwa 'das auch (nur) eines einzigen Großen ging nicht (dahin)'; der Sinn ist mit Goetze, *AM* 134f. zweifellos, daß keiner der Großen im Kampfe gefallen ist, also letztlich auch *pait* 'ging' = 'starb, fiel'. Zu *hwek-* 'schlachten' und *pug-* 'hassen' vgl. *AfO* 16.317f. (1952–53). Schwierig *sak-* bzw. *sek-* 'wissen' wegen zu großer Auswahl: kaum zu got. *saíƕan* 'sehen' usw., eher mit Benveniste, *BSL* 33.140f. (1932) zu lat. *sāgīre* 'spüren, ahnen' oder zu **seg'h-* in ἔχω 'halten, besitzen' usw. als 'geistig besitzen' oder zu lat. *secare* 'schneiden' neben *scire* 'wissen' (Vaillant, *BSL* 42.84ff. [1946])?

Wurzelhaftes *k* auch bei *hunink-* 'zerschlagen, beschädigen' mit kausativem Infix *-nen-/-nin-* zu **huk-* für **ūg-* von **u̯āg-/ūg-* in toch. AB *wāk-* 'sich spalten, bersten' (Van Windekens, *Lexique* 155) und ἄγ-νυμι 'ich zerbreche' (tr. mit kaus. -νυ-). Ebenso *lak-* bzw. *lag-* 'neigen, beugen, verbiegen; schief schlagen (Zahn)' zu ὀ-λόγ-ινον 'mit Zweigen' (Hes.), aksl. *loza* 'Zweig' u.a. zu **log'-* 'biegsam' (IEW 691 'Rute, Gerte?'). Wurzelhaft auch *nink-* 'heben' Couvreur, *Ḫ* 173.

Trotz dieser wurzelhaften *-k-* hat sich eine starke Vorliebe im Heth. für die *k*-Erweiterung gezeigt; die k-Erweiterung ist bei *hurk-* (und **wark-* zur selben Wurzel) ererbt, wohl auch bei *dug-*, vielleicht bei *hark-* 'umkommen'.

Walter Petersen, *Language* 9.12–34 (1933), hat sich als Erster ausführlich für nähere heth.-tocharische Beziehungen ausgesprochen. Daß er dabei insbesondere in der Annahme einer heth.-toch. Einheit gegenüber einer solchen der übrigen idg. Sprachen zu weit gegangen ist, hat er *Language* 10.205f. (1934) selbst bekundet. Es befremdet jedoch etwas, wenn man bei Porzig, *Gliederung* 183 (1954) liest, daß "bisher keine speziellen Übereinstimmungen" zwischen Toch. und Heth. gefunden seien: zunächst scheinen das Toch. und Heth. die einzigen idg. Sprachen zu sein, in denen die vierfache Reihe der Mediae (aspiratae) und Tenues (aspiratae) als einfache Reihe der Tenues erscheint (für 'Sturtevants Gesetz' gibt es zu viele Ausnahmen, so daß es mir unannehmbar ist; Näheres anderwärts). Ferner sind die Hinweise auf die 2. und 3. sg. prt. bei Petersen, *Language* 9.28f. (1933) sehr beachtlich. Auch die lexikalischen Isoglossen gehen weit über heth. *tekan-*, bh. *takam-* (vgl. *AO* demnächst) und toch. A *tkaṃ*, B *keṃ* 'Erde' hinaus.[1] Einiges habe ich im Anschluß an Petersen und Van Windekens *KZ* 72.245 (1955) zusammengestellt.[2] Dazu noch die *st*-Reste (S. 122f.) und heth. *malk-* zu toch. AB *mälk-* (S. 121). Darüber hinaus zeigt sich nun im Heth. und noch mehr im Toch. eine das übliche Maß weit überschreitende Vorliebe für die hier behandelte *k*-Erweiterung: in beiden Sprachen ist nur ein kleiner Teil ererbt. Ich kann dies hier in extenso nicht vorführen, sondern verweise auf Van Windekens, *Morph.* 226f., wo unter dem irreführenden Titel 'Thèmes en *-tk*' (*tk* ist allerdings im Toch. produktiv geworden) eine größere Anzahl einwandfreier Fälle aufgeführt wird, die sich mit Hilfe des rückläufigen Index bei Poucha, I. 440f. wesentlich vergrößern läßt (für B mit der Liste bei Krause I. 218ff.). Insbesondere sei noch auf toch. AB *särk-* 'übertreffen' hingewiesen, das semantisch wohl besser zu heth. *sark-u-* 'hervorragend, erhaben, mächtig; Held' paßt als zu **ser-* 'strömen, sich rasch bewegen' (Van Windekens, *Lexique* 119). Dies wäre eine weitere ausschließlich heth.– bzw. anatolisch[3]–toch. Isoglosse, wie heth. *kast-* und toch. A *kaṣt* 'Hunger', aus demselben Sachbezirk auch heth. *eku-* und toch. AB *yok-* 'trinken', dazu andere, die weniger sicher sind (vgl. Anm. 2 *loc. cit.*).

Ferner treffen die beiden Sprachen auch in der Vorliebe zu verbalen *t*-Erweiterungen zusammen, die auch nur zu einem kleinen Teil ererbt sind. Zunächst fällt im Heth. *wen-tsi* 'er beschläft (außerehelich)' auf neben 3. pl. prt. *wen-t-ir* (m.E. richtig mit Sturtevant, *Language* 6.218 [1930] zu **gh^u^en-* 'schlagen, töten', heth. sonst *kwen-/kun-* ds., wo der *k*-Anlaut wegen *ku-* bewahrt ist; semantisch zu vergleichen lat. *uiolāre* 'gewaltsam behandeln' und 'schänden'). Ferner stellte Sommer (bei Friedrich, *Wtb.* 103) heth. *kart-* 'abschneiden' (*kartant-* 'abgeschnitten') sicher

[1] Man entschuldige, daß ich nun mit Hinweisen sparsam bin, doch ist mit den neuen Arbeiten, die Petersen noch nicht zur Verfügung standen, alles leicht zu überprüfen: A. J. Van Windekens, *Lexique étymologique des dialectes tokhariens* (Louvain 1941); *id.*, *Morphologie comparée du tokharien* (Louvain 1944); Wolfg. Krause, *Westtocharische Grammatik*, I: Das Verbum (Heidelberg 1952); Pavel Poucha, *Thesaurus linguae Tocharicae dialecti A*, I (Praha 1955), II: *Chrestomathia Tocharica* (Praha 1956).

[2] *Vergleichende Laut- und Formenlehre des Hethitischen* 222 (Heidelberg 1956).

[3] Wegen lyk. *hri* 'über' : heth. *ser.* = ἐνί : ἐν, Pedersen, *Lyk* 24. – Da mir Otten in seiner Besprechung meines Anm. 2 angegebenen Buches *DLZ* 77, Spalte 496 (1956) sagt, daß ich den Gedanken der 'anatolischen' Sprachen (Keilheth., Bh., Luw., Pal., Lyk., Milyisch und etwas abseits Lyd.) übernommen habe (von Sturtevant), so sei dem hinzugefügt, daß ich den Gedanken mit 20 Einzelheiten gestützt habe (232f.).

richtig zu ai. *kar-t-ati* 'er schneidet', das allerdings jünger ist als *kṛ-ntati* ds. Dennoch ist die *t*-Erweiterung hier alt: arm. *k'ert'em* 'ich ziehe die Haut ab', lit. *kertù* 'ich schlage heftig', also zu *(*s*)*ker-* 'schneiden', IEW 938, 942. Als sicher diesem Typ zugehörig, aber nicht mit ererbter *t*-Erweiterung, möchte ich noch folgende zwei Fälle betrachten:

mitaye- bezeichnet eine andere Art des Befestigens als *termaye-* 'festnageln', zu **mei-/mi-* 'befestigen' in ai. *mi-noti* 'er befestigt', *su-me-ka-* 'fest; wohlgegründet', lat. *moe-nia* pl. 'Stadtmauern' u.a., IEW 709.

mutaye- 'entfernen, beseitigen' zu **meu-* 'fortschieben' in lat. *mouēre* 'fortbewegen', lit. *máuti* (3. sg. prt. *móvė*) 'abstreifen' (Ring vom Finger, Handschuh von der Hand, Pantoffel vom Fuß) u.a., IEW 743.

Unsicher, aber doch wohl idg. ist *saktaye-* 'gesund machen' (einen Verletzten); kann zu heth. *sak-* 'wissen' (S. 126) gehören, vgl. lat. *medēri* 'heilen' zu μήδομαι 'ich ersinne', aw. *vi-mād-* 'Arzt', lat. *medicus*. Anderseits steht auch heth. *sakiya-* zur Verfügung, ein Verbum feierlicher Willenseröffnung durch Götter oder Könige, auch magischen Rezitierens, vgl. aksl. *baliji* 'Arzt', aksl. *vračь* 'Arzt' (serb. *vrač* 'Wahrsager'!), got. *lekeis* 'Arzt', die letztlich zu Verben des Sprechens gehören : aksl. *o-bavati* 'besprechen, beschwören', russ-ksl. *bajati* 'erzählen; besprechen' und 'heilen', russ. *vraka* 'Geschwätz', *vratь* 'lügen', λέγειν und ἐρεῖν 'sprechen'.

Schwierig wegen der unsicheren Bedeutung *sartaye-* 'bestreichen' (??); wenn richtig oder ähnlich zu **ser-/sor-* (eine Farbbezeichnung, IEW 910f. 'rot, rötlich') in lit. *sar̃tas* 'fuchsrot' (Pferd), lett. *sarks* 'rötlich', fraglich ai. *sāra-* 'Baummark'.

Unsicher auch *ispart-*, weil sich die Grundbedeutung nicht fassen läßt: (einem Überfall) 'entkommen', (von einem Gerücht) 'aufkommen, entstehen', (zur Regierung) 'emporkommen'. Es könnten verschiedene idg. **sp*(*h*)*er-* herangezogen werden, wobei sich einschlägige Bedeutungsentwicklungen als möglich rekonstruieren ließen.

Vom toch. Material, wo der Anteil von ererbten *t*-Erweiterungen größer ist als bei *-k-*, sei nur ganz weniges genannt (vgl. Anm. 1):

A *ărt-* B *ārt* 'lieben', heth. *ara-* 'Freund', ἔρως 'Liebe', sonst ohne sichere Anknüpfung.

AB *lut-* 'entfernen, beseitigen' zu **leu-/lu-* 'abschneiden, trennen, loslösen' in λύω 'löse, befreie; vertilge' usw., IEW 681.

A *met-* B *mait-/mit-* 'sich aufmachen, gehen' zu **mei-/mi-* 'wandern, gehen' in lat. *meare* 'gehen, aksl. *mi-nǫ* 'ich gehe vorüber' u.a., IEW 710; nicht mit Van Windekens, *Lexique* 60 zu got. *maitan* 'hauen, schneiden' usw.

Genannt sei noch A *wät-* 'setzen, stellen; errichten', dessen Übereinstimmung mit heth. *wedantsi* 'sie bauen' m.E. kein Zufall ist. Und das part. praet. pass. heth. *wedant-* 'gebaut', toch. A *watunt* (cas. obl.) 'errichtet' zeigt, daß auch im Toch. – allerdings mit starker Einschränkung (vgl. Pedersen, *Toch.* 110f.) – ein sonst im Präsens aktives *-nt-* beim passiven Partizip des Präteritums verwendet wird. Wenn auch diesem *nt* im Hinblick auf die eigenartige Stellung dieses Suffixes im Toch. wenig Gewicht beizumessen ist, so ist m.E. doch zuzugeben, daß toch. A *wät-* und heth. *wed-* (oft *wet-*, intervokalisch auch *witt-*) den Anforderungen einer brauchbaren Etymologie (Übereinstimmung in Form und Bedeutung) genügen. Anderseits liegt aber Beziehung von heth. *wed-* zu *we-/u-* 'her-' nahe, wie dies für *ú-en-zi* = *we-ntsi* 3. pl. 'sie kommen (her)', *ú-wa-te* = *wate* 'bring!' u.a. verschiedentlich behauptet wurde. Ich könnte es für möglich halten, daß heth. *wed-* 'bauen' als '*her-setzen' eine unmittelbare Ableitung von *we-* 'her' ist, ähnlich wie *uptsi* (S. 123). Dann aber hätte das Tocharische an der Änderung des Zielpunktes **u̯e-* 'weg' zu *we-* 'her' teil gehabt oder teil bekommen.

Keineswegs will ich nun etwa Petersens Hypothese einer toch.–heth. Einheit aufwärmen. Aber so viel scheint mir doch klar: spezielle Übereinstimmungen zwischen Heth. und Toch. sind vorhanden.

UNIVERSITÄT WIEN

JERZY KURYŁOWICZ

MORPHOLOGICAL GEMINATION IN KELTIC AND GERMANIC

SCHOLARS have always felt uneasy about the pretended Keltic change of stop plus *n* resulting in *kk*, *tt*, *pp* (from *k*+*n*, *t*+*n*, *p*+*n*) and *gg*, *dd*, *bb* (from *g* or *gh*+*n*, *d* or *dh*+*n*, *b* or *bh*+*n*). Not only is such a progressive assimilation, which reminds us of similar Prakrit developments,[1] unheard of in the European branch of IE, but what is more, a different and apparently phonetic treatment of these clusters is very well attested. E.g.[2]:

MI *brén* 'fetid, putrid', W *braen*, MB *breyn*, NB *brein* < **mrakno-*; MI *blén* 'groin', W *blaen* 'point', C *blyn* 'summit', MB *blein* 'summit' < **mlakno-*; OI *srón* 'nose' W *ffroen*, MB *froan*, NB *fron*, also W *trwyn*, OC *trein* < **s(p)roknā-;* MI *tón* 'bottom, lower part', W *tin* < **tuknā-*; OI *mén* 'open mouth', W *min* 'lip', C *myn*, *meyn*, B *min* 'snout' < **mĕ̄kno* or **mēknā-*.

MI *gráin* 'disgust', W *graen* 'asperity, grief, grievous' < **gragni-*; I *stán* 'tin', W *ystaen*, NC *stean*, B *stean*, Gaulish-Lat. *stannum* < **stagno-*; I *súanem* 'rope', W *hoenyn*, *hwynyn* 'hair; snare' < **sogno-*; OI *fén* 'carriage', W *gwain* (plur. *gweiniau*), Gaulish *covinnos* (uocant quorum falcatis axibus utuntur) < **u̯egno-*; MI *cuilén* 'whelp, little dog', W *colwyn*, OC *coloin*, B *kolen* < **koligno-*.

OI *én* 'bird', W *edn* ,OC *hethen*, MC *ethen*, NC *eđanor* 'auceps', OB *etn-*, MB *ezn*, NB *evn*, *ein* < **petno-*; in W *llwdn* 'young animal', MB *lo*(*e*)*zn*, NB *loen*, whatever their origin, the root of I *loth* 'colt' has been enlarged by a nasal suffix.

MI *móin* 'moor' < **moudni-*; W *blwyddyn* (with another vocalism: OC *bliþen*, MC *blythen*, *blethen*, B *blizenn*) has an ancient plural *blynedd* < **blidnii̯ās* (after numerals).

[1] Sanskrit *agni-*, *vighna-*, *yatna-* > Prakrit *aggi-*, *viggha-*, *jatta-*, etc.

[2] Abbreviations I = Irish, W = Welsh, C = Cornish, B = Breton; O = old, M = middle, N = new or modern.

MI *ten*(*e*) 'fire', W, C, B *tan* < **tepnet-*; OI *súan* 'sleep', W, C, B *hun* < **sopno-*; MI *cúan* 'haven' < **kopno-*, cf. ONorse *hǫfn*.

OI *domun* 'world', *domain* 'deep', W *dwfn* (f. *dofn*), C *down*, B *doun* 'deep', Gaulish *Dubnoreix* (proper name) < **dubno-*.

For these and other examples (of *-kn-*, *-gn-*) cf. Pedersen, *Vgl. Gramm.* 1.125, 103, 135, 113, 93, 117.

Hence it is evident that we must count with a double treatment of the consonantal groups stop+*n*. According to Stokes and Zupitza, followed by Pedersen (*op. cit.* 159) and by Walde-Pokorny (*Vgl. Wtb.*) both treatments are phonetic, the assimilation *-kn-* > *-kk-*, *-gn-* > *-gg-*, etc., taking place immediately before the (prehistorically) stressed vowel. But as long as independent clues concerning the prehistoric accentuation are not forthcoming, this explication remains an otiose hypothesis, although the respective IE formations (nouns in *-no-*, *-nā-*, *-ni-*, *-nu-*, verbs in *-ne/o-*, *-nā-*, *-nu-*) were as a rule stressed on the suffix. It is not surprising that other opinions concerning the aforesaid change have been reserved or even negative, thus Thurneysen (*Handbuch d. Altir.* p. 88) or M.-L. Sjoestedt (*L'aspect verbal et les formations à affixe nasal en celtique*, 1926, p. 19, 20).

To deal with this phonetic dilemma writers had recourse to an overall expedient, the so called *expressive gemination.* Putting aside onomatopœic creations and sound metaphors, the chief bulk of expressive word-forms is represented by hypocoristic transformations of proper names and of common names denoting persons (especially family members), more rarely animals, and quite exceptionally inanimate objects. Nicknames ('sobriquets') are closely related to pet names. Adjectives are liable to undergo such transformations chiefly when they refer to persons (signifying e.g. physical or moral defects).

But once the more or less determined criteria of expressive word-formation are abandoned, this expedient to account for abnormal phonetic forms becomes illusory. Nobody will dispute the difference between the Protogermanic gemination, an important chapter of Germanic morphology, and the Greek gemination which approximately covers the above named semantic range (Schwyzer, *Griech. Gramm.* I, p. 315).

It seems that Keltic ranges together with Germanic in assigning a grammatical rôle to the doubling of stops. If this is true, then neither the older phonetic explanation nor the more recent semantic one can pass muster. We are obliged to admit a *morphologic* gemination. IE heritage seems improbable as traces of a morphological alternation *simple stop*: *double stop* have been preserved neither in Indo-Iranian nor in Greek.[3] Therefore the question of its *Keltic* origin becomes predominant.

The doubling of stops in inherited IE roots is a peculiar feature of both the Keltic

[3] In this respect IE sharply differs from the Semitic group, where the doubling of the second or the third radical consonant may constitute a special morph : Arabic *ḳatala* versus *ḳattala*.

and the Germanic[4] languages. But the latter group offers much richer linguistic data, permitting to distinguish several chronological layers of gemination, and its evolution from a morphologically restricted phenomenon to an almost facultative means of 'expression'. As it is rather probable that the fragmentary Keltic materials represent the traces of a similar development, an analysis of the Germanic data may be expected to throw light upon the neighbouring group.

Germanic with its ablaut-series of the strong verb is particularly suitable for a study of primary derivational processes. Now it seems that not only vowel gradation but also the doubling of the final root-consonant belongs to the primary formations centering upon the strong verb.

The Germanic III class of strong verbs includes a series of forms with double consonant, nasal or liquid. Thus *brinnan, -ginnan, hlimman, krimman, linnan, rinnan, spinnan, swimman, winnan; bellan, gellan, hellan, kerran, quellan, skellan, skerran, swellan, wellan* 'to boil', *wellan* 'to roll, turn'.

The double consonant goes back to an original group consisting of final radical consonant plus present suffix. According to *WP*, Falk-Torp, *Wortschatz*, etc., the geminate continues *-nu̯-* in *brinnan, linnan, rinnan, spinnan, winnan* and perhaps *-ginnan; -ln-* in *hellan, quellan, skellan, swellan, wellan* (both verbs) and perhaps in *bellan* and *gellan*[5]; *-rz-* in *kerran, skerran.* The double *m* of *hlimman, krimman* and *swimman*[6] has not been accounted for.

The double consonant, originally restricted to the present tense, was generalized in the whole conjugation already in the prehistoric period, cp. the past-present Goth. *kann, kunnum* etc.

Direct evidence for this origin of the geminate is supplied by certain archaic primary derivatives which according to the well-known IE rule of word-formation are built upon the verbal root, not upon the present tense. E.g.:

brinnan 'to burn' : ON *bruni* 'conflagration'; OE *bryne* (*-i*-stem)
hlimman 'to sound etc.' : weak verb I ON *hlymja* 'to crash, make noise' weak verb II OHG *hlamôn* 'to rush, roar'
krimman 'to press, clutch, pinch' : weak verb ON *kremia* 'to press, pinch'; weak verb II OSwed. *krama* 'to clutch'; ON *krǫm* 'consumption'

[4] In Germanic, like in Keltic, double stops never proceed from simple stops+*n*. For the regular phonetic development cf. ON *botn* 'bottom'; ON *ogn* and Goth. *aúhns* 'oven'; OE *swefn* 'sleep, dream', ON *svefn*; ON *þegn* 'thane, man', OS *dheg(a)n*, OHG *dëgan*; Goth. *uslukns* 'open'; etc. There are, according to Wissmann (*Nomina postverbalia* p. 97), quite a number of Germanic verbs with *-nō-* suffix corresponding to the *-nā*-verbs of other IE languages. But no Germanic verb with final geminated stop corresponds to a *-nā*-verb of another language.

[5] Cf. Goth. *kinnus, kinnaus* 'chin' < **kinus, kinnaus* < **kinus, *kinnis* < **kinu̯iz.* Progressive assimilation of *ln* > *ll* is solidly testified to in Germanic : Goth. *wulla* 'wool' = Sanskrit *ūrṇā-* (< **u̯l̥̄nā-*); Goth. *fulls* 'full' = Sanskrit *pūrṇa-* (< **pl̥̄no-*); OHG *wëlla* 'wave' (< **u̯elnā-*), cf. OSl *vlъna* < **u̯l̥̄nā-*). The cluster *ln* does not occur in Protogermanic.

[6] A progressive assimilation **su̯em+n-* or **su̯em+u̯-* is scarcely probable.

rinnan 'to run' : Goth. *runs* (f. -*i*-stem) 'run(ning)' = OE *ryne* m.; ON *run* 'connexion between two lakes'; Goth. *garunjo* 'flood, inundation'
spinnan 'to spin' : ON *spuni* 'spinning'; OE, MHG *spinel* 'spindle'
swimman 'to swim' : MHG *swamen* 'to swim'
bellan 'to bark etc.' : ON *belja* 'to bawl' (**baljōn*); ON *bylja* 'to threaten'
hellan 'to sound, call' : weak verb II **halōn* 'to call, fetch' (OE, OF, OS, OHG); ON *hjala* 'to talk to', *hjal* n. 'talk'
kerran 'to creak, cry' : weak verb II ON *kura* 'to growl'; ON *kura* 'complaint'
quellan 'to swell' : Danish *kval* 'steam'
skellan 'to sound' : ON *skjal* n. 'talk'; ON *skal* n. 'noise'
swellan 'to swell' : OE *swile* 'swelling'; OHG *swilo* m. and *swil* n. 'weal'
wellan 'to bubble, boil, effervesce' : weak verb I ON *ylja* 'to warm'; ON *ylr* 'steam'; OHG *walî* 'tepor'
wellan 'to roll, turn' : MLG *walen;* ON *valr* 'round'.

The relation between the derived forms and the respective strong verbs is comparable to that of *spurnan* 'to spurn, kick' and the *n*-derivative **spuran-* (ON *spori*, OE *spora*, OHG *sporo*) 'spur', built upon the root **spur*, not upon the present stem *spurn-*.

But the productiveness of certain vocalic suffixes is responsible for the ever increasing penetration of the geminate into deverbative derivatives, both verbs and nouns. The chief respective categories are:

1) the causative-iterative verbs in -(*i*)*ja*- (weak verbs I): **brannjan*, **kannjan*, **rannjan* (Goth. etc.); ON *skella* (< *skellan*); Goth. *ufswalleins* < **swalljan* (< *swellan*); ON *vella* (< *wellan*)

2) the iterative and intensive verbs in -*ō*- (weak verbs II) : OE *crammian*, MHG *krammen* (< *krimman*); ON *bulla*, OHG *bullôn* (< *bellan*); ON *karra* (< *kerran*); ON *kurra* (< *kerran*); Norw. *skarra* and MLG, NHG *scharren* (< *skerran*); Swed. *skorra* and MLG *schurren* (< *skerran*); a weak verb III Goth. -*kunnan* is derived from the past-present verb *kann*

3) nouns in -(*j*)*o*- (Germ. -*a*-) : ON *gjallr* and *gallr* (< *gellan*); ON *skjallr* = OE *sciell* (< *skellan*); ON *sullr* (< *swellan*)

4) nouns in -(*j*)*ā*- (Germ. -*ō*-) : Goth. *winna* (< *winnan*); ON *skǫll* (< *skellan*); OE *wiell* (< *wellan* 'to boil')

5) nouns in -*i*- : OE *hlemm* (< *hlimman*); Goth. *wunns* f. (< *winnan*); ON *skellr* = OHG *scal*(*l*) (< *skellan*)

6) weak nouns in Germ. -(*j*)*an*-, -(*j*)*ōn*- : *brinno* (< *brinnan*); OE *hlimme* (< *hlimman*); ON *krumma*, *krymma* (< *krimman*); Goth. *rinno* (< *rinnan*); Goth. *winno* = ON *vinna* (< *winnan*); ON *bjalla* = OE *belle* (< *bellan*); ON *vella* and *olla* (< *wellan* 'to boil').

The new procedure and the inherited one must have, during a certain span of time,

coexisted side by side, creating a contrast between simple and double consonant, the latter being perceived as 'expressive' not in virtue of its phonologically marked character but as the carrier of the primary semantic function (causative, iterative, etc.), whereas the secondary functions were still, during a certain time, rendered by not geminated forms. This temporary opposition, growing productive, called forth the creation of geminated forms outside the narrowly circumscribed, etymologically justified, original domain. E.g.:
kurōn : *kurrōn* (< *kerran*) = *tugōn* : *tukkōn* (< *tiuhan*).

Outside the original domain the gemination invaded derivatives with pregnant semantic value of the derivational suffix. Where this value had been weakened or neutralized by the root, the doubling of the final root-consonant did not take place. This fact is to be held responsible for the incomplete extension of the gemination, the chief morphological stages being the following:

a) The living derivatives (groups 1–6) of the above verbs (*brinnan* etc.) replace, as a rule, the simple consonant by the corresponding geminate.

b) The derivatives 1–6 of other strong verbs frequently geminate the final root-consonant.

c) Other derivatives, chiefly denominative, with suffixes 1–6 may also adopt gemination.

d) Not motivated (primary) words with inflexional suffixes corresponding to the derivational suffixes 1–6 (-(*i*)*ja*-, -*ō*-, -*ē*-; -(*j*)*a*-, -(*j*)*ō*-, -*i*-, -(*j*)*an*-, -(*j*)*ōn*-), *sporadically* geminate the final root-consonant.

Group b) is best illustrated by weak -*ōn*-verbs and by weak nouns. Cf. the iterative and intensive verbs in -*ōn*:

**glīsan* (supposed by the Norw. adjective *glīsen*): ON *glissa* 'to grin'
hnīpan 'to pinch, push' : ON *hnippa* 'to push'
snīþan 'to cut' : MHG *snetzen* 'to chip, carve' (OHG *snetzeri* 'sculptor')
wīpan 'to wind' : OHG *wipfôn* 'to lose one's way'
wrītan 'to engrave, draw' : OHG *rizzôn* 'to scratch'
driupan 'to drip' : OE *droppian*, OHG *tropfôn*
liugan 'to lie' : **lukkōn* 'to allure, entice' (ON, OE, OHG)
sliupan 'to slip' : OHG *slophôn* (supposed by agent-noun *slophâri*)
striukan 'to stroke' : OE *stroccian*
tiuhan 'to drag, draw' : OHG *zocchôn* 'to snatch' (without gemination *zogôn*)
sūpan 'to sip' : OE *soppian* 'to sop'
brekan 'to break' : OHG *brockôn*
teran 'to tear' : OHG **zerrôn* (in *gizerrôt*) 'to cut off'
tredan 'to tread' : OHG *trettôn* 'to trample'
hlahjan 'to laugh' : OFrisian *hlakkia* (intensive), ON *hlakka*
stapjan 'to step' : OHG *stapfôn*

swarjan 'to swear' : ON *svarra* 'to buzz etc.'

The strong verb of **likkōn* 'to lick' (OE, OS, OHG) is not attested.

One of the chief functions of the Germanic nominal -*n*-suffix was the formation of deverbative nouns. Gemination is attested in cases like:

driupan 'to drip' : OE *droppa* 'drop', OHG *tropfo*
fliugan 'to fly' : OHG *floccho* 'flake'
slūkan 'to swallow' : OHG *slucko* 'glutton'
smiugan 'to cling to, to press against' : OHG *smocko* 'shirt'
snûfen, *snûben* (MHG) 'to snore, snort' : OHG *snupfe* 'rheum'
sūpan 'to sip' : OE *soppe* 'sop'
stëhhan (OHG) 'to sting' : OE *sticca* 'stick', OHG *stëcko* (without gemination *stëhho*)
brekan 'to break' : OHG *brocko* 'fragment, crumb'
gedan 'to weed' : OHG *jëtto* 'weed, darnel'
kresan 'to crawl' : OHG *kresso* 'groundling, gudgeon'
fregnan 'to ask' : OE *fricca* 'herald'
hafjan 'to lift' : OHG *hepfo* 'leaven' (also without gemination *heve*)
stapjan 'to step' : OHG *stapfo* 'stride, pace'.

This alternation between simple and double consonant inside the *motivated* (deverbative) -*n*- stems with gemination (functioning as 'expressive' forms) tends to spread to other *motivated* -*n*-stems, viz. of denominative origin (group c). Nicknames and hypocoristic names are often formed from substantives or adjectives by transferring them to the weak declension, in which case gemination is readily adopted as an additional 'expressive' feature. If the basic appellative noun is already weak, gemination alone may function as the constituent morph.

E.g. ON *farri* 'tramp, vagabond' < **fari* agent-noun < *fara*; ON *goddi* nickname < *goþi* '(heathen) priest'; OHG *zickî*(*n*) 'kid' < **zëcko* < *ziga;* OHG *Berri* '(name of) a constellation' < **berro* < *bëro* 'bear'; OHG *roggo*, *rocko* 'rye' < **rugi-*; ON *futta* 'cunnus' < *fuþ*.

Maybe Germ. *Knappe* and *Rappe* were originally hypocoristic forms (< *Knabe*, *Rabe*).

Hypocoristic proper names are built by adding the inflexional suffix -*n*- to the *hypocoristic root*, and geminating the final radical consonant. Thus in German:

full name	hypocoristic root	hypocoristic name
Friedrich	*Frid-*	*Fritz* (< *Fritt*(*o*))
Karl	*Kal-*	OHG *Kallo*
Ludwig	*Lud-*	*Lutz* (< *Lutto*)
Sig (*-bert*, *-frid*, *-mâr*)	*Sig-*	OHG *Sikko* (< *Siggo*)
Swedish *Lars*	*Las-*	*Lasse*

Perhaps ON *krabbi*, OE *crabba*, NLG *krabbe* < **krabban-* continue a hypocoristic geminated form of **krabita-* inherited by German (*Krebs*).

As a *tertiary* stratum one may regard geminated *-n-* stems whose inflexional suffix is not motivated by derivation. In such a case gemination has probably been induced by semantic contact with words belonging to the more fundamental layers. Fluctuation between simple and double consonant is frequently characteristic of the forms belonging to this last group.

The relatively recent origin of group d), partly also of c), is betrayed by the frequent coexistence of the geminated and non-geminated forms.

Difference between two dialects: ON *boli*, OE *bula* 'bull' – MLG and NHG *Bulle;* ON *kraki* 'hooked stick' – OHG *kracco;* OF, OS *skap*, OHG *skaf* 'tub, pail' – ON *skeppa* 'bushel'; OHG *scrato* 'faun' – ON *skratti* 'wizard'; ON *spari* (and *sparri*) – OHG *sparro* 'rafter, spar'; OS, OHG *waga* 'cradle' – ON *vagga.*

Inside the same dialect: ON *staka* and *stakka* 'skin, hide'; OHG *bahho* and *backo* 'cheek etc.'; MHG *zëche* and *zëcke* 'tick'; OHG *zota* and *zotta* 'tuft (of hair)'. – With simultaneous shortening of long vowel : OE *crúce* 'jug' but *crocca* 'pot'; OHG *hâko* 'hook' and *hacko* 'uncinus, furca' (OE *haca*, OS *haco* with simple consonant).

In denominative and unmotivated *-ōn*-verbs the doubling is also frequently optional : E *to gloat* < **glotian* but ON *glotta* 'to grin', NHG *glotzen* 'to stare'; OHG *hlamôn* 'to rush, roar' but ON *hlamma;* ON *skopa* and OSwed. *skoppa* 'to tease, jeer'; MHG *klaffen* and *klapfen* 'to sound, clap'; Frisian *dufen*, *duven* and *dubben* 'to push' (ON *dubba*, OE *dubbian*).

In a similar way copious examples illustrating the phases b), c) and d) may be quoted for suffixes of groups 1), 3), 4), 5).[7]

To sum up, the expressive function of the gemination must have developed along the following lines:

In group a) the two formative processes, e.g. the suffixation of *-ōn* (weak verbs II) and suffixation plus doubling, enter into a semantic opposition. The spread of the doubling to group b) is not entailed by the iterative (intensive) sense of the verbs b), it is seized upon as an already existing alternative offering the possibility of differentiation with respect to the hitherto employed formative. Now if the renewal of a formative process results in a differentiation, the new form is the carrier of the primary semantic function, the secondary functions being, at least temporarily, rendered by the old form. This accounts for the transitory coexistence of geminated and non-geminated forms, even for the same root.

[7] The *direct* origin of a given form is sometimes doubtful. Masculine *-a*-stems, feminine *-ō*-stems, and weak stems of both genders, may be derived from weak verbs, e.g. OHG *kouf* 'purchase' from *koufôn* (Goth. *kaupon*). Therefore the double consonant of such stems may go back directly to geminated *-ō*-verbs : OHG *brocko*, *tropfo*, *stapfo*, OE *soppe*, cf. *brockôn*, *tropfôn*, *stapfôn*, *soppian*. On the other hand, verbs in *-ōn* derived from geminated stems in *-a-*, *-ō-* are also to be expected. In all such cases the choice between the given alternatives is often rather difficult.

The sound symbolism, the association of intensity (or iteration) with the repetition of the final stop, is secondary. The doubling in **druppōn* is by its nature clearly distinct from the geminate in *atta, mamma*, originating in 'Urschöpfung'.

Expressiveness in this sense can attach itself not only to gemination but also to nasalization, vowel lengthening, inflexion, coalescence of suffixes, and so on. The last phenomenon is especially frequent : OHG *fugililî* = *fugil-il-î* 'small bird' is more expressive (in the above sense) than *fugil-î;* MHG *zickelîn* 'kid' = *zick-el-în* more expressive than OHG *zick-în;* and so forth. The new formation process is more 'expressive' than the old one.

If gemination under b) is a formal reinforcement of the chief morph *-ō-*, its introduction into c) is comprehensible. The spread of the doubling takes place along formal lines: not only the iterative morph *-ō-* but also verbal derivational morphs other than the iterative one (e.g. the *-ō-* of denominative verbs) may adopt gemination as auxiliary characteristics. Up to that moment the doubling is restricted to a number of semantic categories represented by the derivational suffix *-ō-*. But the stage c) differs from b) in that no specific semantic value can be ascribed to the totality of geminated forms, consisting of two or more distinct subgroups. The expressiveness of the doubling becomes more vague and diffuse than it is in b). But its semantic rôle in b) and c) is revealed by the fact that, limited to verbs with derivational *-ō-* suffix, it is not adopted by all such verbs. We must therefore admit that the semantic value of the *root* or rather the relation between suffix and root is an important factor explaining the presence and the absence of gemination inside the motivated *-ōn-* verbs.

At any rate the rôle of the root becomes unlimited in d) where the suffix, a mere exponent of the inflectional type, loses all semantic value. Here at last we face something which reminds us of expressiveness in the *traditional* sense of the term : a spontaneous phenomenon conditioned by emotional factors, independent of special grammatical structure, except that it must be clothed in a grammatical form, i.e., join an inflexional type. But other than in the case of 'Urschöpfung' the forms under d) are produced by grafting gemination on already existing words, not by creating words with gemination.

The phase investigated by the adherents of expressiveness in the traditional sense is just the last one (class d) where expressiveness is based upon a lexical value and not upon one (class b) or several (class c) grammatical values. Therefore the variety of possible associations increases enormously and the gemination loses its faculty to 'express' a *determined* semantic shade. It is apt to express any shade and thus to become, in a certain measure, an *optional* accessory morph.

There have been, in the history of language, cases of similar development. Cf. e.g. the fate of the Indo-Iranian nominal suffix -(*a*)*ka*-. In Pehlevi *-ak* can be attached to any noun whatever without changing its sense : *kām-ak* 'desire' = *kām* (*Grundriss* *d. ir. Phil.* I, 2, p. 173). The same suffix plays the part of an empty morph in Sanskrit, e.g. *yaka-* '(this) who' = *ya-* (Bloch, *L'Indo-Aryen*, p. 111).

An interesting point was raised nearly a century ago by Gerland (quoted by Martinet, *La gémination consonantique*, p. 146): no geminated intensive forms are derived from roots ending in liquid, nasal, or *s*. Although there is of course no *phonetic* obstacle to geminate these sounds, one can guess at the underlying *morphological* difficulty. From a certain moment on Proto-Germanic has known strong verbs with roots in *rr, ll, nn, mm* (cf. supra) but not with roots terminating in a double stop. The doubling of *r, l, n, m* would mean in many a case a deformation of the verbal root and cause a confusion between derivatives of the strong classes III and IV. At least the doubling must have been avoided for the following roots: *beran* 'to bear' but OHG *barrên* (*parrên*) 'to be numb, stiff'; *helan* 'to hide' : *hellan* 'to sound'; *quelan* 'to suffer pains, to die' : *quellan* 'to swell'; *skeran* 'to cut, shear' : *skerran* 'to scrape'; *stelan* 'to steal': **stalljan* 'to set up' and **stilljan* 'to still'; *þweran* 'to twirl': *þwerran* (ON *þverra*) 'to dwindle away'.

As regards the verbal roots in *-s* we must keep in mind the possibility of *s* > *z* (Vermeer's law) > *r* (in West Germanic), hence the same morphological obstacle to doubling as in the case of original *r*. Both *-ōn-* verbs and weak agent-nouns were characterized by the zero grade and the accompanying 'grammatical change' (Verner's law).

It must, however, be stressed that Gerland's rule is not absolutely valid. Instances of geminated *s* or liquid do occur: OHG *kresso*, ON *svarra*, perhaps a few others.

The contrast between the gemination *rr, ll, nn, mm* encountered in the old stock of strong verbs, and the doubling of stops in the living and productive derivational categories, is most instructive and speaks in favour of our explanation of the Germanic doubled stops. The doubling of liquids and nasals being already morphologically pertinent (as a feature of the *verbal root*) it could often not be turned to account to form derivatives from strong verbs in simple *r, l, n, m*. On the other hand, the gemination of stops, being proper only to derivatives, never to strong verbs, is clearly more recent than the rise of *rr, ll, nn, mm* in strong verbs. The fact alone that there are no primary verbs in *TT* (double stop), disposes both of the theory of phonetical doubling (*TT* < *Tn*) and of the theory of expressive doubling in the traditional sense. If the latter were correct, the total absence of strong verbs like **gebban*, **lessan*, **waddan*, and so on, would be inexplicable.[8]

The lack of grammatical gemination in Gothic constitutes an enigma unsatisfactorily explained by the solemn character of the text. Now although expressive forms (in the old sense) may not have found a place in the translation of the New Testament, an occasional iterative verb in *-ōn* or a weak substantive designing an

[8] Therefore OHG *backan* 'to bake' must be considered as a derivative from *bakan* attested in OHG, MHG (*bachen*) and OE (*bacan*). It may be a contamination from *bakan* + **bakkōn*.

inanimate object, i.e. words with *morphological* gemination, could surely be expected.[9] The only acceptable hypothesis accounting for this state of things is that morphological gemination is a feature proper to North and West Germanic only, developed during the period of the linguistic community of these two dialectic groups between approximately 200 and 600 A.D. (after the departure of the Goths towards the Black Sea).

The *phonetic* aspect of the Germanic doubling is of secondary importance. The fact that the geminates *kk*, *tt*, *pp* seem to correspond to all three modes of articulation (IE *k*, *g*, *gh* = Germanic *h*, *k*, *g*) may be accounted for by the assumptions a) that the oldest stratum of the respective forms goes back to a period when Verner's law still represented a living alternation between the voiced and the voiceless fricatives; b) that the gemination of a fricative was accompanied by 'strengthening', i.e., simultaneous occlusion (cf. analogical developments in OIrish, Thurneysen, *op. cit.*, 82, ONorse, OE).

As long as the couples *g*:*h*, *đ*:*þ*, *ƀ*:*f* followed the rules of privative opposition (surd fricative never before stress except initially), i.e., before the disappearance of the inherited IE accentuation, the triangular system of the Germanic consonants presented the following form:

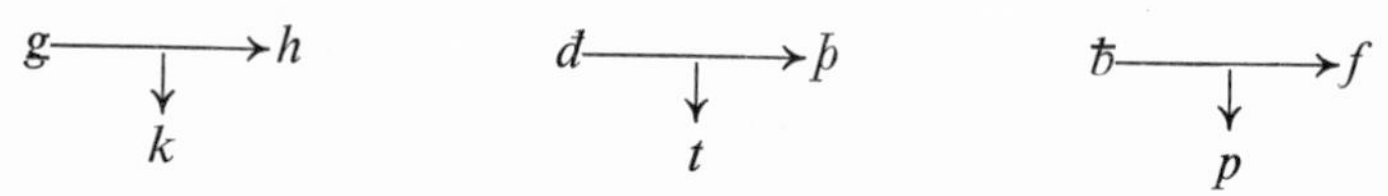

Verner's law having established a close relation between *đ* and *þ* etc., we must admit 1) that *đ* etc. and not *d* (occlusive appearing initially and after nasal) etc., were the chief allophones; 2) that *h*, *þ*, *f*, being of restricted occurrence, were the marked members of the opposition *đ*:*þ*, etc.,; 3) that therefore *k*, *t*, *p* were the sole representatives of the Germanic *stops*.

If gemination entailed occlusion, we should then understand why the doubling of both *đ* and *þ* resulted in *tt*.

There is no *objective* phonemic criterion recommending a system *t*—*d* (↓ *þ*) with *d* as the chief variant of the phoneme *d*/*đ*, at least not for the period preceding the fixation of the Germanic accent.

The only representatives of doubled consonants being originally *kk*, *tt*, *pp*, the historical geminates *gg*, *dd*, *bb* must belong to a younger layer. Their appearance is

[9] Besides forms belonging to a), already quoted (*brannjan* etc.), those to be investigated are: *andstaúrran*, *faírra*, *qaírrus*, *qrammiþa*, *skatts*, *smakka*, *stamms*, *wamme*. The double *r* of the first three words is according to Brugmann, whose opinion is followed in *WP* 1.685, 2.31, and 628), to be accounted for by the haplological loss of an intermediate vowel. The etymology of *skatts*, *smakka* is unknown, that of *wamme* uncertain. But *qrammiþa* (for *krammiþa*) and *stamms* may represent cases of non-etymological gemination. We find, however, no example of a *doubled stop* in the forms 1–6 derived from strong verbs.

conditioned by the fact that in the more recent stages of phonetic evolution the stops *g, d, b* have reached the status of chief variants (or even independent phonemes). The doubling of *h, þ, f,* dialectal and restricted to West Germanic, is still younger.

Resuming the Germanic data analysed here one is tempted to clothe them in a more general formula (the symbol of nasal or liquid):

verbal root	$-t_1t_1$	$-t_2t_2$	$-t_3t_3$ . . . .
primary derivatives	$-t_1-$	$-t_2-$	$-t_3-$ +vocalic suffix
new formative process	$-t_1t_1-$	$-t_2t_2-$	$-t_3t_3-$+vocalic suffix

Hence a transitory opposition $-t_1t_1-:-t_1-$, $-t_2t_2-:-t_2$, $-t_3t_3-:-t_3-$ . . . . . . spreading outside its originally restricted sphere.

The primordial condition of such a development is of course the existence of a new type of verbal roots, unknown in IE, viz., of roots with geminated final consonant resulting from *progressive* gemination. *Retrograde* assimilation would have had no morphological consequence, an opposition like $-t_1t_1-$ (from t_2+t_1):$-t_2-$ being isolated and accordingly not productive.

Returning to our starting-point, i.e., the Keltic doubled stops, we must therefore ask, in the first place, whether verbal roots in geminates resulting from progressive assimilation did exist in Keltic. This question ought to be answered in the affirmative.

Progressive assimilation in Keltic is certified by a number of reliable etymologies. The chief cases are the same as in Germanic: *-ln-* > *-ll-*, *-rs-* > *-rr-*, perhaps *-ls-* > *-ll-*, the first being the most important (for examples see Pedersen, *op. cit.*, I.156, 82, 85). We may overlook *-rp-* > *-rr-*, *p* as morphic element being practically without importance.

Verbs in *-ll-*: OI *at-baill* 'to die' (< **bal-n-*); *cell-* 'to turn' (< **q^{u}el-n-*); *ad-ellaim* 'to visit' (< **el-n-*); *fillim* 'to turn, inflect' (< **u̯el-n-*); W *gallaf* 'to be able' (< **gal-n-*). Verbs in *-rr-*: MI *cirrim* 'to cut off, mutilate', *corrán* 'sickle'. According to the current opinion this form goes back to **kerp*, but identification with **kers* (ἀκερσεκόμης = ἄκαρτος τὰς κόμας) is also phonetically acceptable. There are moreover examples of *-nn-* < *-n+n-*: OI *senn* 'sonare, to play (an instrument)' < **su̯en+n-*; W *mynnu* (C 1. p. sing. *mennaf*) 'to want' < **men+n-*, cf. OSl *pomęnǫti* < **men+n-*.

Outside the present system the old verbal root is better preserved in OI than in Germanic where inflexions like **fregnan* : **frah* are exceptional. E.g.:

OI *benaid* 'to strike' : subj. *-bia-*, past tense *-bí*, passive *-bíth*, abstract noun *béim(m)*
OI *bongid* 'to break' : subj. *-bóss-*, past **beb(a)ig*, passive *-bocht*, abstract n. *búain*
OI *guidid* 'to ask, pray' : subj. *-gess-*, past *-gáid*, passive *-gess*, abstract n. *guide*

But the progressive assimilation *-l+n-* > *-ll-* etc. in the present produced a new kind of roots, the old root, which appeared outside the present tense, being felt only as a modification of the fundamental form with geminate, e.g. *ball-* : subj. *-bel-(a-)*. The diffusion of the new root (=old present stem), its penetration into the primary derivatives, was favored by the early decline of the vowel gradation (ablaut). And a temporary contrast between simple and double consonant within the primary derivatives became the starting-point of morphological gemination.

We may therefore assume that the origin and the fate of the gemination in Keltic were much the same as in Germanic. But the scarcity of the Keltic materials does not allow to establish a close connexion between the primary verbs and the geminated forms. Nevertheless one may tentatively group the extant examples into several categories proposed above for Germanic.

Weak verbs in *-āi̯e/o-*:

MI *gataim* 'to steal' < **gaddā-*, cf. strong verb Germanic *getan* 'to get' (relation of the root-vowels as in OI *gabim* : Germanic *geban*)

MI *slacaim* 'to beat' (in *slactha* 'beaten'), *slacc* 'sword', NI *slacaire* 'batterer', cf. strong verb Germanic *slahan* 'to strike'

MI *bocaim* 'to shake', NI *bogadh*, cf. OE *cwacian* and (causative) *cweccan* 'to quake', probably from a strong verb V or VI

MI *glaccaim* 'to seize', *glacc* (NI *glac*) 'hand', cf. OE *clyccean* 'to clutch' supposing IE **glek*

Deverbative nouns in *-o-*, *-ā-*, *-i-*:

OI *accai* (dat. sing.) 'fettering, chaining' < **pakki-*, cf. Lat. *pango* 'to fix', *pax*

MI *brocc*, Gaelic (mod.) *bróg* 'grief', cf. OSl *gryzǫ*, *grysti*, Lith. *gráužiu*, *gráužti*, Greek βρύχω; Russ. *grustь* 'grief'

MI *ette*, NI *eite* 'pinion, wing', strong verb Sanskrit *patati*, Greek πέτομαι

NI *grág* 'croaking', cf. OE **crácian* (> NE *to croak*), ON *kráka* 'crow', *krákr* 'raven'

NI *grug* 'wrinkle', MI *grucánach*, cf. Germanic *kriukan* 'to wriggle, crawl' in Norw. dial. *krjuka*, OHG *kriochan*; MLG *kroke* 'wrinkle'

OI *lacc* (voiced stop) 'limp, weak', primary verb Greek λήγω

MI *lúta*, NI *lúda* 'the little finger', cf. Germanic **lŭ̄tila-* 'small, little' < *lūtan* 'to bow, sink, fall'

OI *reicc* (infinitive from dat. sing.) 'to sell', cf. Lith. *perkù*, *pir̃kti* 'to buy'

MI *robb* '(animal) given to butting', cf. Germanic *raupjan* 'to rip, pluck' and the ON intensive *ruppa*

NI, Gaelic *smug* 'rheum', cf. Lat. *emungo* 'to blow one's nose'.

The above list contains only etymologies admitted by Walde-Pokorny.

The Keltic data at our disposal are too incomplete to allow a distinction between the derivational group c) and the unmotivated one d). We may, however, safely admit hypocoristic gemination for nouns of chiefly primary character designing persons or animals.

I *fracc* 'woman', Gaelic (mod.) *frag* 'a kind wife', W *gwrach* 'old woman', MB *groach*, NB *grac'h* (< **u̯ragg-*)

OI *macc* 'son', OBrit. *Maccus* (proper name)

W *merch* 'girl', C *myrgh*, B *merc'h* (< **merggā* if related to Lith. *mergà* 'girl')
MI *lelap* 'child' (NI *leanabán*) presuppose **lelabb-*
NI *bocán*, MI *boccánach* 'goblin' (< **bukk-*)
MI *catt* 'cat', W *cath*, C *cath*, B *kaz* (< **katto-*), if the word is Keltic
W *hwch* f. 'hog, pig', C *hoch*, B *houc'h* 'hog, pig' and (related) OI *socc-ṡail* 'lolligo' (< **sukkā-*)
OI *mucc* 'pig', Gaelic *moch*, Gaulish *Mocco* (proper name).

Notice also Gaulish *Eppius*, *Eppo*, hypocoristic proper names from compounds with *Epo-*. Irish name *Tuatán* (*t* < *tt*) < *túath*.

Coexistence of simple and geminated root-consonant, although of course not so frequent as in Germanic, is well attested in Keltic:
MI *brocc*, Gaelic (mod.) *brόg* 'grief' (< **broggo-*) – and MI *brόn* 'grief', W *brwyn* 'smarting pain' (< **brogno-*)
MI *crocenn* 'skin', NI *croiceann*, C *cro(g)hen*, B *kroc'hen* (< **krokko-*) and W *croen*, plur. *crwyn*, OC *croin* (**krokno-*)
MI *ette*, NI *eite* 'pinion, wing' (< **pettiā-*) but OI *én* 'bird', W *edn*, OC *hethen*, MB *ezn* (< **petno-*).

The above examples show, at the same time, the difference between a doubled stop and the group stop+*n*.

Cf. furthermore OI *macc* 'son' but W *mab;* MI *lelap* and *lenab* 'child' (NI *leanabán* and *leanbh*); NI *bocán* but W *bwg*(*an*).

As regards the phonetic aspect of gemination the Brittonic branch and Gaulish present the same problem as Germanic. The gemination of intervocalic *b*, *d*, *g* is *pp*, *tt*, *kk* (hence *f*, *þ*, *x*) whereas the Goidelic group distinguishes between voiceless and voiced geminates (*kk* : *gg* . . . . . .). Cf. Gaulish voiceless geminates beside voiced simple stops in hypocoristic forms like *Vigellius* : *Viccius*, *Gaberius* : *Gappius*, and so on (C. Watkins, *Language* 31.16 [1955]). In our opinion it is the phonetic consequence of an early weakening (spirantization) of intervocalic *b*, *d*, *g*. Their reinforcement (gemination) must have engendered a surd (geminate) simply because the corresponding voiced stop had ceased to exist.

In Goidelic spirantization affects the voiceless and the voiced stops simultaneously, and the corresponding geminates become simple stops.

Keeping in mind the above facts and remarks we can now sum up the problem of the Keltic and Germanic doubled stops in a certain number of formulae:

1) A phonetic change of stop+*n* to double stop has never taken place, neither in Keltic nor in Germanic. The theory of assimilation contains, however, a grain of truth inasmuch as the progressive assimilation *l*+*n* > *ll* (beside *r*+*s* > *rr*, *l*+*s* > *ll*) was the chief source of a new class of primary verbs, the verbs with doubled final root-element (*ll*, *nn*, *rr*, maybe *mm*).

2) The geminates resulting from the progressive assimilation of the root-element and a suffix (chiefly *n*) do not at first appear outside the present system of the conjugation nor in derivation. But the new conception of the verbal root (roots with geminated final element) favours the spread of the double consonant both in the conjugation and in the derivatives of the respective verbs.

It is the first step in the general process of replacing the verbal root by the present stem.

3) The contrast *-ll-* : *-l-*, *-nn-* : *-n-* between the old and the new derivatives, accompanied by semantic differences, is turned to account outside its originally rather narrowly circumscribed sphere according to the proportion:

$$l : ll = n : nn = T : TT \ (T = \text{stop}).$$[10]

4) The double consonant (stop) may be called *expressive* inasmuch as it underlines the *primary function* of the derivational suffix. The expressiveness is not arbitrary but morphologically conditioned and concerns at first only primary derivatives.

5) The further evolution of the linguistic rôle of the doubling has been illustrated above by the categories c) and d), the last phase being the loss of its *morphological* character in favour of a *lexically* determined feature.

6) It seems that the study of this last stage as expressiveness *par excellence* has largely contributed to a certain disregard of the stages b) and c) which seem older and more fundamental than d).

7) Even the expressiveness of phase d) is to be strictly distinguished from the expressiveness of 'Urschöpfung', although in marginal cases, e.g. in hypocoristic forms subject to unsystematic mutilations, the two kinds of expressiveness may coincide and become undistinguishable.

8) The true linguistic problem, as regards Keltic and Germanic gemination, lies therefore somewhere in the middle between the two explanations proposed up to now. It is the *morphological* consequence of the assimilation $l+n > ll$ that accounts for the special status of the doubling in certain categories, i.e., its expressiveness in the new sense.[11]

UNIVERSITY OF KRAKÓW

[10] *Structurally* a bipartite proportion is sufficient to establish a morphological rule. The relation *sit* : *sat* (pp. *sat*) = *spit* : *spat* (pp. *spat*) differs from *heed* : *heeded* = *mend* : *mended* = *beg* : *begged* = *pack* : *packed* ... only by its restrained range and the improductiveness of the respective morph. On the other hand, no distinction is to be drawn between an isolated ablaut like *choose* : *chose*, or *fly* : *flew*, and a 'suppletive' relation like *go* : *went*.

[11] Martinet has not drawn the full consequence of the fact stated by him *op. cit.* 131: "La concomitance fréquente, dans les mots d'une même catégorie sémantique, de la gémination et d'un suffixe donné dont on sait qu'il est caractéristique de cette classe, et ceci dans plusieurs classes sémantiques différentes, a pour nous ceci d'intéressant qu'elle montre que la gémination n'apparaît pas arbitrairement, mais qu'elle caractérise certaines familles sémantiques particulières."

W. P. LEHMANN

A SYNTACTIC REFLEX OF THE INDO-EUROPEAN LARYNGEALS

VIRTUALLY all of the evidence for the Indo-European laryngeals has been phonological, though some morphological patterns have been adduced.[1] Since evidence based on a later level of analysis than the phonological is particularly welcome in supporting phonological reconstructions, even an infrequent reflex at the morphological or syntactic level is worth note. I suggest here that the Germanic pattern of using the neuter plural of pronouns, adjectives, and participles in references to nouns of differing genders is such a reflex.

The pattern is well described. Krause gives Gothic examples; Grimm and Behaghel list examples from the various Germanic languages, such as the following:[2] Gothic: Luke 1.6 *wesunuh þan garaihta ba* 'and they were both just' (Zacharias and Elizabeth); Old High German: Tatian 2.2 *siu uuarun rehtiu beidu fora gote ... inti beidu framgigiengun in iro tagun* 'both of them were just before God ... and both were advanced in their days' (Zacharias and Elizabeth); Old Saxon: *Heliand* 458 *Giuuitun im thō thiu gōdun tuuē, Ioseph endi Maria bēðiu fon Bethleem* 'went then the two good ones, both Joseph and Mary, from Bethlehem'; Old English: Genesis 811 *and wit her baru standað* 'and we two stand here bare'; Old Icelandic: *Njáls saga* 6 *Gunnhildr fann þat ok mælti til hans, er þau váru tvau saman*: 'Gunnhild found that out and said to him when the two of them were alone together.'

Despite its general occurrence, no explanation for the origin of the pattern has been widely accepted. Behaghel, following Meringer, suggests that the masculine dual in -*ō* was used in these patterns in Indo-European and that this ending coincided with that

[1] See my *Proto-Indo-European phonology*, especially p. 24 (Austin, 1952).

[2] Wolfgang Krause, *Handbuch des Gotischen*, 126–7 (München, 1953); J. Grimm, *Deutsche Grammatik* 4.429–31 (Gütersloh, 1898); O. Behaghel, *Deutsche Syntax* 3.39–41 (Heidelberg, 1928). The various handbooks give examples and present a descriptive analysis of the pattern; as for example O. Erdmann, *Grundzüge der deutschen Syntax*, 9–10 (Stuttgart, 1886–98), O. Behaghel, *Die Syntax des Heliand*, § 198 (Vienna, 1897), and so on.

of the neuter plural in Germanic, adding however that W. Schulze had expressed reservations towards this suggestion.[3] While Streitberg accepts this explanation, Krause rejects it and suggests that the pattern is probably to be explained purely on a syntactical basis. For, according to Krause, the Gothic forms such as the neuter plurals *þō* and *twa* are to be derived from Indo-European **tō* and **du̯ō*, rather than from duals; the dual ending, Indo-European **-ōu̯*, Krause finds in Gothic *ahtau* 'eight.'[4] Phonological evidence then points to an ending identical to that of the neuter plurals for this pattern.

Before the laryngeal theory was developed, no probable reason could be advanced for the use of a neuter plural for nouns of various genders. Indo-Europeanists were, to be sure, aware of the use of neuter plurals in a collective sense.[5] But no neuter noun plurals of masculine or feminine nouns, such as Latin *loca* for *locus*, were attested in Germanic, and accordingly there was no apparent basis for explaining the Germanic syntactic feature as a reflex of a collective use. It is now clear from recent comparative Indo-European study that the explanation of *loca* and similar forms as aberrant neuter plurals was a consequence of our limited information on pre-Indo-European. These forms are rather reflexes of collectives with endings from pre-Indo-European *-eh*. After loss of the *-h*, this ending came to be generalized in the neuter plural.[6] In his discussion of *-h* Sturtevant cites other forms ending in long vowels, such as Vedic Sanskrit *purū* 'many', which give evidence of the collective *-h*. By this explanation *-h*, which in pre-Indo-European was a collective marker, came to be a neuter plural ending after the Indo-European gender system was established. Relatively few substantival forms, such as Latin *loca* to *locus* 'place', Greek μῆρα to μηρός 'thigh', were preserved in which the early Indo-European use of *-h* is reflected.

In Germanic on the other hand the early Indo-European pattern of using *-h* as a collective was maintained syntactically. By this pattern, a form of the modifier was chosen which reflected a collective rather than a plural meaning. The Germanic passages, such as those listed above, refer to two or more items or individuals taken as a unit. Other passages are clearly collective in force, such as Gothic: Mark 3.31 *jah qemun þan aiþei is jah broþrjus is jah uta standandona insandidedun du imma, haitandona ina* 'his mother and his brothers came and (collectively) standing outside sent to him, calling him.' Old High German: Otfrid II.1.4 *Er sé joh hímil wurti joh érda ouh so hérti, ouh wíht in thiu gifúarit, thaz si̯u éllu thriu rúarit*. 'He created sea and

[3] Behaghel, *DS* 3.39; R. Meringer, "Beiträge zur Geschichte der idg. Declination," *KZ* 28.216–239 (1887), esp. 238–9; H. Hirt maintains this view; see his *Indogermanische Grammatik* 3.322 fn. 1 (Heidelberg, 1927).

[4] W. Streitberg, *Gotisches Elementarbuch*[6] § 236.3 (Heidelberg, 1920); Krause, *HG* 127.

[5] See Brugmann, *Gdr.* 2.1. §467 and 511 (Strassburg, 1906). The bibliography is huge, but J. Schmidt's *Die Pluralbildungen der indogermanischen Neutra* (Weimar, 1889) is the most comprehensive treatment.

[6] See E. H. Sturtevant, "Indo-Hittite collective nouns with a laryngeal suffix," *Language* 24.259–61 (1948) and *A comparative grammar of the Hittite language*[2], 81–2 (New Haven, 1951).

heaven and also the solid earth and introduced something into them, that concerns all three.' By contrast, when neuter forms are not used, individuals rather than a grouping are emphasized, as in *Heliand* 461, the continuation of the passage cited above: *thar scoldun sie is geld frummean* 'there they (each) were to perform his service.'

Accordingly we explain the Germanic use of neuter plural pronouns, adjectives, and participles in referring to nouns of various genders as a survival from Indo-European syntactic patterns which were in use before the development of the neuter gender. An *-h* was used to indicate collectives. In most Indo-European dialects, as in Germanic, the subsequent gender distinction became predominant, with the loss of this syntactic pattern. It survived however in Germanic, and we can equate these forms, like Gothic *þō* and *twa*, with Indo-European neuter plurals though their etyma of a previous period ended in a laryngeal *-h*.

THE UNIVERSITY OF TEXAS

MICHEL LEJEUNE

OBSERVATIONS SUR LES INSCRIPTIONS VÉNÉTO-LATINES

DU POINT de vue épigraphique et linguistique, la romanisation de l'Italie ancienne se caractérise par l'extension de l'alphabet latin aux dépens des alphabets locaux, et par l'extension de la langue latine aux dépens des parlers locaux. Mais, dans nos inscriptions, celle-ci apparaît comme postérieure à celle-là. La période de transition entre textes en langue et écriture locales, d'une part, textes en langue et écriture latines, d'autre part, se manifeste, généralement, par des *textes en langue locale et en écriture latine* (mais jamais par des textes en langue latine et en écriture locale). A une époque qui se situe environ entre 150 et 50 avant notre ère, on trouve, un peu partout, des documents de ce type, dont les représentants principaux sont la loi municipale de Bantia (Ve. 2)[1] et la rédaction la plus récente des Tables Eugubines (Ve. 239): ainsi, en pays lucanien (Ve. 195), campanien (Ve. 7), volsque (Ve. 222, etc.), marse (Ve. 224, etc.), pélignien (Ve. 202, etc.), marrucin (Ve. 218, etc.), ombrien (Ve. 232, etc.), capénate (Ve. 356, etc.). Il est même des parlers (volsque, etc.) que nous ne connaissons qu'à travers des inscriptions de ce type, faute d'avoir des textes en écriture locale.

b) Il faut ajouter que la délimitation entre inscriptions en 'parler local' et inscriptions latines n'est pas toujours aisée à définir avec rigueur: d'une part, parce qu'un certain nombre de formes peuvent être ambiguës,[2] d'autre part, parce qu'il existe des rédactions mixtes entremêlant l'une et l'autre langue de façons diverses; ainsi à Cumes (Ve. 7), à Corfinium (Ve. 214), à Luco (Ve. 228a), etc.

c) Si la délimitation entre 'alphabet local' et alphabet latin est plus aisée en général,

[1] Le sigle Ve., ci-après, renvoie au tome I [1953] du *Handbuch der Italischen Dialekte* de Emil Vetter.

[2] En particulier, certaines formes de noms de personnes, là où une désinence caractéristique ne distingue pas la déclinaison locale de la déclinaison latine. C'est ainsi que, parmi les urnes funéraires vénètes inscrites en alphabet latin, nous n'avons retenu comme vénéto-latines que celles qui présentent des datifs sing. en *-OI* (2e. décl.), *-AI* (1e décl.), *-EI* (3e décl.).

bien que beaucoup de signes soient à cet égard ambigus, il reste que, dans un petit nombre de cas, une caractéristique de l'écriture indigène peut être introduite dans l'écriture latine,[3] et que, plus souvent, dans les inscriptions tardives en alphabet local, le sens de l'écriture, ou la forme des lettres, ou l'orthographe même[4] subissent l'action de l'alphabet latin, déjà employé sur le même site à la même époque.

Ces rédactions mixtes ou ces graphies mixtes étaient, au reste, facilitées par la parenté ('italique') des langues en présence, et par la parenté (étrusque) des écritures en présence.

Nous nous proposons, ici, d'examiner d'ensemble les documents de cette période de transition sur le domaine vénète.[5]

2 Nous réunissons, d'abord, les textes qui appartiennent à cette catégorie. Ils proviennent: du sanctuaire d'Este (**a**, **b**), du sanctuaire de Làgole, sur le haut-Piave, près de Pieve di Cadore (**c**-**g**), et de nécropoles ou de tombes isolées: à Este (**h**-**q**), à la lisière des Préalpes et de la plaine au Nord-Ouest de Trévise (**r** : Montebelluna, **s** : Covolo), sur le moyen-Piave en amont de Belluno (**t** : Canevói). Deux de ces textes sont connus depuis le XVIIIe s.: **q**[6] et **t**[7]; puis, publication, par Ghirardini, de **r** et **s** en 1883, de **a** et **b** en 1888; publication, par Callegari, de **i** en 1928, de **h**, **k**, **l**, **m**, **n**, **o**, **p** en 1933; publication, par G. B. Pellegrini, de **c** en 1950, de **f** en 1952, de **d**, **e**, **g** en 1954. Sauf **t**, qui est perdu, nous avons personnellement revu et republié

[3] Par exemple: non-séparation des mots (cf. ci-dessous, **h**, **m**, **p**, **t**); introduction sporadique d'une 'ponctuation' locale (cf. ci-dessous, **d**, **e**, **m**, **p**); usage d'une lettre locale sans équivalent exact en latin (ainsi signe *ś* du lépontique dans une épitaphe en écriture latine à Levo: PID. II, p. 108) ou d'une lettre latine diacritée, sans qu'on sache si elle remonte ou non à un plus ancien alphabet local (ainsi signe *đ* en pélignien à Corfinium: Ve. 213); formes angulaires données aux tracés normalement arrondis de lettres latines (cf. ci-dessous, § 5); etc.

[4] Ainsi lorsque, dans un texte tardif en langue et écriture locales, on trouve *s* employé, au lieu de *ś* qu'on attendrait, sous l'action de l'écriture latine, laquelle n'a pas de signe propre de 'sifflante forte' (p. ex. *esanekoti* au lieu de **eśanekoti* dans l'épitaphe gauloise de Briona en écriture lépontique, PID 2.337).

[5] Notre hommage s'adresse, en particulier, à J. Whatmough éditeur du tome II des *Praeitalic Dialects of Italy*, et qui, précisément, a consacré un article aux urnes funéraires d'Este (*Class. Phil.* 29.280–292 [1934]) parmi lesquelles figurent les documents **h**, **k**, **l**, **m**, **n**, **o**, **p** de la présente étude.

[6] L'urne appartenait, dès la fin du XVIIIe s., à la collection Obizzi ,villa del Cataio (sur la route de Padoue à Monselice et Este). Elle y est signalée en 1789 par Lanzi, en 1842 par Cavedoni. En 1880, Gamurrini la publie, avec la fausse indication de provenance 'Mantova', d'après de médiocres copies trouvées dans les papiers de Lanzi; et c'est d'après Gamurrini qu'est ensuite reproduit ce texte d'une inscription réputée perdue, jusqu'au moment où E. Vetter retrouve et identifie l'urne à Vienne (*Glotta*, 25.257–262 [1936]).

[7] L'urne de Canevói se trouvait appartenir, en 1781, au chanoine Doglioni, qui la décrit minutieusement dans une lettre, conservée au musée de Belluno. D'après cette lettre, qui lui fut communiquée par un érudit local en 1896, Lattes publia l'inscription en 1901 dans les *Rendiconti dell' Istituto Lombardo* (Ser. 2, vol. 34.1131–1134 [1901]). Le chanoine Doglioni mourut en 1804, et, une trentaine d'années plus tard, sa famille étant éteinte, les biens en furent dispersées; l'urne est demeurée jusqu'à présent introuvable.

(souvent avec de nouvelles lectures) toutes ces inscriptions.[8] Les documents sont conservés au musée d'Este, sauf **c** – **g** (musée de Làgole), **q** (Kunsthistorisches Museum, Wien), **r**, **s** (Musée de Trévise) et **t** (perdu).

Dédicaces sur bronze à Este[9]

a) PID. 5 = **M** V (plaque)
lignes 6–7 : [*vda*.]*n*[.] *vo*.*l*.*t*[*i*]*i*[*o*.*n*.]*mno*.*s*. [*do*]*na*.*s*.*to kela*.*g*.[ ] |
[*śa*.*i*.]*nate*.*i*. *re*.*i*.*tiia*.*i*. *o*.*p* [*vo*].*l*.*tiio len*[*o*]
ligne 8 : [*D*]*O*[*NVM*] *DEDIT LIBENS MERITO*
lignes 9–10: . . .], *kn*, *mn*, *ml*, *sr*, *sl*, *bl*, *gr*, *g*[. . . | . . .] *n*, *p*[*l*, *v*]*hn*, *pn*, *pr*, *br*, *śl*, *śn*, *tr*
ligne 11 : [———], *V*, *R*, *E*, [–], *G*, *D*, *H*, *O*, *I*, *N*, *K*, *M*, [—]

b) PID. 7 = **M** XXI (plaque)
ligne 3 : *MEGO DONASTO*
ligne 6 : [*A*], *B*, *C*, *D*, *E*, *F*, *G*, *H*, *I*, *K*, *L*, *M*, *N*, *O*, [*P*], *Q*, *R*, *S*, *T*, *V*, *X*.

Dédicaces sur bronze à Làgole

c) Pe. 13 = **AB** 14 (plaque)
. . . *T*]*RIBVSIATIN* . *D* . *L*[. *M* .]

d) Pe. 72 = **AB** 11 (manche de simpule)
V.*OLSOMNOS ENNICEIOS* | *V* . *S* . *L* . *M* . *TRVM*(*VSIATEI*)

e) Pe. 66 = **AB** 12 (manche de simpule)
FV[–]*V*.*S*. .*I*.*OVONICVS* . *TRVMVSIA* | [*TEI* .] *DONOM*

f) Pe. 52 = **AB** 13 (piédestal de statuette)
L . *APINIVS* . *L* . *F* . *TRVMV*[*SIA*]*TEI* . *V* . *S* . *L* . *M* .

g) Pe. 64 = **AB** 10 (manche de simpule)
[–]*E TRV*

Épitaphes sur urnes de terre-cuite à Este[10]

h) Ca. 1933/36 = Wh. 10 = **T** XXVII

[8] Nous donnons en italiques minuscules les textes en écriture vénète, en italiques majuscules les textes en écriture latine. — L'ensemble de la bibliographie est donné dans nos articles, à quoi nous renvoyons par les sigles ci-après: **M** = *Rev. Ét. Anc.* 55.58–112 (1953); **T** = *Rev. Ét. Lat.* 31.117–176 (1953); **U** = *Rendiconti dei Lincei*, ser. 8, vol. 9.21–33 (1954); **V** = *Rev. Ét. Anc.* 56.61–89 (1954); **AB** = *Rev. Ét. Lat.* 32.120–138 (1954), (avec renvoi à nos articles antérieurs sur Làgole). Autres sigles: PID = vol. I [1953], par R. S. Conway, des *Praeitalic Dialects of Italy;* Ca. = Callegari, *Not. Sc.* 1928, p. 13–17, et 1933, p. 123–143; Wh. = Whatmough, *Class. Phil.* 29.280–292 (1934); Pe. = G. B. Pellegrini, *Rendiconti dei Lincei*, ser. 8 ,vol. 5.307–332 (1950), (pour Pe. 13); *ibid.* vol. 7.58–74 (1952), (pour Pe. 52); *Atti del II Convegno Internazionale di Linguisti*, Milano 1953 (pour Pe. 64, 66, 72). Dans tous les cas, nos références se font par ces sigles et par le *numéro* du texte dans le travail cité.

[9] Notes critiques. Dans **a**, le texte ici donné s'écarte de celui de **M** sur deux points: lecture *leno* (et non *veno*) à la ligne 7 (cf. *Rev. Ét. Anc.* 56.86 [1954]); lacune d'une lettre entre *E* et *G* à la ligne 11.

[10] Notes critiques. Nous avons préféré, dans **n**, restituer *LEMETO*[*RI*]*NAI* (plutôt que *LEME-*

ligne 1 : *LEMONEI*
ligne 2 : *LEMONEI ENNONIOI* (écrit sans séparation des mots)

i) Ca. 1928/19 = **T** XXVIII
GENTEI . IVANTIOI

k) Ca. 1933/55 = Wh. 28 = **T** XXIX
EGETOREI . CRVMEL[ONIOI]

l) Ca. 1933/44 = Wh. 18 = **T** XXX (urne réemployée)
ligne 1 : *VANTAI*
ligne 2 : *IVANTEIAI . FREMAISTINAI*

m) Ca. 1933/46 = Wh. 20 = **T** XXXI (urne réemployée)
ligne 1 : *FO[VGONT]AI OST.INAI* (écrit sans séparation des mots)
ligne 2 : *FOVGON[ ]A[ ]O[ ]ONAI*

n) Ca. 1933/58 = Wh. 19 = **T** XXXII
P[RI]MAI . RV[TILI]AI [.] LEMETO[RI]NAI

o) Ca. 1933/47 = Wh. 21 = **T** XXXIII
FOVGONTAI . FVGISONIAI . PRIGDINAI . EGO

p) Ca. 1933/43 = Wh. 17 = **T** XXXIV
FREMA . .I.VANTINA : KTVLISTOI VESCES (les deux derniers mots non séparés)

q) **T** XXXV
FOVGONTAI . EGTOREI . FILIA . FVGENIA . LAMVSIOI

Épitaphe sur urne de terre-cuite à Montebelluna[11]

r) PID. 156 = **U** II
ligne 1 : *OSTIANCO . USEDICA*
ligne 2 : *ostiianko . u[śedika]*

Épitaphe sur urne de terre-cuite à Covolo

s) **U** VII
FEMA . MARTRICAI

Épitaphe sur urne de bronze à Canevói

t) PID. 157

TO[R]NAI, texte de **T**, où l'autre possibilité était d'ailleurs indiquée); et nous avons préféré, dans **p**, laisser en un mot *KTVLISTOI* (que nous interprétions, non sans hésitation, dans **T**, par *K TVLISTOI*).

[11] Notes critiques. Nous préférons résoudre en *-an-* la ligature que, moins vraisemblablement, nous résolvions, dans **U**, en *-ai-* (**U**: *OSTIAICO* et *ostiiaiko*). Suffixation celtique; cf., à Làgole, *iion.ko.s.* (**AB** 16), *resun.ko.s.* (**AB** 17), [ ]*a.i.son.ko.s.* (**AB** 19), [ ]*n.ka* (**AB** 54), et voir Holder, III, 607. Ici, nom individuel féminin en *-ō* (thème à nasale); la souche *Osti-* paraît d'ailleurs vénète, non celtique. Mais le patronyme est celtique dans tous ses éléments (souche *Ux-*, suffixe *-edo-*, dérivation patronymique en *-iko-*).

ENONI . ONTEI . APPIOI . SSELBOISSELBOI . ANDETICOBOS ECVPETARIS (les deux derniers mots probablement non séparés)

3 Dans l'examen des phénomènes de transition, liés à la romanisation, nous négligerons ici (mais en en soulignant l'intérêt) la transformation du système anthroponymique; nous avons étudié ailleurs[12] ces données, qui concernent les institutions au même titre que la langue.

Nous examinerons successivement : l'alphabet latin en tant que transposition de l'alphabet vénète dans les documents '*vda*' (§ 6); les inscriptions juxtaposant un même texte en deux écritures (§ 7); les inscriptions juxtaposant un énoncé vénète en alphabet local et un énoncé latin en alphabet latin (bilingues au sens strict : § 8); enfin les inscriptions en écriture latine dont la langue est, totalement ou partielle ment, vénète (§ 9), appartenant à la catégorie définie au § 1*a*, et qui nous fournissent de précieuses informations sur la valeur phonétique de certaine signes de l'écriture locale (§ 10).

Des interférences linguistiques définies au § 1*b*, il sera question à propos des textes vénéto-latins (§ 9). Des interférences graphiques définies au § 1*c*, nous disons un mot tout de suite (§§ 4–5).

4 À l'époque où les deux écritures sont, concurremment, en usage, il s'est, certainement, exercé une action de l'écriture latine sur l'écriture vénète. Mais les marques de cette action sont inégalement aisées à mettre en évidence.

a) Les *fautes de ponctuation*[13] qu'on relève, sporadiquement, dans les inscriptions vénètes, n'y apparaissent pas sensiblement plus nombreuses à date récente qu'à date ancienne,[14] et il y aurait quelque arbitraire à les imputer, pour la période de transition, à l'influence de l'écriture latine (qui ignore la ponctuation syllabique). En revanche, les cas, d'ailleurs très rares, où l'écriture vénète tardive, en plus de la

[12] Dans *Word* 11.24–44 (1955). On y ajoutera d'utiles remarques de J. Untermann, *BzN* 7.173–194 (1956).

[13] Rappelons que sont ponctués en vénète (c'est à dire précédés et suivis d'un point, ou d'un petit tiret vertical): 1°) les signes des voyelles *u*, *o*, *a*, *e* (les exemples manquent pour *i*) lorsque ces voyelles sont initiales de syllabe (c'est à dire initiales de mot, ou, pour *o*, *a*, *e*, en hiatus dans le mot après une autre voyelle); 2°) les signes des phonèmes (seconds éléments de diphtongue ou consonnes) qui appartiennent à la partie descendante (c'est à dire postvocalique) de la syllabe.

[14] La datation des textes vénètes est souvent très incertaine. Eléments *internes* de datation: caractères de l'écriture (mais ce critère est d'application souvent difficile et imprécise); présence d'éléments anthroponymiques celtiques (ce qui implique une date postérieure à 300) ou romains (ce qui implique une date postérieure, en gros, à 125). Eléments *externes*: nature du support de l'inscription (p. ex. facture des vases, type des urnes, etc.); contexte archéologique. — Pratiquement, c'est seulement pour Este que le contexte archéologique a permis l'établissement (Ghirardini) de la chronologie générale d'un site vénète. Tous les textes atestins appartiennent soit à ESTE–III (450–300: période preceltique), soit à ESTE–IV (300–125: période marquée par des influences celtiques), soit à l'époque romaine (postérieure à ESTE–IV).

ponctuation syllabique, emploie des points comme *séparateurs de mots*,[15] relèvent, certainement, de l'influence latine. Nous en avons mis en évidence[16] un exemple sûr à Gurina[17] et signalé deux autres exemples possibles (mais non certains) dans des fragments de textes à Gurina[18] et à Este.[19] A l'action du latin ressortissent aussi les séparations de mots par des blancs, que l'on constate sporadiquement[20] à Idria,[21] à Làgole[22] et à Este.[23]

b) Le *sens* de l'écriture ne donne, par lui-même, que des indications incertaines. Il est vrai que le sens rétrograde est, de beaucoup, le plus fréquent dans les documents anciens; même dans ceux qui sont tracés boustrophédon, la ligne initiale est, presque toujours, orientée de droite à gauche;[24] l'écriture rétrograde est l'écriture vénète 'classique'.[25] Cependant, même à date ancienne, il y a quelques exemples de textes

[15] Rappelons que l'écriture vénète use de la *scriptio continua*, sans autres exceptions que celles signalées ici. — A propos de la ponctuation, irrégulière, à Làgole, d'un *ś*- initial dans **AB** 52 = Pe. 48, d'un *s*- initial dans **AB** 17 = Pe. 41, voir *Latomus* 12.7 n. 3 (1953), et cf., plus bas, la note 42.

[16] *Rev. Ét. Anc.* 55.94 sv. (1953).

[17] Plaque votive PID. 166 (dont la lecture correcte, à cet égard, n'avait pas été reconnue), portant (avec *d* et *m* de forme latine, non vénète) *.a. .t.to . dona.s.to . .a. .i.su.m.* ('Atto donauit deum').

[18] Fragment de plaque votive PID. 171, portant, s'il s'agit d'une fin (?) de dédicace, . . .]*ua*. ; mais voir les réserves exprimées (p. 97, n. 89) dans l'article cité à la note 16, réserves que nous serions disposé à formuler, aujourd'hui, de façon encore plus nette.

[19] Fragment de plaque votive jusque là inédite; mais voir les réserves exprimées dans l'article cité à la note 16.

[20] Voir *Rev. Ét. Anc.* 54.64 (1952).

[21] Écuelle de bronze PID. 164a; mais les deux mêmes mots sont écrits sans séparation sur le pot de bronze 164b. Nous avons revu ces textes en 1952 au Musée d'Histoire Naturelle de Vienne (Autriche).

[22] Dans **AB** 33 = Pe. 36; cf. aussi, mais les cas sont particuliers, la seconde ligne de **AB** 66 = Pe. 4, et **AB** 28 = Pe. 5.

[23] Urne PID. 136e = T XXI, laquelle produit plusieurs indices d'influence latine (sens direct de l'écriture; *s*- au lieu de *ś*-, voir plus bas § 4*e*).

[24] Il ne semble pas que ce fait, à nos yeux significatif, ait été, jusqu'ici, relevé. A titre d'exemple, nous donnons ici une liste des textes boustrophédon *sur pierre* (avec l'indication: 'dir'., ou 'rétr.', ou '?' du sens de l'écriture aux lignes qui suivent la première). — *Avec ligne initiale rétrograde*, à Este: PID. 110 (2: dir.; 3: rétr.); 111, face principale (2 et 3: rétr.); 112 (2: dir.); 114 (2: dir.); 115a (2: dir.); 117 (2: dir.); 118 (2: dir.); 120, faces A et B (2: rétr.); 121 (2: rétr.); 122 (2: rétr.); 123, faces A et B (2: rétr.); 124 (2: ?); 125 (2: dir.); obélisque (inconnu des PID) *.e.go K*[. . . | . . .]*io.i.* (2: ?); obélisque PID. 147, faussement attribué à Padoue (2: rétr.). À Padoue, PID. 146 (2: ?). À Roganzuolo, PID. 158 (2: rétr.). Au Monte Pore, PID. 159 (2: rétr.). À Pozzale, PID. 160 (2: rétr.). À Lozzo, PID. 161 (2: rétr.). — Un seul exemple connu *avec ligne initiale de sens direct*, à Este: PID. 119 (2: dir.); c'est, d'ailleurs, le plus ancien de nos obélisques funéraires (vers 450).

[25] On peut la dire classique parce qu'elle est, de beaucoup la plus répandue. Ainsi, au sanctuaire d'Este, sont écrites de droite à gauche: toutes les dédicaces sur plaques; seize sur vingt-deux des dédicaces sur épingles (exceptions: PID. 24, 26, 28 et Cordenons 23, qui sont de sens direct; PID. 17 et 20, avec première ligne directe, seconde rétrograde); sept sur dix des dédicaces sur piédestaux de pierre (exceptions: PID. 110, boustrophédon, première ligne rétr., seconde directe, troisième rétr. PID. 107 et 108, tracées selon trois côtés d'un carré, avec variation de sens à chaque ligne). — On peut la dire classique, surtout, à cause de son caractère 'officiel': sur les 'tablettes alphabétiques' d'Este, c'est de droite à gauche que sont présentés les éléments rituels et immuables de ce type d'offrandes: liste des consonnes, et lettres *a*, *k*, *e*, *o* de la formule magique (seize fois répétée) *a ke o*.

écrits de gauche à droite;[26] et cette pratique, tout en demeurant rare, n'a jamais dû s'éteindre complètement. Elle a, très certainement, reçu un sensible renforcement à partir du moment où l'écriture latine a commencé d'être connue. Mais le sens direct, dans une inscription, ne peut être retenu comme un indice d'influence romaine que si d'autres indices corroborent cette interprétation.

c) On peut aussi, avec prudence, tirer des indications de la *forme des lettres*. — En regard de l'*a* caractéristique des inscriptions d'Este, de Padoue et de Vicence, *tous* les autres sites vénètes (dont les textes sont plus ou moins tardifs) présentent, pour *a*, un tracé latinoïde. Il serait hasardé d'invoquer une action du latin. Dans l'ignorance où nous sommes des conditions dans lesquelles l'écriture s'est diffusée dans les diverses régions vénètes, il demeure plus plausible, jusqu'à nouvel ordre, de supposer, en ce cas, une autre 'école' de scribes, sans faire intervenir l'influence de Rome. En revanche, le *a* latinoïde qui figure à Este dans le pseudo-texte PID. 140,[27] celui qui, à lui seul, constitue l'inscription d'une minuscule plaque votive d'Este,[28] et celui qui paraît à Padoue sur une stèle funéraire tardive[29] sont, à coup sûr, des latinismes graphiques. — Latinismes aussi, le *m* avec, à droite et à gauche, des jambage verticaux égaux, tel qu'il apparaît sporadiquement à Làgole[30] et probablement aussi à Gurina;[31] ou le *d* latinoïde qu'on trouve une fois à Gurina.[32] Mais la chose paraît moins sûre pour le *t* latinoïde qu'on trouve une fois à Vicence.[33]

[26] À Este, le plus ancien des textes en sens direct (obélisque funéraire PID. 115) date de la période ESTE–III (450–300) et doit être antérieur à la fois aux dédicaces du sanctuaire (cf. note 25) et aux urnes funéraires inscrites (parmi lesquelles T II, III, VII, VIII, XI, XII, XIII, XV, XIX, XXI, XXII, XXIIIb sont écrites de gauche à droite). — À Padoue, c'est sans doute du Ve s. que datent les inscriptions sur vases PID. 150, 151 (écrites en sens direct), très antérieures aux deux textes sur pierre écrits de gauche à droite (PID. 143, 144). — On ne possède aucun texte vénète archaïque hors d'Este et de Padoue.

[27] Peson de métier à tisser, en terre cuite, provenant de la nécropole de Morlungo, avec inscription gravée avant cuisson: pseudo-texte, où se lisent quelques mots ou fragments de mots, et des lettres sans signification; certaines de ces lettres sont de type latin, comme le *a*; d'autres sont des souvenirs de l'écriture archaïque d'Este: nous avons vu un *h* archaïque dans ce que Conway lit *e* (face b, ligne 1, avant-dernière lettre), et nous reconnaissons un θ archaïque (carré avec croisillons, comme dans la liste des consonnes des tablettes alphabétiques) dans ce que Conway lit *x* (face b, ligne 2, seconde lettre).

[28] PID. 14.

[29] Cordenons 91; voir PID. 142, remarque.

[30] Voir, sur les formes de *ś* et de *m* à Làgole, *Rev. Ét. Anc.* 54.71 et n. 43 (1952). On a des *m* de type latin dans **AB** 63 = Pe. 3, **AB** 65 = Pe. 12, **AB** 67 = Pe. 35.

[31] Il s'agit de la plaque PID. 166, où nous proposons de lire *.a. .i.su.m.* plutôt que *.a. .i.su.ś.*, avec un *m* latin. En fait, à en juger par la plaque PID. 167 (sur quoi, *Rev. Ét. Anc.* 54.267–274 [1952]), l'accusatif sg. et l'accusatif pl. sont tous deux possibles. Si l'on admet que la finale d'acc. sg. pouvait être, à Gurina, non seulement en *-n* (dont on a deux exemples, PID. 167 et 169), mais aussi en *-m*, de même que les deux finales coexistent à Làgole, l'interprétation par *-m* dans PID. 166 a pour elle les autres marques d'influence latine que manifeste ce texte tardif (présence de *d* de forme latine; mots séparés par des interponctions). Au reste l'accusatif pluriel, dans PID. 167, est en *-s*, non en *-ś*.

[32] Dans le verbe *dona.s.to* de PID. 166.

[33] PID. 157: sur un vaste linteau de pierre, inscription dédicatoire d'un monument; gravure soignée; écriture angulaire, orientée de droite à gauche; ponctuation correcte; rien ne dénonce un texte tardif.

d) On peut tenir compte, aussi, du *style graphique*: celui du vénète est, en principe, angulaire; le *r* est un triangle à peu près isocèle, dont la base est verticale; le *o* est un losange, le *b* un losange barré verticalement, le *θ* un losange pointé. L'action de l'écriture latine a contribué à *favoriser*, pour ces lettres, un tracé arrondi:[34] semi-circulaire pour *r* (à l'instar du *D* latin), circulaire pour *o* (et, conséquemment, pour *b* et *θ*). Mais le style arrondi n'apporte qu'une *présomption* de date tardive et d'influence romaine, non une preuve. Parmi les obélisques funéraires d'Este,[35] tous antérieurs à l'époque romaine, il y a six 'mains' angulaires,[36] neuf 'mains' arrondies[37] et trois 'mains' qui tracent *r* en demi-cercle, mais *o* en losange.[38] On ne retiendra donc le style courbe comme indice d'influence latine que si, pour un texte donné, d'autres indices engagent à cette hypothèse.

e) L'écriture latine possédait des lettres pour rendre tous les sons[39] notés par l'écriture vénète, sauf dans le cas du signe de sifflante forte *ś* (voir § 10); à une exception près (texte **t**), c'est par *S* que le latin rendait, aussi bien *ś* du vénète (textes **p, r**)

Le verbe 'donauit' est, normalement, *dona.s.to* en vénète, mais présente occasionnellement une forme (à assimilation régressive) *tona.s.to* (cf. *Rev. Ét. Anc.* 54.64 [1952]), attestée une fois à Este (PID. 28) et quatre fois à Làgole (**AB** 15 = Pe. 69; **AB** 16 = Pe. 11; **AB** 17 = Pe. 41; **AB** 19 = Pe. 7). La dédicace de Vicence présente trois exemplaires du *t* vénète normal (en forme de *x* latin), notamment, dans la désinence du verbe; mais la consonne initiale du verbe a la forme d'un *t* latin (haste verticale, dont le haut rencontre, en son milieu, un trait supérieur légèrement incliné). Plutôt que de lire, ici, *tona.s.to*, avec deux formes différentes (l'une atestine, l'autre latinoïde) de *t*, nous préférons lire *dona.s.to*, en admettant que, pour noter *d*, l''école de Vicence' a choisi (de préférence au *z* étrusque) une des formes étrusques de *t*. On observera qu'à Padoue (où *t* est noté par la consonne *θ* de l'étrusque), on ne connaît aucun signe pour *d*; doit-on supposer que, pour *d*, l''école de Padoue' a choisi (de préférence au *z* étrusque) le *t* étrusque, qui restait disponible? En ce cas, dans PID. 142, interpréter par *plede.i.* le premier mot. Ce qui donne quelque corps à cette hypothèse est la dédicace PID. 33 d'Este, écrite selon l'orthographe padouane avec *θ* pour *t*, mais où le verbe est écrit *tona.s.θo*.

[34] On rencontre même, dans la dédicace **AB** 16 = Pe. 11 de Làgole, laquelle a pour *o* et *r* des formes arrondies, des *s* également arrondis à la latine.

[35] On notera, pour Este: style angulaire pour *o* et *r* sur toutes les épingles votives; style angulaire pour *o* et arrondi pour *r* sur toutes les plaques votives (sauf deux: PID. 2 et 6a, où *r* et *o* sont angulaires); style généralement angulaire sur les piédestaux votifs; style angulaire sur les pierres funéraires PID. 111 (face principale = première main) et PID. 127, mais style arrondi sur les pierres funéraires PID. 111 (face latérale = seconde main) et PID. 126, 128; style généralement angulaire sur les urnes funéraires, mais *o* angulaire et *r* arrondi dans **T** XI et XVIII, style arrondi dans **T** II, III, VIII, XIII, XXV, XXVI.

[36] PID. 115 (ESTE–III), 117 (ESTE–III), 123 (IIIe s.), 124, 125.

[37] PID. 112 (ESTE–III), 113, 115a, 116 (ESTE–III), 118, 119 (vers 450), 120 (vers 300), 122 (ESTE–III), 125a. On voit que ce style s'est manifesté, depuis notre texte le plus ancien (PID. 119), pendant une longue période.

[38] PID. 114 (qui, à la ligne 2, présente aussi deux *o* ronds), 121 (IIIe s.), 147; sur d'autres exemples de cette association des deux styles à Este, voir note 35.

[39] Elle a aussi un signe *X* répondant au groupe *-.g.s.-* du vénète; sur les urnes latines d'Este, *FVXSIA* (**T** LXXXIII, LXXXVII) répond à vén. *vhu.g.siia* (PID. 18, 23), cf. *LOXINA* (urne **T** LV; ce serait, en vénète **lo.g.sna*) et *lo.g.sii(a)* (PID. 25). Mais nous n'avons pas d'exemple du signe latin *X* introduit, en place de *-.g. s-* dans une inscription en écriture locale (à moins de lire *sex.*, et non, comme nous le préférons, *set.*, le second mot de l'épitaphe sur urne PID. 136e: voir plus bas).

que *s*; il en est résulté, en vénète même, à l'époque de transition, une tendance[40] à substituer *s* à *ś*: à Este, par exemple, au patronyme abrégé *śet* de l'épitaphe sur pierre PID. 123 (IIIe s.) répond le patronyme abrégé *set.* de l'épitaphe, plus tardive,[41] sur urne PID. 136e.

5 Inversement, à l'époque de la romanisation commençante, l'écriture vénète, encore en usage, a pu influencer l'écriture latine. Mais cette influence est modeste.

a) On a quelques exemples de *scriptio continua* pour le vénète noté en écriture latine (textes **h**; **m**; **p**; **t**). On a aussi quelques exemples de *ponctuation* qui évoquent l'usage vénète; ponctuation finale dans *FV*[–]*V.S.* (**e**), qui serait correcte en vénète (*-o.s.*); pontuation intérieure dans *OST.INAI* (**m**), qui serait incorrecte en vénète (**.o..s.tna.i.*); ponctuation, à trois reprises, d'une semi-voyelle initiale, dans *V.OLSOMNOS* (**d**), dans *.I.OVONICVS* (**e**), dans *.I.VANTINA* (**p**), souvenir altéré de l'usage vénète de ponctuer les voyelles initiales.[42]

b) Aucune action du vénète sur le *sens* de l'écriture latine; tout au plus peut-on rattacher à des habitudes graphiques locales quelques rares exemples de *lettres inversées*.[43]

c) Aucune action du vénète sur la *forme* des lettres latines.

d) Mais action sporadique du vénète sur le *style* graphique latin: certaines lettres latines, normalement arrondies, deviennent, à l'occasion, angulaires.[44]

6 Venons-en, maintenant, aux textes eux-mêmes.

La situation du vénète est à part, en ce sens que l'alphabet complet,[45] ou l'alphabet réduit aux consonnes,[46] ou divers groupements de lettres[47] y constituaient, par eux-

[40] Même tendance en gaulois: voir note 4.

[41] Avec ponctuation irrégulière, écriture de gauche à droite, et blanc entre les mots.

[42] Encore faut-il noter que nous n'avons pas d'exemple de voyelle *i* initiale ponctuée en vénète (voir note 13); seuls cas: PID. 6b (où il n'est pas sûr que ...].*i.tona* soit un mot complet; exempli gratia [.*a*].*i.tona*), PID. 127 (*iθuria*, écrit sans ponctuation); PID. 144 (où il est improbable que ...].*i.θo.s.* soit un mot complet). — Autre tentative d'explication de ces ponctuations initiales incorrectes, dans l'article cité à la note 15.

[43] Par exemple le *N* de *DONASTO* dans **b**; etc.

[44] Par exemple, *R* et *D* à la ligne 11 de **a**; *O* et *S* à la 1.3 de **b**; *R*, *B*, *S* et *D* dans **c**; *O* et *S* dans **d**; *D* dans **e**; *R* dans **g**; *O* à la ligne 1 de **h**; *S* et *C* dans **r**; *C* dans **s**; etc. On notera que le *D* latin introduit dans PID. 166 (voir note 32) est angulaire comme ceux de **a**, **c**, **e**.

[45] Une fois, dans la partie supérieure de la tablette **M** I, abécédaire complet (toutes les lettres, de plus, sont 'ponctuées'), mais avec omission accidentelle de *n*, et ligatures d'une part de *θ*, *i*, *k* (ce qui rend le *i* non apparent), d'autre part de *ś*, *r* : *a*, *e*, *v*, *d*, *h*, *θ*, *i*, *k*, *l*, *m*, < *n* >, *p*, *ś*, *r*, *s*, *t*, *u*, *b*, *g*, *o*.

[46] Liste: *v*, *d*, *h*, *θ*, *k*, *l*, *m*, *n*, *p*, *ś*, *r*, *s*, *t*, *b*, *g*, sans aucune faute ou variante, à la ligne du bas de la partie inférieure (de structure constante) des tablettes **M** I, II, III, IV, V, VI, VIII, XV, XVI; la seule où une mutilation du bronze n'ait pas fait disparaître une portion de la liste est **M** I; comme il n'y avait que quinze consonnes, mais seize cases à remplir, la dernière case (à gauche) est garnie avec un signe quelconque, *a* dans IV, *e* dans I et II, *ii* (une des notations vénètes de yod) dans III.

[47] D'une part, formule, seize fois répétée à la partie inférieure des tablettes **M** I à XVII (dans la

mêmes, des *textes* rituels, dans des documents nommés à Este *vda*,[48] et associant des préoccupations pédagogiques (ou le souvenir de telles préoccupations) avec des croyances magiques.[49]

A l'époque de transition, nous voyons[50] un alphabet latin (l'alphabet de 21 lettres des deux derniers siècles de la République) assumer, par équivalence, le rôle de l'alphabet vénète sur les plaques votives d'Este, soit en s'y juxtaposant dans **a**,[51] soit en s'y substituant dans **b**.[52]

7 Un document funéraire de l'époque de transition (**r**) est, non pas bilingue mais 'digraphe': il juxtapose l'inscription en caractères vénètes et l'inscription en caractères latins du nom et de l'adjectif patronymique de la défunte.[53] Sur cette urne de Montebelluna, les deux inscriptions ont été tracées avant cuisson et de la même main: juxtaposition, donc, évidemment intentionnelle, et destinée à faciliter la lecture de l'épitaphe au moment où une forme de culture locale et la culture romaine coexistent en Vénétie.

8 Un seul document (**a**) est, à proprement parler, bilingue, c'est à dire présente

plupart des cas, avec des lacunes plus ou moins étendues dues aux mutilations du bronze, mais sans aucune variante): *akeo*, que nous avons interprétée par *a ke o* ('*a* et *o*', première et dernière lettre de l'abécédaire vénète, cf. grec τὸ ἄλφα καὶ τὸ ὦ). — D'autre part, dans la partie supérieure des tablettes **M** I à XIV (ici encore, lacunes plus ou moins étendues), liste des 'groupes', dont le type pourrait être: *vhr, vhl, vhn, vh, dr, dn, dl, θr, θl, θn, kr, kl, kn, kv, mr, ml, mn, pr, pl, pn, śr, śl, śn, sr, sl, sn, tr, tl, tn, br, bl, bn, gr, gl, gn*, mais avec des variations de tablette à tablette (interversions ou omissions); nous avons expliqué cette liste comme étant celle des groupements (graphiques) des consonnes de l'abécédaire tels que jamais (en raison des règles de ponctuation syllabique du vénète) le premier élément n'a à en être ponctué, quand ces groupements figurent dans un mot entre deux voyelles. — Sur ces deux faits, voir *Rev. Phil.* 26.199–204 (1952). Sont arrivés, indépendamment, à des interprétations anlogues: pour le premier fait, O. Haas, pour le second, M. S. Beeler.

48 L'interprétation de ce terme a été trouvée par O. Haas (*Die Sprache*, 2.227 [1954]); il y a reconnu le nom même de l' 'alphabet' en vénète, formé (avec, à la fin, un suffixe *-ā-* de dérivation) des noms des deux premières consonnes de l'alphabet, *v* et *d* (ceci étant lié à l'attention particulière, que manifestent nos tablettes, pour l'alphabet réduit aux consonnes). Le nom *vda* est, dans nos dédicaces d'Este, appliqué, d'une part aux tablettes (il se lit dans **M** V, VI, VII), d'autre part aux épingles (il se lit dans **V** XII, XIII, XIV); or les épingles présentent très souvent (voir détail dans PID) un remplissage des portions non occupées par la dédicace au moyen de lettres diverses, dépourvues de signification, mais sûrement pourvues de valeur magique.

49 Voir *Rev. Phil.* 26.199–204 (1952).

50 Mais ceci avait échappé en grande partie à Conway, du moins pour la ligne 11 de **a**.

51 La ligne 11 de **a** nous présente presque sûrement (onze lettres subsistantes; place pour une dizaine de lettres dans les lacunes du bronze) l'alphabet républicain latin de 21 lettres, mais dans un désordre qui paraît voulu, et qui est comme le reflet du complet désordre que manifeste, aux lignes 9–10, la 'liste des groupes' vénète (cf. note 47). La tablette est bilingue (voir § 8). Les lignes 1–5 (non reproduites au § 2) sont conformes au type général (liste des consonnes; formule *a ke o* seize fois répétée).

52 La tablette n'a que deux lignes écrites (données au § 2): l'une fournit l'alphabet latin républicain (substitut de l'alphabet vénète des documents de l'époque antérieure, dans le même rôle rituel); l'autre fournit un début de dédicace en langue vénète et écriture latine (§ 9), méconnu par Conway.

53 Ce type de désignation est vénète (et aussi celtique) mais non latin. Voir aussi note 57.

côte à côte (abstraction faite des alphabets considérés comme textes, voir § 6) une formule en langue et écriture latine (ligne 8) destinée à servir de traduction approximative à certains éléments, au moins, de la formule votive en langue et écriture vénètes (lignes 6–7): *[D]O[NVM] DEDIT* répond à peu près à vénète *dona.s.to*[54] et *LIBENS MERITO* répond à peu près à vénète *.o.p vo.l.tiio leno.*[55]

9 La plupart des textes réunis au § 2 sont en langue vénète et en écriture latine (textes **b**/3; **c** à **q**; **r**/1: voir § 7; **s** et **t**).

Les épitaphes, selon le formulaire vénète, ont, pour la plupart, au datif (finales vénètes[56]: *-AI*, en première déclinaison; *-OI* en seconde; *-EI* en troisième) le nom individuel du défunt, suivi ou non d'un adjectif dérivé du nom du père (pour les hommes, et les femmes mariées ou non mariées)[57] ou du nom de l'époux (pour les femmes mariées),[58] la tombe pouvant être désignée, au nominatif, soit (**o**) par le pronom vénète (identique au pronom latin) *EGO*[59], soit (**t**) par un substantif signifiant 'monument funéraire', comme *ECUPETARIS.*[60] Il arrive aussi que, comme dans certaines épitaphes en écriture vénète,[61] le formulaire funéraire comporte, au nominatif, le nom de la personne qui a rendu les honneurs funèbres, et au datif celui du défunt; c'est le cas[62] dans nos textes **p**, **q**, **s**; figure en plus, dans **p**, un mot de nature

[54] Le verbe de dédicace (3e sg.), toujours avec désinences moyennes, est, en vénète, soit *dona.s.to* (lat. *dōnāuit*), soit *doto* (lat. *dedit*), soit (vénète septentrional) *doto dono.n.* (lat. *dōnum dedit*), soit (vénète septentrional) *tole.r.*; voir *Rev. Phil.* 26.206–207 (1952).

[55] Cf. aussi (vénète septentrional) *pe.r. vo.l.te.r.ko.n. vo.n.ta.r.*; dans ces deux formules, il semble que l'adjectif *vo.l.tiio* (instrum.), *vo.l.te.r.ko.n.* (accus.), corresponde à peu près, pour le sens, à *LIBENS;* l'idée exprimée par *MERITO*, à supposer qu'elle se retrouve en vénète, serait alors impliquée par *leno* ou *vo.n.ta.r.;* sur ces formules, voir *Rev. Phil.* 26.212 (1952), avec correctif apporté (cf. note 9) dans *Rev. Ét. Anc.* 26.86 (1954).

[56] En écriture vénète (nombreux exemples): *-a.i.*, *-o.i.*, *-e.i.*.

[57] En vénète méridional, l'adjectif patronymique est, le plus souvent un dérivé en *-yo-*; ceux de nos textes seraient, en écriture vénète (dat. sg.), *.e.n.noniio.i.* (**h**), *iiuva.n.tiio.i.* (**i**), *krumeloniio.i.* (**k**), *vhugisoniia.i.* (**o**), *lamusiio.i.* (**q**); cf. aussi, à Làgole, le dérivé en *-eyyo-* qui serait, en écriture vénète (nomin. sg.) *.e.n.nike.i.iio.s.* (**d**); mais, en vénète central et septentrional, il est, le plus souvent, un dérivé en *-ko-*, ainsi celui qui (**t**) s'ecrirait en vénète (dat. pl.) *.a.n.detikobo.s.*; cf. aussi nomin. sg. *.u.śedika* (**r**). Cf. *Word* 11.35–39 (1955).

[58] Adjectif en *-nā-* dérivé du nom de l'époux (cf. *Word* 11.39–44 [1955]), avec, dans les textes vénéto-latins, latinisation en *-INA;* les exemples de nos textes seraient, en écriture vénète (dat. sg.), *vhrema.i.s.tna.i.* (**l**), *.o.s.tna.i.* (**m**); le détail de la 1.2 reste obscur), *lemeto.r.na.i.* (**n**; cf. note 10), *pri.g.dna.i.* (**o**); cf. (nomin. sg.) *iiuva.n.tna* en **p**.

[59] Exemples fréquents à Este et Padoue.

[60] Cf. sur deux épitaphes de Padoue (avec nom du défunt au datif) *.e.kupeϑari.s. e.go* (PID. 142), *.e.go ... .e.kupeϑari.s.* (PID. 141).

[61] Este, urnes T XXV, XXV*bis*, XXVI, stèles PID. 115*a* et 123; sur ces deux derniers textes, cf. *Atti dell' Istituto Veneto* 112.255–264 (1953/54).

[62] Dans **q**, c'est ensemble à sa mère (*FOUGONTAI*) et à son père (*EGTOREI*) – les deux noms étant en asyndète, cf. **t** – que leur fille *FVGENIA* rend les derniers devoirs; le patronyme du père (*LAMVSIOI*), peut-être omis par inadvertance après *EGTOREI*, a été ensuite, gauchement, ajouté en fin de texte.

et de sens obscurs, *VESCES*, dont on a l'équivalent en écriture vénète (*ve.s.ke.ś.*) sur une autre urne d'Este, dans un contexte de même structure syntaxique.[63] Un dernier type de formulaire, dont on n'a pas, jusqu'ici, de parallèles dans les épitaphes en écriture vénète, mais dont rien ne permet de croire que la structure soit influencée par le latin, apparaît en **t**: 'tombe (nomin.) d'Ennonios (génit.) pour (datifs) O., A., (et) lui-même'.[64] Rien de latin, donc, que l'écriture dans ces textes, sauf, peut-être,[65] le nom de parenté *FILIA* en **q**, sauf aussi, certainement, en **n**, la substitution du groupe romain: prénom + gentilice à la désignation par un nom individuel local.

La dédicace vénéto-latine d'Este (**b**), laissée en suspens après le second mot, n'est autre que la formule votive fréquente *mego dona.s.to* ... du vénète (lat. *mē dōnāuit*).

Les dédicaces vénéto-latines de Làgole (**c** – **g**) sont, non point bilingues (§ 8), mais mixtes. La formule votive est le plus souvent latine: *D*(*onauit*) *L*(*ibens*) *M*(*erito*) en **c**, *V*(*otum*) *S*(*oluit*) *L*(*ibens*) *M*(*erito*) en **d** et **f**; mais il y a chance que *DONOM* (sans verbe exprimé), en **e**, soit le nom vénète du 'don',[66] plutôt que le mot latin correspondant, qu'on s'attendrait à voir écrit par *-VM*. Le dédicant porte une désignation vénète (nom individuel + adjectif patronymique) à flexion vénète (nomin.sg. en *-o.s.*) en **d**, une désignation vénète à flexion latinisée (nomin.sg.-*VS*) en **e**, une désignation proprement latine en **f**. L'indication de la divinité, en revanche, est toujours faite par son nom local,[67] fléchi à la vénète: thème en *-i-*, accusatif (à côté de '*dōnāre*') en *-IN*[68] ou datif en *-EI*;[69] les formes abrégées (**d**, **g**) témoignent d'un usage graphique local[70], largement attesté dans les dédicaces en écriture vénète.[71]

[63] T XXVI: *vho.u.gota gra.i.ko.i. ve.s.ke.ś.*

[64] D'autre part, sont vénètes la structure onomastique, les thèmes et la flexion des noms, la désignation du 'monument funéraire' (voir note 60) et le remarquable réfléchi redoublé (dat.) qui serait en écriture vénète (mais on n'en a pas d'autre exemple) *śe.l.bo.i.śe.l.bo.i.*.

[65] Mais rien, dans le phonétisme du vénète, ne s'oppose à ce que *FILIA* soit un terme vénète aussi bien que latin.

[66] En vénète septentrional, à Làgole (et sans doute à Gurina: voir note 17), la nasale finale, dans les textes en langue et écriture vénète est tantôt *-n* (comme, toujours, à Este et à Padoue), tantôt *-m*, soit par l'effet d'une diversité dialectale du vénète lui-même, soit sous l'influence du celtique cisalpin, soit sous l'action du latin (discussion: *Rev. Ét. Lat.* 29.86–95 [1951]). Ainsi, à Làgole, *-n* dans **AB** 16, 17, 18, 19, 52, mais *-m* dans **AB** 40, 41, 47, 48, 49, 50, 53, 54, 56, 58, 59, 63, 65; sur le nombre, un exemple sûr de *dono.n.* (**AB** 52) et neuf exemples sûrs de *dono.m.* (**AB** 47, 48, 49, 53, 54, 56, 58, 59, 65).

[67] Il s'agit d'une divinité probablement masculine, à laquelle succède, à l'époque proprement romaine, un Apollon (**AB** 1 à 6); outre une épithète (*śa.i.nati.s.*) qui est commune à la divinité de Làgole et à la déesse d'Este, il existe à Làgole un double nom divin, *tribu.s.iiati.s.* | *trumu.s.iiati.s.*, la première forme étant rare (**AB** 14, 19, 31), la seconde d'usage courant. Les trois mots sont des thèmes en *-i-* qui peuvent, a priori, être soit masculins soit féminins. Le seul argument en faveur d'une divinité féminine serait à tirer de **AB** 63, où paraît figurer un doublet Trumusia de Trumusiatis; mais l'interprétation du texte reste discutée.

[68] Cf. *tona.s.to tru*[*mu.s.iiati.*]*n* (**AB** 17), *tona.s.to tribu.s.iiati.n.* (**AB** 19), et aussi **AB** 18. Sur la nasale finale, cf. note 66.

[69] Cf. *trumu.s.iiate.i.* (**AB** 47 etc.).

[70] On n'en a, pour Este, que des exemples rarissimes (**V** XIX, XX).

[71] Pour *TRV* (**g**), cf., en écriture locale, *tru* (**AB** 21); pour *TRVM* (**d**), nous n'avons pas encore de

10 Aisément interprétables, puisqu'en même temps que la connaissance du latin nous avons une suffisante connaissance du vénète plus ancien, les faits envisagés ci-dessus illustrent bien les effets divers de la concurrence des deux écritures, puis des deux langues, à l'époque de la romanisation.

Mais ils ont aussi l'intérêt de fournir éventuellement un moyen de contrôler[72] les valeurs phonétiques des lettres de l'alphabet vénète, les mêmes mots ou morphèmes nous étant livrés avec la graphie locale et avec la graphie latine.

Le premier problème[73] que les textes vénéto-latins achèvent d'élucider[74] est celui de la double valeur d'un signe qui, dès l'origine, signifie *.i.* (c'est à dire *i* second élément de diphtongue), et qui (à partir, semble-t-il, de 300 environ), à Este et ailleurs, assume aussi la valeur *h* (dans le digramme *vh*, valant *f*). Les datifs en *-AI*, *-OI*, *-EI* des textes vénéto-latins excluent qu'on transcrive (comme encore Conway) par *-ah*, *-oh*, *-eh* les finales vénètes correspondantes en écriture locale; *FREMAIST-* (**I**) ne laisse pas d'hésitation sur les valeurs différentes du signe après *v* et après voyelle dans vén. *vhrema.i.s.t-* (Conway: *vhremah.s.t-*). Etc.

Une seconde question qui reçoit de nos textes vénéto-latins quelque lumière est celle des deux sifflantes *s* et *ś* que l'alphabet vénète a héritées de l'alphabet étrusque,[75] ou, pour mieux dire, la question des emplois, distincts ou non, de ces deux lettres en vénète.[76] Si, d'une part, il semble y avoir constance dans certaines orthographes, par exemple pour *śa.i.nate.i.* (épithète divine, au datif) dont on a une quinzaine d'exemples, toujours avec *ś-*[77], en revanche il semble y avoir flottement entre les abréviations de noms propres *set* (   ) et *śet* (   ) à Este,[78] peut-être aussi entre les

rapprochement sûr en écriture locale; autres abréviations: *trumu* (**AB** 24 à 28), probablement *trum[u.s.]* (**AB** 29), *trumu.s.iia* (certain, **AB** 65; possible, **AB** 63?), *trumus.iiat.* (**AB** 16). On notera que cet usage local s'est maintenu pour le culte romain ultérieur dans le sanctuaire de Làgole, où nous trouvons des dédicaces à *AP* (= *Apollini*: **AB** 1, 2, 3).

72 Il existe encore un autre moyen de contrôler les valeurs que la philologie moderne a, au départ, assigné aux lettres vénètes en fonction des valeurs des lettres étrusques correspondantes, et, accessoirement, en fonction de considérations linguistiques ou combinatoires. Ce moyen est fourni par la confrontation des noms de personnes des inscriptions vénètes préromaines avec les noms de personnes fournis, pour la Vénétie, par les sources classiques (essentiellement, par les inscriptions latines).

73 Voir *Rev. Phil.* 21.204 et suiv. (1951).

74 La première élucidation, partielle, du problème, est due à F. Sommer, *IF* 42.90–132 (1924), article que Conway a eu grand tort d'ignorer ou de négliger. Un des éléments qui ont orienté Sommer sur la bonne voie est une épitaphe d'Este (= PID 126), qui a dû, en fait, être régulièrement ponctuée, mais dont les points ne sont à peu près plus visibles, et où une finale *-e.i.* de datif paraissait être écrite *-ei.*

75 Une complication, accessoire, de la question des sifflantes résulte de l'existence à Làgole de deux tracés différents (mais qu'on ne trouve jamais ensemble dans un même texte) pour le signe de sifflante forte; voir *Rev. Ét. Lat.* 32.137–138 (1954).

76 Nous réservons pour une étude séparée l'examen détaillé de cette question.

77 À Este, tablettes votives **M** III et V; épingles votives **V** XIX (deux ex.), XX (deux ex.), XXI, XXII; dédicaces sur pierre PID. 100 et 106. A Làgole, avec forme usuelle de *ś*, **AB** 16 (peu probablement aussi **AB** 63); avec forme locale de *ś*, **AB** 52, 53, 54, 57 (?), 61.

78 Mais il s'agit là de nos propres interprétations. Dans **T** XXI où nous lisons *set* (   ) en écriture vénète, Callegari et Conway lisaient *SEX* (   ) en écriture latine. Pour PID. 123 où nous isolons

formes d'accusatif pluriel *.a..i.su.s.* et *.a..i.su.ś.* (?) à Gurina;[79] d'autre part, c'est la lettre latine *S* qui répond à vén. *ś*, en fin de mot dans *VESCES* (**p**) = *ve.s.-ke.ś.* (**T** XXVI), sans doute aussi[80] entre voyelles dans *VSEDICA* (**r**). La translitération latine (**t**) *SSELBOISSELBOI* d'une forme vénète (non attestée en écriture locale, mais qui ne peut avoir été que *śe.l.bo.i.śe.l.bo.i.*) apporte un argument décisif en faveur de l'existence en vénète, jusqu'à l'époque de la romanisation, d'une sifflante forte, phonétiquement distincte (et sans doute aussi phonologiquement) de la sifflante normale.

Pour un dernier ordre de problèmes (valeurs des lettres vénètes tirées du *θ*, du *φ*, du *z* et du *χ* de l'alphabet étrusque), les inscriptions vénéto-latines nous apportent sinon des preuves décisives, du moins certaines présomptions. Employée dans les seuls textes de Padoue et dans deux textes (patavinisants) d'Este,[81] la lettre *θ* y répond à *t* des autres documents vénètes;[82] s'agit-il d'une particularité purement graphique ou s'agit-il aussi d'une particularité phonétique? Le nom padouan du 'monument funéraire', *.e.kupeθari.s.* (PID 141, 142) se retrouve à Canevói, en lettres latines: *ECVPETARIS* (**t**), et un certain nombre de noms de personnes avec *-θ-* à Padoue se retrouvent avec *-T-* dans les textes vénéto-latins d'Este.[83] On peut objecter à ces rapprochements que, s'il y a eu prononciation particulière, à Padoue, du *t* vénète, elle a pu être étroitement limitée à la région de Padoue et exclure Canevói comme Este.[84] On peut objecter aussi (voir ci-dessous pour les occlusives sonores) qu'en tout état de cause, *T* demeurait la meilleure approximation en alphabet latin pour une spirante interdentale sourde par exemple (à supposer que telle eût été la réalisation du *t* vénète à Padoue).

Les caractères vénètes[85] issus des lettres *φ*, *z*, *χ*, de l'alphabet étrusque, représentent

śet ( ) (cf. *Atti dell' Istituto Veneto* 112.255–259 [1953/54]), aucune interprétation n'a été proposée par ailleurs.

[79] En PID. 167, la lecture [. . . *dona.s.*]*to .a..i.su.s.* ('. . . dōnāuit deōs') est sûre (cf. *Rev. Ét. Anc.* 54.267–274 [1952]); mais en PID. 166, après *dona.s.to*, la lecture *.a..i.su.m.* ('. . . deum') nous paraît plus probable que la lecture *.a..i.su.ś.* '(. . . deōs'), voir note 17.

[80] Dans la version vénète (§ 7) de l'épitaphe, le patronyme n'est lisible que partiellement; mais les vestiges qui subsistent pour la seconde lettre favorisent *ś* (et excluent *s*).

[81] Épitaphe PID. 127; épingle votive **V** XIX = PID. 33.

[82] Désinence verbale *-.s.θo* (PID. 33, 155, 156) répondant à *-.s.to*. Épithète divine *ś*(*a*)*.i.naθ*(*e.*)*i.* (PID. 33) répondant à *śa.i.nate.i..* Souches de noms de personnes: *vho.u.go.n.θ-* (PID. 33) = *vho.u.go.n.t-* (**V** VIII etc.) et *FOVGONT-* (**o, q**); *ge.n.θ-* (PID. 144) = *GENT-* (**i**); *iuva.n.θ-* (PID. 149) = *iiuva.n.t-* (**M** III etc.) et *IVANT-* (**i, l, p**); *lemeθor-* (PID. 33) = *lemetor-* (**M** XX etc.) et *LEMETOR-* (**n**); *voθ-* (PID. 150) = *vot-* (**V** XXI etc.); etc.

[83] Voir note 82.

[84] Cependant, on pourrait trouver, dans les inscriptions proprement latines de Padoue même (cf. note 72), des noms de personnes apparentés aux noms qui figurent sur nos inscriptions vénètes: ainsi, le gentilice *MVSTIVS* (CIL. V 2822) pourrait continuer un patronyme vénète **mu.s.θiio.s.* dérivé d'un nom individuel masc. **mu.s.θo.s.*: le féminin correspondant (nom individuel au datif) *mu.s.θa.i.* figure dans l'épitaphe PID. 149b; etc.

[85] Sauf nous-même, qui les transcrivons par *b*, *d*, *g* respectivement, les philologues contemporains

étymologiquement, en toutes positions, des occlusives sonores i.e., et aussi, entre voyelles (au moins pour *φ* et *z*; pas d'exemple clair pour *χ*), des 'occlusives sonores aspirées' i.e. Dans les inscriptions vénéto-latines, ces lettres vénètes sont rendues, respectivement, par *B*, *D*, *G*: *TRIBVSIATIN* (**c**) = *tribu.s.iiati.n.* (**AB** 19, cf. 31); dat.pl. *-OBOS* (**t**) = *-obo.s.* (**M** I, **V** XXII), etc.;[86] *DONASTO* (**b**) = *dona.s.to* (**M** I etc.), *DONOM* (**e**) = *dono.m.* (**AB** 47, etc.), etc.;[87] *MEGO* (**b**) = *mego* (**M** I etc.), *EGO* (**o**) = *.e.go* (PID 112 etc.), *FOVGONTAI* (**o**) = *vho.u.go.n.ta.i.* (**V** VIII, etc.), etc.[88] L'hypothèse d'une prononciation spirante de ces sonores en vénète, et de transpositions seulement approximatives par *B*, *D*, *G* de l'alphabet latin[89] demeure théoriquement possible; mais il ne faut pas oublier que les Vénètes ont tiré leur écriture d'un alphabet étrusque dépourvu de consonnes occlusives sonores, et que l'approximation a bien plus de chances de s'être manifestée à ce moment-là, par l'usage des lettres *φ*, *z*, *χ*, de l'étrusque, pour des occlusives *b*, *d*, *g* du phonétisme vénète.

ÉCOLE DES HAUTES ÉTUDES, PARIS

(même s'ils conviennent que des occlusives sont par là notées en vénète) continuent à user des transcriptions *φ*, *z*, *χ*, par référence aux transcriptions des caractères étrusques correspondants.

[86] Le premier exemple est étymologiquement obscur; dans le second, *-b-* vénète continue un **-bh-* intérieur; de même dans *SSELBOISSELBOI*.

[87] Dans ces exemples il s'agit d'un ancien **d-* initial; mais **-dh-* intérieur est vén. *-d-* dans *lo.u.derobo.s.* (**V** XXII), etc.

[88] Ancien **-g-* probable dans *.e.go* (d'où *mego*), sûr dans *vho.u.g-* (**bheug-*).

[89] Lorsqu'elle se manifeste, cette hypothèse est, le plus souvent, une conséquence plutôt qu'une justification de la transcription (encore courante, voir note 85) par *φ*, *z*, *χ*. Chez Martinet (*Word* 6.26–41 [1950], repris dans *L'économie des changements phonétiques*, 332–349 [Berne 1955]), elle est intégrée à une thèse beaucoup plus générale sur le consonantisme italique; cette thèse nous paraît formuler une vue possible, mais non très probable, sur cet ensemble compliqué de données.

YAKOV MALKIEL

THE SEMANTIC LINK BETWEEN LATIN *BI(S)*- AND ROMANCE *BES*-, *BIS*-

THE METHODS of linking Latin to Romance have changed considerably in the course of one century, although the transitions have seldom been abrupt. For the most part, a set of assumptions and a correlated operational technique deemed reputable at a given time, after encountering severe criticism from a new group of front-line scholars, continued for a while to hold their own, with decreasing momentum, at less advanced centers of learning, much as linguistic forms on their wane are known to withdraw gradually to less exposed zones. With this qualification in mind, one may safely contend that, say, sixty years ago in centers of research (and until recently, at outposts) it was a widely accepted practice to project isolated Romance formations, often rather irresponsibly, into the parent language by means of crudely reconstructed bases; that forty years later the recoil from the abuses of this earlier method led to a scrupulousness bordering on timidity in piecing together the Latin antecedents of Romance, the new assumption being that few innovations, beyond those long ago identified, had their roots in the earlier layers of Latin; and that the moment has now arrived to chart a new course by trying with a firm, yet cautious hand to moor traditional Romance speech forms in the solid ground of documented Latin.[1] Let me try to exemplify this latest, I should think very healthy, way of thinking by sketching the semantic relation of the Latin twin prefixes *bi*- and *bis*- (on whose scope the Latinists seem to entertain few doubts) to their multifarious Romance descendants.

[1] See *Rom. Phil.* 9.50–68 (1955–6), especially p. 59, for a rebuttal of M. L. Wagner's extreme skepticism with regard to the untapped wealth of Latin resources ("der lateinische Wortschatz war nicht unbegrenzt... unbegrenzt ist aber die innere Wortschöpfungsmöglichkeit des Romanischen"). C. de Boer, Adolf Tobler et le latin, *Mélanges... M. Roques*, 1.15–20 (Paris, 1950), points out in a very friendly vein that the pioneer concerned, as an essentially "logical" syntactician, did not recognize the need for a deep and solid Latin foundation as an invariable guarantee of safety in his probing into the above-ground structure of Romance, especially French.

The point at issue is this: to the Latinists *bi*(*s*)- presents no semantic problems, because the primary meaning 'twice', in the vast majority of cases, is clearly perceptible (e.g. *biceps*, known to Cicero and Ovid, 'two-headed, with two edges or summits'; *bipedālis*, favored by Cato and Caesar, and its successor, *bipedāneus*, preferred by Columella and Pliny, 'two feet long', etc.). In the remainder of the cases, this imagery is at least discernible underneath the thin disguise of a figurative meaning, e.g. (gloss) *bidentātiō* 'harrowing', lit. 'cutting with a two-pronged instrument' (adj. *bidens* 'with two teeth, two points' occurs as early as Lucretius and Vergil), Late Lat. *bispelliō* 'cunning man', lit. 'man with two skins'. The Romance languages, particularly the French and Italian dialects, contain an appreciable number of relics of this older use.[2] Yet wherever *bis*- has become truly productive in the Romance vernaculars,[3] the newly coined formations suggest not a duality or cleavage, but a gradually widening spectrum of pejorative or depreciative ideas. Such is the semantic discrepancy between Latin and Romance that some founding fathers of our discipline were not even certain whether OFr. *bes*-, the most characteristic and vigorously developed representative of the Romance set, was an authentic offshoot of Lat. *bis*-.[4] When this initial uncertainty vanished, it became the fashion to assert that, although there undeniably existed a direct genetic link between Lat. *bi*(*s*)- and Romance *bes*- (and vars.), the gamut of meanings that *bes*- and its equivalents displayed in languages like

[2] Cf. W. Meyer-Lübke, *REW*[3] 1082 (*bichordium), 1083 (*bicongius*), 1084 (adj. *bicornis incūs*, comparable to Pliny's *ūnicornis*; subst. *bicornia), 1090 (*biferus*), 1092 (*bifidus*), 1093 (*bifurcus*), 1103 ([*]bilancia, based on fem. *bi-lanx*), 1109 (*bīnātī), 1114 (*bīrotium), 1115 (*bīrotus*), 1121 (*bisacchium*; cf. A. Schiaffini, *Problemi del lessico italiano* 189 [Rome, 1952]), 1122 (*bisacūtus), 1123 (*biscoctum*), 1127 (*bislūca), 1128 (*bisluscus*), 1129 (*bisocca), 1131 (*bissextus*), 1132 (*bissus), 1137 (*bitōnsiāre), 1137a (*bitortiāre). Add Ven. *bigòlo* 'arnese di legno per portar sulla spalla due secchie' < [*]bicollu (A. Prati, Etimologie, *AGI* 17.273–5 [1910–3]), recently endorsed by Rohlfs; and Sp. *bisojo*, Murc. *bizuejo*, Fr.-Comt. *biseuil* 'squinting', which Meyer-Lübke, inconsistently, listed s.v. *oculus*, just as he split his scanty information on *bisau(ul)us 'great-grandfather' between the entries 837 and (Supplement) 9647; on *bisoculus, whose connection with Sp. *bizco* 'id.' remains to be ascertained, see O. Deutschmann in *Rom. Jb.* 1.144 (1947–8) and Corominas, *DCELC* 1.465a. *Bīgae* and *bīmus*, likewise preserved in Romance, have here been left out of the reckoning because their prefix must have become unanalyzable at the Latin stage. The quantity of the *i* in *bi*- (especially among some inferred formations) raises special problems which fall beyond the scope of this paper.

[3] The variant *bi*- became unproductive at a fairly early date. Cf. the parallel replacement of *dī*- and *dē*- by *dis*-, and of *ē*- by *ex*- (or *a*-). *Bis*- shows no signs of vitality in Rumanian; M. L. Wagner, *Historische Wortbildungslehre des Sardischen* (Berne, 1952), makes no mention of it. For Raeto-Romance note Surs. *bavuork* < *bifurcu* and *bert* < *birotu*.

[4] Thus, F. Diez, *Grammatik der romanischen Sprachen* 2.357–8 (Bonn, 1838), after mentioning the still unexplained tendential shift, within French and Italian, of *bes*- to *ber*- (and even *bre*-), *bar*- (OFr. *bre-tauder*, *bar-long*, *ber-lue*; It. *ber-lusco*, *ber-nocchoi*, *bar-dosso*, *bar-lume* beside *bis-canto*, *bis-cazza*, *bis-dosso*), argued thus: "Begrifflich passt es nicht zu *bis*-, Verwechslung mit *mis*- muss gleichfalls abgelehnt werden. Vielleicht starke Abkürzung von *en-biais*, *de-biais* 'quer'." Later, in his *Etymologisches Wörterbuch der romanischen Sprachen* 56–7 (Bonn, 1853), despite having garnered additional evidence (It. *biscantare*, OProv. *beslei*, OFr. *besivre* alongside Cl.-Fr. *bertouser*; Sp. *bisojo*, Piedm. *besanca* alongside *berlichè* and *berlaita*), Diez felt even less certain about the ancestry of the formative (Lat. *bis*- or *vice*? Gmc. *mis*-? Bret. *besk* 'cropped, clipped'? Fr. *biais* 'slanting, askew'?).

Old French and Italian represented a sharp departure from the Latin norm.[5] Even a specialist of Rohlfs's caliber, only three years ago, contended that the "old Latin meaning" underlies solely Group I of the formations adduced, tied together by the image of duality (It. *biscotto* 'biscuit', lit. 'twice baked', *bidente* 'pitchfork'), whereas several other groups represented "semantic shifts in various directions".[6] Is this statement valid, or can the roots of the new developments (as distinct from their ultimate ramifications) be laid bare within the rich and easily accessible growth of documented Latin?

It would seem that they can, and that one of the changes underlying all further developments was the extension of the primeval image of 'duality' to include the idea of 'duplicity'. Of this incipient widening of scope there is ample evidence in a variety of Latin sources. Thus, *bicors*, in the early Christian writer Commodianus (1.11.8), signifies not only 'with two hearts', but also 'dissembling'. *Bilinguis*, a favorite with Ennius, Plautus, and Varro, means 'double-tongued' not only with the familiar connotation of 'conversant with two languages', but also with a hint at deceitfulness. Though *bisulcus*, viewed in isolation, is a descriptive adjective devoid of emotional overtones ('two-furrowed, two-cleft, forked'; common in Pliny), the Plautine compound *bisulcī linguā* 'with a cloven tongue' within the given context has sometimes been understood to mean 'deceitful' or at least to have a vituperative connotation (*Poenulus*, v. 1034: "*Bisulci* lingua quasi proserpens bestia").

[5] For the most detailed and penetrating older discussion turn to A. Darmesteter, *Traité de la formation des mots composés dans la langue française*... 104–5, 108–11 (BÉHÉ, Vol. 19; Paris, 1874). The author toys with the idea of an immanent, panchronic tendency of speakers to indulge in the shift from 'diversity' via 'duplicity' to 'perversity', but gratuitously burdens his argument with material tapped from other languages, pays insufficient attention to readily available Latin data, and makes a serious blunder by positing, as a semantic link, the idea of 'séparation, déchirement' (p. 110). Darmesteter found a supporter in E. L. Adams, *Word-Formation in Provençal* 419, 465–6 (New York and London, 1913), despite the paucity of pejorative formations at hand (*bistensar* 'to delay, disturb', *beslei* 'injustice'); otherwise the prefix in that language is either functionally unprecise (e.g. *bescambi* 'exchange', he might have added: perhaps originally 'unfavorable exchange'; *bestor* 'bastion, turret') or simply suggestive of duality (*bescalon*, presumably replacing **bes-escalon* 'double step'; *bescuig* 'biscuit'). Meyer-Lübke hazarded a different interpretation in his *Historische Grammatik der französischen Sprache* (II): *Wortbildungslehre* § 248 (Heidelberg, 1921), setting aside *bescuire* 'to bake twice' as a relic and selecting *bestourner* 'to turn, twist' as the leader word for the series OFr. *besjugier* 'to judge wrongly', *besloier* 'to act unfairly' (postverbal: *besloi*), *bestondre* 'to shear badly', *bestordre* 'to twist out of shape', and, conceivably, **besveoir*, judging from *besvue* 'blunder, oversight'. His argument was that the image of repetition may have engendered the idea of incorrectness. Despite the excellency of stray observations (note the comment on the replacement of *oblif* < *oblīquu*, *oblong* by *beslif*, *beslong*; and, in § 229, on the respective shares of Italian and of Latin learning in the transformation of OFr. *bes-* into Mod. Fr. *bis-*: *biscotte*, *biscuit*; *bisaïeul*, *biscornu*, *bistourner*), the kernel of Meyer-Lübke's reasoning lacks conviction.

[6] G. Rohlfs, *Historische Grammatik der italienischen Sprache* § 1006 (3.234–5 [Berne, 1954]). Less felicitous examples quoted by the author are learned *bisesso* and learned and hybrid *bisillabo*. On this hybrid derivational pattern (Med. Lat. *bigamus* vs. Gr.-Lat. *digamus* in Tertullian) see B. Migliorini, Le lingue classiche, serbatoio delle lingue europee moderne, *LN* 16.34 [1956]).

One may set off a further category of graphic adjectives which, in the relatively few passages transmitted to us, fail to show any noticeable deterioration of meaning, but which, against the background of existing tastes, customs, superstitions, and scales of value, at least clearly offered the potentiality of assuming a derogatory meaning on the colloquial level. Examples in point include, on the one hand, *bicōdulus* 'two-tailed' (Laevius, apud Apuleium) and similar designations of anatomic anomalies, e.g. *bicomis* 'with a double mane' (Vegetius, *Mulomedicina*), *bicorpor* 'double-bodied' (Naevius, Cicero) beside *bicorporeus* (Firmicus Maternus), *bifax* 'with a double face' (gloss: διπρόσωπος), *bifrons* 'with two foreheads' (an epithet of Janus in the *Aeneid* 7.180, 12.198), *bimembris* 'half man, half beast' (Ovid, Juvenal, speaking of a Centaur); on the other hand, *bigamus* 'twice-married' (Ambrosius, Jerome, Isidore), *bigener(is)* 'hybrid, mongrel' (Varro and Paulus ex Festo), *bimarītus* 'husband of two wives' (Cicero, Jerome, *Glossae Isidori*), *bimātris* (or *-er*) 'having two mothers', patterned on διμήτωρ (Ovid, in reference to Bacchus; Hyginus; *Anthologia Latina*: *bī-*), *binūbus* 'doubly married man' (Cassiodorus), *biuira* 'woman married to a second husband' (Varro); to some extent, also *binōminis* 'bearing two names' (Ovid) alongside *binōmius* (Paulus ex Festo).

In other words, one has to start from situations in which uniqueness is – or at least was – the rule, anatomically (a human being has one heart, one face, one forehead, and one tongue) or socially (each member of the Roman society had one spouse, also, of course, one mother, and bore one fixed set of names). Under these conditions, duality (and plurality) became departures from the standard, and these aberrations, understandably, were rated as defects. Eventually, the new derogatory value may have spread from some such particularly well-remembered formations to the prefix itself, a demonstrably common process in many languages, giving that prefix a connotation similar to that of *ill-* in English and of *mal-* (beside *mes-*, *menos-*) in Romance.[7] On this assumption alone does Darmesteter's masterly characterization of OFr. *bes-* fit into a meaningful historical context:

> BIS- ajoute au mot avec lequel on le combine une idée de défectuosité choquante, de vice qui frappe et blesse l'esprit, quelquefois aussi de bizarrerie grotesque et baroque. Les mots *biscornu*, *bévue*, *berlue* ['trouble visuel'], par exemple, emportent l'idée de quelque chose de risible, de ridicule. Dans le vieux français *besloyer*, *besjugier*, BIS- dit plus que MALE- et marque mieux la violence de l'injustice. BIS- est donc une particule éminemment péjorative, et les diverses nuances de sens dont elle est susceptible donnent à cette signification péjorative une physionomie bien caractérisée.[8]

The few examples adduced suffice to delimit the chronological layer in which *bis-* began to develop in the new direction. The record begins with Ennius, Plautus, and

[7] On the relation of Gallo-Rom. *mes-* to *menos-* in Provençal, Catalan, and Spanish, see my article Préstamos y cultismos, to appear in *RLiR* (1957).

[8] *Traité de la formation des mots composés* 108–9.

Varro and includes Lucretius, Cicero, Vergil, and Ovid, extending, at the other extreme, to Vegetius, Cassiodorus, Isidore of Seville, and the glossographers. The texts, which afford not only a very fragmentary, but, in addition, a biased view of the spoken language, show continued productivity of *bis-* 'two-, twice-' down to the closing centuries of Antiquity; they shed little, if any, light on the gradual recession of *bi-* before *bis-*.[9] Yet given the early evidence, however vestigial, of the figurative use of *bis-*, one may safely aver that we are dealing not with a Romance semantic innovation, nor even with a distinctly Late Latin feature, but with a trait transplanted, with varying success, from the Republican metropolitan into the provincial varieties of Latin.

The chronological distance separating the bulk of the Latin from the earliest Romance examples may account for the fact that the two sets fail to match very closely, either lexically or grammatically. Recall that the rate of attrition among derogatory words is usually accelerated. One change is particularly conspicuous: Lat. *bi-* ordinarily served to form nouns: *biduum*, *biennium*, and especially *bīmus*, *bipēs*, the two last-mentioned of very ancient coinage on comparative evidence; *bis-* (var. *bī-*) was originally restricted to certain categories of numerals (cardinal, ordinal, distributive): *bissex*, *bissēnī*, *bissext-us* or *-ilis* 'containing one intercalary day', *bīnī*, etc. Neither *bi-* nor *bis-* (*bī-*) functioned as preverbs on any major scale, even though Servius' statement to this effect (commentary to *Aeneis* 2.330) was probably too categorically worded.[10]

Conversely, the typical (though hardly anywhere the exclusive) Romance function of *bes-*, *bis-* is to introduce a verb; cf. OFr. *bescuire* 'to bake twice or thoroughly', *besjugier* 'to misjudge', *besleiier* 'to treat unfairly', *besorder* 'to sully', *bestencier* 'to dispute' (*REW*³ 8652), *bestondre* and vars. 'to shear carelessly', *bestordre* 'to twist out of shape', *bestorner* 'to turn upside down, alter, corrupt';[11] It. *bis-cantare* 'to trill, troll

[9] Examples of late coinage or, at least, late introduction: *bicamerātus* 'doubly arched' (Jerome, Augustine), *bicinium* 'duet' (Isidore), *bifestus* 'doubly festive' (Prudentius), *binoctium* 'space of two nights' (Ammianus), *bipeda* 'flagstone two feet long' (Palladius), *birota* 'cabriolet' (*Codex Theodosianus*), *biuertex* 'with two summits' (Statius, Sidonius Apollinaris).

[10] Even if one discounts past participles like *bifidātus* 'cleft into two parts' (Pliny) beside *bifidus* 'id'. (Ovid, Columella, Pliny) and *bifissus* (Solinus), *bifōrmātus* (?) 'two-shaped' (Cicero) beside more common *bifōrmis*, and an occasional present participle like *bipatēns* 'opening in two ways' (Vergil), there remains the crucially important verb *bipartiō* (var. *bipertiō*) *-īre* 'to bisect' (Varro, Cicero, Columella). This verb, rather than the prototype of It. *bistornare* 'to pervert' (Meyer-Lübke, *Romanische Formenlehre* § 618), must be regarded as the leader word.

[11] See K. Nyrop, *Grammaire historique de la langue française* 3.212 (Copenhagen, 1908). Observe that among the pejorative formations *bes-* may simply reinforce the inherent derogatory meaning of the radical, as in *bes-order*, *bes-tordre*, or else inject a note of disparagement originally absent, as in *bes-jugier*, *bes-tondre*. On *bestorner* see E. B. Ham's ed. (1947) of *Renart le Bestorné* and the various critiques that it has provoked; also *Les Neuf Joies Nostre Dame* (ed. 1952), p. 159: "Tu iez Eva la *bestornée*". For further examples of the prefix see J. Haust, *Étymologies wallonnes et françaises* 25–6 (Liège, 1923): Liég. *bèraudi* 'cage, grenier' < 'échafaudage'; and the excellent collection of Piedmontese formations by G. Toppino, *Il dialetto di Castellinaldo* § 248 (*St. Rom.* 10.45–6 [1913]).

out', *bescazzare* 'to frequent gambling dens', *bischizzare* 'to indulge in fancies, build castles in the air', (obs.) *biscontare* 'to miscalculate', *biscurare* 'to neglect', *bislessare* 'to parboil', *bistondare* 'to make roundish', *bistrattare* 'to treat badly', OGen. *bescurar* 'to neglect', *berzignar* 'to cheat' (modeled on *ingegnare*), Lomb. (Milan) *bestirà* 'ritirare', *barlüśì* 'splendere', *barloǵà* 'allucciare', Tusc. (Versilia) *baluccicare*; OSp. *biscocha* and *bisassada* (Berceo, *Duelo*, 14c). Sometimes the semantic thread linking these formations to the Latin stock is recognizable; thus, the group suggestive of 'twilight, dim light': Sp. *vislumbrar* intr. 'to loom', tr. 'to glimpse', Ital. *baluccicare, barloǵà, barlume* 'glimmer', *a barluzzo* 'at dawn', *barlüśì, berlusco* (Umbr. *balusco*) 'squinting', Rom. *balucano* 'short-sighted', Fr. *berlue, bévue* unmistakably recalls *bicolor* (Vergil, Ovid), *bicolorus* (Vopiscus) 'two-colored'. Nevertheless, the distance, in terms of grammatical category, is considerable. It is a fair guess that the coexistence of the preverbs *des-*, (*e*)*s-*, and *mes-*, of similar configuration and function, was instrumental in accelerating this shift, if not in setting it in motion.

The knot of the further semantic threads one can hardly hope to unravel with accuracy; at this point, the former provinces of the Empire show great divergencies. For Italian, Rohlfs sets off the following schema of secondary functions:

(a) relegation to greater distance, especially in kinship terms (cf. OFr. *bes-aive, -aïeul, -ante, -oncle*; Sp. *bisabuelo, biznieto*, also *tatar-abuelo* 'great-great-grandfather', involving Lat. *ter-ter*): *biscugino* 'second cousin', (obs.) *bisgènero* 'niece's husband', *bisnipote* 'grand-nephew, great-grandson', *bisnònno* 'great-grandfather';[12]

(b) 'weakening' (the intensity of a quality or the impact, momentum of an action, cf. OFr. *beslong*): *bislungo* 'longish', *bistondo* 'roundish', *biscantare* 'to trill';

(c) 'suggestion of inferiority or disapproval': *bistorto* 'crooked, tortuous, deceitful', *bistrattare* 'to ill-treat, snub', *andare a bisdosso* 'to ride bareback', *bisunto* 'carelessly greased'.[13]

This subdivision is not free from arbitrariness (*biscantare* may also be interpreted as 'faulty singing', *bistondo* as 'imperfectly rounded out', etc.). But even more scrupulous attempts at semantic classification probably would not be immune to criticism. Nyrop, more cautious in this respect, was satisfied with breaking down a string of Old French formations into substantives (e.g. *besaive, beslei)*, adjectives, in part substantivated (e.g. *besaigue, besistre, beslourd, bes-, ber-* > *bar-long*), and verbs (e.g. *besjugier*).

The number of unknowns in the pan-Romanic history of this prefix remains impressive. The origin of the by-forms *ber-*, *bar-*, characteristic of French and Italian (especially on the dialect level[14]), has not yet been satisfactorily elucidated. Several

[12] There seems to be little point in associating (as does Rohlfs) with this close-knit group coll. *cose e biscose*, still less the grammatical term *bisdrucciolo* 'stressed on the fourth syllable from the end' (patterned on *bibreuis* < δίβραχυς, *bilongus*, etc.).

[13] Cf. the geographical proper names *Bis-arno*, *Pietra Bis-mantova*.

[14] Among other abnormal alterations, note Fr. *brouette* 'wheelbarrow' < **berouette* (related to

important words tentatively associated with the prefix lack a transparent etymology. It is uncertain whether the luxuriant growth of the prefix in some territories (France, northern Italy) and its decay or rarity in others (Spain, Portugal) is attributable to the inner stratification of Vulgar Latin, to the parallel pressure, unevenly distributed, of Gmc. *mis-*, or to the second of these two factors as a concomitant of the first. The routes of diffusion within the Franco-Italian zone of highest frequency and the prongs into surrounding areas have not yet been identified with any degree of specificness.[15] Finally, the intricate relation, on the Romance plane, of *bis-* to *trēs-*, *trī-*, *ter-* 'thrice' and, indirectly, to *trā(n)s-*, *trā-*, and even *(in)ter-*, *(in)trō-* awaits painstaking examination.[16]

Yet amid all these embarrassing admissions of ignorance, it is comforting to report that the initial phase of the semantic transformation of *bi(s)-* seems amenable to sharply focused observation. The beginning of the process must be placed squarely within the bounds of Latin. The more advanced and more richly diversified Romance phase does not bring with it any real innovation, but only the heightening, in racy, unrestrained speech, of a semantic effect traceable to the period of Ennius and Plautus.

Once again, the relationship of Romance to Latin is seen in its conspicuous complexity. Aside from representing a late state of Latin, along a single straight vertical, Romance speech contains several additional ingredients. Thus it shows in full blossoming some very old tendencies within substandard Latin, archetypal trends obscured, for a while, by the increasingly conventional character of Rome's literary idiom. This situation confirms a tenet of nearly every well-informed Romanicist's creed: only if compounded of linguistic analysis as practiced by an expert grammarian, of social analysis as undertaken by a seasoned historian, and of stylistic analysis as handled by a deft philologist, can our research in language history do full justice to the wide range of significant facts.

UNIVERSITY OF CALIFORNIA

birotus); and the metathesis of *bis-* to *śbi-*, in the present-day dialect of Rome: *śbillongo, śbinnonno* (mentioned, but left unexplained, by Rohlfs). The radical involved may also show an anomaly, especially apheresis: to the Old Genoese and Old Provençal examples quoted, add Eng. *basgual* 'uneven' (Meyer-Lübke, *Romanische Formenlehre* § 540), based on *(ae)quālis* (*Phil. Quart.* 27.112–22 [1948]).

15 The relationship between OFr. *beslourd* (late fifteenth century), Mod. Fr. *balourd* (1597, beside m.f. *balorde* 1611, m.f. *balourde*, until the close of the seventeenth century) 'dull, thickheaded' (*balourdise* 'doltishness'), and It. *balordo* raises delicate problems of transmission and adaptation; see O. Bloch and W. von Wartburg, *Dictionnaire étymologique de la langue française*² 54a (Paris, 1950). Curiously enough, some of the earlier estimates of diffusion were so liberal as to have been in need of sober reappraisal; cf. Meyer-Lübke's analysis of the descendants of **bicornia* in *Romanische Formenlehre* § 540 as against *REW*³ 1083.

16 On OFr. *bestondre, bestouser, bretauder* (E. Gamillscheg, in *ZRPh.* 40.146 [1919–20]), and their Gascon counterpart in relation to OSp. *(tr)es-*, *tras-quilar* 'to shear' see my forthcoming separate monograph. On the 'valeur expressive' of *b-* in *balourd* see A. Martinet, *Economie des changements phonétiques* 4.58 (Berne, 1955).

GORDON M. MESSING

LATIN *POPLES*
'BACK OF THE KNEE'

THE ETYMOLOGY of Lat. *poples* 'back of the knee' has never been satisfactorily explained. According to the Latin etymological dictionary of Ernout-Meillet, the word is a reduplicated form of obscure origin; the etymological dictionary of Walde-Hofmann accepts none of the various proposed etymologies and expressly rejects any attempts to link the word with a presumed Osco-Umbrian **poplo-*, IE *$q^{u}oq^{u}lo$-, on the ground that this is unlikely in the case of a name for a part of the body.

In a recent article on this word in *AJP* 75.186–189 (1954), Eric P. Hamp defended anew precisely that etymology which Walde-Hofmann had dismissed as unlikely. For special reasons which will be apparent presently Hamp posits, not IE *$q^{u}oq^{u}lo$- but IE *$q^{u}eq^{u}lo$-, the base from which is derived Gk. κύκλος, Ved. Skt. *cakrá-ḥ*, OEng. *hwēol*, Eng. *wheel*. Whether with *e* or *o* vocalism in the first syllable, this represents a reduplicated form from IE *$q^{u}el$- 'turn' (instead of IE **pel-* 'turn' which has been assumed by other etymologists of Lat. *poples*). Hamp justified his etymology semantically through such forms as Span. *rodilla* 'knee' (ultimately from Lat. *rota* 'wheel') and OChSlav. *kolěno* 'knee' (cf. OChSlav. *kolo* 'wheel'). For the form, he pointed to Alb. *sjetullë* 'armpit' which he derived from the same IE base via an intermediate Proto-Albanian *$q^{u}et(u)l\bar{a}$ and tied the meanings together by assuming the initial meaning to have been 'hollow of a (major) joint'.

While this etymology seems to me most unlikely from all points of view, it is curious to note that Hamp might have cited a startlingly close semantic parellel: OHG *hahsa* MHG *hehse* Germ. *Hächse* Eng. *hough* 'back of the knee' is in fact demonstrably cognate with Skt. *kakṣā*, *kakṣaḥ* 'armpit'.

In considering Hamp's etymology, it might first be objected that an Osco-Umbrian **poplo-* for expected **peplo-* is not an attested development. The shift of IE *e* to Osco-Umbrian *o* as far as our evidence goes is confined solely to the base *$q^{u}e\eta q^{u}e$,

Osc.-Umb. **pompe* 'five' (seen in the proper name adduced by Hamp: Osc. Πομπτιες cf. Lat. *Quinctius*). It is of course always possible that such a shift did occur regularly or sporadically elsewhere before a labiovelar, but at all events this is not represented in our fairly limited corpus; see C.D. Buck, *A Grammar of Oscan and Umbrian*, § 37.

From a semantic point of view one might further object that Hamp's examples apply only to terms meaning 'knee'. Such terms can easily be derived from the meaning 'wheel' because of the protruding and obvious circle formed by what we significantly call the 'knee-cap'. Here one could compare Lat. *patella* 'knee-cap', originally 'small round dish', or Fr. *rotule* 'knee-cap' ultimately from Lat. *rota* 'wheel'; the second element of Germ. *Kniescheibe* 'knee-cap' means 'disk' or the like. On the contrary, the 'back of the knee' has very little reason to be named from its circularity, and I know of no pertinent examples.

Finally, Hamp's Albanian examples do not, to my mind, clinch the case. Gustav Meyer's etymology of Alb. *sjetullë* 'armpit' (*Etym. Wörterbuch d. alb. Spr.* 403) tried to make the best of a great profusion of forms. Meyer cited *shetulle*, *sjetull*, *shketullë*, *sqetullë* (here in modernized spelling). The geographical distribution of these forms, according to Meyer, is perhaps not reliable. It is at least apparent that *sjetullë* is a common form in the Geg dialects (the only form to be found in P. Fulvio Cordignano's Albanian-Italian dictionary which is based on Geg). Angelo Leotti's Albanian-Italian dictionary which is largely drawn from Tosk materials lists both *sjetullë* and *sqetull*. Stuart E. Mann lists both *sjetullë* and *sqetullë* in his Albanian-English dictionary of 1948. The recent Albanian official dictionary, *Fjalori i Gjuhës Shqipe* (Tirana, 1954), which is avowedly normative in character, lists *sjetulle* without any definition but with a cross-reference to *sqetull*, evidently the form currently preferred. In the Geg dialect of Borgo Erizzo as recorded by Carlo Tagliavini (*L'Albanese di Dalmazia* 244) the form *thjetull* occurs, clearly related to *sjetullë*, as the initial *th-* (from *s-*) is a special development of this dialect.

At most this seems to demonstrate that *sjetullë* occurred both in Geg and Tosk dialects, while *sqetull* was apparently Tosk.[1] Hamp's claim for the greater antiquity of forms in *sj-* on the basis of its occurrence in the Albanian of southern Italy cannot be allowed, for reasons to be mentioned presently, and in any case it is difficult to see how forms in *sq-* or the like could have developed from those in *sj-* rather than vice versa.

Meyer correctly rejected Schuchardt's phonetically impossible previous explanation of *sjetullë* (*KZ* 20.252, from Lat. *scūtula* 'shoulder blades', found in Celsus) and

[1] It is a pity that there is no entry under *axilla* in the Latin-Albanian dictionary of Franciscus Blancus of 1635 (*Le Dictionnaire albanais de 1635*, ed. by Mario Roques, Paris, 1932), possibly because the number of words beginning with the letters *A* through *E* is, as Roques remarks (38), "exagérément réduit." The form *sjetullë* (in modernized spelling) appears as the equivalent of Gk. μασκάλη in the word-list of Theodore Kavalliotis (1770) published by Gustav Meyer in *Alb. Studien* (Vienna, 1895).

preferred a blend of Late Lat. *scapula* and *spatula* 'shoulder-blade, shoulder'. He was evidently aware of the obvious objection to this, the fact that *spatula* is maintained in its original sense in Alb. *shpatullë*. Perhaps for this reason he suggested diffidently that another possibility was to be seen in Lat. *axilla* 'armpit' which in Isidore already appeared in the form *ascilla*, cf. It. *ascella*; this could have yielded an Alb. **shqelë* which, under the influence of *shpatullë*, was altered to *shqetullë*, while the forms in *sj-* were derived through an intermediate **shtj-*.

Meyer was certainly on the right track. The word *axilla* (which replaced *āla* in this sense) is a term of extremely specialized meaning, and it has derivatives with the same meaning in the principal Romance languages except Portuguese and Rumanian.[2] Moreover, it was borrowed into Goidelic Keltic with the same meaning: OIr. *oxalaib* (gloss) MidIr. *ochsal*.[3] Given the specialized meaning of the word, its wide attested circulation in the Romania, and the large number of Latin borrowings within Albanian, it seems most likely that *sjetullë* which continues this same specialized meaning is derived from *axilla*, despite admitted phonetic difficulties.

The shift of *axilla* to *ascilla* or (often) *ascella* is well attested.[4] If Meyer's blend of forms is not acceptable, one could as easily assume that *ascella* had a variant in Eastern Romance, **ascetula*, testifying to a conflation of the similarly employed formants *-illus* and *-tulus*. Meyer's derivation of *sjetullë* from the (on this reasoning) older forms in *shq-* or *sq-* is reasonable. Possibly, the loss of the older forms in S. Italy can be satisfactorily explained through the influence and conflict in bilingual communities of dialect Italian forms derived from the same Latin etymon: cf. Sic. *ašiḍḍa* or *šiḍḍa*.[5]

To return now to Lat. *poples*, we must point out from a methodological standpoint that Hamp's approach is open to criticism. In the earliest heyday of Indo-European studies a comparativist was at liberty to cast his nets far and wide: he could indiscriminately compare forms drawn from any of the IE languages and dialects and from any phase of their development. Since then, we have grown aware in more sophisticated fashion that individual words have their own private histories and must be considered within the framework of the language to which they belong and the total vocabulary of which they are a part. Any etymology of *poples* is worthless unless it takes into account its formation, its usage within Latin and its relation to other elements of the Latin vocabulary.

[2] The argument advanced here would admittedly be strengthened if *axilla* were further attested in Eastern Romance (for Rum. *subsuoară* see *REW*, *s.v. subāla*). Sp. Port. *sobaco* has been variously explained.
[3] But in Brythonic Keltic the word was borrowed in the kindred meaning 'wing': Welsh *asgell*, Corn. *ascall*, Bret. *askell*. See Holger Pedersen, *Vergl. Gr. d. keltischen Sprachen* 1.193; Pedersen notes that these latter forms imply *ascilla*.
[4] See Alex. Souter, *A glossary of Later Latin to 600 A.D.*, *s.v.* (Oxford, 1949).
[5] *REW*, *s.v. axilla*.

In form *poples* belongs to a rather limited class of stems in *-it-*,[6] for most of which a satisfactory etymology has not been found: *Quirītes*; *satelles*; *mīles*; *uēles*; *cocles*; *ames*; *caespes*; *termes*. A. Ernout has convincingly explained several of these words in *-es*, *-itis* as Etruscan in origin[7] and suggests that *poples* may very well have a similar explanation.

A study of the occurrences of *poples* is instructive. We are often told that the word first meant 'back of the knee' and then acquired the meaning 'knee'. Yet the earliest occurrence, if this is indeed in L. Accius,[8] runs:

Caue lássitudo poplitum [tuum] cursúm levet

'See to it that weariness of the *poplitum* does not diminish (your) speed.' In this rather vague context *poplitum* could perfectly well mean 'knees'; the meaning 'backs of the knees', though equally possible, need not be implied.

Another of the earliest occurrences of the word, Lucretius, 4. 952–3, is as follows (the passage describes the effect of sleep):

bracchia palpebraeque cadunt poplitesque cubanti
saepe tamen summittuntur

'arms and eyelids droop, and the hams, even as you lie down, are often drawn up.'[9] Here again there is nothing specifically in the context which requires us to translate by 'hams' rather than by 'knees', as both hams and knees are necessarily drawn up together.

Bailey's rendering 'hams' really does fit a passage of Columella (6.2.13):

Oleo et sale genua poplitesque et crura [sc. bovis] confricanda sunt

for here *poplites* are specifically contrasted with *genua* ('the knees, hams and shanks should be thoroughly rubbed with oil and salt').

A slight shift of meaning, again, can be glimpsed in such a passage as Virgil, *Aen.* 9.762–3:

Principio Phalerim et succiso poplite Gygen
excipit

'First he catches Phaleris and hamstrings Gyges.' In this context there can be no doubt

[6] Some nouns of this family, *pedes* 'infantryman', *eques* 'cavalryman', *āles* 'bird' are clearly derived from *pēs*, *equus*, *āla;* it has even been conjectured that the second element of these words is a root noun from the verb *īre* 'go': **it-s* 'one who goes'.

[7] *Philologica* 46–7 (Paris, 1946).

[8] Otto Ribbeck's *Tragicorum Romanorum Fragmenta* (Leipzig, 1871); later edition of 1897 not available to me.

[9] Text and translation from Cyril Bailey's edition and commentary in three volumes, here from Vol. I, corrected edition (Oxford, 1950).

that Turnus has severed not the 'back of the knee' but rather the tendon at the back of the knee. An almost equivalent phrase,

succisis feminibus poplitibusque

occurs in Livy (22.51,7), and the meaning 'hamstring' is elsewhere attested.

In human anatomy the hamstring can be defined[10] as "one of the tendons which form the sides of the ham or space at the back of the knee; they are the tendons of the muscles of the thigh"; in quadrupeds, the hamstring is "the great tendon at the back of the hough in the hind leg... the *tendo Achillis* corresponding to that of the heel in man."

In later Latin, as is well known, *poples* was generalized to mean 'knee', though it is worth mentioning that throughout all its history it was a poetic or technical word. (Significantly, it seems not to occur in Latin comedy.)

In summary, then, while *poples* originally meant 'back of the knee', this must be understood in the concrete sense of 'hamstring' or (derived therefrom) 'flesh in the vicinity of the hamstring' (cf. Fr. *jarret*, *couper le jarret*).[11] Thus it is synonymous with Lat. *suffrāgō*, except that the latter word seems to have been originally used almost exclusively for quadrupeds[12] while *poples* could be used either for men or quadrupeds. Perhaps one can reasonably conclude that, insofar as this distinction holds, *poples* was originally a technical term from warfare (cf. the passage of Virgil cited above), since this area was one of the sensitive points, not covered by defensive armor, where a wound could put a warrior out of action. It thus corresponded to Gk. ἰγνύα, Ion. ἰγνύη which occurs once in Homer in just such a context (*Iliad* 13.212).

Consequently, it seems to me that if the original sense of *poples* is in all probability 'hamstring', its etymology must reflect this. A step in the right direction was taken by T. G. Tucker in his *Concise etymological dictionary of Latin* (Halle/Saale, 1931), who derived *poples* from a reduplicated **po-plet-* < **p(e)let-* 'bend' (cf. OChSl. *pletą plesti* 'plait', originally from the idea of bending or twisting; *platŭno* 'linen'[13]; Gk. διπλάσιος 'double', originally of a double fold; Goth. *falþan*, OEng. *fealdan*, Eng. *fold*).

Tucker's explanation accounts for the *-t-* stem and is semantically sound (compare in this connection *suffrāgō*, literally the point at which 'bending in' occurs, clearly from *sub-* and *frango*).[14] It is weakened by the fact that *poples* would be isolated in Italic.

[10] *Shorter Oxford Dictionary*, *s.v.*

[11] These meanings can fit the passages from Accius and Lucretius cited above although, as pointed out already, the later meaning 'knee' may be equally appropriate.

[12] But in later usage it was used for the human ham; cf. the citations *s.v.* in Alex. Souter, *op. cit.*

[13] OChSl. *platŭno* should be separated from the family of OChSl *pletą* according to Max Vasmer, *Russ. etym. Wörterbuch*, *s.v. polotno*.

[14] That the verb **suffrangō* does not occur in its literal sense is of course to be explained by interference with the family of *suffrāgium* 'ballot, voting'.

I should like to modify Tucker's explanation so as to derive *poples* not from the IE base **plet-* but from the base **plek-* or its extended form **plek-t-* which is well represented in Latin: *plicō* (probably for **plecō*, cf. Gk. πλέκω 'braid, twine') or with the *-t-* extension Lat. *plectō* 'plait'.[15]

Assuming on the basis of the preceding discussion that the original meaning of *poples* is 'hamstring', I suggest that an Italic **po-plekts* could have been formed on the base **plekt-* either in the sense 'the bender' (active) or 'that which is bent'; the element **plekts* is comparable to the element **-pleks* actually found in the common *-plex* of *duplex*, *triplex* etc.[16] To revert then to my earlier suggestion that *poples* was originally a technical term of battle, I should like to suggest further that it was a non-Latin term which shows non-Latin development. As such it might have been borrowed in the course of the early Roman warfare with other Italic peoples. The development of original *-kt-* in Osco-Umbrian is to *-ht-*, and the *h* of this new combination was weakly sounded and often lost in Umbrian, as evidenced by its frequent omission: cf. Umb. **rehte,** Lat. *rēctē*, but Umb. **speture,** Lat. (*in*)*spector*. In this case, **po-plekts* would have yielded Osco-Umbrian **poplehts* and Umbrian **poplets* which is precisely the form desired. As a non-Latin form it could the more easily be integrated into the (largely imported) family of stems in *-es*, *-itis*. Perhaps this etymology will be found to satisfy in some degree the various criteria, morphological, semantic, and historical, which have been considered above.

AMERICAN EMBASSY, ATHENS, GREECE

[15] *LEW*, *s.v. plectō*, consider that OChSl. *pletą plesti* come from IE **pleq-* with IE *q* for *k*.

[16] The first element **po-* may be regarded either as reduplication or as the prefix seen in Lat. *po-situs* 'placed' or perhaps in *pōmum* 'fruit' if this is indeed from **po-emom* 'that which is taken off' (scil. from the tree).

ANTHONY G. OETTINGER

LINGUISTICS AND MATHEMATICS

LINGUISTICS, at least in several aspects, is evolving from a humanity into a science. There is a growing recognition of languages as natural phenomena whose secrets may yield to methods of analysis and description akin to those that have proved fruitful in the physical sciences. A concurrent growth of what may be called 'experimental linguistics' is occurring along new lines, in such areas a speech analysis and synthesis, and in the machine translation of languages. Finally, a number of challenging problems of language synthesis arise in the design of automatic calculating and data-processing machines. In this light, a significant growth of interest in the applications of mathematical methods to linguistic problems seems inevitable The present state of the alliance between linguistics and mathematics is briefly sketched in this paper, chiefly by a review of some recent additions to the literature.

In the area where linguistics and the physics of sound intersect, the relation between linguistics and mathematics is clear-cut, since physics is indissolubly and harmoniously wedded to mathematics. Speech analysis and synthesis are now the subject of a rich and growing literature, in which several branches of mathematics play an important role. On the other hand, the most elementary statistics was, until a few years ago, the only mathematical tool used in linguistic studies not directly related to the physics of sound. Whatmough[1] has recently described the status of what he calls the "mechanics of language," and the state of affairs as of the end of 1953 is reflected in the comprehensive *Bibliographie critique de la statistique linguistique*.[2] This bibliography is organized into ten sections, e.g., *Principes et méthodologie*, *Métrique*

[1] J. Whatmough, *Language* chapter XI (Secker and Warburg, London, and St. Martin's Press, N. Y., 1956).

[2] P. Guiraud, *Bibliographie critique de la statistique linguistique*, Revisée et complétée par T. D. Houchin, J. Puhvel, et C. W. Watkins, sous la direction de J. Whatmough (Editions Spectrum, Utrecht/Anvers, 1954).

et versification, *Fréquence des mots*, etc., and the introduction to each section is in itself a valuable commentary on the achievements and the shortcomings of the authors represented in the corresponding section. The compilers noted the absence of any general treatise on statistical linguistics and of any statistics textbook directed toward linguistic applications. The recent appearance of Herdan's *Language as choice and chance*[3] may be hailed as the first effort to fill this gap. The point of view of this work is primarily statistical, while another recent book, *Langage des machines et langage humain*[4] by Vitold Belevitch, draws its inspiration from the design of automatic calculating machines. To see these works, and indeed any contribution of mathematics to linguistics, in proper perspective, the notion of *mathematical model* must be understood.

When applied to the study of phenomena of nature, rather than developed for its own sake, a mathematical system serves as a *model*. In ordinary English, the word 'model' is used in a number of different senses. The specialized sense in which it is used here is closest to that defined by Webster as "a miniature representation of a thing; sometimes, a facsimile." The key idea is that of 'representation,' of 'abstraction,' but a good model may also play more active roles.

An architect's model of a house is not the same thing as the house itself. For example, it may readily be set on a table, or carried about, while a house may not; certainly people cannot live in it. It is useful, however, because it faithfully represents certain selected characteristics of the house. Although its dimensions are not those of the house, the relative proportions of all dimensions are preserved; the texture of various building materials and landscape detail may be faithfully imitated to give an idea of how the house itself will look. Such models play a useful descriptive role, and permit the evaluation of certain qualities of a given house, or the comparison of those of several, prior to actual construction. Mathematical equations are often used in analogous circumstances. Suppose someone notices, as Condon[5] and Zipf[6] did, that the logarithms of the frequencies (f) of words occurring in a large sample text arrange themselves very nearly on a straight line when plotted against the logarithms of the ranks (r) of these words. The equation

$$f = \frac{c}{r}$$

where c is a constant, can be used successfully to represent this relationship, in the limited sense that $\frac{c}{r}$, for a given value of r, gives very nearly the observed frequency. The relation between f and r as expressed by the formula is thus a model for the relation

[3] G. Herdan, *Language as choice and chance* (P. Noordhoff, Groningen, 1956).
[4] V. Belevitch, *Langage des machines et langage humain* (Office de Publicité, S. A., Bruxelles, 1956).
[5] E. V. Condon, Statistics of vocabulary, *Science* 67. 300 (1928).
[6] G. K. Zipf, *Human behavior and the principle of least effort* (Addison-Wesley, Cambridge, Mass., 1949).

between the observed values of frequency and rank. No more can reasonably be claimed for an isolated model of this type, obtained by a process of empirical curve-fitting, than what has been said. It turns out, however, that this formula can be fitted, with varying degrees of accuracy, to rank-frequency data obtained from a variety of different texts. It is natural, as a consequence, to inquire into the reasons why one and the same model should serve so well under circumstances supposed to be different. The formula $f = \frac{c}{r}$ itself obviously cannot serve as an answer to such a question. More sophisticated models are required. How such models operate is readily illustrated by analogy with a common experience.

To determine the best arrangement of two desks and two chairs in an office, one can move these desks and chairs about in the room until a satisfactory arrangement has been found. Another alternative is to draw a floor plan of the room, and then draw desk and chair outlines until a satisfactory layout is achieved. In this model, scaled-down distances and dimensions on paper stand for distances and dimensions within the room, the inclusion of the diagrams for desks and chairs within the actual room, erasure and redrawing of desk and chair diagrams replaces the moving of desks and chairs. So far as physical layout, aisle space, etc., are concerned, the model adequately mirrors the actual room. However, it is important to note that the model does not represent such factors as lighting, window placement, etc. By choice, the model is a floor plan, and it cannot be expected to yield information about those aspects of the room under study to which no model elements correspond.

The discovery that the replacement of concrete objects by diagrams, and of operations on these objects by corresponding operations on the corresponding diagrams can lead to useful results provides the very justification for the use of models. Unfortunately, this discovery must be made anew, at least in part, each time a new model is applied to a new type of situation. In view of the long and fruitful experience of mankind with the use of floor plans as models, their value is usually taken for granted, and the consequent savings in effort realized. Analogous mathematical models, geometry being one example, are of great importance in all branches of engineering, but insofar as they are tools for synthesis, their value to linguistics, which has been a primarily historical and descriptive discipline, naturally appears limited.

The type of correspondence between a concrete system and a model illustrated by the preceding example need not, however, necessarily be used for synthesis. Often, a model is used merely to 'explain,' by imposing a structure on the concrete system, a structure defined by the model elements and the relations among them, even when no direct verification of the independent existence of corresponding concrete elements and relations is possible. Gleason[7] illustrates the use of English itself as a model of this type in the following way:

[7] H. A. Gleason, *An introduction to descriptive linguistics* 4 (Henry Holt, N. Y., 1955).

"Consider a rainbow or a spectrum from a prism. There is a continuous gradation of color from one end to the other. That is, at any point there is only a small difference in the colors immediately adjacent at either side. Yet an American describing it will list the hues as *red, orange, yellow, green, blue, purple*, or something of the kind. The continuous gradation of color which exists in nature is represented in language by a series of discrete categories. This is an instance of structuring of content. There is nothing inherent either in the spectrum or the human perception of it which would compel its division in this way. The specific method of division is part of the structure of English."

Belevitch, in his book, and Mandelbrot[8,9] have attempted to 'explain' the universality of the observed relation between word rank and frequency in terms of a model based on the theory of communication. The model formalizes Zipf's principle of least effort, by assigning a cost to undefined elementary symbols (model elements), then a cost to combinations of these symbols. Mathematical techniques are then used to find that probability distribution of symbol combinations for which the ratio of average information (in the sense of Shannon[10]) per combination to average cost per combination is maximum. This maximum is attained when the negative logarithm of the probability of a combination is proportional to the cost of the combination. It is obvious that the most probable combinations should also be the least costly, but this result specifies a more precise relation between cost and probability. On the assumption of a rule of formation for combinations in terms of elementary symbols, the number of combinations having cost less than or equal to a given cost can be calculated, and a formula correlating rank and probability obtained. A graph of rank versus probability plotted according to this formula bears a remarkable resemblance to those of observed rank-frequency graphs, and therein lies, at present, the only point of contact between this model and reality.

What makes such a model seem superior to the empirical formula of Zipf, is the fact that the structure of the model is presented as a tentative 'explanation' for the observed phenomenon. However, the only verification offered to date of the validity of this explanation, is the agreement between the model formula and observed data. The degree of agreement must not be overemphasized. For one thing, the shape of the observed curve is, to some extent, an artifact. By definition, the first word, in order of frequency, is at least as frequent as the second word, the nth at least as frequent as the $n+1$st. It is hardly surprising therefore that regularity of a very restricted kind (monotonic decrease of frequency with increasing rank) should be observed. Furthermore, the agreement is subject to the adjustment of at least one parameter, which

[8] B. Mandelbrot, An informational theory of the statistical structure of language, *Communication theory*, ed. by W. Jackson 486–502 (Academic Press, N. Y., 1953).
[9] B. Mandelbrot, Structure formelle des textes et communication, *Word*, 10. 1–27 (1954).
[10] C. E. Shannon, and W. Weaver, *The mathematical theory of communication* (University of Illinois Press, Urbana, 1949).

cannot yet be specified independently, but must be obtained from the observed data themselves. All the rest, elementary symbols, costs, criteria for maximization, etc., belong to the model. Whether or not these model elements can ultimately be placed in significant correspondence with observable data remains an open question. Belevitch has attempted to identify the elementary symbols of the model with letters in printed texts, while Mandelbrot (see footnote 9) laudably has been more cautious in this respect, and leaves the problem to physiologists or psychologists.

In spite of these reservations, the model is so reasonable, and the predicted rank-frequency relation so close to observations that the model must be considered highly promising. This impression is reinforced by the success of Belevitch in developing a similar model for the observed rank-frequency relation of letters. The assumption that 'words' are organized as *sequences* of elementary symbols, while fruitful in accounting for the rank-frequency relations of words, fails with respect to letters. However, with the assumption that letters are combinations of *simultaneously* occuring elementary symbols, the same basic model leads to a theoretical rank-frequency curve whose shape is in close agreement with that of observed curves.

Belevitch has not restricted himself to the analysis of words and letters. With a model based on Jakobson's analysis of phonemes in terms of binary distinctive features, he attempts to describe rank-frequency relations for phonemes in much the same terms as for letters. A more speculative argument, based on somewhat recondite properties of binary functions of binary variables, is presented as a possible explanation of the recognition of approximately 40 phonemes in several languages.

The models of Herdan have a closer kinship to the simple 'descriptive' model of Zipf, than to the 'explanatory' models of Belevitch and Mandelbrot. Herdan, like many others, has been struck by, on the one hand, the apparent stability of many characteristics of texts and, on the other, by the variation of other characteristics from author to author or with time. His book represents an effort to express these characteristics quantitatively in a useful fashion. The fundamental assumption underlying the use of statistical tests in linguistics is that given texts can be regarded as random samples from a model population. Insofar as Herdan coolly examines the validity of this assumption with respect to a variety of statistical tests, the circumstances in which these tests can be applied, and the conclusions that can be drawn as a consequence, the book has considerable merit.

Unfortunately, the exposition is frequently obscure, and a strong current of mysticism running throughout the text tends to blur the distinction between fact and fancy. Matters are at their worst with regard to the so-called Principle of Linguistic Duality, claimed to be related to the perfectly respectable concept of duality in projective geometry. The confusion begins with a mistaken view of binary coding as essential to information theory: "The use of a binary code in information theory is itself only a first step towards a deeper understanding of the linguistic mechanism, and could never achieve its ultimate purpose without being 'aided and abetted' at every stage of the journey by the principle which I have called Linguistic Duality." It ends on the following note: "To paraphrase Larochefoucauld's aphorism about hypocrisy being the tribute which vice pays to virtue, we can say confidently from our study of the Nazi use of language that 'Duplicity is the tribute which "Gleichschaltung" pays to Duality.'" The linguist, with good reason, might look askance at the introduction of such 'mathematics' into linguistics. Nevertheless, a solid substratum of scholarship, and many stimulating ideas combine to make the book an important contribution to the mathematics of linguistics.

The introduction of chance into linguistics through the use of statistical models seems to make some linguists uncomfortable. Commenting on Mandelbrot's model of the rank-frequency relation for words, A. S. C. Ross[11] said: "All statements of this kind really imply that the occurrence of a word at a given point in a text is a matter of chance and this is what philologists and students of literature will deny. If an English writer has to express the idea 'teapot' – and whether he has to or not is not in the least a matter of chance – the probability of his using the word 'teapot' is unity, and the probability of his using the word 'kettle' is zero." Such misunderstandings can arise only when the scope of a mathematical model is misunderstood. It is essential to distinguish between a model purporting to account for the way a given writer sets down successive words on a page, and one intended to describe and to explain characteristics that long sample texts possess on the average, which is all that is claimed for the rank-frequency model. It may be a pity or a blessing that this model cannot predict whether an author will write 'teapot' or 'kettle' at a given stage of writing, but it should be understood that it was not intended to do so. Furthermore, large-scale regularities that can be described by a statistical model are not at all inconsistent with the apparent operation of definite rules or deliberate choice in the small. For example, it is not the common practice to decide when to use a preposition by flipping a coin. A preposition is used when the thought to be expressed and the rules of grammar dictate that it be used. Nevertheless, a model[12,13] purporting to describe the distribution of certain prepositions in large text samples on the hypothesis that they have been sprinkled at random on the page, gives results that are in close agreement with observation.

The internal logical consistency of many mathematical models, and the aura of precision about numbers with many decimal places often blind interpreters to the crucial question, namely, what range of reality can the model usefully mirror? Thus, Joos, in a recent review[14] states that "The element which recurs most often in these

[11] Comments on a paper of Mandelbrot (fn. 8, p. 500).
[12] H. H. Josselson, *The Russian word count* 30 (Wayne University Press, Detroit, 1953).
[13] V. Yngve, Gap analysis and syntax, *IRE Transactions on Information Theory*, Vol. IT–2, No. 3, September 1956, pp. 106–112.
[14] M. Joos, *Language*, 32. 294 (1956).

notions is the elementary idea that meaning is simply additive, contrary to its information-theory definition which makes it multiplicative (so that logarithms get added). The illusion that meaning is additive can, however, be accounted for from redundancy." When a mathematician is obscure or vague (and this happens), or uses a common word in a technical sense without adequate warning (and this happens too), he is to blame for any ensuing misinterpretation. Shannon, and other writers on information theory, have, however, made quite clear the exclusive concern of this theory for certain statistical properties of symbol sequences, and the absence in the theory of any elements corresponding to meaning. Such use of misinterpreted mathematical models is particularly dangerous in view of the ease with which laymen often abdicate their common sense when confronted with the authority of supposedly exact mathematical arguments. It is only if the real limitations, as well as the power of mathematical models, are clearly understood by linguists, that mathematics can be used effectively in the service of linguistics.

Algebra is another branch of mathematics of potential value to linguistics. A recent paper by Schützenberger[15] describes conditions under which a discrete sequence of elementary symbols ('letters') has a unique decomposition into groups of these symbols ('words'). Thus, in a text formed as a sequence of the words '+,' '−+,' '−−+,' '−−−,' the words may be recovered even though written together without spaces, as the reader may verify with the sequence '+−−+−+−++−−−−−+.' At least some of the ideas presented in this paper should prove to be of interest in connection with the problem of segmentation of phonemic transcriptions, but this remains to be seen. The theory of semi-groups, a branch of modern algebra, is used by Schützenberger to obtain his results. Techniques of algebra and mathematical logic have been used by Chomsky[16] in a search for models for processes capable of generating all grammatical sentences of a language and no other combinations of elementary symbols, and capable also of characterizing the internal structure of such sentences. Models such as these may prove fruitful in applications to problems of automatic language translation.

A new class of problems of language synthesis has been posed as a consequence of attempts to use automatic machines for the retrieval of technical information from libraries.[17] The objective of research in this field is to develop machines able to search files of documents or abstracts, and to select and deliver all and only those pertinent to a question posed by an enquirer. The synthesis of languages for expressing abstracts and questions in a form suitable for machine use is considered to be of major importance in attaining this objective.

[15] M. P. Schützenberger, On an application of semi-group methods to some problems in coding, *IRE Transactions on Information Theory*, Vol. IT–2, No. 3, September 1956, pp. 47–60.

[16] N. Chomsky, Three models for the description of language, *IRE Transactions on Information Theory*, Vol. IT–2, No. 3, September 1956, pp. 113–124.

[17] J. W. Perry, A. Kent, M. Berry, *Machine literature searching* (Interscience, N. Y., 1956).

The problem of matching natural languages to symbol systems suitable for automatic manipulation recurs frequently in the design of automatic calculating and data-processing machines.[18,19] For example, the operating instructions for such machines must at present be expressed in languages which vary from machine to machine, and bear little resemblance to the languages (e.g., algebra or business English) in which problems to be solved by the machines are originally expressed. The 'programmer' responsible for devising the set of operating instructions must learn a machine language which, more often than not, has been designed by engineers with a view to ease of machine construction, rather than for ease of human use. The development of an adequate symbol system presents difficult problems. As Gleason[20] has pointed out, "the design of an orthography is a difficult and intricate matter about which we as yet know all too little," but what knowledge the linguist has of stable desirable features of natural languages could be of considerable value in this problem of machine design.

COMPUTATION LABORATORY, HARVARD UNIVERSITY

[18] A. G. Oettinger, Chart representations of data-processing systems, *Progress Reports* No. 1 and 2 by the Staff of the Computation Laboratory to the Electronic Research Steering Committee of the American Gas Association and Edison Electric Institute.
[19] A. G. Oettinger, A new basic approach to automatic data processing, *Progress Report* No. 3 by the Staff of the Computation Laboratory to the Electronic Research Steering Committee of the American Gas Association and Edison Electric Institute.
[20] Gleason, *op. cit.* 317.

L. R. PALMER

SOME OBSERVATIONS ON THE LANGUAGE OF LINGUISTS

IN 1867 Michel Bréal stood before the *Société de Linguistique* of Paris to lament the death of Franz Bopp. "The founder of our studies," he said, "Franz Bopp, died a few weeks ago. Up till now all the scholars devoted to our branch of studies could regard themselves as one family whose head was still in their midst. Today Comparative Philology has lost its father."[1] Today the break-up of that unitary family has proceeded so far that the different branches speak mutually unintelligible languages. This is widely deplored. Professor E. Haugen, for instance, in his survey article 'Directions in modern linguistics'[2] writes: "The very growth of an independent group of linguists has promoted a kind of scientific isolation. . . . American linguists are finding it increasingly difficult to read European writings in our field..." (211). "...in Europe a new metalanguage is being shaped which is at least as different from that of our school grammars as is the American metalanguage. The two are as mutually incomprehensible as French and English, and we shall soon need a bimetalingual dictionary to translate from one into the other..." (213). Haugen even points to examples of metadialects and metaidiolects "which make it confusing to follow recent discussion" (ibid.). Sharing as I do Haugen's conviction that all scholars concerned are talking about the same thing, I believe that it has become an urgent task to examine the language of linguists. This is primarily a matter for the philosopher, but I venture to submit some brief prolegomena.

First a quotation from a master of scientific terminology, Carl von Linné (1707–78): "Knowledge implies peculiar ideas and suitable designations, some of which allow in ourselves to imitate certain things, and others which make possible an Intercourse with the rest of Mankind by means of some comprehensible Manner of Parlance" (*Systema, Genera, Species Plantarum*, 1753). Accepting this sound advice concerning

[1] Les progrès de la grammaire comparée, *MSL* 1.72ff.
[2] *Language* 27.211–222 (1951).

comprehensibility, we must decide what rules we should lay down for the contributor of a new term. We should, I suggest, reassert the tyranny of the hearer. It is the responsibility of the proposer of a new term to make it intelligible in the way that all speech becomes intelligible, that is by repetition in the appropriate context of situation, and this in the case of the descriptive linguist is simply the set of operations he is carrying out on his chosen body of speech material. The proposer of a new term must simply make an exhibition of himself. Before the attentive *corona* of metalinguists he must demonstrate his successive operations until he reaches the point at which he finds himself impelled to guide and rivet our attention by means of the new term.

Before submitting a recent example to this simple test, I should first emphasize what seems to me a fact of basic importance often ignored in the highly self-conscious modern procedures of analysis and description. This is what I propose to call the 'item-experience', No speech habits can be acquired, understood or described without first the 'that there' of the primary experience, followed by the 'that there again' which identifies the given perception with some other or others retained in memory. This fundamental problem has been recently discussed by H. H. Price in *Thinking and experience*, especially c. II "Recognition", where I single out his insistence that "the first problem [one] will have to tackle if he begins at the beginning, will be the analysis of primary recognition" (55). Now for the apprehension of the linguistic sign the 'that there again' of the perceived sound-complex is matched again and again with the 'that there again' in the context of situation until there jumps that vitalizing spark which transforms a concatenation of noises into the linguistic sign. This fundamental 'that there again' I propose to call by the convenient Latin adverb *item.* No earthworm or octopus can go about its business without 'item experiences'. No less are speech acquisition and linguistic description at bottom essentially processes of 'itemization'. In describing the speech habits of a given community we proceed from a corpus of recorded gross 'items', the utterances. By the use of various criteria, pause, intonational and rhythmic patterns, minimal utterance and so on we can isolate 'items' at different levels of analysis down to the phoneme and the phonemic feature. But our whole structure of description, it would appear, rests on the elemental 'item-experience'. Failure to realise this has vitiated attempts at complete replacement of 'item-description' by purely distributional statements.

This much said by way of prolegomena, we may proceed to the examination of a new technical term. In a paper[3] which has done much to clarify some of the basis concepts of descriptive linguistics, Mr. W. Haas declares that "the empirical meaning of segment is nothing more than being separately quotable. This is also what is generally meant by a *sound.*" That considerable importance attaches to this new insight was suggested by a preliminary announcement from a distinguished contemp-

[3] On defining linguistic units, *TPS* 1954, 54–84.

orary in the front rank of descriptive linguistics.[4] Let us submit this important new technical term to the sort of examination suggested above. It is a new word uttered by an analyst of speech within the context of situation provided by his technical operations. It is only so that we can apprehend its purport or reference. Unfortunately Mr. Haas has offered no definition, and we are left to assume that the meaning is to be sought within the semantic field plotted in the standard dictionaries of English for this word. We proceed on that assumption.

'Quotability', implying able to be quoted, in order to be applicable to an operation being carried out by the linguist must be transformed into the verbal form 'I quote'. The mise-en-scène of our metalinguistic autopsy will be an 'I quote' operation. We are offered the example of the initial *p* in *pin*. Here two itemizing operations have already been performed, first at the word level and then at the phoneme level. The linguist is asked to demonstrate an act of 'quoting'. He will make the sound [*p*]. The insistent *corona* of observers will object that the said act is adequately described by the statement "I utter [*p*]." What new factor is involved in the expression "I quote [*p*]"? Surely it is the implication that the [*p*] which I now utter is the *same* as other sounds which I remember uttering and hearing on previous occasions. It looks as though 'to quote', in Mr. Haas' own words, is "a practical reference by imitation" to an *item*. It is the use of a token to stand for a type. So Professor Bazell's dictum that "the unquotable is often the unidentifiable" should perhaps be modified to read "the non-identified cannot be quoted". This brings descriptive linguistics back to its starting point – the intuitive apprehension of 'items': [*p*] is a segment, a minimal segment, a phoneme because we can say, repeat, quote, identify, itemize [*p*].[5] Doubtless the Greeks analysed their own language along these common-sense lines and established its phoneme inventory when they adopted and adapted the Semitic alphabet not long after 1000 B.C. It was to these basic units that the Greek theorists gave the name στοιχεῖα.

This brings us to another possible avenue to the reconciliation and reintegration of our studies. Is there not in the new much that is old? The Greeks in their linguistic descriptions found it necessary to add to their analysis in terms of the basic indivisible στοιχεῖον the concept of προσῳδία. This is another word which has come to figure largely in some recent English contributions to linguistic description. Following on Professor J. R. Firth's programmatic paper Sounds and Prosodies[6] a number of his

[4] C. E. Bazell, *Linguistic Form* 55 (1953): "On the importance of quotability see W. Haas, *Trans. Phil. Soc.* 1954 (article consulted in MS)."

[5] Though the new term 'quote' would appear to be purely tautological and nothing more than a restatement of the primary 'item-experience', 'quotability' provides a handy practical laboratory criterion for the delimitation of that class of basic items we call 'phonemes'. It solves the dilemma posed by the differentiation of 'two pins' and 'two bins', which may be stated either in terms of the phoneme opposition /*p*:*b*/ or the phonemic features *zero*:*voice*. The operational boundary between the two modes of description is precisely that of 'quotability'.

[6] *TPS* 1948, 127–152.

pupils have applied this fundamental insight to studies of particular languages. The part played by 'prosodies' in this apparently new technique of linguistic description would appear to be this. The given corpus of utterances is broken down so as to yield the minimal distinctive units. This gives us an inventory of phonemes. But to describe the given speech corpus it is also necessary to state the relationships between the phonemes – their relative length, pitch, stress, intonation patterns, modes of juncture, and so on. These provide handy technical criteria for the delimitation of sentence, phrase, word, and so on. The term prosodies is used by Firth and his pupils to include most of those interphonemic features which others differentiate as 'suprasegmental features' and junctures. Thus Firth writes (*op. cit.*): "...we may abstract those features which mark word or syllable initial, word or syllable finals, or word junctions from the word piece or sentence and regard them syntagmatically as prosodies, distinct from the phonematic constituents which are referred to as units of the consonant and vowel systems."

This extension of the application of the term 'prosody' might seem to be a regrettable dilution of a useful technical term, but there is ancient precedent for this usage. The Greeks, as I have said, not only carried out an adequate phonemic analysis of their own language but also were not slow in devising a scientific terminology. They analysed utterance (λόγος), song (μέλος), and dance along parallel lines and found the ultimate units in the στοιχεῖον, a mysterious term which the Romans still more mysteriously rendered as *elementum.*[7] But if a description is devised primarily to serve the purpose of 'realising' the acts of speech, and the Greeks were always conscious of this practical end, then it is evident that the phonemic representation of an utterance as a row of symbols whose time succession is represented by the arbitrary order left-to-right will not suffice. So the Greeks supplemented their descriptions by additional indication marks to guide the reader in his realisation.[8] These marks were called προσῳδίαι. This term is an abstract noun from the verb προσᾴδειν in the sense 'sing in tune with an accompanying instrument'. The term was subsequently applied to the spoken word with reference to the intonation of the whole utterance as well as the accentuation of individual syllables. This limitation of sense persisted in the Latin calque *accentus*. Laum makes clear that with reference to the syllable the limitation

[7] The most recent paper on this subject known to me is that by H. Koller in *Glotta* 34.161–174 (1955). I have not been convinced by this author's attempt to show that the term στοιχεῖον originated among the musicologists. In the first place the Peripatetic Adrestos, quoted by Koller, himself makes the linguistic analysis the basis of the analysis of μέλος. Further στοιχεῖον is regularly used for the basic indivisible units in technical analyses of language while the corresponding term in music is φθόγγος. Adrestos merely says that they are στοιχειώδεις. Nor does Plato's remark (*Theaet.* 206a) "everyone would agree that these [φθόγγοι] are the στοιχεῖα of music" show that στοιχεῖον was the standard technical term for the musical 'element'. Finally there is no evidence to show that στοῖχος from which στοιχεῖον is allegedly derived, was ever used to designate the musical scale.

[8] In this paragraph I summarize the findings of B. Laum's fundamental study *Das alexandrinische Akzentuationssystem* (1928).

of 'prosody' to the τόνος persisted and the expression δάσεια or ψιλὴ προσῳδία is not found until the Byzantine grammarians. But in so far as the correct 'realisation' of texts depends no less on knowledge of breathing and quantity than on that of accentuation proper, προσῳδία came to include these phenomena too. Herodian appears to have been the first to include under προσῳδία all the modifications to which a sound is subject. By the beginning of the fourth century there is evidence that 'prosodies' included accents, breathing, and quantity. Later still all the written indications including apostrophe, hyphen and comma (ὑποδιαστολή) were subsumed in the term προσῳδία. To insert such marks of pronunciation in a text was described as κατὰ προσῳδίαν στίχειν τὰς γραφάς (Laum p. 27). This is in striking agreement with the modern extended usage which includes junctural features under the heading of prosodies. Even the hyphen (ὑφ'ἓν ἀναγινώσκειν) was justly regarded as a prosody since it indicated to the reader that the elements so joined were to be 'realised with singleness of accent' (ἕνωσις τοῦ τόνου).[9] This extension of the concept should find acceptance among modern theorists, for the hyphen in the English word 'green-house' might equally well be regarded as a prosodic indication since sentences such as "you will find him in the *green-house* at the end of the lane" and "you will find him in the *green house* at the end of the lane" are distinguished only by 'singleness of accent', *greén-hoùse* in the first as against the double accent *greén hoúse* in the second. It can hardly be objected that the Byzantine definitions were superficial and based solely on the indication in the written texts. Earlier authors had remained fully aware of the distinction between the spoken sound and the written symbol. Sextus Empiricus explicitly states that there are three current acceptations of the term στοιχεῖον and he rightly emphasizes that he is concerned with 'the power of the character' (προαγέτω νῦν ἡ ζήτησις μάλιστα περὶ τῆς δυνάμεως),[10] that is to say the spoken sound which the character symbolizes.

It is this uncomfortable man, who had no very high opinion of professional philologers, who will provide us with another example of the sophisticated use of the concept of 'prosody' in linguistic analysis. His purpose is avowedly destructive, and the argument runs as follows. These philologers give themselves airs (κομᾶν καὶ μέγα φρονεῖν) and run down professors of other subjects (ἀεὶ δὲ τῶν τὰ λοιπὰ κοσμουμένων μαθήματα κατατρέχειν). When driven into a corner they evade the issue by accusing their opponents of barbarism or solecism. These men of letters, unable themselves to string together two passable sentences, presume to criticise the great masters such as Thucydides, Plato and Demosthenes. But their science is non-existent. In his attack on the philologers Sextus cunningly saps the very citadel of their pride – their much vaunted system of 'elements'. After showing (1.102ff.) that the concept of double consonants such as ζ (consisting of s+d) is a contradiction in terms and that the true

[9] Laum, *op. cit.* 426.
[10] *Adv. Math.* 1.99.

'elements' are the components of such a composite sound (τὰ συστατικά τοῦ διπλοῦ στοιχείου στοιχεῖά ἐστιν), Sextus turns to the so-called 'dichronous' vowels, which are 'common' in respect of length and shortness. But the letter and the bare character are not indicative of a 'common' nature. α, ι, and υ are neither one thing nor the other until they are uttered with a 'prosody'. When they receive the prosody, they are at one time long and at another short, but never 'common'. The same argument applies to all the so-called prosodies of which the philologists say there are seven – long, short, acute, grave, and circumflex, rough and smooth. Now the short vocalic elements admit of five prosodies, namely short, acute, grave, rough, and smooth; this makes $5 \times 2 = 10$. The long elements admit of six, since we must add the circumflex: $6 \times 2 = 12$. Then there are the 'dichronous' elements with seven possible prosodies apiece: $7 \times 3 = 21$. Hence the total number of such vocalic elements is in fact 43. If we add 17 consonants, the 'elements' now amount to 60 and not the 24 of the philologists.

It should be observed that in this analysis Sextus is operating with units at the level of quotability, and that if we define the στοιχεῖον in this way, his criticism is valid. It is impossible to 'quote' a Greek vocalic element which is neither long nor short, neither acute nor grave nor circumflex, neither rough nor smooth, still less one in which these contradictory qualities 'subsist'. On the other hand, if the concept of prosody is introduced, we may reduce the inventory still more drastically than the philologists' seven vocalic elements. There is a different line of argument, says Sextus,[11] according to which the vocalic elements are fewer than the seven the philologists are always prating about. For if according to them an α subject to lengthening and shortening is not two different elements but a single common one, and likewise with ι and υ, it will follow that ε and η are also one element common in respect of the same 'power'. Likewise with ο and ω. So the philologists are blind and do not perceive the consequences of their own reasoning when they say that there are seven vowels when there are in fact only five in respect of their nature.

It remains to add that this highly sophisticated analysis, a splitting of the linguistic atom, the στοιχεῖον-phoneme, with the aid of the concept of 'prosody', is dated to the last third of the second century A. D. Shall we not plead for some mitigation of that severe judgment according to which "It was the Greeks who debased the science [of language]. They showed how infinitely inferior they were to the Hindus as scientific thinkers and the effect of their muddling lasted two thousand years"?[12]

OXFORD

[11] *Op. cit.* 1.115ff.

[12] B. Whorf, Linguistics as an exact science, *Technology Review* M.I.T. 43.14 = Four articles on metalinguistics, 11ff., a passage quoted with approval by Professor W. S. Allen in *TPS* 1953, 85.

HERBERT PENZL

THE EVIDENCE FOR PHONEMIC CHANGES

I. TYPES OF PHONEMIC CHANGE

IN DIACHRONIC linguistics a great variety of phonetic changes can be observed. Scholars seem to be agreed, however, that there are only very few types of phonemic change. Prehistorical, i.e. reconstructed changes cannot be treated in the same manner as historically attested changes. Only a careful consideration of historical changes enables us to draw any conclusions regarding prehistorical changes. The problems of reconstruction should not be prematurely linked and added to the specific problems of diachronic phonemics.

§ 1.1 *Phonemic Change.* A number of changes affect only the shape of certain morphemes but not the phonemic stock. Among them we notice the loss or replacement of certain phonemes in morphemes (assimilation, dissimilation), e.g. *Tölpel* 'bumpkin' (MHG *dörpære, dörper* > *dörpel*); *Pfennig* (OHG *pfenning*); *Welt* (MHG *werlt, welt*); *Hoffart* 'arrogance' (MHG *hochvart*); *Elle* (OHG *elina*). The sequence of phonemes in a morpheme can be reversed (metathesis): *Wespe* (MHG *wefse, webse, wespe*), *Erle* 'alder' (OHG *erila, elira*). A phoneme can be added to a morpheme: *Obst* 'fruit' (MHG *obez*), *Habicht* 'hawk' (MHG *habech*), *albern* 'foolish' (MHG *alwære*), *niemand* (MHG *nieman*). All these changes could be called distributional; they do not constitute sound-change in the regular sense. Some of them may occur almost with the regularity of a sound-change at a given time in a given language, but they are not gradual, even if possibly produced unconsciously. They seem often sporadic, involving some morphemes but not others with the same structure. Analogical remodeling is a common factor in their occurrence. They may be a factor leading to a phonemic change, however, since any change in incidence or distribution may also result in a change in pattern and stock. The evidence for such distributional changes is usually plentiful and unambiguous; it does not differ from the evidence for phonemic changes which we will consider here. All observable phonetic changes in the history of a language may have some phonemic significance.[1] Thus a phonemic change is any sound-change that gradually affects the contrastive features of the phonemes, their general incidence and patterning, or their allophonic variation.

The phonemic principle makes it necessary for us to view each and every change from the point of view of the entire pattern. This is perhaps the most important new methodological demand in historical linguistics that at the same time presents a distinct advance over an earlier approach that appears too atomistic now. If we thus isolate in this paper certain phonemic changes and do not analyze their pattern impact in detail, we are aware that we are not offering an adequate description of the change. After all, we do not indicate its absolute and relative chronology, its regional origin and spread, and its probable causes either. We are concerned here with its typological classification and the evidence for its occurrence, not with any other pertinent factors.

§ 1.2 *The Phonemic Shift.* All phonemic changes may either occur in all positions or only in specific ones; the latter changes are usually called 'conditioned', the former 'unconditioned'. What is conditioned change diachronically, corresponds synchronically to conditioned allophonic variation.[2] André Martinet[3] subdivides phonemic changes into (1) those that do no affect the number of distinctive features within the language, (2) those that reduce them, (3) those that increase them. Daniel Jones' 29 types of phonemic change are partly based on phonetic criteria.[4] Among attested phonemic changes we distinguish six different types: shifts, mergers (§ 1.3), splits (§ 1.4), monophonemization (§ 1.5), diphonemization (§ 1.6), phonemic loss (§ 1.7). The phonemic shift consists of the change of a phoneme of one sound-type to a phoneme of another sound-type. Any such shift may result in a whole series of interconnected changes, but the pattern adjustment may also not exceed some allophonic variation which is not recoverable historically. The change from the high back rounded vowel phoneme /u/ to a high front rounded vowel phoneme /ü/ in French, *tu*, *dur*, *duc* is an example of a shift. Another example is the change from an apical lenis spirant /þ/ to an apical lenis stop /d/ in Old High German: *ther* or *dher*, later *der*; *thing*, later *ding*. In both cases the 'terminal' phoneme is of a different

[1] R. Jakobson, "Prinzipien der historischen Phonologie," *TCLP* 4.247 ff. (1931) labeled sound-changes as 'phonologisch' or as 'ausserphonologisch'. N. van Wijk, *Mélanges van Ginneken* 94 ff., rejected this dichotomy.

[2] Charles E. Osgood and T. E. Sebeok, *Psycholinguistics* 148 (1954).

[3] *Économie des changements phonétiques* 175 (1955). Henry M. Hoenigswald, "Sound change and linguistic structure," *Language* 22.138 (1946), differentiated between: phonemic change without loss of contrast; unconditioned and conditioned mergers with loss of contrast; secondary rearrangements induced by a primary loss of contrast; borrowed contrasts.

[4] D. Jones, *The phoneme: its nature and use*, chapter 32, pp. 233–252 (1950).

type than the 'initial' one and not identical with any phoneme already in the language: neither /ü/ in French (Latin) nor /đ/ in most Middle and Upper German dialects of Old High German existed before the phonemic change. In a shift the number of phonemes remains the same, since the loss of one or more units of the initial pattern seems compensated by the addition of one or more units in the terminal pattern. The formula to express a phonemic shift is: /A/ > /*x*/.[5] A. Martinet considers all phonemic changes that affect the pattern as part of a chain, which, from the point of view of the change in question, would either seem to be a 'drag-chain' or a 'push-chain'.[6] Most shifts represent what R. Jakobson called 'Umphonologisierung', i.e., a change from one phonemic distinction between two phonemes to another phonemic distinction between them.[7]

§ 1.3 *The Phonemic Merger*. Another important and most frequent type of phonemic change is the merger, the coalescence of two phonemes. This can either occur in all positions (unconditioned change) or only in some special phonetic environment (conditioned change). The result of the merger may be the exclusive occurrence of either one of the two contrasting units or the emergence of a new, possibly intermediate type. Two well-known examples for merger in the history of German are the medial and final coalescence of the two sibilants /s/ and /z/ in late Middle High German, e.g. *es* from earlier *ez* 'it' and *es* 'of it, of him', and the coalescence of the allophones of /a/ and /e/ before *i* sounds in Old High German (primary umlaut of /a/), e.g. OHG *gesti*, plural of *gast*. The phonetic identification of the initial sibilant phonemes /s/ and /z/ has been a moot question, but at any rate a single terminal phoneme /s/ results, in contrast with the other new sibilant /š/ which developed from the cluster /sk/ in Middle High German (see below § 1.5). The Old High German [e] allophones of /a/ before *i*-sounds and the [e] allophones of /e/ in its rare occurrences before *i*-sounds, e.g. in *felis* (NHG *Fels*) 'rock', *krebiz* (NHG *Krebs*) 'crab', *pelliz* (NHG *Pelz*) 'fur', merged; thus a suspension of the contrast between /a/ and /e/, in the terminology of the Prague school a 'neutralization', resulted in that position. The /e/ phoneme prevailed however. Our formulas for merger will have to be:

$$\begin{matrix} /\mathrm{A}/ \\ \\ /\mathrm{B}/ \end{matrix} > /A/; \qquad \begin{matrix} /\mathrm{A}/ \\ \\ /\mathrm{B}/ \end{matrix} > /B/; \qquad \begin{matrix} /\mathrm{A}/ \\ \\ /\mathrm{B}/ \end{matrix} > /x/$$

This indicates that the terminal phoneme may be either one of the two initial

[5] We use Roman capitals for the phoneme in the initial pattern (A B), Italic capitals for the corresponding more or less identical phonemes in the terminal pattern (*A B*), and lower case Italics (*x*) for a new terminal phoneme which is not identical with any initial phonemes.
[6] A. Martinet, "Function, structure, and sound change," *Word* 8.1ff. (1952).
[7] *TCLP* 4.255ff.

phonemes or a phoneme that is different from them.[8] Partial or limited merger (neutralization), e.g. before a phoneme /X/, we can express as follows:

/AX/ > /*BX*/; /BX/ > /*AX*/

This indicates the merger of /A/ and /B/ only before /X/ with the terminal prevalence of /*B*/ or /*A*/, respectively. Most mergers represent what R. Jakobson called an 'Entphonologisierung' of some distinctive feature.[9]

§ 1.4 *The Phonemic Split.* A third most important type of phonemic change is the split, a bifurcation of two phonemes out of the allophones of one initial phoneme. Striking examples are provided by the results of umlaut in late Old High German, when all rounded back vowel phonemes developed rounded front vowel phonemes from their allophones before former *i*-sounds:[10] /a/ and /ä/, /ā/ and /ǟ/, /ō/ and /ȫ/, /o/ and /ö/, /ū/ and /ü/, /u/ and /ü/, /au/ and /eu/, also /ë/ and /e/, e.g. MHG *maht*, pl. *mähte* (OHG *mahti*), *nāmen* (OHG *nāmun*) 'they took', *næmen* subj. (OHG *nāmin*), *schōne* adv. 'beautifully' (OHG *scōno*), *schoene* adj. 'beautiful' (OHG *scōni*), *hūt* 'skin', pl. *hiute* (OHG *hūti*), *übel* (OHG *ubil)* 'evil'. Our formula for a phonemic split is as follows:

/*A*/
/A/ >
/*x*/

/*x*/ in this formula designates the new phoneme, which is often /*A'*/ from an allophone [A'] of /A/. All splits represent what R. Jakobson (see footnote 9) calls a 'Phonologisierung' (a phonemization or phonemicization).

§ 1.5 *Monophonemization.* Another phonemic change consists of the change from a cluster to a single phoneme. This often resembles a phonemic shift (§ 1.2). As examples we quote the development of a groove sibilant /š/ from an earlier cluster consisting of a slit sibilant and a velar stop (/sk/) in Middle High German and in Middle English: MHG *visch* (OHG *fisk*), ME *fish*, *fissh* (OE *fisc*) (see § 3.4). In English and in German the cluster /ng/ developed into a single velar nasal phoneme /ŋ/: *singen*, *to sing*. The formula for such a change is as follows:

/AB/ > /*x*/

The new phoneme /*x*/ may represent /*A'*/ or /*B'*/, i.e. be the reflex of allophones [A'] or [B'] appearing in the initial cluster: e.g., /ŋ/ developed from the allophone

[8] See Osgood-Sebeok, *loc.cit.*, for factors determining the likelihood of merger between two phones.
[9] *TCLP* 4.250ff.
[10] Herbert Penzl, "Umlaut and secondary umlaut in Old High German," *Language* 25.233ff. (1949).

[ŋ] of /n/ appearing before /g/ (or /k/); thus /ng/ ([ŋg]) > /ŋ/ is an example for /AB/ > /*A'*/.

§ 1.6 *Diphonemization.* A single phoneme can develop into a cluster of two phonemes: /A/ > /*XY*/. Also this change resembles a phonemic shift (§ 1.2). The terminal cluster can contain two phonemes already found in the pattern. An example for this change is the New High German diphthongization where Middle High German /ī/ became /ai/, /ū/ became /au/, /ǖ/ became /oi/: *Wein* (MHG *wīn*), *Haus* (MHG *hūs*), *Leute* (MHG *liute*) (§ 3.4).

§ 1.7 *The Phonemic Loss.* Another phonemic change is the loss of a phoneme either in some positions only or everywhere: /A/ > 0. It could be labelled 'merger with zero'.[11] As examples we can cite the Old High German loss of the phoneme /h/ in clusters as /hl/ /hr/ /hw/ /hn/, e.g. *laut* (OHG *hlūt*), *Ross* (OHG *hros*), *wer* (OHG *hwer*), *neigen* (OHG *hnīgan*), or the loss of /h/ in intervocalic position in late Middle High German: e.g. in *sehen* (§ 3.5).

The rise of a new phoneme by borrowing, e.g. the appearance of nasalized vowels in French loan-words in German (*Cousin*, *Bonbon*), or the adoption of /f/ in Russian, cannot be considered a counterpart to phonemic loss because the borrowing of foreign phonemes is not a sound-change from initial zero.[12]

II. EVIDENCE FOR SYNCHRONIC AND DIACHRONIC ANALYSIS

§ 2.1 *Orthographic Evidence.* In historical linguistics diachronic analysis must be preceded by synchronic analysis. The former can only be based on the comparison between two or more successive stages of a language that have been analyzed synchronically. The evidence for the synchronic and diachronic analysis is the same. There are several types of such evidence. Their careful consideration, which seems to have been somewhat neglected, is of great importance for the methodology of historical linguistics.

Orthographic evidence (§ 3) must be mentioned first. The relationship between symbol and sound, between the graphemic and the phonemic system is a basic problem in historical linguistics. Alphabetic writing itself in its inception used to involve a certain 'phonemic' interpretation of the sounds on the part of scribes and authors, particularly if they wrote their own native language or dialect, when they would attempt to render the essential units of their phonemic system and would not be aware of allophones. Thus the use and distribution of graphemes is important evidence in synchronic analysis. The known derivation of the symbols and their

[11] Hoenigswald, *Language* 22.139.

[12] R. Jakobson, *TCLP* 4.254,261; D. Jones, *The phoneme* §§ 735–739.

original values can be used for general phonetic identifications (§ 2.5). Occasionally recorded transliterations into another alphabet, e.g. into the Cyrillic, Arabic, or some phonetic alphabet, may be helpful. Diachronic interpretations are facilitated by the observation of changes in the orthographic system, of internal orthographic fluctuation or of a modern discrepancy between symbol and pronunciation.[13] Not every change in spelling implies a change in pronunciation; e.g., the Middle English use of 'ou' for Old English 'u' is simply due to the different spelling-practice of the Anglo-Norman scribes. Not only the analysis of orthographic systems, but also the study of all deviations from them, namely of occasional spellings ('naive spellings'), provides evidence. Their synchronic analysis reveals the discrepancy between the traditional orthography and the phonemic system of its user.

The term 'occasional spellings' suggests a minority-type of orthography which occurs together with the majority-type in identical or contemporaneous texts. Occasional spellings may represent just graphical errors, e.g. dittography, mistakes in copying, or only graphical variants, which are determined by the orthographic system with which the scribe or naive writer is familiar. They may reveal historical or dialectal variants for individual words: e.g. *jest* 'just', *gould* beside *gold*, *loom* beside *loam*. Synchronic analysis has to screen these spellings carefully within a given text and separate them from spellings that reveal the writer's or scribe's phonemic distribution or phonemic changes (see below § 4).[14] Diachronic analysis centers on the relevant differences between the conventional orthography and the observed individual deviations.

§ 2.2 *Orthoëpic Evidence*. Statements by grammarians at different times offer one type of evidence to the synchronic and diachronic analyst that orthography itself cannot supply (§ 5): phonetic identifications of the values designated by the symbols. Certain characteristics of Latin, Greek, Sanskrit sounds can be ascertained from the descriptions of native grammarians.[15] With the notable exception of the First Grammatical Treatise written about Old Icelandic phonemes in the middle of the twelfth century, evidence of this kind is not found for the Germanic languages until we reach early modern times. Then grammarians describe foreign sounds in terms of their native language; they describe the correct pronunciation and dialectal usage as to spelling and pronunciation; they describe the correlation sound: symbol

[13] C. L. Wrenn, "The value of spelling as evidence," *TPS* 1943, 14ff. speaks of the 'diachronicness' of English orthography (p. 16).

[14] Herbert Penzl, *Language* 18.148–151 (1942). R. E. Zachrisson, *Pronunciation of English vowels 1400–1700* 52ff. (1913) distinguished between "phonetic doublets" (historical variants), "irregular spellings due to miswriting, analogical transference, mechanical transference of symbols", and "phonetic spellings", which he defined as "deviations from the traditional spelling by which a sound-change is denoted."

[15] E. H. Sturtevant, *The pronunciation of Greek and Latin*[2] § 5 (1940).

to facilitate the teaching of reading and spelling. They are often interested in normalizing or reforming the orthographic evidence mentioned above (§2.1). They are usually themselves decisively influenced by the orthography.

Occasional and systematic representations of speech or dialect characteristics by deviant spellings in literary works can provide evidence equivalent to the observations of grammarians, e.g. the rendering of rustic American English in Lowell's *Biglow Papers*. The German schoolmasters' transcriptions of German dialects in conventional orthography for the Deutscher Sprachatlas as well as scholars' phonetic or phonemic field-notes or the phonetic recordings of a speech-atlas can also be interpreted by what Charles F. Hockett[16] called the analyst's 'philological method'.

§ 2.3 *Metrical Evidence*. Evidence is supplied by the structure of lines of poetry, either by the appearance of stressed or quantitatively marked syllables in a determined sequence, by the pattern of alliteration, or by the demands of assonance and rime (§ 6). Synchronic analysis of texts provides a description of these metrical patterns; diachronic analysis compares their observed differences at different times.

Similar to the evidence of alliteration, assonance, and rime is that furnished by puns in literary works. Puns may be homonymic or only show a partial correspondence in pronunciation.[17]

§ 2.4 *Comparative Evidence*. Comparative data provide important evidence for the analyst. Internal comparison considers distributional and structural facts, or other parallel sound-changes of the language itself. We often assume a symmetrical structure of the phonemic pattern and draw inferences from correlated features.[18]

The comparison may also concern the corresponding historical values of other dialects of the same language or of related languages within the same branch or within the same language family. We can call this 'syncomparative' analysis. The comparison may involve a contrastive treatment of later attested stages of the same or related languages: this constitutes 'diacomparative' evidence. It may pertain to the values that could have developed out of a reconstructed system of protophonemes and thus be 'protocomparative', which is actually COMPARATIVE in the narrowest sense. Also all modern dialectal values in their present areal distribution can be interpreted diachronically as 'neocomparative' material. Significant alternations at a later stage will often provide comparative evidence for an earlier stage of the same language or dialect. All diachronic interpretation implies a comparison, of course. The comparative evidence reveals that diachronic considerations can be fruitful also

[16] *Language* 24.119f. (1948).

[17] H. Kökeritz, *Shakespeare's pronunciation* 53–157 (1953); Sturtevant, *Pron.* § 10.

[18] Sturtevant, *Pron.* § 11: "Having discovered, therefore, that Latin ē was closer than ĕ, we expect to find ō closer than ŏ."

for supplementing or revising synchronic analyses. The terminal value can be used to determine the initial values. All historical comparative data consist in turn of orthographic, orthoëpic, metrical, and contact material. The method of direct contact or field-work can only be applied to neocomparative data.

§ 2.5 *Contact Evidence.* While syncomparative evidence concerns simultaneous or roughly simultaneous correspondences in related languages, further data for analysis are provided by the actual interchange, the loan and borrowing of words from one language to the other. The adoption of the alphabet or single letters of another language yields important evidence for the initial values linked to the letters. Accurate transliterations of words or sentences into different writing systems provide a welcome key to the corresponding values of the symbols (see above § 2.1). Loans based partly or totally on the written form or presumably provided by a third language as an intermediary must, of course, be interpreted differently from direct borrowings based on the spoken form in the contact between speakers of the two languages. The actual borrowing of foreign phonemes is a rare occurrence (§ 1.7). Ordinarily, we can observe in such direct loans the rendering of the foreign phoneme by corresponding native phonemes. In historical linguistics, of course, the graphic reflexes of the correspondences have to be subjected to synchronic analysis. Under favorable circumstances both the initial and the terminal values of phonemic changes that are involved in the borrowings can be isolated by diachronic interpretation of such reflexes in a foreign pattern.

III. ORTHOGRAPHIC EVIDENCE AND PHONEMIC CHANGES

§ 3.1 *Orthography and Shifts.* The orthographic system expresses all distributional changes, since they concern the incidence of phonemes, for which symbols are available (§ 1.1). It often indicates phonemic shifts (§ 1.2). The Old High German change from /þ/ to /d/ is clearly rendered, particularly in initial position, by the replacement of 'th' or 'dh' by the letter 'd': *der* for earlier *ther* or *dher*. Originally the digraph which Latin scribes used to transliterate the Greek theta was employed to render the OHG apical spirant unknown to Latin; the prompt rendering of the new OHG value may be due to the convenient availability of the symbol 'd' which agrees more or less with its Latin value. The French phonemic shift from /u/ to /ü/ in *tu, dur*[19] is not reflected by any orthographic change: the initial symbol 'u' remains constant.

§ 3.2 *Orthography and Mergers.* Orthography indicates phonemic mergers and their

[19] A. G. Haudricourt and A. G. Juilland, *Essai pour une histoire structurale du phonétisme français* 100–113 (1949).

results, e.g. by noncontrastive use of two formerly contrasting symbols or by the use of one symbol instead of two initial ones. The terminal use of one symbol only indicates the prevalence of the phoneme initially designated by it. The OHG spellings *gesti* 'guests' (sing. *gast*), *eltir* 'older' (*alt* 'old') with the 'e' symbol as found in *herza* 'heart', *helfan* 'help' indicate the merger of /e/ and /a/ before *i* and the replacement of /a/ in that position. The merger of /s/ and /z/ in medial and final positions in late MHG was first shown by the indiscriminate use of 's' and 'z' and their graphic variants.[20] Reverse or inverse spellings ('umgekehrte Schreibungen') always indicate a phonemic coalescence (see § 4.2).

§ 3.3 *Orthography and Splits.* Orthography gives often belated recognition to a phonemic split (§ 1.4) by the creation of new symbols derived from the old ones or by consistently contrastive use of two available symbols. In Middle High German most scribes use special diacritics or digraphs to render the new umlaut phonemes: e.g. *ä æ oe ü* in *mähte, næmen, schoene, übel.* The late OHG merger of the diphthong /iu/ and the umlaut of /ū/ provided a digraph symbol 'iu' for /ǖ/: *hiute* (OHG *hūti*) 'skins' like *hiute* (OHG *hiutu*) 'today'. This practice is already found in the orthographic system of Notker III. The phonemic split of Old English *k* was expressed by a contrastive use of the two available symbols 'k' and 'c' in some manuscripts, e.g. in that of the Rushworth glosses to the gospel of St. Mathew; *kining, cild,* since 1200 by the symbols 'k (c)' and 'ch', respectively: *king, child.*[21]

§ 3.4 *Orthography and Cluster Changes.* The development of clusters into single phonemes and of single phonemes into clusters is often indicated by a change in orthographic practice. Middle English spellings *s ss sch sh ssh* for historical /sk/ indicate its change to a single phoneme, similarly such Middle High German spellings as *sch sg sh ss* (*s*): e.g. *sharp* (*sarp, ssarp, scharp*), *fissh*, MHG *scharpf* (OHG *scarpf*).[22] The change from /ng/ to /ŋ/ is not expressed by the orthography; the digraph 'ng' remains in German and in English. The New High German diphthongization is indicated by the replacement of 'i' 'u' 'iu' symbols from the 12th century on by the digraphs 'ei' 'ou(au)' 'eu', respectively:[23] *wein* (HMG *wīn*), *hous, haws, hauss* (MHG *hūs*), *leute* (MHG *liute*) (§ 1.6). A similar development in Early Modern English is not reflected by any change of the orthography: *wine* (ME *wīn*), *house* (ME *hous, hūs*). The French change from clusters of vowel plus nasal to nasalized vowel

[20] O. Behaghel, *Geschichte der deutschen Sprache*[5] § 380.7 (1928); V. Michels, *Mittelhochdeutsches Elementarbuch*[3, 4] § 184 (1921); V. Moser, *Frühneuhochdeutsche Grammatik* 3.3 § 146 (1951); Friedrich Kauffmann, *Geschichte der schwäbischen Mundart* 210 (1890).

[21] Herbert Penzl, "The phonemic split of Germanic *k* in Old English," *Language* 23.34–42 (1947).

[22] R. Jordan, *Handbuch der mittelenglischen Grammatik* § 181 (1934); V. Michels § 109; Karl Weinhold, *Mittelhochdeutsche Grammatik*[2] §§ 206, 210 (1883).

[23] K. Weinhold §§ 105ff., 118; Michels § 91; Kauffmann §§ 76, 82.

phonemes is not shown by the orthography, which still retains the digraph spelling: e.g. *danser, pain, bon.*

§ 3.5 *Orthography and Phonemic Loss.* The orthography usually reflects the loss of a phoneme. The OHG loss of initial /h/ is indicated by spellings without 'h' (§ 1.7): *nigan, lut, ros, wer.*[24] The MHG phonemic loss of intervocalic /h/ is not reflected by a regular orthographic loss, only by occasional spellings (§ 4): *sehen* (MHG *sehen*), *Vieh* (MHG *vihe*), *Stahl* (MHG *stahel*).[25] But the Modern German 'h' with the value zero signifying vowel-length, e.g. in *gehen* (MHG *gēn*), *mahlen* (MHG *maln*) 'grind', indicates this postvocalic 'merger with zero' orthographically. It constitutes a reverse spelling (§ 3.2). The Late Latin loss of /h/ in all positions is also reflected by the alternation of the symbol 'h' and zero: e.g. *onurem, hedernam.*[26]

The borrowing of foreign phonemes is usually accompanied by the adoption of foreign orthographic symbols: e.g. *Cousin, Bonbon* in Modern German with French orthography.

IV. OCCASIONAL SPELLINGS AND PHONEMIC CHANGES

§ 4.1 *Occasional Spellings and Shifts.* Occasional or naive spellings (§ 2.1) render most readily all distributional changes found in colloquial speech: e.g. such Early Modern English and American English spellings as *nex* 'next', *husbon* 'husband', *myssomer* 'midsummer', *wrytyn* 'writing', *orphants* 'orphans', *meten* 'meeting', *of* 'have'.[27] Some of these spellings show loss (or addition) of phonemes in fast, unstressed forms. The *-en, -yn* spellings indicate the change of /ŋ/ (/ng/?) to /n/ in the suffix *-ing.* The traditional orthography usually reflects the forms of slow, careful speech.

Medieval scribes or copyists sometimes unintentionally, sometimes intentionally but inconsistently, substitute symbols either representing their own phonemes or at least their usual orthographic practice for those found in the original text. We find substitutions of the symbol 'd' for a presumable 'th' or 'dh' in the OHG Monsee Fragments, the Freising MS. of Otfrid, in the MS of 'Christ and the Samaritan Woman'. This reveals the diffusion of the phonemic shift from /þ/ to /d/ in OHG dialects: e.g. *thaz, ther* and *daz, der* (Christ and the Samaritan Woman); *dhuo* and *duo* 'da' (Monsee).

[24] W. Braune and W. Mitzka, *Althochdeutsche Grammatik*⁸ § 153 (1953).
[25] Moser, *Frühnhd. Gramm.* 1.1 § 10 (1929).
[26] R. L. Politzer, "The phonemic interpretation of Late Latin orthography," *Language* 27.151–154 (1951).
[27] H. C. Wyld, *A history of modern colloquial English*³ 69f., 289f. (1937); George Ph. Krapp, *The English language in America* 2.215, 232 (1925).

§ 4.2 *Occasional Spellings and Mergers.* Occasional spellings indicate general (unconditioned) or limited (conditioned) phonemic merger. They may do this preceding a general orthographic change. They may reveal the phonemic change the orthography does not show through any adjustment. They may reveal a dialectal change that is not reflected by the established spelling, which rather shows the phonemic pattern of another dialect or of the standard language. Graphic confusion of the symbols 's' and 'z' in late Middle High German and Early New High German manuscripts preceded the orthographic readjustment by the general adoption of 's' symbols (§ 3.2). All reverse spellings are really occasional at first (§ 3.5). Such spellings as OHG 'hr' for /r/ indicate the loss of the /h/: e.g. *hrinnit* for *rinnit* 'flows'.[28] Occasional spellings readily show the merger with already existing phonemes: e.g. the merger of /sj/ and /š/ in Modern English is shown by such 15th century spellings as *conschens* 'conscience', *ishu* 'issue', *condishon* 'condition', *pashens* 'patience'.[29] Such 1st century forms in inscriptions indicate an early substandard merger of *ae* and *e* in the Latin of Rome and Pompey: *etati* 'aetati', *maeae* 'meae', *saenatus* 'senatus', *Clarie* 'Clariae' (dat.).[30] Numerous occasional spellings indicate the merger of the rounded front vowels /ö/ /ü/ and their unrounded counterparts /e/ /i/ in High German dialects since the middle of the 12th century. 'e' 'i' are written for the historical umlauts: *werter* 'Wörter', *gresser* 'grösser', *yber* 'über', *vnglick* 'Unglück', *anzinden* 'anzünden.' Also reverse spellings are numerous: *bösser* 'besser', *moer* 'Meer', *schüff* 'Schiff', *kürche* 'Kirche'; some of the 'ö' and 'ü' spellings may indicate new roundings or hyperforms.[31]

Phonemic splits are not as readily reflected by occasional spellings, since no contrastive symbols are ordinarily available, but they must have preceded a general orthographic adjustment wherever it took place (§ 3.3).

V. ORTHOËPIC EVIDENCE

Certain morpheme-bound (distributional) changes such as additions, omissions, or substitutions of phonemes are described in the statements of grammarians, and illustrative forms are often quoted as vulgarisms or dialectal. Elphinston (1765, 1787), e.g., 'generally' heard *Lunnon* for *London*; he called *proddestant* 'protestant', *pardner* 'partner' London vulgarisms. Noah Webster in *Dissertations on the English Language* (1789) attacked the New England pronunciation *kiow* for *cow*.[32]

Orthoëpic evidence reveals the occurrence of the various types of phonemic

28 Braune-Mitzka § 153, Anm. 1.
29 H. C. Wyld, *HMCE*, pp. 69, 293.
30 Sturtevant §§ 4, 132; F. Sommer, *Handbuch der lat. Laut- und Formenlehre* § 61 (1948); Max Niedermann, *Historische Lautlehre des Lateinischen*³ § 31 (1953).
31 V. Moser 1.1 § 65f.; F. Kauffmann 79, 81; H. Penzl, *Language* 32.354f. (1956).
32 Wyld, *HMCE* 302, 313; Krapp 2.210.

changes. The statements of grammarians in the Early New High German period reveal that the Middle High German contrast between /s/ and /z/ has survived medially after long vowels and diphthongs in some dialects as one between a lenis written 's' and a fortis written 'ss' 'sz': e.g. Standard German *reisen* 'travel', *reissen* 'tear'.[33] The phonemic development of the cluster /ng/ into a velar nasal /ŋ/ is confirmed by Valentin Ickelsamer in his *Teutsche Grammatica* (1537), who deplores the orthography 'ng', since neither sound is completely heard in *Engel angel franck* but rather a fusion ('zusammen schmeltzung').[34] Orthoëpic evidence is obviously of particular importance, whenever the orthography fails to indicate a phonemic change. The Early Modern English change of Middle English /ī/ and /ū/ into diphthongs is also not expressed by the orthography but attested by descriptions of British grammarians like Salisbury (1547, 1567), Hart (1569), Gill (1621), and of French grammarians like Bellot (1580), Mason (1622), Festeau (1693).[35] Some of the latter sources clearly indicate a merger of Middle English /ī/ and Middle English /oi/ during their time (see below § 6).

VI. METRICAL EVIDENCE

The synchronic analysis of the distribution of stress and quantity is aided by the rigid pattern of some verse lines (§ 2.3). For the recognition of phonemic changes the analysis of rime is of particular importance. Even assonances may yield some phonemic information. Such Otfrid rimes as *quad*: *sprah* and *ward*: *tharf* have been interpreted as indicating that his final 'd' still represents a spirant rather than a stop; thus the shift from /þ/ to /d/ has not been completed finally in spite of the misleading orthography.[36] The impure rime *hart*: *anbracht* of the Nürnberg poet Jakob Ayrer (1543–1605)[37] probably indicates a uvular *r*. The rime *zit*:*geleit* by Heinrich von dem Türlin (1215) may still be impure but it reveals the diphthongization of /ī/.[38]

On the whole, only poetry with predominantly pure rimes can reveal phonemic shifts, mergers, and splits, since only there occurrence or nonoccurrence in rime position can indicate sameness or difference. The nonoccurrence of certain types of rimes indicates, if statistics make mere chance unlikely, a phonemic split or a phonemic distinction; the occurrence of rimes indicates phonemic merger. Rimes may not

[33] Moser 3. 3 § 146, Anm. 9.

[34] Johannes Müller, *Quellenschriften und Geschichte des deutschsprachlichen Unterrichts bis zur Mitte des 16. Jhd.* 139 (1882).

[35] Zachrisson, *Pron. of Engl. vowels*, 129ff., 205ff.

[36] Braune-Mitzka § 167, Anm. 4; J. Franck, *Altfränkische Grammatik* § 92 (1909); but see W. Wilmanns, *Deutsche Grammatik*³ 1. § 83, Anm. 1 (1911).

[37] Herbert Penzl, *Language* 18.299–302 (1942): review of W. A. Kozumplik, *The phonology of Jacob Ayrer's language based on his rhymes.*

[38] Michels § 91.

always reflect the pattern of the poet's own dialect. Isolated rime-words may represent historical variants. Some rimes may reflect an earlier phonemic stage of the language (traditional rimes), particularly if the orthography still provides rimes for the eye: e.g. Modern English *hand*: *wand*. The results of more recent splits or coalescences may be rarely reflected by rimes if the orthography seems to disagree: such French rimes as *nous*:*loup*, *talent*:*grands* are considered incorrect; rimes of the *water*:*quarter* type are very infrequent in Modern British English.[39] Another type of rime may reflect the phonemic pattern of another, presumably more prestigious dialect or the standard language (literary rimes). The analyst will have to decide whether any given rimes of a poet are genuinely dialectal or just traditional or literary. Middle High German rimes of the classical period reveal what the orthography with its uniform symbol 'e' does not indicate: there are two short *e* phonemes in the language which do not rime. Only in certain dialects and in certain positions, e.g. in Bavarian before *b d g t*, do /e/, the result of the historical umlaut, and /ë/, the old Germanic *e* sound, merge, as rimes show: *heben* 'lift': *lëben* 'live'; *stete* 'place': *bëte* 'prayer, request'.[40] Classical Middle High German shows no rimes of final -*z* and -*s*; they appear in the 13th century, e.g. Meier Helmbrecht shows *hūs* 'house': *ūz* 'out'.[41] This indicates the merger of the two sibilants in final position. Rimes confirm the orthographic and orthoëpic evidence for a merger of the reflexes of ME /ī/ and ME /oi/ since the 16th century: *swine*:*groin* (Shakespeare); *smile*:*coil* (Suckling); *toil*:*isle* (Waller); *join*:*divine*:*line* (Pope).[42]

VII. COMPARATIVE EVIDENCE

§ 7.1 *Proto-Comparative Data.* All prehistoric reconstructed phonemic changes are exclusively based on proto-comparative evidence, e.g. the Germanic Consonant Shift or the Old High German Consonant Shift. The initial values of a phonemic change, e.g. of 'th' in Old High German (which became /d/), can sometimes be established by comparative evidence. Syncomparative evaluation reveals the existence of an interdental or postdental, nonsibilant, voiceless spirant in cognate morphemes in Old Icelandic, Gothic, Old English, Old Frisian, Old Saxon, Old High German: e.g. OIc. *þjōfr*, Go. *þiubs*, OE *þēof*, OFrs. *thiāf*, OS *thiof*, OHG (Franc.) *thiob* 'thief'. This evidence can be used for the reconstruction of a proto-phoneme *þ, a voiceless, nonsibilant, interdental or postdental spirant. The umlaut variation of velar vowels in the Germanic languages can be compared, and postulated for the prehistoric stage.

[39] O. Jespersen, *A Modern English grammar* 1.13.27 (1909); C. L. Wrenn, *TPS* 1943, 34–37; H. C. Wyld, *Short history of English*[3] § 214 (1927).
[40] K. Zwierzina, *ZfdA* 44,249ff. (1900).
[41] A. Schirokauer, *PBB* 47.97–100 (1922).
[42] Wyld, *SHE* § 270; *HMCE*, pp. 224, 249–251.

The feasibility of such a reconstruction confirms by its consistency the assumption of initial palatal allophones of long or short *a o u* before *i*-sounds in the Germanic languages. Reconstructed proto-phonemes can support the results of historical synchronic and diachronic analyses.

§ 7.2 *Diacomparative and Neocomparative Data.* Diachronic analysis presupposes 'diacomparative' data from different periods, preferably within the same dialect or language but by no means excluding available allotopic evidence. Other phonemic changes can furnish evidence. The common dialectal change of *-ing* to *-in* makes the initial value [ŋ] more likely than [ŋg], thus provides evidence for the change from the cluster to a single nasal phoneme.

Evidence from modern dialectal conditions and from modern areal distribution, i.e. 'neocomparative' material (§ 2.4) is of special importance, since it can be directly observed in the field, not only through its written reflexes. We can compare the modern sounds and their relation to modern orthographic symbols to the earlier symbols and their presumable sound-values. We find, e.g., that Modern French orthography still has the symbol 'u' in *tu dur*, which is pronounced as [ü]: this definitely proves the completion of the phonemic shift from /u/ to /ü/. The fact that Modern German 's' is pronounced like a dorsal or like an apical sibilant at the present time has been used for phonetic identification attempts of the respective values of OHG and MHG 'z' and 's'. Modern German and Modern English 'ng' are pronounced like a single velar nasal in final position: *sing*. But English shows a morphophonemic variation between the single sound and the cluster in such sets as *long* [ŋ], *longer* [ŋg], and it contrasts *finger* with the cluster and *singer* from *sing* with the simple nasal. Thus modern pronunciations confirm the assumed terminal values of phonemic changes, while sometimes their relation to the modern orthographic symbols or an internal phonemic alternation throws light on earlier or initial values. Neocomparative evidence can show the completion of phonemic shifts, splits, and mergers, also the presence of foreign phonemes of marginal status (§ 1.7). The modern areal distribution can also sometimes indicate which values are terminal and which initial or, as it is usually stated, which are archaic and which innovations. This modern dialectal diffusion and differentiation has been used to postulate intermediate stages of a sound-change, but this seems more of a problem of historical reconstruction, which we shall not take up here.

VIII. EVIDENCE FROM CONTACT BETWEEN LANGUAGES

It is tempting to look for proof of a completed shift of French /u/ to /ü/ among French loan-words in Middle High German and Middle English, since the orthography does not indicate the phonemic shift. MHG forms like *natiure* (OF *nature*), *aventiure* (OF *aventure*), *creatiure* (OF *creature*), *hürten* (*hurten*) (OF *hurter*) 'attack, push foward', *kabütze* (OF *capuce*) 'monk's hood' reveal by the spellings 'iu' (for /x/) and 'ü' rounded palatal vowels. Only the western dialects of Middle English had a sound phonetically identical with the French sound. The diphthong /iu/ written 'ew' 'eu' renders French 'u' in *glew*, *mewe*, *deuk*;[43] early ME *hurten*, *hirten*, *herten* renders French *hurter*, and Modern English /i/ is found in unstressed syllables in *minute*, *lettuce*, *conduit*, /ī/ in *pedigree* from *pied de grue*. Thus also the English evidence points to a rounded palatal vowel, and indicates the completion of the shift to /ü/ in French.

The adoption of certain orthographic symbols (§ 2.5) can throw light on the values in both languages. The use of the OHG symbol 'z' to render the Old Slovenian sibilants *s z*, but of the symbol 's' to render Old Slovenian sibilants *š ž* in the Freising documents[44] proves that the phonetic differences between the OHG sibilants /z/ and /s/ did not consist in voice participation or fortis and lenis articulation but rather in the manner and place of articulation. The MHG reflexes 's' and 'z' of Old French *s* and *c* in loan-words reveal the phonemic contrast between the two sibilants but admit of no specific phonetic identifications or conclusions because of the ambiguity of the MHG 'z' symbol: *birsen* (OF *berser*) 'to hunt', *garzûn* (OF *garçon*) 'page'.

Sometimes we can be more specific in our synchronic and diachronic analyses. E. H. Sturtevant[45] has pointed out that OE *strǣt*, *strēt* from Latin (*uia*) *strāta* has preserved the dental stop *t* better than most Romance languages and reveals the long quantity of the Latin stem vowel. OHG *keisur* from Latin *caesar* suggests a late diphthongal pronunciation of 'ae' as the basis for the OHG sound value. Thus, evidence through contact between languages can be valuable for phonetic identifications, which other evidence supplies even less readily.

IX. CONCLUSIONS

The innumerable phonetic changes found in the history of languages represent not more than six types of phonemic change, which could even be further reduced to these three major types: phonemic shift (including cluster changes); phonemic merger (including phonemic loss); phonemic split. All reconstructed sound-changes and their special problems have been excluded from our consideration here, since we are at first concerned with methodological clarification, which must come from the synchronic analysis of both the initial and the terminal values of historical

[43] Karl Luick, *Historische Grammatik der englischen Sprache* §412 (1921); Jespersen *MEG* 1.3.815; Karl Brunner, *Die englische Sprache* 1.156f., 241 (1950).
[44] W. Braune, *PBB* 1.527–534; also Primus Lessiak, *Beiträge zur Geschichte des deutschen Konsonantismus* 83ff. (1933).
[45] *Pronunc.* § § 3c, 130e.

phonemic changes and their diachronic interpretation. Only one major aspect of phonemic change has been dealt with: its evidence. The various types of evidence have been analyzed as to how they can reveal the various types of phonemic change. Orthography and its deviations (the occasional spellings) reveal shifts and mergers but they indicate often only belatedly phonemic splits. Orthoëpic evidence is often tied to the orthography but can reveal all phonemic changes, even specific phonetic values. Evidence from rimes is sometimes particularly useful in detecting phonemic mergers and splits. Among the comparative evidence not proto-comparative reconstruction, but rather data from the structure of the language and from other sound-changes as well as from present-day dialects or the standard language (neo-comparative data) throw light on historical shifts, mergers, and splits. The evidence from loan-words can sometimes reveal shifts where orthography and orthoëpic evidence fail to provide satisfactory data.

We cannot expect that all types of evidence can be found for each phonemic change within the history of a language. It is necessary, however, to make use of all available evidence and to correlate its data. Interpretation and even speculation has often taken the place of the missing data. It is imperative that the description of each assumed phonemic change should contain a discussion of the evidence, its type, scope, and conclusiveness.

UNIVERSITY OF MICHIGAN

GORDON E. PETERSON

THE DISCRETE AND THE CONTINUOUS IN THE SYMBOLIZATION OF LANGUAGE

SPOKEN language is a code of great complexity. Because of this complexity the code is not easily defined nor completely described, but it has been considered from many points of view. Those who believe in the precepts of their particular disciplines as dogma find truth and falsehood in the descriptions, but there are those who recognize the limitations and incompleteness of all specialized descriptions of a process so complex as language.

To describe a process is to represent it symbolically, or to provide some form of map or schematic. Certainly it is rare, if indeed possible, to provide a complete representation of all aspects of any process. In fact, it is in many respects the selection of aspects or parameters of importance or interest which makes the construction of mathematical and physical models useful. The model may be restricted to information which is significant or important under the conditions of interest.

Language is not a random process in any of its many aspects. Within a code the maximum information per symbol is transmitted when any symbol is equally likely to occur. But if the speech source were in all instances equally likely to generate any symbol, each elementary symbol would constitute an independent utterance. We know language to be very different from this elementary statistical model. Language involves system and structure. The symbols are not equally probable, nor are their occurrences statistically independent of each other.

Speech serves primarily as a representation or symbolization of portions of the real world. It is generally recognized that the representations are often inadequate or inaccurate. The speech itself is a part of the real world, and as such its physical properties may be analyzed.

Portions of the world may also be symbolized by visual means. These may vary from pictorial and graphic representations in which there is some evident correspondence with reality, to arbitrary representations such as orthographic and mathemat-

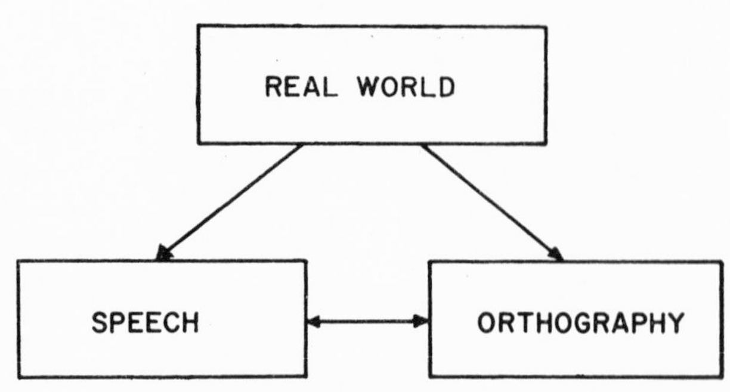

Figure 1. Symbolization and reality.

ical symbolization. Frequently some degree of correspondence may be observed between orthographic representation and spoken language. The relationships between the real world, speech, and orthography are indicated schematically in Figure 1; the function of representation is indicated by the direction of the arrows. These representations hold, of course, regardless of whether there is a correspondence among the individual structures of the systems involved. The only requirement is that at some unit level the language must symbolize reality. The arrows may be considered as an extension of the real world, and usually the speech or orthography may be considered in some respects as a meta-language of the one for the other. Additional meta-languages of various forms might also be represented by additional rectangles and arrows in the diagram.

When we examine the physiological production and the acoustical waves of speech, we do not find simple discrete symbols. Rather, in general, the basic parameters of speech show continuity over short intervals of time. If a human listens to this continuous type of signal he is able to represent it by a sequence of discrete symbols, as a phonemic transcription. We know from many types of tests that this representation is fairly adequate, and that another individual may be able to generate continuous speech which is very similar to the original from an examination of such a symbolic sequence.

Such discrete systems have long been considered to represent essential elements or units within the continuum of speech. At the physiological level these elements are considered to be basic articulatory positions or movements with associated breath pressure patterns; at the acoustical level they are considered to be basic patterns in frequency and time. The perceptual process is based primarily upon these physiological and acoustical properties. The results of acoustical studies have emphasized that in continuous speech the inter-effects among the elements are considerable, so that the elements are often neither distinct nor easily observable instrumentally. Thus in continuous speech the elements are often distorted in formation. The distortions are exemplified in the allophones of phonemes. Complexities in the management and control of the vocal system account for many of the inter-effects which are observed; but prominent effects may also be the result of linguistic conditioning and learning.

In printing, the notation is essentially discrete, and a printed phonemic sequence is essentially a discrete representation of the elements within the continuity of speech. In the cursive writing of phonemic sequences, however, a continuous representation is employed. In this representation the inter-effects, of course, are a function of the properties of the code, and have no particular relation to the inter-effects which occur within the physiological or acoustical patterns of the speech signal.

Spoken language does not involve single linear sequences of elements. The code is structurally multi-dimensional and several concurrent sequences of elements normally occur. For example, the oscillations of the vocal cords normally produce the excitation of the vocal cavities for vowel formant production; and simultaneously the fundamental frequency of the vocal cord oscillations forms another coded sequence within the speech signal. Printing, however, is only a schematic or summary of the articulatory and acoustic multi-dimensional complex of speech. In the printing of a language the letters, the word spaces, and the marks of punctuation normally follow in a unidimensional series, so that information which may appear in a multi-dimensional simultaneity in speech will normally appear in a unidimensional sequence in printing.

In general, orthographies have been plagued by the powerful forces of linguistic change. The history of literacy provides continuous examples of the slow but unrelenting divergence of speech from any established orthography.[1] These changes are not confined to allophonic changes within phonemic contrasts, of course, but phonemic systems themselves alter with time in diverse ways. According to this writer's orientation it may be said that the allophonic structure, the number, the allowed sequences, and the distribution of phonemes within a language may all be altered with time.

When through education specific orthographic sequences are perpetuated for morphemic representation, not only may the orthographic symbols fail to approximate the phonemic structure of the language, but the spelling may fail to approximate the phonemic sequence of which the words are composed. In such a course of linguistic change there would appear to be only a few basic alternatives. The speech and the spelling may be left to follow their own divergent courses. The most likely outcome of this rather primitive approach to literary is orthographic chaos, followed by orthographic revolution; then as the spoken language alters further, new confusions develop and additional changes in orthography become imperative.

[1] What follows will be essentially uninteresting to those who see all dialects of any language and all diachronic phases of each language as basically identical, with coherent systems throughout. Here the viewpoint is operational: what cannot be demonstrated systematically is freely recognized as speculation – with the burden of proof on the author, not the reader.

Let us next consider whether it would be possible to maintain a coherent relationship between orthography and speech by *stabilizing the speech* so that it will conform to the orthography which has already been stabilized through convention. This procedure would require the general use of intensive educational programs in articulation and pronunciaction; perhaps with modern educational facilities such is possible. This solution, however, is distasteful to many. It is often explained that languages are natural systems, perhaps even beautiful, and that their artificial alteration is both homely and ineffective. A firmer objection, however, lies in the recognition of the tremendous and diverse forces of language change; like other bio-physical systems, languages are subject to change. In the world of today, with the great interchange of cultures, attempts to stabilize spoken language can only seem weak and provincial. This point of view is not to be taken as argument against acquiring the cultured patterns of a given dialect; which often is impelled with considerable force. To attempt to discourage speakers from this process is, in fact, to attempt to counteract one of the strong forces of linguistic change.

A much more reasonable solution to the problems of relating speech and orthography would appear to be systematically to change the orthography; surely it is better that early writings should be obscure (as the speech), than that all writings, old and modern, should be confused in their relation to speech. In the concept of the Academy of Letters should be a recognition of the dynamics and of the immediate values of spoken language. If such an Academy is to adjust adequately the written form of the language to follow the spoken form, however, it must continually analyze current speech and must ever be on guard against the inherent conservative forces of orthography.

A less promising approach would be to attempt to perpetuate *phonetic writing* rather than phonemic writing. Under this plan, education in the techniques of phonetic transcription would become universal in education. Since phonetic change appears to be incessant, the desire would be to have all major phonetic changes reflected promptly in the phonetic system of orthography.

Descriptive phonetics, of course, is essentially of a discrete and quantified character. It is not possible to designate with separate symbols all gradations of sound formation, for these are infinite. Thus the problem of developing a coherent and flexible phonetic notation is an exceedingly difficult, if not impossible task. When a symbol is chosen to represent a specific articulatory position or an articulatory region, arbitrary subdivisions of an articulatory continuum are normally involved. As a result it frequently occurs that phonemic boundaries are found at different locations from those employed, even in refined phonetic notations. Sometimes the phonemic subdivisions are even more refined than the common phonetic classifications employed by phoneticians.

Allophonic variations within a phoneme tend to be generally less conspicuous to a native speaker than do variations which are phonemically distinctive. Thus in the daily phonetic transcription of a particular language, one would expect writers to become increasingly inexact. The obvious result would be the gradual but determined degeneration to phonemic notation. The subsequent divergence of speech and orthography would then follow as before.

As long as arbitrary and discrete symbols are employed in a phonetic notation, there is no systematic way in which to define gradations and boundaries without extremely elaborate coding. This suggests the use of symbols which provide a *pictorial representation of the physiological positions* and activities of the vocal system. Alexander Melville Bell developed a schematic system of this nature which has been used widely.[2] The basic difficulty with such systems, however, is that the vocal mechanism is too elaborate and too complex for its essential details to be encompassed within individual symbols. Further, it is not possible to predict what phonetic details may become important within any particular language. Thus in routine use such pictorial notation would be expected to become increasingly stereotyped, and again this essentially phonetic orthography would degenerate to a phonemic system, with the customary eventual divergence of writing and speech. At this point it seems wise to return to the concept of an Academy which could recommend and guide orthographic and spelling change. Actually, linguistic chance is usually sufficiently slow that when properly directed such an influence should be entirely adequate.

Do the recent advances in acoustical analysis provide more effective and futuristic solutions to the orthographic problem?

Speech is generated by a complex coordination of muscular movements and breath pressures. The acoustical waves which result may be highly intelligible; for example, under optimum acoustical condition, almost 100 per cent of the monosyllables produced by a normal speaker of a given dialect may be identified by another speaker of the same dialect serving as a listener. Much information may be derived from visual cues alone, as is evidenced by the ability of trained deaf listeners to understand speech without acoustical data, but the details of the positions and movements of the vocal cavities are much more completely represented in the acoustical waves than they are in what may be observed by watching the face of the speaker. Thus, as Pollack has shown, auditory stimuli normally make a much greater contribution to speech intelligibility than do visual cues.[3]

Sound spectrographic techniques provide a means of *automatically converting the acoustical waves of speech to visible patterns.* These patterns represent both the phonetic details and the continuities of speech. It is possible to construct concurrent patterns which show the phonetic structure, the fundamental voice frequency, and the energy distributions; durations, of course, are inherent in the lengths within the

[2] Alexander Melville Bell, *Visible speech* (London 1867).
[3] W. H. Sumby – Irwin Pollack, Visual contribution to speech intelligibility in noise, *JASA* 26.212–215 (1954).

patterns. A fourth trace may be added for the feature of nasalization by inserting an acoustical probe in the nose.

These multiple patterns might form the basis of an entirely new form of printing. The printer would in essence be a spectrographic analyzer which would mark each page according to the speech inserted into it. Modern techniques of duplicating material could be employed to copy the originals.

The procedure is illustrated in Figure 2 which shows four parallel analyses of an utterance. The bottom trace is of the fundamental voice frequency, based on the tenth harmonic of a narrow band spectrogram. The second pattern is the regular broad band analysis, extending to 3500 cps. The third pattern above is an amplitude trace made on an approximately logarithmic scale, and the fourth pattern shows the nasal output through a probe-tube microphone. This four-trace pattern is related in some respects to descriptive phonetic notation, where diacritical and parallel markings above and below the articulatory notations may be employed to represent pitch, stress, and nasalization. The simplifying morphemic and syntactic markings now present in much orthography would not appear in such a system of 'speech printing'. The reader would have a much closer representation of the corresponding speech, however, and thus would have much more linguistic information available to him.

Such patterns are continuous; they can be drawn easily and as such may be employed in a system of writing.[4] In the broad band analysis (second pattern from below in Figure 2), four basic formations are involved; blanks, random striations, vertical strokes, and curved lines progressing horizontally. These correspond to the essential types of sound structure which occur in speech. The inter-effects in the writing will now in general resemble the inter-effects in the speech. In the nasal trace (top pattern) a strong nasal component may be noted on the vowels associated with the nasal consonants. The weaker markings in this fourth trace are normally observed on oral sounds; they are probably due both to structure-borne and to air-borne sound at the nares.

In such a system of speech printing the patterns would automatically alter as language change occurred; it is reasonable to assume that the writing would follow in form. The writing system would thus essentially be of an acoustic-phonetic nature. A sample of such writing, based on the patterns of Figure 2, is shown in Figure 3.

Would such an orthography be unreasonably complex for the general intellectual abilities of the human? This is unlikely:

a. The orthography would represent the distributions in frequency and time of the speech we hear. Anyone who learns to talk learns to distinguish these patterns.

[4] A rather discrete type of schematic spectrographic notation was suggested in R. K. Potter – G. A. Kopp – H. C. Green, *Visible speech* (New York 1947). The suggestion was for a phonetic notation rather than for a universal orthography. In the system submitted there the transitions and continuities were not retained, as is here proposed.

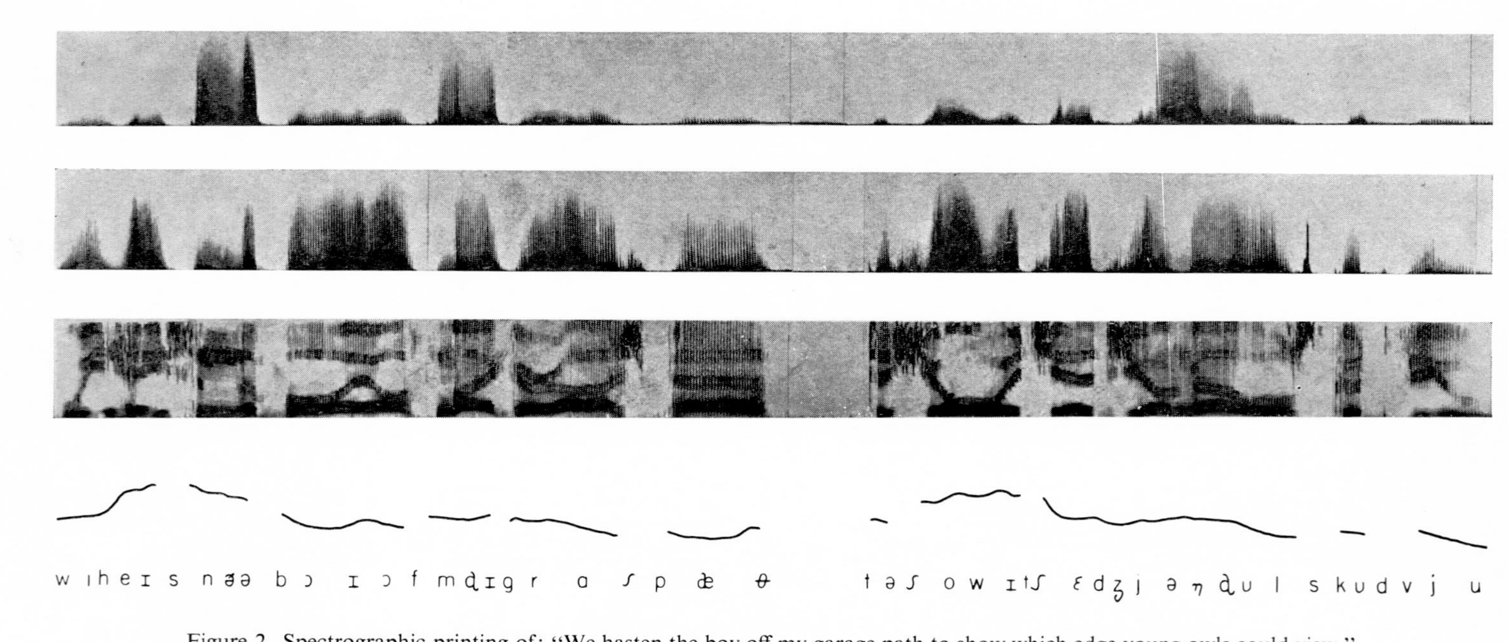

Figure 2. Spectrographic printing of: "We hasten the boy off my garage path to show which edge young owls could view."

From above downward the patterns represent:

A. Nasal output through a probe tube microphone. B. Overall amplitude. C. Broad band spectrum analysis. D. Fundamental voice frequency.

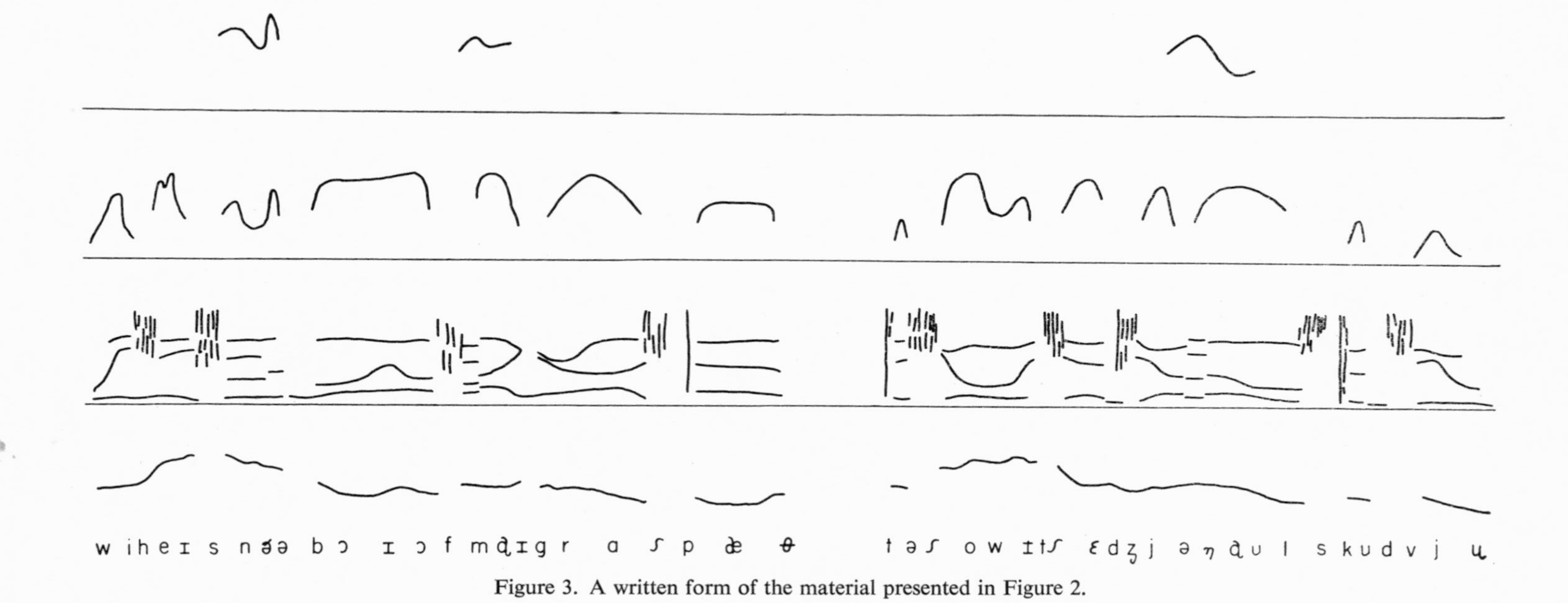

Figure 3. A written form of the material presented in Figure 2.

To represent them spatially in an orthography is a relatively simple transformation; the basic instrumental simplicity of the sound spectrograph gives considerable support to this point of view.

b. Since the orthographic patterns would have a basic correspondence to the sounds of speech, their forms and shapes would be more meaningful and inherently reasonable than are the arbitrary symbols of discrete alphabets. Thus it might actually take the beginner less time to learn the basic patterns found in the spectrographic analysis of a language than to learn the shapes of the letters – and certainly it would take him less time to learn the patterns than that required to learn to spell a language such as English.

While acoustical writing might solve many of the problems of universal orthography, it would appear to be a somewhat trivial accomplishment relative to the development of automata. The control of instrumental operations by means of speech is one of the essential objectives of communication technology. Such control can only be achieved by the automatic recognition of words and the larger units of sentence structure. Similar word and syntactic recognition is essential to the automatic translation of spoken language. Recognition of the complex acoustical patterns of speech at the word level, however, involves much more elaborate and complicated pattern identification and storage techniques than does recognition at the phonemic level. Automatic speech recognition at the phonemic level would permit the storage of words in terms of elementary discrete phonemic symbols for operational and translational purposes, and in general would provide a much more basic and flexible management of speech signals for control purposes.

Thus *automatic phonemic recognition* is an essential objective in the development of automata. In addition to providing the basis for machine control and the translation of spoken languages, however, the reduction of continuous speech to phonemic sequences would make possible automatic speech writing with discrete symbols. Here ultimately may lie a basic force for spelling change, since it is not likely to be economical to insert a computer of sufficient complexity to convert phonemic sequences to a poorly related orthography.

One of the great and fundamental problems facing those interested in speech processes is the systematic reduction of the continuous parameters of speech production and waves to discrete symbols. This transformation is, of course, also fundamental to the practical objective of speech automation. Current techniques in linguistic analysis, based largely upon concepts of physiological phonetics, represent such an operation at the level of human skill, in which the operation of an individual auditor is interposed between the speech signal and its symbolic representation. The rigorous mathematical and systematic statement of the process should reduce the skill to a science, which in the case of individual languages may be prescribed for machine operations.

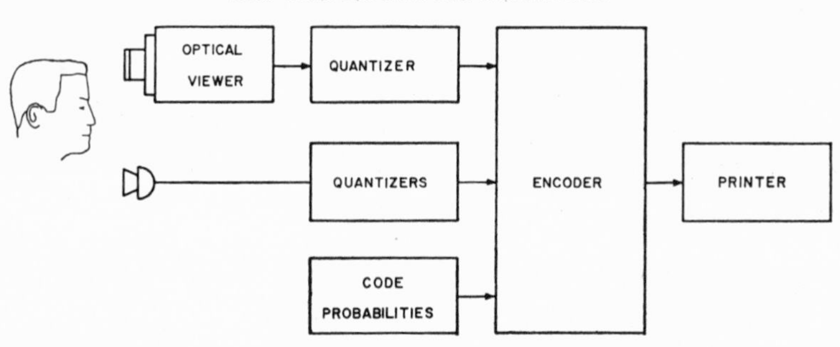

Figure 4. The basic operations of automatic speech recognition.

The *mathematical description* of the transformation of the parameters of speech and associated inter-effects to discrete symbolization is a field which at present very seriously lacks systematic theoretical formulation. The problem has only begun to attract earnest scientific attention, and it will undoubtedly receive an increasing emphasis during the coming years. The formulation probably should relate both to physiological and acoustical processes. In particular, there is much reason to consider the physiological representation of most consonants as simpler than their corresponding acoustical representations; on the other hand, the representation of the vowels by means of formants is much simpler than the detailed description of the vocal tract required for their specification.

Obviously, a great deal of experimental study will yet be required before rigorous procedures for converting the physical processes of speech to symbolic notations can be developed. However, as in all science, it is essential that theoretical formulations and experimental evidence develop in parallel. At the present time, there is a special need for the mathematical theory of speech processes. In essence this involves a mathematical representation of the physiological formations and the acoustical waves of speech, the mathematical representation of inter-effects within each of these systems, and the development of mathematical techniques for reducing combinations of the various continuous parameters of speech to discrete elements.

The second great problem in the technical study of language concerns the mathematical description of the principles which govern distributions and combinations of symbols. In the broad sense, the problem concerns all levels of linguistic structure, including phonemics, morphemics, and syntax, with associated inter-effects at all levels. In any one language, we know that in some aspects the system may be incoherent and incomplete. The problem as defined here, however, relates not to specific languages, but to a general mathematical and physical methodology for language description.

The general processes involved in automatic speech recognition for speech writing are indicated in Figure 4. Since the optical information essentially concerns articulation, only one process of quantification is involved. In the acoustical wave, however, there is contained information about all basic parameters, such as articulation, nasalization, and fundamental voice frequency. Thus several somewhat parallel quantification operations are required in the acoustical portion of the system. The encoder must base its decisions not only upon the optical and acoustical information, but also upon stored information concerning the statistical properties of the various components of the language as spoken.

Eventually, automata which can learn languages independently of human adjustment will doubtless be developed. Such devices must obviously have great capacity for signal analysis and storage and must be equipped with highly flexible output systems. From the organization and parameter values assumed by such an instrument, it should be possible to derive a basic description of a spoken language – in fact, after the machine has learned the language, the values of the internal parameters of the instrument should provide a valuable metalinguistic representation of the speech which has been presented to it. Only through further research on the type of processes and systems suggested in Figure 4, however, can we learn the nature of certain of the basic components essential to such automata.

In summary, speech is continuous and ever changing, but there are fundamental purposes for reducing it to discrete codes. While in the distant future automata may achieve such reduction without human aid, in the immediate future research should define the basic processes and operations required.

Acknowledgement: The author wishes to express his appreciation to Mr. William D. Chapman, of the Speech Research Laboratory, for the construction of the continuous amplitude display circuits which were employed in constructing Figure 2.

UNIVERSITY OF MICHIGAN

JAMES W. POULTNEY

IMPERFECT INDICATIVE AND HISTORICAL INFINITIVE

IN GLOTTA 35. 114–133 (1956), Anton Mayer published an article advocating the view that the Latin imperfect indicative arose from a combination in which the locative of an *s*-stem verbal noun was followed by the finite verb **bhwām*, **bhwās*, **bhwāt*, etc.[1] Thus *vehēbam* would be from **vehesi bhwām* with syncope of *i*, loss of *s*, and compensatory lengthening of *e*, and the characteristic imperfect meaning developed from 'I was (engaged in) carrying.' This explanation is not new; it had been offered by O. Hoffmann, *Rh. M.* 73. 227–231 (1920–24), and favored as the best of several possibilities by R. G. Kent, *Forms of Latin* 120. The interest of the theory for the present paper consists in the fact that, if acceptable, it provides a new explanation for the origin of the historical infinitive. First, however, it is necessary to make certain remarks in amplification and support of Mayer's article.

The old view that the imperfect originated in expressions like **agēns fuam* may be ignored as too difficult phonologically.[2] W. Petersen, Language 3. 175–183 (1927), suggested that O. impf. 3 pl. *fufans* originated from **bhubhwānt*, originally an injunctive in *ā* to a reduplicated perfect stem (with imperfect value 'they were' corresponding to the present value of the perfect 'they are' < 'they have become'), subsequently reanalyzed as an unreduplicated form with suffix *-bhwā-*, whence the whole Italic imperfect indicative arose. Mayer apparently accepts this explanation for O. *fufans* but naturally not for the Latin imperfect. Against **bhubhwā-* as the source of the imperfect either in Oscan or in Latin the most serious objection is that the reduplication of the perfect tense normally had an *e*-vowel not only in Sanskrit and Greek[3]

[1] From the disyllabic base **bhewā-* seen in Lith. *buvaũ*, early Latin *fuam*, of which the former has the same preterit value seen in the Latin suffix *-bam*, while *fuam* is a subjunctive derived from **bhuwām* in its injunctive use.

[2] Rejected by Mayer 130, and Buck, *Comparative grammar of Greek and Latin* 278.

[3] Cf. Skt. *babhūva* (< *bhebh-*), Gk. epic 3 pl. πεφύασι. It is true that Skt. *dudhāva*, *pupāva*, *suṣāva* belong to verbs from roots of the same type as **bhū*, but there is nowhere any evidence of a perfect

but in early Latin as well.[4] Mayer's explanation of the imperfect therefore appears the most plausible, and it may be mentioned in passing that he offers a satisfying refutation of the objection sometimes made against it by those who call attention to the short radical syllable in *dabam* (pp. 123–30). By any theory which views the imperfect as originally a periphrastic combination, the combination must have been made before *bh* became differentiated in Latin into initial *f* and medial *b*, the enclitic nature of the second element being the ground for the medial development *bh* > *b*.[5] The diversity among infinitive formations in the various IE languages is so great that it is impossible to give a detailed account of the prototypes of these infinitives in proto-IE or even in the prehistoric stages of the separate branches. But it is altogether reasonable to believe that the Latin active infinitive was in origin the locative of an *s*-stem. This view applies especially to the third conjugation, where numerous verbs like *fero*, *rego*, *lego*, *tego*, etc., show full grade of the root, the same grade seen in the Greek *s*-stems γένος, λέχος, τέγος, etc. It may also be mentioned that *-sĭ* satisfies the conditions of Sievers' Law (if this law was still operative in the period in question), which would call for *-bhwām* after a short syllable in contrast to *-bhuwām* after a long syllable. The spread of *-si* to verbs of other conjugational classes was a natural accompaniment of the development of nouns indicating action into formal categories of the non-finite verb.[6] For the periphrasis consisting of an *s*-stem verbal noun in the locative

of **bhū* with a *u*-vowel in the reduplication. To cite O. *fufans* as evidence would merely be circular argument. The choice is rather between forms based on reduplication **bhe-* and forms with no reduplication at all, and in fact the perfect forms of the base **bhewā* may have developed independently in Sanskrit and Greek, a suspicion which is strengthened by the *ū* in the radical syllable of *babhūva* when viewed in contrast with *dudhāva*, etc.

[4] Aul. Gell. 6.9. 2–8 cites *peposci*, *memordi*, *pepugi*, *spepondi*, *cecurri* as early forms. The reanalysis of **bhubhwā-* offered by Petersen as the source of the imperfect would in any case have had to belong to a period considerably earlier than the period when perfect forms of the type cited by Gellius were replaced by forms with identical vowel in reduplication and radical syllable.

[5] Whether we must place it back in the period of 'Italo-Celtic' unity is another matter. Thurneysen *Grammar of Old Irish* 398 (Dublin, 1946), denies connection between the Irish *f*-future and the Latin *b*-formations, since IE *bh* should yield Irish *b*. W. Petersen, *Language* 8. 134–135 (1932), had sought an escape from the difficulty through the apparent development *bh* > OIr. *f* when in postconsonantal position.

[6] How much place we must give to verbal nouns in *-ā*, *-ē* as sources of the first element is uncertain. If we start from loc. sg. in *-āi*, *-ēi*, the long diphthongs should change to *-ai*, *-ei* in preconsonantal position, not yielding the desired result, while on the other hand Hirt's *casus indefinitus* (*Idg. Gr.* 4.98) is too uncertain a solution. The future in *-bo*, which is limited to the first and second conjugations (with the fourth in early Latin) might be an argument for believing that the Latin *b*-tenses originated outside of the third conjugation, but there is no objection to the view that first the infinitive in **-si* was generalized through all the conjugations, and subsequently the *b*-tenses developed in the manner described above, the imperfect being used in all conjugations, the future in *-bo* in all except the third, where *ē*-forms of subjunctive origin already functioned as futures and later displaced the *b*-forms from the fourth conjugation. Another matter is the problem of making O. *fufans*, the only recorded imperfect indicative form in the Italic dialects, fit the explanation adopted here for Latin. One solution is simply to separate it from the Latin formation in *-bam*, *-bas*, etc. as Mayer (pp. 121–22) does. But it is difficult to escape the conviction that not only *fufans* but also the Oscan-Umbrian *f*-perfects

case plus the verb ‘be’ in the sense ‘be engaged in’ a partial parallel occurs in Avestan *aēte spāna biš hapta nmāna pairi. tačahi bavąn* ‘sobald die Hunde zweimal sieben Häuser umlaufen können,’[7] where however the action is shown as potential rather than progressive.

The theory offered here to account for the historical infinitive is that it originated when two or more infinitives occurred in sequence, with **bhwām, -ās, -āt* used after only one of them. It is well known that the historical infinitive is especially frequent in series of two or more, and in fact single examples are infrequent in early Latin.[8] Narrations of exciting or dramatic actions, especially battles, often call for a series of verbs in quick succession. Perfects or historical presents may be used for the main actions, but there is need for a past tense indicating events which continue to recur as an accompaniment to the main action. Imperfects are not infrequently used in our Latin texts in close succession one after another without producing an impression of prolixity, but during the stage when the combination of infinitive plus **bhwāt* was developing, if the theory of its origin adopted here is correct, the repetition of **bhwāt* (virtually a form of the copula) after every one of a series of half a dozen or more infinitives would have been as unnatural and tiresome as the repetition of *est* or *erat* with every one of an equally long series of predicative adjectives or ablatives of quality.[9]

The notion that the historical infinitive originated through an ellipsis had been expressed by ancient grammarians cited by Quint. 8.6.21, and had been revived by Jänicke, *Jb. cl. Ph.* 151, 134–138 (1895). Here the verb supposed to have been lost through ellipsis was *coepi*, and Kretschmer, *Glotta* 2. 272–273 (1910), rightly con-

are somehow related to the Latin *b*-tenses. The lack in O. -U. of an infinitive of the type of Latin *-re* < *-si* is less serious than may at first appear. Like the classical Skt. infinitive in *-tum*, which alone survived from among a variety of Vedic infinitives, the O.–U. infinitive in *-om*, morphologically an accusative form, may easily be the only formation surviving from a prehistoric stage in which another type, a locative in *-si*, furnished the basis for several periphrastic tenses. The O.–U. *f*-perfect agrees in a morphological, though not in a semantic sense, with the Latin *b*-future. Both appear to contain a stem **bhwe/o-*, perhaps with ‘aoristic’ or ‘punctual’ value ‘become,’ which would explain both the development in O.–U. as perfect and in Latin (through subjunctive use) as future.

7 Reichelt, *Awestisches Elementarbuch* 342 (Heidelberg, 1909).

8 So Bennett, *Syntax of Early Latin* 1.423. Pp. 419–21 contain discussion of conflicting theories on the origin of the historical infinitive. Kretschmer, *Glotta* 2.270–287 (1910), in regarding the construction as a variety of ‘Nominalsatz’ made an advance over most earlier attempts. See also M. Schuster, *Festschrift Kretschmer* 224–243 (Vienna, 1926), who further developed Kretschmer’s theory from a psychological viewpoint.

9 Cf., for example, Plaut., *Capt.*, 647–48 (Aristophontes speaking) *macilento ore, naso acuto, corpore albo, oculis nigris, subrufus aliquantum, crispus, cincinnatus*, where the force of the single verb *est* in 646 (Hegio speaking) carries over. For the omission of formative elements in a series of verbs I am indebted to my colleague, Dr. Thomas O. Lambdin, who directed my attention to a similar phenomenon in Egyptian: A. Gardiner, *Egyptian Grammar*^{2}, 397 (Oxford, 1950): “Omission of both subject and formative element. – Such omissions occur in passages where there is a sequence of parallel verbs, and where consequently subject and formative element are alike superfluous. Ex. *ʿḥʿ·n ꜣg·n·f ʿt·f nb im·s, nḥm ꜣw·f sʿḳ r ḏꜣtt(?)·f* ‘then he belaboured all his limbs with it, took away his asses, and drove (them) into his estate.’ Understand *nḥm.n.f, sʿḳ.n.f.*”

demned the theory on the grounds that the characteristic meaning of *coepi* would be inadmissible in a large proportion of passages containing the historical infinitive, and that the failure to repeat *coepi* with every infinitive in a series is an altogether different thing from its total omission. Conceivably the same objections might be made against the theory offered in the present paper. But the semantic content of *coepi*, like that of, for example, *possum* or *uolo*, is such that the dependence of every infinitive in the series upon it would be clear and its omission would vitally affect the sense. With **bhwāt* it is quite otherwise. Its omission would be scarcely more shocking than that of the present forms of the verb 'be', and the past sense in the proper environment could be as easily inferred as in the case of the historical present. Because of its enclitic nature **bhwāt* would seem no longer to belong to the entire series of infinitives but to be a part of one word only. The new imperfect form was not an integral part of the series, but could be omitted at will, making possible a new type of sentence in which the infinitive alone, with nominative subject, could have much the same value as an imperfect indicative.

The following passages are given in full as being especially illustrative of the use of historical infinitives in series: Plaut., *Merc.*, 43–52 *leno importunus, dominus eius mulieris, ui summa ut quidque poterat rapiebat domum. obiurigare pater haec noctes et dies, perfidiam, iniustitiam lenonum expromere; lacerari ualide suam rem, illius augerier. summo haec clamore; interdum mussans conloqui: abnuere, negitare adeo me natum suom. conclamitare tota urbe et praedicere omnes tenerent mutuitanti credere. lacerari* and *augerier* are in oratio obliqua, *credere* depends on *tenerent*, and the remaining infinitives are historical. *Trin.* 835–37 *circumstabant nauem turbines uenti, imbres fluctusque atque procellae infensae frangere malum, ruere antemnas, scindere uela.* Caes., *B. G.*, 3.4 *Breui spatio interiecto, uix ut eis rebus quas constituissent collocandis atque administrandis tempus daretur, hostes ex omnibus partibus signo dato decurrere, lapides gaesaque in uallum conicere. Nostri primo integri uiribus fortiter repugnare neque ullum frustra telum ex loco superiore mittere, ut quaeque pars castrorum nudata defensoribus premi uidebatur, eo occurrere et auxilium ferre, sed hoc superari, quod...* Sall., *C.*, 6. 4–5 *igitur reges populique finitumi bello temptare, pauci ex amicis auxilio esse, nam ceteri metu perculsi a periculis aberant. at Romani domi militiaeque intenti festinare parare, alius alium hortari, hostibus obviam ire, libertatem patriam parentisque armis tegere*; the next five principal verbs are imperfect indicative. Tac., *Agr.*, 38 *Britanni palantes, mixto uirorum mulierumque ploratu trahere uulneratos, uocare integros, deserere domos ac per iram ultro incendere, eligere latebras et statim relinquere*; *miscere in uicem consilia aliqua, dein separare*: *aliquando frangi aspectu pignorum suorum, saepius concitari.*

It is unfortunate that the theory of the imperfect as a combination with the infinitive as its first element cannot be proven, for the view of the historical infinitive here suggested is fully dependent on the correctness of this former theory. No other theory of the imperfect would give the necessary support unless we fall back on the notion that the first element was a verbal noun in *-ā*, *-ē* (see note 6 above), and then argue that these verbal nouns were in the process of being displaced by infinitives in *-si* at the time when the periphrastic *bh*-tenses were developing; a hazardous piece of speculation at best. If the prior element of the imperfect really was an infinitive, then the theory here offered provides an easy explanation for two striking features of the historical infinitive, its tendency to appear in series and its close functional equivalence with the imperfect, its past as opposed to present value being especially apparent from the secondary tense sequence which regularly follows it. Naturally once the historical infinitive gained its independent status, it could appear singly, and it was no longer necessary for any imperfect form to stand in its immediate vicinity. The fact that a similar construction with present value scarcely[10] exists may be explained by the fact that there was no need for a present periphrasis consisting of infinitive plus *est* and corresponding to the past periphrasis of infinitive plus **bhwāt*; simple present forms with durative aspect filled the need, and there was no objection to using them in long series.

THE JOHNS HOPKINS UNIVERSITY

[10] A few examples show present time with reference to habitual action: e.g., Verg., *G.*, 1.199–200 *sic omnia fatis in peius ruere ac retro sublapsa referri*, on which Ladewig-Schaper (*Vergils Gedichte*[7], Berlin, 1882) in note give several other examples.

JAAN PUHVEL

THE SEA IN HITTITE TEXTS

1. A HISTORICAL SURVEY

WHEN THE Hittite armies first poured south through the Cilician Gates on the route which was to be their principal avenue of political expansion throughout the history of the Hittite empire, they had in all likelihood their first contact with the Mediterranean Sea. To a land-locked people centered on the bleak highlands in the great bend of the Halys river this contact with the south and the sea was an event of intense significance. Generations earlier the forebears of those Hittites had probably occupied regions bordering on the Black Sea, or the Caspian, or both, depending on the still unknown route of their migrations into Asia Minor. It is reasonable to assume that a word denoting these large bodies of water existed in their language ever since, and was readily applicable to the new expanse on their widened horizon. But while later to Xenophon's men, straining north by the same route, the eventual sight of the Euxine meant a joyous reunion with an ever-present element of their lives, the reaching of the Mediterranean must have been a discovery to the Hittites, and Telipinus in his Edict celebrates it in solemn phrases which recur verbatim in recounting the feats of the three early kings Labarnas, Hattusilis, and Mursilis: *nu-uš a-ru-na-aš ir-ḫu-us i-e-it* 'and he made them (viz. his conquered lands) boundaries of the sea', i.e. extended his demesne to include the coastal lands (KBo III 1 I 7, 16, 26 = 2BoTU 23A).[1]

The earliest variations on this theme actually antedate Telipinus and go back to the oldest extant records in Hittite. The Anittas text[2] is suspected of being an

[1] For the bibliographical abbreviations in this article, see the list in J. Friedrich, *Hethitisches Wörterbuch* 7–13 (Heidelberg, 1952). It is a pleasure to record here my thanks to Professor H. G. Güterbock of the University of Chicago, who in the course of the investigation answered time-consuming queries with the utmost patience and kindness.

[2] Cf. B. Hrozný, L'invasion des Indo-Européens en Asie Mineure vers 2000 av. J.–C., *ArchOr* 1.273–99 (1929); H. Otten, Zu den Anfängen der hethitischen Geschichte, *MDOG* 83.33–45 (1951). Since local campaigns of early kings are involved, Bossert (*JKF* 2.338 [1953]) believes that *aruna-*

artificial literary royal inscription, like that of Naram-Sin (cf. e.g. H. G. Güterbock, *ZA* NF 10.139–45 [1938]); but it is in any event very archaic. The word *a-ru-na-aš* occurs in a fractured context in the main copy of the text (KBo III 22 Vs 32 = 2BoTU 7), to which corresponds –]*u̯a-aš a-ru-na*[– in the fragment KUB XXXVI 98 a. 3 (cf. Otten, *MDOG* 76.43–5 [1938)]. Line 38 of the same passage reads: *ud-ne-e ḫu-u-ma-an-da* URU *za-al-pu-az an-da a-ru-na* 'all the countries from (the town of) Zalpuwas in the interior (?) to the sea (?)'. The text which follows the Anittas inscription on the same tablet in the version KUB XXVI 71 = 2BoTU 30 shows (IV 14) LUGAL-*uš a-ru-na-an ar-ḫa-an IṢ-BAT* 'the king took the sea as his frontier (?)' or 'the king seized the limit (coast, region) of the sea(s) (?)'. It may belong to the Ammunas text which follows Anittas also in KUB XXXVI 98 b Rs. 7, or to yet another text which follows Ammunas in KUB XXVI 71.

Later important references to the sea in concrete historical and geographic terms occur in the Annals of Mursilis II:[3] *uḫ-ḫa*-LÚ-*iš* of Arzawa, the sick enemy of Mursilis, left his capital without a fight and (KBo III 4 II 31–2 = 2BoTU 48) *a-ru-ni pár-ra-an-da* ... *pa-it na-aš-kán a-pí-i̯a an-da e-eš-ta* 'went across the sea, and he stayed therein'. Some of his people fled to Mount Arinnanda, others to Puranda, (ibid. 36) *ku-i-e-eš-ma-kán* NAM.RA.MEŠ *a-ru-ni pár-ra-an-da IT-TI* I *uḫ-ḫa*-LÚ *pa-a-ir* 'but other colonists went with U. across the sea'. Mursilis pursued the populace to Arinnanda, which was (KUB XIV 15 III 40 = 2BoTU 51A; KUB XIV 16 III 35 = 2BoTU 51B) *me-ik-ki* (*na-*)*ak-ki-iš a-ru-ni-i̯a-aš-kán pár-ra-an-da pa-a-an-za* 'very steep, and it stretches out to the sea'. He besieged the mountain till the people surrendered. The following spring *Uḫḫazitis* with his two sons still (KBo III 4 II 51) *a-ru-ni an-da e-eš-ta* 'was in the sea', but died there (ibid. 52); one of his sons (53) ŠA(G) A.AB.BA-*pít e-eš-ta* 'stayed in the sea', while the other (54) *a-ru-na-az ar-ḫa ú-it* 'came forth from the sea' and went to Puranda, where he was defeated by Mursilis.[4]

One further occurrence in the detailed Annals is KBo IV 4 IV 5 (= 2BoTU 58B): *a-ši-ma-kán* URU *a-ri-ip-ša-aš* Š[A(G) A.A]B.BA *ki-it-ta-ri* 'but the aforementioned (city) Aripsa lies in the sea'.

Except for a fragmentary passage in the Milawata letter (KUB XIX 55 Vs 13 EGIR?-*pa a-ru-na-an* 'again (?) the sea', Sommer AU 198), the next important historical occurrence appears in the autobiography of Hattusilis III (KUB I 1 IV 36; Götze, Ḫatt. 34): *na-an-kán* A.AB.BA *ta-pu-ša up-pa-aḫ-ḫu-un* 'and I banished him (viz. Urhi-Tesupas) across the sea'.

in the Anittas text in conjunction with Zalpuwas refers to the present-day Tuz Gölü, the large salt lake southwest of the great bend of the Halys.

[3] The following survey, combining materials from the 'ten-year Annals' with the 'detailed Annals', comprises materials treated by Götze, AM p. 50–66, and Sommer, AU p. 310–3.

[4] The sequel is fragmentary, and the restorations by Götze and Sommer, who joins KUB XXIII 125, vary sharply. The same phrases with the word 'sea' recur.

In the mythological and poetic texts the sea appears as the scene of action in the Illuyankas myth, when the storm-god sets out to face the dragon (KBo III 7 III 22): *na-aš nam-ma a-ru-ni za-aḫ-ḫi-i̯a pa-it* 'then he went to the sea for battle'.

In the Hittite Gilgameš fragments[5] the sea figures in KUB VIII 50 III 8, where Uršanabi addresses the hero: *ku-it* ᴰGIŠ.GIM.MAŠ *nu-u̯a-kán a-ru-na-an p[a-ri-i̯a-an] pa-a-i-ši nu-u̯a ag-ga-an-na-aš ú-e-te-n[a-aš] ku-u̯a-pí a-ar-ti nu-u̯a* GIM-*an i-i̯a-ši* 'What, Gilgameš? Will you go across the sea? Now when you come to the waters of death, how will you do then?'

Furthermore KUB VIII 59.4–10 contains in a fragmentary state the following:

(4) [GIM-]*an-ma* ᴰGIŠ.GIM.MAŠ-*uš a-ru[-ni a-ar-aš*
'but when Gilgameš came to the sea'

(5) [*na-*]*aš a-ru-ni ḫi-en-ik-ta*
'those he consigned to the sea'

(6) [*tu-*]*u-u̯a-za e-eš šal-li-iš a-r*[*u-na-aš*
'be far (?), great sea'

(8) [...] *a-ru-na-aš-kán* ᴰGIŠ.GIM.MAŠ-*un* 'the sea Gilgameš...'

(10)]*a-ru-na-an*[

This repetitional structure from line to line brings to mind the Sumero-Akkadian prototypes of this epic.

In the Ullikummi epic[6] the entire scene is connected with the sea. Early in the poem Impaluri, vizier of the Sea, (KUB XVII 7 II 8) *a-ru-ni i-i̯a-an-ni-eš* 'went to the Sea', and converses with his master in a fragmentary passage (lines 9–15). The Sea sends Impaluri to invite Kumarbi to a feast, and Kumarbi (KUB XXXIII 102 II 21) *a-ru-na-aš* [É-]*ri an-da* [*pa-it*] 'went to the Sea's house'. Later, as Kumarbi's son, the diorite monster Ullikummi, had grown fast on the shoulder of the giant Upelluri, (KUB XVII 7 IV 27–8) *na-aš-kán a-ru-ni gi-nu-u̯a-aš ... ar-ta-at ú-i-te-na-za-aš-kán ar-ḫa ú-it* 'in the sea on his knees ... he stood, out of the water he stood', and the sea reached up to the place of the belt (line 30). When the sun-god looked down from heaven and saw Ullikummi, he wondered (KUB XVII 7 IV 35): *ku-iš-u̯]a-kán* DINGIR-*LUM nu-tar-ri-i̯a-aš a-ru-ni an-da* [*ar-ta-ri* 'what swift god is standing in the sea?', and he went to the sea to investigate (line 37). The sea is mentioned in the sequel in Bo 2527 II 5–7,[7] where Ištar goes down to it and vainly tries to lure the deaf stone-monster with song. In the ensuing battle against Ullikummi the seventy gods who assisted Tešub in his fight fell down into the sea (KUB XXXIII 106 I 13). At length the power of Ullikummi was broken with the help of Ea, the Babylonian god of magic, and Tešub (KUB XXXIII 106 IV 22) *kat-ta a-ru-ni a-ar-aš* 'went down to the sea' to engage the monster in a final, presumably successful battle.

[5] Cf. Friedrich, *ZA* NF 5.24–6 (1929).
[6] Cf. Güterbock, *The Song of Ullikummi* (New Haven, 1952).
[7] Otten, *Mythen vom Gotte Kumarbi, Fragment* 12 *II* (Berlin, 1950).

In another fragmentary text of the Kumarbi cycle of Hurrian myths[8] Kumarbi sends his vizier Mukišanu to invite the Sea to a banquet; the vizier (KUB XII 65 III 4) *a-ru-ni kat-ta-an-da pa-it* 'went down to the Sea' and delivered the message. Thereupon, *ma-a-an šal-li-iš a-ru-na-aš ud-da-ar IṢ-ME* (ibid. line 9) 'when the great Sea heard the words', he goes straight to Kumarbi's abode, is seated with the latter, and they eat and drink.

One further, even more broken text (KUB XXXIII 109 and 94) shows Kumarbi again in the Sea's house, and it appears that the Sea gives Kumarbi his daughter in marriage.

In the Hedammu myth, where Ištar seduces with her physical charms the serpent of that name, the sea is mentioned a number of times, but always in very fragmentary context (KUB VIII 64.4, XXXIII 88.13, XXXIII 86 II 13, VIII 65.8, 13, 16, 19, XXXIII 85.2). Cf. Friedrich, *ArchOr* 17.230–54 (1949).

In the beginning of the story of Appu we read (KUB XXIV 8 I 7–10; cf. Friedrich, *ZA* NF 15.214 [1950]): URU-*aš ŠUM-an-še-it* URU[*šu*]-*du-ul* URU*lu-ul-lu-ụa-ịa-aš-ša*[-*an*] KUR-*e a-ru-ni* ZAG-*ši e-eš-zi nu-k*[*án*] *še-ir* LÚ-*aš* I*ap-pu ŠUM-an-še-it* 'there is a city called Šudul, in the land of Lulluwa by the sea, and up (there lived) a man named Appu'. The people of Lullu, known from Assyrian and Haldian sources, lived on the mountainous borderlands of Assyria and Persia; here the country and the reference to the sea are probably purely legendary.

The most famous instance in a religious text is found in the Prayer of Muwatallis KUB VI 45 III 14: *ša-ra-a-kán u-ụa-ši ne-pí-ša-aš* DUTU-*uš a-ru-na-az* 'up thou risest, sun-god of heaven, from the sea'.[9] This may go back to the traditions of a people living on an (eastern) litoral, and the figure of the 'sun-god in the water': DUTU *ú-i-te-e-ni* (KBo V 2 II 13), DUTU *ME-E* (KUB V 6 I 6, II 14) points in similar direction. The conception of the sun as the 'lord of judgment' in the same passage is profoundly influenced by the Mesopotamian image of Šamaš; but this very syncretism of one aspect serves to underline a contrast of another: the idea of the sun rising from the sea is foreign to both Babylonia and Egypt, where the sun is traditionally depicted as rising from the mountains,[10] and must represent a genuine Hittite tradition.

A section of Mursilis' prayer to Telipinus[11] reads (KUB XXIV 2 I 8): *nu-za-kán*

[8] See Güterbock, Kumarbi 32–3, 82–5, 95, Transkription 30–2 (Zürich, 1946).

[9] On the Hittite solar deities in this and other connexions, see e.g. E. Tenner, Tages- und Nachtsonne bei den Hethitern, *ZA* NF 4.186–90 (1929); O. R. Gurney, *AAA* 27.10–11 (1940); E. Laroche, *Recherches sur les noms des dieux hittites* 105–7 (Paris, 1947).

[10] Cf. e.g. '(When) thou art risen over the mountains thou dost scan the earth' in a Šamaš-hymn from the Library of Aššurbanipal, or 'to worship the sun when he rises from the mountains in the east' from an Egyptian tomb inscription of the reign of Tuthmosis III. The same is seen in Hurrian traditions, e.g. the story of the hunter Kešši (KUB XVII 1 II 14): *n*[*u* GIM-*an l*]*u-uk-kat-ta* D[U]TU-*uš-kán kal-ma-ra-az ú-it* 'when it dawned and the sun-god rose from the mountain...' (cf. Friedrich, *ZA* NF 15.238 [1950]).

[11] Cf. Gurney, *AAA* 27.16 (1940).

ma-a-an na-ak-ki-iš ᴰ*te-li-pí-nu-uš še-ir ne-pí-ši* DINGIR.MEŠ-*aš iš-tar-na ma-a-an a-ru-ni na-aš-ma A-NA* ḪUR.SAG.MEŠ *ṷa-ḫa-an-na pa-a-an-za na-aš-ma-za I-NA* KUR ᴸᵁ́KÚR *za-aḫ-ḫi-ịa pa-a-an-za* ... 'Now, noble Telipinus, whether thou art up in heaven among the gods; whether thou art gone to the sea or to the mountains to roam, or art gone into the enemy's country to battle...'.

In a quaint building ritual for the royal palace[12] we find (KUB XXIX 1 I 24): LUGAL-*u-e-mu ma-ni-ya-aḫ-ḫa-u-en* ᴳᴵŠ*tal-lu-ga-an-ni-en* ᴳᴵŠDAG-*iz a-ru-na-za ú-da-aš* 'to me, the king, the Throne has brought from the sea the assigned sceptre'. Ibid. line 51: *ma-a-an-ma* LUGAL *an-da-an pár-na ú-iz-zi* ᴳᴵŠDAG-*iz* ÁᴹᵁŠᴱᴺ-*an ḫal-za-a-i e-ḫu-ta a-ru-na pí-e-i-mi* 'when the king enters the house, the Throne calls the Eagle: "Come, I send you to the sea" ' (cf. Güterbock, *RHA* 14.22–23 [1956]).

The sea is found in the company of divinities in KUB XXI 38 Vs 15, where a crusty old Hittite Tawannannas, perhaps Queen Puduḫepa, is chiding in a letter a presumably wealthy foreign monarch for demanding some material gift in connexion with a marriage project: *ma-a-an A-NA* DUMU ᴰUTU *na-aš-ma* DUMU ᴰU *Ú-UL ku-it-ki e-eš-zi na-aš-ma a-ru-ni Ú-UL e-eš-zi tu-uq-qa Ú-UL ku-it-ki e-eš-zi* 'if the son of the sun-god or the son of the storm-god has nothing, or the sea has nothing, do you (then) have nothing?'.[13] With this implicit reference to the wealth of the sea one may compare the astrological omen text KUB VIII 1 III 12 *a-ru-na-aš a-aš-šu ḫar-ak-zi* 'the goods of the sea will perish',[14] which is the literal equivalent of the Akkadian *hiṣib tāmti iḫalliq*. In another, broken omen text (KBo II 19 I 9) we find *a-ru-na-aš-ša la-a-ḫu-ṷa-i* 'and the sea pours (?)'.

We have already seen cases where the sea was termed 'great' (Gilgameš and Kumarbi fragments); with this epithet it figures in the lists of witnesses at the end of Hittite treaties; from the numerous examples I select:[15]

KBo IV 10 II 4 (end of list): *šal-li-iš a-ru-na-aš* ḪUR.SAG.MEŠ ÍD.MEŠ TÚL.-MEŠ *ŠA* KURᵁᴿᵁ*ḫa-at-ti* 'the great sea, the mountains, rivers, springs of Ḫatti-land'.

KBo V 3 I 59:[16] *ne-pi*[*-iš*] *te-e-kán šal-li-iš a-a-ru-na-aš* 'heaven, earth, the great sea'.

KBo V 9 IV 18:[17] ḪUR.SAG.MEŠ ÍD.MEŠ TÚL.MEŠ A.AB.BA GAL AN *Ù* KI 'the mountains, rivers, springs, the great sea, heaven and earth'.

[12] See B. Schwartz, A Hittite ritual text, *Orientalia* N.S. 16.23–55 (1947).

[13] Cf. Sommer, AU 258–60: Forrer (see ref.) thought that the 'son of the sun-god' refers to Pharaoh, 'son of the storm-god' to the king of Mitanni-Ḫurri, and 'the sea' to the Mycenaean thalassocracy of Aḫḫiyawa; the point would thus be 'even if the great monarchs of the world were paupers, it would not follow that you are one, so do not ask for a gift from me'. Yet the same general idea is clear also without these elaborate identifications.

[14] Perhaps fish and seafood in general are meant here, since the next paragraph mentions famine. Cf. Friedrich, Aus dem heth. Schrifttum 2.28 (*Der Alte Orient* 25.2 [1925]).

[15] Further references are given by Sommer, *OLZ* 1921.197–201; Laroche, Recherches 72.

[16] Suppiluliuma's treaty with Huqqanaš; cf. Friedrich, Staatsv. 2.112 (1930).

[17] Mursilis' treaty with Duppi-Teššub of Amurru (Friedrich, Staatsv. 1.24); a close parallel is found in the Egyptian version of the Hattusilis-Ramses treaty, which also mentions the 'great sea' (cf. S. Langdon and A. H. Gardiner, *JEA* 6.194 [1920]).

We find the sea in similar company in 2BoTU 14β, 11, a text which is a mixture of myth and history:[18] ÍD.MEŠ-*uš* ḪUR.SAG.MEŠ-*uš* *a-ru-nu-uš-ša* 'rivers, mountains, and seas'.

In the beginning of a ritual designed to attract gods from foreign countries we find a similar enumeration (KUB XV 34 I 1–3; cf. L. Zuntz, *Atti del Reale Istituto Veneto* 96–2.488 [1936–37]): [*ma-a-a*]*n* $^{\mathrm{LU.MEŠ}}$AZU DINGIR.MEŠ *IŠ.T[U* 8? KA]S.-MEŠ [*ú-el-lu-?*]*u-u̯a-az* ḪUR.SAG.MEŠ ÍD.MEŠ [*a-r*]*u-na-az* TÚL.MEŠ-*az* *pa-aḫ-ḫu-e-na-az* [*ne-p*]*í-sa-az* *tág-na-a-az* *ḫu-it-ti-i̯a-an-zi* *nu* *ki-i* *da-an-zi* 'when the seers draw the gods by eight ways, from the field (?), mountains, rivers, sea, springs, fire, heaven, and earth, then they take this'.

From such animistic invocation of elements of nature the next step is to a concrete personification of the sea as a deity. The sea is conceived as a person in the Ullikummi and Kumarbi epics quoted above. In these passages it is treated as a male divinity,[19] but we must remember that these are Hurrian myths. According to KUB XVII 8 IV 20 the sea, in more clearly Anatolian context, is the daughter of the goddess Kamrusepas.[20] In any event the outright divine character of the sea is very sporadically attested, and the use of the divine determinative is excessively rare. Examples are ^{D}*a-ru-na-an-na* (KUB XX 1 II 32), ^{D}*a-ru-na-an* (KUB XX 1 III 5, 11), ^{D}*a-ru-ni* (ibid. 16), in a festival ritual, and the fragments discussed by Güterbock, Kumarbi p. 85, 95 fn. 19, 122: KUB XXXIII 89.15 ^{D}A.AB.[BA], KUB XXXIII 108.17 ^{D}U-*aš* ^{D}*a-ru-na-an* *tar-aḫ-zi* 'the storm-god overcomes the sea(-god)'; these latter instances reflect Hurrian traditions.[21]

Turning to secondary cases, we find a city ^{URU}*a-ru-u-na*^{KI} mentioned in KBo I 5 IV 43,45, a festival ^{EZEN}*arunitaš* in KUB XXV 27 I 29, and a ^{D}*arunitti* in ABoT I 14 IV 11–2. A derivative adjective *arunumaneš* (nom. pl.) 'maritimi' appears in the fragment KUB VIII 14 I 14 (cf. Sommer, HAB 169–70).

Thus the Hittite notion of 'sea' is expressed by the graphic equation A.AB.BA = *aruna-*. The case usages are in most instances unequivocal, notably when the ending is formally unifunctional, as in the case of the ablative *arunaz*(*a*), the dative *aruni*, or the archaic directional dative *aruna* (KUB XII 60 I 11, XXIX 1 I 51). In other cases the syntax has to provide a criterion of differentiation, so with the probable accusative plural *arunuš*, where the ending *-uš* tends to impinge on the nominative plural *-eš* as well. Notably *-aš* may denote nominative, vocative, or genitive singular, and genitive, dative (or, less commonly, nominative and accusative) plural. Hence *arunaš* in the Edict of Telipinus may also be genitive plural 'of the seas'. So also

[18] Cf. Güterbock, *ZA* NF 10.113 (1938).

[19] Cf. Güterbock, Ullikummi p. 53.

[20] This is one of the several cases where the sex of a Hittite deity is a matter of controversy, see e.g. Otten, *JKF* 2.62–73 (1951), Laroche, Recherches 87, on Pirwa; Laroche 106fn. 3, on the chthonic solar deity; Laroche 82–3, Güterbock, *Orientalia* N.S. 12.338 (1943), on Inaras.

[21] Some further cases are mentioned in KUB XXVII, p. 5.

the ending *-an* may be accusative singular or an archaic genitive plural, generally used in words denoting living beings, and spilling over occasionally into the genitive singular.[22] I have alternatively proposed to translate *arunan* in KUB XXVI 71 IV 14 as such a genitive, since it makes good sense in the context. It would be quite unique as used of other than living beings; but we are dealing with a text of unusually ancient character, and may expect archaic anomalies.[23]

The expression *aruni anda* in the Ullikummi passage KUB XVII 7 IV 35 means literally 'in the sea', but the same phrase (= ŠA(G) A.AB.BA) and *arunaz arḫa* 'from the sea' in the Annals of Mursilis seem to mean 'on an island' and 'from an island'.[24] As such they may be copied from the Akkadian *qabal tāmtim*, literally 'the midst of the sea' or 'in the midst of the sea', hence 'island' or 'on an island'. But we may also note that similar formations have yielded words for 'island' in other IE languages: e.g. Lat. *insula* 'island', if compared with Gk. ἐνάλιος 'in the sea', and Old Slavonic *otokŭ*, *ostrovŭ*, bahuvrihi compounds like Gk. ἔνθεος, made up of **obŭ* 'around', *tokŭ* 'course, stream', and a cognate to *struja* 'stream'. In Hittite, however, we have no noun form for 'island', but only those adverbial phrases.

2. PRELIMINARIES TO AN ETYMOLOGY

Turning now to the problem of the wider connexions and the etymological background of the word *aruna-*, let us take up first the so-called Indic hypothesis. The much-discussed listing of Vedic divinities of the Mitannian ruling class in the treaty between Suppiluliuma and Mattiwaza (see e.g. Laroche, Recherches 118–9) presents the variant graphies *u-ru-wa-na-aš-ši-el* and *a-ru-na-aš-ši-il* for the god Varuna.[25] This variation precipitated the connecting of Hitt. *aruna-* directly with the Indic god. Varuna is a sea-god in post-Vedic tradition, and the importance of his early relations to water has been convincingly demonstrated (H. Lüders, *Varuṇa* I [Göttingen, 1951]). So Kretschmer (*WZKM* 33.1–22 [1926], *KZ* 55.75–78 [1927]) maintained that we have originally an Anatolian god *Aruna* 'Sea', taken over by Indic peoples in the Near East, and changed by popular etymology (*urú-* 'broad', *váras-* 'breadth') to *Uruwana*, *Varuna*. This view was justly criticized (see Benveniste, *RHA* 1.206–7 [1932]). Any such attempt ignores the fact that Hitt. *aruna-* is hardly ever a deity in the texts, but a common word for 'sea', and that the sporadic and hesitant divine

[22] E.g. LUGAL-*an aška* = LUGAL-*u̯aš aška* 'to the king's gate' (Code 71). See H. Ehelolf, *ZA* NF 9.173–81 (1936); Sommer, HAB 162, 187; HuH 48–9; H. Pedersen, Hitt. 32,193.

[23] A parallel may be present in the word for 'foot', if *pa-ta-a-na* and GÌR.ḪI.A-*na* contain a genitive plural; GÌR-*an* (KUB IX 4 I 33) is probably genitive singular. Cf. Otten, *ZA* NF 16.230–1 (1952), 17.124 (1955).

[24] Cf. P. Kretschmer, *Glotta* 33.8–9 (1954). In this case the island was probably Alasiya, i.e. Cyprus, opposite the presumable location of Arzawa in the Cilicia Tracheia region. It is likely to be also the place 'across the sea' where Hattusilis III banished Urhitesupas.

[25] *Arawna* in the OT (2Sam. 24.16), and *wrn* in a legal papyrus have also been connected (cf. W. Feiler, *ZA* NF 11.222–225 [1939]; *WZKM* 46.235 fn. 4 [1939]).

character is due mostly to the relatively late influence of Hurrian epic poetry. This same fact also invalidates the converse approach, which attributes primacy to *Varuna*: it would account for the loss of the initial phoneme by pointing to the alternative absence of *w*- in words of presumed Hurrian character like ^{UZU}*u̯a-ap-pu-uz-zi-i̯a* (KUB XXVII 1 I 39): ^{UZU}*ap-pu-*[*uz-*]*zi-i̯a* (KUB XXVII 1 I 43).[26] This Hurrian phonetic vacillation is instructive enough for the Mattiwaza passage, but has nothing whatever to do with the origin of Hitt. *aruna*-, except that the resulting random homophony may have beguiled the contemporaries as well as so many modern scholars, and even prompted a secondary identification.

We may thus safely conclude that *aruna*- is a native Hittite word. Laroche (Recherches 72) suggests Hattic origin, because of the suffix *-una*- in divine names like Zašḫapuna, Karuna, Šuwašuna (cf. Sommer, *IF* 55.178 [1937]). Forrer (*Glotta* 26.193–6 [1938]) terms it vaguely 'Luwian', connecting *arinna* 'fountain', extracted from ^{URU}TÚL-*na* = ^{URU}*arinna*, and the mountain Arinnanda which we saw in the Annals of Mursilis as being in Luwian territory (Arzawa).[27]

[26] *u̯appuzzi*- 'tallow'; cf. Ehelolf, *ZA* NF 9.173 fn. 1 (1936). Feiler (*WZKM* 46.235) thought that *a-ru-na-aš-ši-il* lost its *w*- by being drawn through popular etymology to the deified Hittite *aruna*-.

[27] Forrer considered Arinnanda to be a Luwian neuter plural 'springs', and also discussed W. Brandenstein's derivation of Gk. *Lerna* from a 'Hattic' **lē-arinna* 'the springs'. But Luwian nom. pl. neuter ends in *-a* as in Hittite (cf. Otten, *Zur gramm. und lexik. Bestimmung des Luvischen* 120 [Berlin, 1953]). *-anda* is simply the very common local suffix. Forrer also cites from Bo 523 the Luwian forms *a-ru-na-a*, *a-ru-ú-na*, and a '3rd pers. pl. imperative' *a-ru-na-in-du*. A comparable form *a-a-ru-na-an-du* is found in KUB XXV 38.15. Forrer's text has been published as KUB XXXV 132, but is not included in Otten's *Luvische Texte in Umschrift* (Berlin, 1953). It seems unlikely that there is other than a homophonous relationship to Hitt. *aruna*-. HH *ʾa-ru-na* in the Çiftlik inscription HHM XXXI 17 is preceded by the ideogram 'to eat', and followed by 'to drink'. It is probably as infinitive in *-una*. Such non-Hittite Anatolian infinitives are found also in the 'Glossenkeilsprache' (e.g. *taparuna* 'to overcome' KUB XIX 29 IV 21; *paššuna* 'to swallow' KUB XXIV 7 III 31; *lau̯arruna* 'to break' KUB XXIV 3 II 30) and in Palaic (see below), while in Luwian proper the only infinitive form so far is one in *-uu̯an* (cf. Otten, Bestimmung 23). In view of the very common HH development of intervocalic *d* > *r* (cf. e.g. Friedrich, *ArchOr* 21.135–9 [1953]; Bossert, *JKF* 2.335–9 [1953]) one may compare *ʾa-za-tu-u* 'may they eat' in the Sultanhan inscription HHM LXXI 49 c (see Gelb, HH 3.24–5; Bossert, Königssiegel 230), the root being that of Hitt. *edmi* 'I eat', *adanzi* 'they eat', infin. *adanna*. The Luwian forms of this verb are *a-az-za-aš-ta-an* in KUB IX 31 II 26 (Zarpiya-ritual, 2nd pers. pl. act. imperative, Hitt. *ezza*(*š*)*ten*) and *ni-iš az-tu-u-u̯a-ri* (2nd pers. pl. pres. middle in prohibition, ibid. line 28). Cf. e.g. Sommer, HAB 85; Laroche, *RHA* 9.20 (1948); Otten, Bestimmung 46–7; Friedrich, *Corolla linguistica* 44 (Wiesbaden, 1955). A Palaic correspondence to this HH infinitive 'to eat' is suspected by Bossert (*BiOr* 12.53 [1955]) in the ritual text KUB XXXV 165 Vs 23, emended by KUB XXXII 17.9: [(*a-ru-u-*)]*na-am-pí*; in line 22 Bossert restores *a-ḫu-nu-uš-ši-am-pí*, containing the infinitive seen in *a-ḫu-u-na* 'to drink' (KUB XXXV 165 Rs 22; Hitt. inf. *akuu̯anna*). Cf. further Palaic *a-ḫu-u̯a-*(*a-*)*an-ti* 'they drink' (KUB XXXII 18 I 9, 18; Hitt. *akuu̯anzi*), *a-ta-a-an-ti* 'they eat' (ibid. line 7, 8). Laroche (*RHA* 13.74–5 [1955]) sees in KUB XXXV 165 Vs 15, 20 *a-ti-a-pa-an az-zi-ki-i* the Palaic *ad*- 'eat' and its iterative, corresponding to Hitt. *azzik*-. See Bossert, Königssiegel 77–92; Otten, *ZA* NF 14.119–45 (1944), *AfO* 15.81–2 (1945–51), *Wissenschaftliche Annalen* 2.328 (Berlin, 1953); F. Cornelius, *WZKM* 52.272–87 (1955); Kammenhuber, *OLZ* 1955.352–78, esp. 363–5; Friedrich, *Gedenkschrift ... Kretschmer* 1.108–9 (Wien, 1956). Thus the *d* : *r* variation may be present in Palaic also, though Kammenhuber (*RHA* 14.15–16 [1956]) disputes Bossert's interpretation of

A further indication of 'Luwian' origin might be the hapax *arunumaneš*, when compared with the (probably pre-IE, but non-Hattic) derivative suffix *-uman* in the Cappadocian tablets from Kültepe-Kaneš. In Hittite proper the use of the gentilic suffix *-umna-* is sporadic, and perhaps an imported provincialism. Note that *nešumnili* occurs only once, in the 'second Arzawa letter' from Tell el-Amarna (and lately LÚ.MEŠ*ne-šu-me-ni-eš* 'the men of Nesa' in KBo VII 38.10), whereas the normal Hittite variant is *nešili* or *našili*. Kaneš was on the fringe of Luwian territory, and the dialect of Ištanuwa seems to have been a variety of Luwian, so that *kanešumnili* and *ištanumnili* would be in sympathy with this interpretation (cf. *luium(a)nas* in the Code, § 21). Less so are *palaumnili* relating to Palaic, i.e. a northern Anatolian language, and the pronominal adjective *kuenzumna-* 'cuias'. Cf. Laroche, Onomastique 104, 108–110; Goetze, *Language* 29.263–4 (1953), 30.351–2 (1954); A. Kammenhuber, *RHA* 14.9, 17–19 (1956).

The only other flimsy evidence in support of strictly Luwian character would seem to be the one passage (KUB XVII 8 IV 20) where the sea is said to be the daughter of the goddess Kamrusepas. The latter (cf. e.g. Laroche, Recherches 67–8) was the deity of healing and magic, and is frequent in Luwian texts, e.g. the conjuration against illness KUB XXXV 88 III 14: D*kam-ru-ši-pa-aš*.

More important is Forrer's connexion of *arinna-*, *aruna-* with Skt. *riṇā́ti* 'flow', *árṇas-* 'flood, wave'. Kretschmer, in dealing with *aruna-* (*WZKM* 33.10), was reminded of Ved. *arṇavá-*, but thought non-IE origin of *aruna-* more likely. W. Couvreur, *De hettitische Ḫ* 98 (Louvain, 1937) adduced OIr. *rían* < **reinos* 'sea', Gaul. *Rēnos*, and especially Skt. *árvant-* 'swift'. Juret's *Vocabulaire étymologique de la language hittite* 44–45 (Limoges, 1942) takes up the comparison, and the connexion with *árṇas-* has been endorsed most recently by Mayrhofer, *Kurzgef. etym. Wb. des Altind.* 51 (Heidelberg, 1954).

While a comparison of *arinna* with Skt. *riṇā́ti*, OIr. *rían*, and the other cognates from the same root (Gk. ὀρίνω, Lat. *rīuos*, OSl. *rinǫti*, *rivati*, *rěka*, Goth. *rinnan*, OE *rīþ*) might be considered, that with *aruna-* should be rejected outright as phonematically unfeasible. But the coupling of *aruna-* with Skt. *árṇas-*, *arṇavá-* raises very interesting possibilities. *árṇas-* is quite frequent in the Rig-Veda, denoting a surging, billowing mass of water, more specifically 'flood' or 'sea' (e.g. *árṇaso* . . . *samudrā́d* RV 1.117.14). *arṇavá-* is an adjective seen in RV 10.910.1: *samudró arṇaváḥ* 'surging sea' (cf. 10.191.2, 1.19.7, 10.58.5, 3.53.9), but also a noun in e.g. *apā́m* . . . *arṇavám* 'flood of waters' (1.56.5, 1.85.9; cf. 10.65.3, 5.32.1, 5.59.1). In the later language it is a frequent term for 'sea'. *árṇa-* 'id.' is an adjective in *apó árṇā* (RV 1.174.2, 3.32.5), but a noun in 3.22.3 (*árṇam*), 5.41.14 (*árṇāḥ*). A derivative adjective from *árṇas-* is the Rig-Vedic hapax *arṇasá-* (5.54.6).

(*a-ru-u-*)*na-* and his restoration of *a-ḫu-nu-* in KUB XXXV 165 Vs 22–3. From Luwian there is only the very scanty and indirect evidence discussed by A. J. van Windekens, *KZ* 72.245 (1955).

These words are related to the verb *r̥ṇóti*, *r̥ṇváti* 'stir' (both in RV), and the various present formations seen in *r̥cháti*, *íyarti*, *rante* (all in RV), *árti* (TS). The Greek correspondents are ὄρνῡμι 'stir', ὀρούω 'rush', while the Hittite *arnuzi* 'bring' may belong rather with Gk. ἄρνυμαι 'win', Arm. *aṙnum* 'take'. We have basically a root **H̯er-*, and the initial vowel of the Greek forms affords an indication of an *o*-colored laryngeal.[28] A straight verbal derivative is seen in Vedic *r̥tá-* 'stirred' (different from *r̥tá-* 'due, fitting, right', from a verbal root related to Gk. ἀραρίσκω 'fit', Arm. *aṙnem* 'make'). But the unquestionably related *īrṇá-* 'id.' points to an alternative laryngeal suffix as well (**H̯r̥H̯nó-*), and the present *ī́rte* 'stir' may well stand for a root class middle present **H̯r̥H̯tói̯*. The Sanskrit accent on the root syllable is due to analogical levelling in a whole later category (cf. Whitney, *Sanskrit Grammar* 628). This second laryngeal may be identified by an important new criterion and give added support to the latter. I am referring to Martinet's phonological discussion of the labiovelar characteristics of the IE *o*-colored laryngeal (or laryngeals, denoted A^{w}),[29] where the (subsequently phonematic) labial element *w* is shown to remain in other than preconsonantal positions, yielding oppositions like *-eA^{w}t- > -ōt- : *-eA^{w}e- > -āwe-. The *w* generally persisted prevocalically, and thus the 3rd person plural *r̥ṇvánti* may be reconstructed as *A^{w}r̥-n-A^{w}-énti, to which the original 3rd person singular was *A^{w}r̥-n-éA^{w}-ti > IE **r̥nṓti*; Skt. *r̥ṇóti* and *r̥ṇváti* are secondary formations.[30] The *w*-element of the derivatives RV *árvan(t)-* 'swift', 'courser', Av. *aurva(nt)-* 'swift',[31] Gk. οὖρος 'fair wind' < *ὀρϝος, OIcel. *ǫrr* 'swift' < **arwa-* is likely to be a reflex of the laryngeal. In relating Hitt. *aruna-* to this root, we may consider the following two possibilities, either one of which, if substantiated, has important consequences for Hittite phonology:

1. *aruna-* is the phonematic equivalent of Vedic *árṇa-*, i.e., *A^{w}erA^{w}no-, and the *u* in *aruna-* is a vocalization of the labial component of the labiovelar laryngeal. A parallel is found in the vocalization of this element in labiovelar stops in Greek (γυνή, κύκλος). This would introduce a new element into the discussion of Hittite reflexes of the laryngeals, and especially of the *o*-colored variety, for which the evidence is notoriously ambiguous. This evidence will be treated in detail in the aforementioned monograph. It will be sufficient here to postulate tentatively that one variety of *o*-colored laryngeal in a position between non-syllabics was generally lost in Hittite, but that its labial component was capable of being merged with the syllabic allophone of the IE phoneme /w/.

[28] Indo-Iranian, Germanic, and Hittite materials do not admit any differentiation of original *a* and *o* quality, but Greek points to *o*.

[29] *Word* 9.253–67 (1953), 12.1–6 (1956); *BSL* 51.42–56 (1955); cf. E. Hamp, *Word* 11.399–403 (1955).

[30] The mechanism of this development and the whole complex of these questions will be discussed in my forthcoming monograph on the role of laryngeals in IE morphology.

[31] Goetze, *JCS* 8.80 (1954) interprets the divine name *Uruwanda/Runda* as '**o/erwont-* (skr. *árvant-*, aw. *aurvant* 'swift, brave')'.

2. *aruna-* is the equivalent of Ved. *īrṇá-*, i.e. *A^wr̥A^wno-*, and *aru-* is thus a reflex of the weak grade of a *seṭ* root in cases where laryngeals were lost in Hittite. To my knowledge no such forms have been isolated so far in Hittite. In the absence of contrasting evidence it is impossible to decide whether the quality of the *o*-colored laryngeal(s) has had any influence on the phonematic shape of *aru-*. Obvious parallels are the Greek results αρα, ανα, and the Balto-Slavic accent features, which point to the loss of one syllable in an original dissyllabic reflex.

The nearest Hittite parallel is the word *daluki-* 'long'. Although Specht (*Der Ursprung der idg. Dekl.* 126 [Göttingen, 1944]) tried to explain away the *u* as evidence for a *u*-stem base, and account for the peculiarities evidenced by Gk. δολιχός and other forms in similar fashion, his manner of handling parallels, and his entire method should not deter us from stressing primarily the preponderance of the *seṭ* nature of the root. This is overwhelmingly clear from Skt. *dīrghá-*, Av. *darəya-* 'long', Gk. ἐνδελεχής 'lasting'.[32] Schwyzer (*Gr. Gramm.* 1.278) explains the ι in δολιχός by svarabhakti, adducing πινυτός : πεπνυμένος; but it may be rather the same kind of peculiar vowel coloring as in Aeolic πίσυρες 'four'. We have basically a root **del-H̯-*, and an infixed variety **dlenH̯-*, the relation of which to the normal **dl̥-n-eH̯-* is the same as that of Gk. ῥέμβομαι to Skt. *vr̥ṇákti*. Thematic derivation with a nominal *-gh-* determinative yielded the types **dl̥H̯ghó-* (*dīrghá-*), **dolH̯ghó-* (δολιχός), and **dlonH̯ghó-* (*longus*). Gk. ἐνδελεχής perhaps reflects a noun *δέλεχος, and the quality of the second ε is no more a trustworthy phonological criterion than that of μέγεθος as compared with μέγας. Thus the Greek evidence sheds no conclusive light on the quality of the laryngeal involved, and full grade forms of the type Skt. *drā́ghiyāṅs-*, which would settle the issue in many other IE languages, are found only in Indo-Iranian. Therefore *daluki-*, while being a plausible parallel, does not provide a definitive check for the suppositions enuntiated regarding *aruna-*.[33]

Another parallel is possibly present in the noun *kaluti-* which means 'line, row, list, circle, group'. By imagining some connexion with 'line, thread' we might compare Gk. κλώθω 'spin', which is in ablaut with κάλαθος 'basket'; thus *kaluti-* would stand for **kl̥A^wdhi-* (cf. Gk. κλῶσις 'spinning', but also 'line, clue'). That only **kl̥A^wdhi-* may be postulated here supports the weak grade alternative. **kolA^wdhi-* is impossible, because the extended root form is distinctly verbal, and thus only the suffixed variety **kl-éA^w-* may have the determinative *-dh-* (cf. Gk. πλήθω). In contrast, the nominal **dolA^wghó-* was not subject to these limitations.

This may implicate Luwian as well as Hittite in such patterns, as *kaluti-* has

[32] Cf. full grade in the Skt. comparative *drā́ghiyāṅs-*; further OSl. *dlŭgŭ*, Lith *ìlgas* (with obscure loss of *d-*); and with nasal infix Lat. *longus*, Goth. *laggs*, Pers. *dirang*.

[33] If **dolH̯ghi-*, only A^w is possible; in **dl̥H̯ghi-*, a different laryngeal would indicate that *alu* is the general reflex of the weak grade of *seṭ* roots, regardless of the quality of the laryngeal.

Luwian affinities because of the 3rd pers. sg. *kalutitti* (KUB XX 59 V 3) beside the normal, frequent *kalutiịazzi, kalutezzi* from the denominative verb *kalutiịa-* (cf. Friedrich, *RHA* 8.8 [1947]; Güterbock, *Orientalia* N.S. 25.121 [1956]). KUB XXV 37 II 33, 35 has *ka-lu-ut-ta-ni-ta, ka-lu-ut-ta-an-ni* in the Ištanuwa dialect, probably a local variety of Luwian (cf. B. Rosenkranz, *Beiträge zur Erforschung des Luvischen* 20–21 [Wiesbaden, 1952]; see also Laroche, *JCS* 2.113 [1948]; *RHA* 9.22 [1948]; *Onomastique* 115).

Ḫaluga- 'message', *ḫalugatalla-* 'messenger' likewise present the sequence *alu*, but there is no acceptable etymology. Goetze (*Mélanges ... Pedersen* 490 [Copenhagen, 1937]) and Pedersen (*Hitt.* 177 fn. 1) compared Gk. κέλευθος, but this connexion collapses with the unacceptable assumption of guttural origin for Hitt. *ḫ*. E. Polomé (*Language* 28.451 [1952]) believes that the word is non-Indo-European.

This does not, however, exhaust the possible approaches to Hittite *aruna-*, but what follows enters the domain of pure hypothesis. Since *a* is the normal Hittite reflex of IE **m̥*,[34] we may posit a tentative **m̥ru-no-*. A parallel is provided by Gk. ἄλευρον, ἀλετρίς beside Mycenaean *me-re-u-ro* (PY Un 718.10), *me-re-ti-ri-ja*, (PY Aa 62), i.e. μέλευρον, μελέτριαι (**m̥l-* beside **mel-*),[35] although the attractive alternative connexion of ἀλέω, ἄλευρον with Arm. *alam* 'grind', *alewr* 'flour' makes difficulty (cf. Frisk *GEW* 70). Such **m̥ru-no-* may conceivably be related to IE **mori* 'sea', but this is a remote possibility.

Yet perhaps *aruna-* is in origin a name for the Black Sea, since this is likely the first large body of water with which the Hittites came into contact. Here we are reminded of Vasmer's brilliant interpretation[36] of (Πόντος) Ἄξεινος, the earlier well-attested name of the euphemistic Εὔξεινος, as a loanword from Scythian, connected with Av. *axšaēna-*, OPe. *axšaina-*, Sakian *āṣṣeina-* 'dark (blue)' (lit. 'not bright', cf. Av. *xšaēta-* 'bright', Bartholomae, *IF* 5.360 fn. 1); cf. further Sakian *aṣṣänaka-* '(dark) dove', borrowed in Toch. B *ekṣinek* (E. Schwentner, *KZ* 71.89 [1953], 73.238 [1956]; cf. Gk. πέλεια 'dove': πελιτνός 'dark', Goth. *dubo* 'dove': OIr. *dub* 'black'). The dark waters of the Euxine have impressed ancients and moderns alike; the Μαύρη Θάλασσα of Modern Greek was called Πόντος μέλας by Euripides (Iphigen. 107). It may therefore be plausible to see in **m̥ru-no-* a cognate of Gk. μόρυχος 'σκοτεινός'· μορτός· μέλας, φαιός (Hes.).[37]

[34] See e.g. H. Kronasser, *Vgl. Laut- und Formenlehre des Heth.* 53 (Heidelberg, 1956).
[35] Cf. e.g. J. Chadwick, *TPS* 1954.14; C. Gallavotti, *PP* II (fasc. 47), 150-151 (1956).
[36] *Acta et Commentationes Universitatis Dorpatensis*, Series B, Vol. 1.3–6 (1921); cf. Boisacq, *RBPhH* 3.315–6 (1924); also Vasmer, *Die Iranier in Südrussland* 20, 60 (Leipzig, 1923), *Reallex. der Vorgesch.* 12.241 (1928). Vasmer's interpretation was disputed by A. C. Moorhouse, *CQ* 34.123–8 (1940), but his objections were refuted by W. S. Allen, *CQ* 41.86–8 (1947). Further Moorhouse, *CQ* 42.59–60 (1948), Allen, *ibid.* 60.
[37] Acc. to Specht, *Ursprung* 119, IE **mori* 'sea' comes from the same root. Further cognates in Pokorny, *IEW* 734.

Such an approach may provide a hypothesis also for the origin of the desperately obscure Gk. ἀμαυρός, μαυρός, μαῦρος 'dark', (ἀ)μαυρόω 'darken'. It is practically post-Homeric, the only occurrence in the Epic being Od. 4.824, 835. It is perhaps not overbold to postulate a Scythian **maurva-* < **morwo-* 'dark' (type of Av. *haurva-* < **sol-wo-*), which came into Greek by the same route as the model of Ἄξεινος, but was supplanted by the latter as a name of the Black Sea, thanks to the fancies of popular etymology which set to work on Ἄξεινος. That it belatedly regained its place in the Greek name of the Euxine would be an exquisite piece of historical irony in etymology.

This implies an assumption that the *i* and *u* epenthesis,[38] which notably characterizes Avestan, and is attested also in Sakian, Ossetic, and other northern Iranian dialects, was present in Scythian at an early date; for the borrowings into Greek cannot well be later than the founding of Milesian colonies in the Pontic region in the 7th century B.C. The existence of epenthesis in Scythian is well attested.[39] That early traces of certain generally later Iranian phonetic developments were present in Scythian is made probable by Ἄξεινος itself, where the Greek ει denotes long close *e*; thus the Scythian prototype should have been **axšēna-*, with monophthongization of the diphthong which persisted much later in Avestan and Old Persian.[40] It is then reasonable to believe that epenthesis may also have had an early beginning in Scythian and is reflected in Gk. (ἀ)μαυρος < *(ἀ)μαυρϝος < Scyth. **maurva-*.

This quest for the origin of Hittite *aruna-* has taken us far afield, but it is essential that all reasonable possibilities be explored. If this study shall have made a small contribution towards a definitive future solution of the history of *aruna-*, its purpose has been amply fulfilled.

HARVARD UNIVERSITY

[38] Cf. H. Reichelt, *Stand und Aufgaben der Sprachwissenschaft* (*Festschrift ... Streitberg*), 278 (Heidelberg, 1924); Iranisch 33 (*Gesch. der idg. Sprachwiss.*, 2. Teil, 4. Band, 2. Hälfte [Berlin und Leipzig, 1927]).

[39] Cf. Vasmer, *Die Iranier in Südrussland* 39–40; Iranisches aus Südrussland, *Streitberg Festgabe*, 368 (Leipzig, 1924); RLV 12.243; J. Harmatta, *Studies in the language of the Iranian tribes in south Russia* 34–6 (Budapest, 1952).

[40] Cf. H. Jacobsohn, *KZ* 54.254–86 (1927).

ERNST PULGRAM

LINGUISTIC EXPANSION AND DIVERSIFICATION

I

RECENTLY I had occasion to argue that linguistic expansion can take place in three basic ways: by diffusion, infiltration, and migration. The essential difference among these lies in the manner in which human carriers participate, and in their number. In the case of migration whole tribes or nations permanently displace themselves for some social or cultural reason; infiltration implies a movement of but a restricted number of individuals, small especially in relation to the area they occupy permanently and to the number of natives with whom they come in contact; diffusion necessitates no permanent displacement of carriers at all but describes merely the passing on of linguistic items or features across a linguistic boundary, with the result that this boundary, consisting of one or several or all isoglosses of a dialect, is either shifted or obliterated.[1]

Now I should like to examine, in general terms, what the linguistic results of each of these three types of expansion will be, that is to say, what will be the condition of a language after its spreading over a new territory. Since I am here principally interested in linguistic expansion rather than effacement, I shall mainly speak of cases in which the moving language is actually successful in superseding the native one and takes its place, in the manner in which Latin, for example, originally an unimportant dialect of prehistoric Latium, replaced the idioms of the regions where today Neo-Latin, Romanic languages are spoken. (Of course, not all linguistic spread will be as strikingly triumphant as that of Latin.)

I shall call the superseded idiom the SUBSTRATUM language. Where the imported language does not replace but leaves obvious traces upon the established dialect, it becomes a SUPERSTRATUM. In modern France, for example, the substratum is Keltic and the most important superstratum is Germanic. The language which

[1] Cf. Ernst Pulgram, "On prehistoric linguistic expansion," *For Roman Jakobson* 411–417 (The Hague, 1956).

emerges from such encounters as the linguistic coin of the realm, whether it be the new one influenced by the native substratum or the native one modified by the spreading superstratum, I shall call the MAINSTRATUM. In France this is Latin.

This terminology is therefore founded not just on chronological criteria (indeed in regions where more than a three layers occur it would be difficult to decide which was sub and which was super and which was main on the basis of chronology alone) but is rather established upon the now prevailing result of the repeated superposition of linguistic structures. The enduring layer, as viewed from the present moment, is the mainstratum, regardless of whether it is situated at the beginning or the middle or the end of the series, all others are sub- or superstrata in relation to it. If, for example, France should ever become an English-speaking country, then English would be its linguistic mainstratum, with all other idioms relegated to the position of more or less effective substrata.

(a) *France*
Germanic
LATIN
Keltic

(b) *Austria*
GERMANIC
Latin
Keltic

(c) *Spain*
Arabic
Germanic
LATIN
Iberian?

(d) *Italy, Tuscany*
Germanic
LATIN
Etruscan
Mediterranean?

(e) *Italy, Latium*
Germanic
Etruscan
LATIN
Mediterranean?

(f) *Italy, Campania*
Germanic
LATIN
Oscan
Etruscan
Greek
Mediterranean?

(g) *Sicily*
Norman (Old French)
Arabic
LATIN
Greek
Sicel (Italic)
Mediterranean?

FIG. 1

Fig. 1 illustrates the relation of these strata in various parts of Europe. Needless to say, within the larger national and linguistic regions each locality with its local dialect may have a stratification peculiarly its own, and one that need not be exactly repeated in the wider dialect or language area within which it is generally counted. In fact, each speaker can be said to have a stratum history of his own. But the reasons for our not calling each micro-dialect or idiolect a language are obvious in view of our definition of language as an instrument of cooperation among at least two and generally a great many more individuals. I have also omitted in my illustration some strata whose influence is less telling and scarcely exceeds occasional lexical borrowings (e.g. Slavic in some regions of Austria, French and Spanish in Campania, especially Naples). The names of the mainstrata are printed in small capitals. The question mark after Mediterranean and Iberian indicates that these are mere names and that we have no factual knowledge of the languages so called – unless Etruscan is part of the Mediterranean stratum which can otherwise be dimly recognized in a number of non-Indo-European words and names of the Mediterranean area, and unless Basque is an Iberian type of language. A name's position at the bottom of the list is no indication of its primacy but only means that we can recede no farther into prehistory without giving rein to pure fancy.

The speakers of the substratum language are by definition the eventual recipients and users of the imported language. Since cultural mutation through a process of learning can be accomplished only over a more or less extended period of cultural co-existence, that is, in terms of linguistics, through bilingualism of a certain intensity and extensity, it follows that the new language will be subjected in the mouths of the native learners to certain modifications which have been gathered under the term INTERFERENCE.[2] (Obviously interference effects also the substratum language while it is still in use, but for the present purposes concerned with language expansion I need not deal with the fate of the vanishing idiom.) The manner and degree of substratum interference vary widely according to non-linguistic factors which either favor or inhibit it. Among these are, one, the manner of expansion of which I spoke above: the greater the number of substratum speakers in relation to the number of speakers of the expanding language, the greater the interference of the first upon the second; and two, the cultural conditions of receptivity or hostility: a generally superior culture accompanying the new language is likely to increase the linguistic receptivity in the learners whereby phenomena of interference will be reduced in number and intensity – *but* if the new language is brought and perhaps forcefully imposed by hated albeit culturally superior conquerors, interference may become strengthened through political and patriotic resistance and other forces of xenophobia.

Also purely linguistic factors play a rôle. But whether near relationship between the strata is or is not going to be conducive to interference cannot be stated in the form of a rule, because an argument can be made both ways. One could say that substratum speakers prompted by pressure or desire to learn a closely related language can achieve the goal easily and may quickly learn to speak it well; but one might also maintain that precisely the ease of acquisition invites a relaxation of effort and calls forth a stronger hold and greater persistence of interference phenomena, which operate without being impeded or remedied. (This argument applies also to language learning by students and can be adduced to 'explain', for example, why an Italian either does, or does not, learn Spanish more quickly than a German.) Naturally, one acquires a passive or reading knowledge of a language related to one's own more easily; but I am not concerned here with this type of language learning alone, or even chiefly.

[2] A term coined and defined by Uriel Weinreich, *Languages in contact* 1 (New York, 1953).

Not all parts of the expanding language spread with equal ease and thoroughness, and one may establish a hierarchy in this.[3] The spread of non-structural items is achieved with less total expenditure of energy than that of structural features. Among the latter, phonemic, morphemic, and syntactic phenomena form in this order another ascending scale of difficulty. In other words, a lexical loan which concerns merely the inventory of a language can occur more easily than the transfer of a phoneme, or a morpheme, or a grammatical construction, any of which upset and alter the structure of the borrowing language and require of the learner not only an effort of memory but also a behavioral adjustment. Hence the total energy required for linguistic expansion is determined jointly by the type and number of transferred features, the time within which, and the area over which the spread occurs, the number of carriers involved and their socio-cultural relationship to the learners, and the relationship among the languages themselves. This implies a formula of such complexity, containing so many and such varied imponderables and non-quantifiables, that it will not lend itself to making predictions, nor, of course, to experimentation. We can only employ it for subjecting to *a posteriori* analysis already known cases of linguistic spread, or at best apply it against linguistic events, especially of prehistory, in which one or the other ingredient is unknown (e.g. the manner of expansion – diffusion, infiltration, or migration) and may be plausibly conjectured from the known facts and the known results.

II

One may be certain that the total energy needed to spread Latin over the Romania, or Proto-Indo-European (PIE) over most of Europe and parts of Asia, was enormous. We know fairly well how Latin expanded from Latium. In terms of carriers the process must be classified as infiltration (by colonists, merchants, soldiers, administrators, and, later, missionaries and clerics) and not as either seeping diffusion or sweeping migration. We know also for certain that neither were there in existence in prehistoric Latium, the original home of Latin, the proto-dialects of modern Italy in some embryonic form, nor in Roman Italy the proto-dialects of French, Spanish, Portuguese etc., all waiting to be carried off by migrating social units into the regions in which we know them now. It is as certain as can be that, as Roman arms conquered Italy piece by piece in the early centuries of the Republic, and as the local non-Latin dialects were gradually superseded by Latin, these idioms did not disappear on the day when the last battle for political supremacy was fought and generally lost by their speakers, but rather maintained themselves through periods of bilingualism of varying length. In consequence of this perseverance they imposed upon ultimately victorious Latin some of their peculiarities through interference. If we today know

[3] For details on the following paragraph see my article cited above.

very little about such varied forms of Latin local dialects, the reason is that we know very little about spoken Latin, our sources giving us almost exclusively Classical Latin, a standard written language unreceptive and inimical to dialectal diversity.

As the Roman legions extended their conquests beyond the confines of Italy, the same linguistic process, mutatis mutandis, took place. Once more we know little about the kind of Latin each region or locality spoke after its linguistic acculturation, again because of the insufficiency of the record. Indeed we do not even know what kind of Latin was received by the various localities, though one may suspect that not all inhabitants of the Roman state learned the same kind of Latin from their conquerors.

There are two principal reasons for this view, which are essentially valid also outside the history of Latin. The first one, often advanced to explain, at least in part, the variety of the Romanic languages, is that the conquests of eventually Latinized territory took place at widely separated dates, anywhere between the fifth century B.C. and the second century after Christ, and that therefore it is impossible to assume that the 'same' Latin reached the various areas, because Latin, like any other language, could not but undergo considerable changes in these centuries, however blurred and levelled out they may be in the classical or attempted classical writings we possess. (This theory does of course not suffice to explain why a larger linguistic area, like France, which was conquered and colonized within a few years during which Latin was not altered by major changes, shows nonetheless great dialectal diversity. Here our knowledge, however meager, of different Keltic substrata must be called upon.) The second reason is that the victorious 'Romans' had come to be, precisely because of their continued conquests, ethnically and also linguistically a less and less homogeneous lot. If we knew, for instance, that a legion recruited mainly in Campania from among the natives of that region conquered a certain district of Gaul and that thereafter the 'Roman' newcomers to this area were generally from the same region and spoke the same dialect, then we could make a case for the transfer of Campanian Latin to this locale and derive the peculiarities of its Neo-Latin dialect from the Latin dialect of Campania. Unfortunately we have no records of a Roman legion or army so uniformly constituted, by accident or design, in regard to its soldiers' origin or speech, or of colonization occurring in this manner, nor do we have the slightest reason to assume that the historical facts were such. (Some want to see in the name of the town *Huesca* in northern Spain not far from Zaragoza, a remembrance of *Osca* and the Oscans, and connect some features of the modern local dialect with ancient Oscan. I doubt the validity of this reasoning, or at least its inevitability. Even if Huesca does go back to an older Osca, one should not overlook that, after all, it takes only one man of Oscan origin to name a town after his homeland, whereas it takes a lot of people to furnish an Oscan linguistic substratum.)

But it may well be that the citizens of Rome of various origins and dialects, when thrown together in military service or as civilians in a foreign country, used some kind of empire-wide lingua franca, a koinë, and that the natives learned this speech rather than any genuine Latin dialects. We have little factual information on all this, and may never obtain more. In any event, the possibility, or even the probability of the existence of such a koinë does not provide sufficient grounds for denying altogether the existence of Latin local dialects.

Any dialect of, for example, France is therefore the result of some kind of Latin superimposed upon a local Keltic substratum (and even though we know but little of the Keltic dialects of Gaul we are certain that there were several, and surely more than the three corresponding to Caesar's *partes tres*) and subjected to interference from it. Next occurs, over most of France, interference from German superstrata, mainly Frankish, but also Burgundian (to which, according to some Romanic scholars, the characteristics of the Franco-Provençal dialects are due), Visigothic, etc., overlaid by all kinds of borrowings from other European idioms. It is therefore clear that any French dialect, like any other dialect in the world, is not something that came to its present location in its present or some ancestral form from somewhere else, from an original *Urheimat*, but rather that it is the immeasurably complex product of an innumerably vast series of factors which in this unique sequence and quantitative and qualitative mixture could be present only in this one area and could deliver this unique linguistic result only in this one area, and nowhere else on earth.

III

I shall now apply the preceding views to a consideration of the spread and the diversification of PIE. From what I have said concerning the rôle of nonlinguistic factors, it is clear that, at least as far as the type of spread is concerned, our knowledge of PIE differs radically in kind and in manner of acquisition from our knowledge of Latin and the Romanic languages. The latter is derived from political and linguistic history, of which we possess a fair though by no means full documentation; the former takes us into prehistory, where historic and linguistic documentation is lacking, apart from occasional fortuitous scraps of secondary evidence: the records are anthropological and archaeological, and information useful to us is therefore not direct but inferential.

The details of the argument on the PIE homeland and the manner of the spread of PIE may be read elsewhere;[4] here I shall merely offer the conclusions, which are: (1) The question of the *Urheimat* of so-called pre-divisional PIE is specious as long as it is connected with some PIE people or ethnic Proto-Indo-Europeans, and as long as one deals with PIE itself as though it were the absolute beginning of something

[4] *Op. cit.*, and in a forthcoming book of mine entitled *The tongues of Italy: prehistory and history* (Harvard University Press).

and not just one segment of an unbroken development; (2) the best archaeological information available at present does not point to vast migrations of PIE-speaking tribes or nations out of the east over central, western, and southern Europe, but rather makes it appear that the spread of PIE is due to infiltration, over a protracted period, reaching in fact into our times, of its speakers or of speakers of its dialects into heterogloss regions.

From these findings, together with what I have said in the preceding pages of this article, follow a number of deductions.

One of them concerns the origins of the ancient Indo-European (IE) dialects – Keltic, Italic, Hellenic, Germanic, etc. For example, the question as to where Italic came from, where it was spoken before it arrived and was finally recorded in Italy, I should now answer by saying: Italic did not 'come' from anywhere, it originated in Italy, exactly as, for reasons just stated, French did not come from anywhere into France but just grew there, the unique product of the many factors which made it. Now something did come to Italy, as something came to Gaul, because to the best of our knowledge without this something Italy would not have been Indo-Europeanized or Gaul Latinized. But this something in Italy was not Italic any more than it was French in Gaul, and it was not imported by conveniently so named Italici or Proto-Italici any more than Frenchmen or Proto-Frenchmen migrated to France. Rather was it some kind of IE in Italy and some kind of Latin in France, superimposed upon an unknown (Mediterranean?) and a Keltic substratum, respectively.

One might argue that Italic is Neo-PIE as French is Neo-Latin, and that therefore an Italic type of IE was imported to Italy and a French type of Latin to Gaul. The spuriousness of the proposition as it concerns an alleged French Latin is patent; and unless factual ignorance makes a theory more palatable, I do not see why a parallel opinion concerning an Italic IE should enjoy greater favor among theorists. This reasoning is applied not only to Italic. Virtually all IE dialects known are extracted from PIE in this peculiar way. The mode of transfer is generally supposed to have been mass migration in Völkerwanderung style, allowing certain 'IE' tribes or nations to acquire land and subdue the inhabitants of Europe by military conquest. This view then gives rise to theses on the physical and mental and moral superiority of the 'Indo-Europeans', who are furthermore endowed with a superior language. Such a concoction of hypotheses is not only unsupported by the known facts, but is indeed – and this is even worse – unnecessary.

The term 'pre-divisional' or 'pre-ethnic' PIE makes therefore little sense, because PIE was not really divided in any sense of the word (even though a literal interpretation of the genealogical tree might invite such a view, and even though certain schematic illustrations show a PIE pie cut up into its post-divisional portions) and because ethnic considerations do not enter the problem at all. As for the ethnic or racial argument, we simply do not know any ethnic or even national or tribal units which severally dispersed from the PIE homeland and carried with them the IE dialects to their ultimate locations – the Italici with Italic to Italy, the Hellenes with Hellenic to Greece, the Kelts with Keltic to Gaul, etc. As for the dialectal argument, there is no reason whatever to assume that PIE, wherever, whenever, and by whatever persons it was spoken, already contained a dialectal division corresponding to the later IE dialects, or that dialects of PIE were geographically arranged in their tight little homeland in such a way as to presage their future relative locations in the wide world.

I do not say that such a development is impossible. But I reject a hypothesis of this kind because there is no shred of evidence for it (a hypothesis being, to my mind, a provisional thesis that must have some chance of survival built into it, and not a mere invention), because similar linguistic phenomena of expansion, e.g. of Latin, whose mechanics we know, behave altogether differently, and because good sense and general linguistic theory rebel against it, especially when the arguments exhibit an unpleasant *ad hoc* flavor and an IE supremacy tinge.

In the place of marching Italici and Kelts and Hellenes, whether or not prefixed by Proto-, I put the movement of some persons (I do not know how many or whether they were brave warriors or adventurers or refugees or pioneering homesteaders on the way west), who come from somewhere (I do not know exactly from where, but probably, in consideration of archaeologically detectable cultural movements, from the east), and who bring with them some new type of dialect or dialects (I do not know exactly what they were like, but they were of the IE variety in any event). These dialects were planted in an alien and no doubt already linguistically diversified (unless it were fallow) soil. The harvest, in all places where one grew under favorable enough conditions, that is to say, where IE superseded a substratum instead of being absorbed by the native tongue, was something which was again IE. But owing to the varied soil, the differences of historical and cultural climate, indeed the probable diversity of the seed itself, in short, because of the multiformity and multiplicity of factors which combine, as I said, to produce a unique linguistic issue in each locale, there grew up diverse linguistic crops. In all of them the PIE ancestry is visible, but they are not all alike.

This thesis throws also some light, I believe, upon such questions as to whether there existed or not a so-called pre-divisional Italo-Keltic, or Balto-Slavic, or Osco-Umbrian unity. The conventional way of putting the question is this: Was there a society (some even think of it as an ethnically homogeneous society) which spoke a language that later divided into two branches?, or, more concretely: Was there spoken somewhere outside of Italy, say, in Austria, a language which may be called Italo-Keltic and whose speakers then divided into two branches, one moving southward – the Italic-speaking Italici, one westward – the Keltic-speaking Kelts?

According to what I have said so far, it seems that the question is wrongly put. For even if the view is correct that there prevailed in the region under consideration a prehistoric language whose southern and western offshoots appear historically as Italic and Keltic, it would make as little sense to call this unknown language Italo-Keltic or by any other name that contains either of the words Italic and Keltic as it would to speak of a Hispano-Portuguese language prevailing north of the Pyrenees prior to the penetration of Latin into the Iberian peninsula. Note that I do not mean to imply that we *must not* name this language of Austria Italo-Keltic because it would be false or misrepresent a truth; I merely propose not to employ this name because without proper warning it would be misunderstood, as it has been, and give rise, as it has, to a number of wholly unwarranted inferences.

If there are any legitimate questions to be asked concerning a possible Italo-Keltic unity I should phrase them this way: Are the Keltic and Italic dialects related, and if they are, to what degree, and how did they come into the lands where we find them attested, and how do we best account for their differentness and their likeness? The answers would be as follows. First, yes, they are related, all of them belonging to the IE family; and in so far as such relationship is measurable they are more closely akin to each other than each is to other IE languages; second, they do not come from anywhere as such, all ready-made, but they have grown individually into the shape in which we first see them precisely in the place where we first find them, that is to say, the first and all subsequent documents we have of them are unthinkable anywhere but where they are; third, these different places of origin and kinds of development account also for their differentness from one another; fourth, the great likeness and certain striking agreements have to be explained, to the extent that the evidence lets us see the light, in terms of cultural history and through the manner of expansion and diversification which I discussed, and not through an unattested linguistic unity which even as a hypothesis is unwarranted and unnecessary, especially under the name Italo-Keltic; this is so because, fifth, such a terminology is apt to misrepresent the facts for reasons already stated, there being nothing deserving the name Italo-Keltic before the formation Italic and Keltic, which, by definition, occurred after and not before the alleged Italo-Keltic stage.

IV

Do I mean to say, then, that no language can expand without being in some way modified by interference, that in fact after it has spread over new territory it may well be preferable to call it by a new name? Now the first part of this question concerns a question of facts, and the answer is Yes, a language is so modified. But the second part refers to preference and convenience, and whatever the answer may be, it will not contain a statement on verities but only one on definitions. Involved here is the problem as to how similar two forms of speech must be to be called by the same name, or how different they may be without having to be called by different names. Hence the question is not whether Latin is or is not PIE, whether French is or is not Latin or, for that matter, PIE, but whether it is convenient or not to use different names. If it is, we are at once brought face to face with the next question, namely, when does PIE cease and Latin begin, and when does Latin cease and French begin?

A language, by definition, serves for human communication and cooperation by means of a conventional system and arrangement of vocal symbols. (This is not a complete definition of language, but it will do for the moment.) Now we know that this peculiar structure is subject to change. Time alone is an agent of this change, so that even without any substratum or superstratum interference a language will in the course of centuries undergo alternations to such an extent that speakers of the 'same' language, but a certain span of time apart, could not understand one another if they had an opportunity to converse. (While for the past our knowledge concerning this behavior of speech is necessarily based on written records, in the future, stored recordings may bear out this statement also acoustically.) Such a condition should really cause us to give a new name to the new language; hence we properly distinguish PIE and Latin and French. But on occasion we may be reluctant to do this, not only because it is useful to indicate in the name the continuity which really exists between an older and a newer stage, but also because we are at a loss as to where to cut the chain and to establish the boundary within this continuum.[5] Terminologically we often bypass the dilemma by speaking of, for example, *Old* English and *Middle* English and *Modern* English. Of course, Old English and Modern English are no more alike than Latin and Italian, and this nomenclature which is due to historical circumstances should not mislead us in matters of linguistic reality.

Sometimes the accidents of documentation help us in establishing more firmly a terminological and linguistic chronological boundary. For example, in the history of Latin the written language continued with a fair degree of uniformity far into the Middle Ages; indeed during the Carolingian Renaissance, and again in Humanism of the Renaissance, it even experienced a revival and, in terms of Ciceronian Latin, a purification. But since at the same time the spoken Latin vernaculars in the different parts of the Romania distanced themselves ever more from this kind of petrified Latin, and since there arose ultimately the desire and the necessity not only to speak

[5] The same dilemma also faces a person throughout the ages of his life. Am I or am I not the 'same' being as I was at the age of two? Biologically I partly am and partly am not. Socially and legally I am in so far as I bear the same name; but my status of responsibility changed at the age of twenty-one. Some societies and religions take cognizance of this kind of transition by changing a person's name for biological reasons (at puberty) or social reasons (at marriage), sometimes several times during his or her life. Especially a woman's name is, in our western societies, notoriously unstable. Also choosing 476 A.D. as the beginning and 1492 A.D. as the end of the Middle Ages is arbitrary and due merely to the fact that these dates, among many other possible ones, were by agreement and convention adjudged significant enough (the end of the Roman Empire and the discovery of America) to provide convenient milestones in an otherwise indivisible continuum.

but also to write in these vernaculars, we find throughout the Romanic world, in the ninth and tenth centuries, the beginning of a new set of written languages. They render, as far as this was possible under the tutelage of powerful and jealous Mother Latin, the varied spoken languages of the Latinized world. These turned out to be quite different from Latin at the time of their first appearance, after many years, even centuries, of an unwritten underground development that hitherto had borne the stigma of vulgarity. Hence we seem to witness, as it were, the real birth of new languages, and we have neither troubles nor scruples in naming the first and subsequent monuments in these languages not Latin but Spanish, French, Italian, etc. Of course, this birth is an optical illusion, meaning not the birth of a language (languages are never born in this way) but only its appearance in written form which we can now finally perceive. There lay behind it a long and unbroken oral development which, unfortunately, is not accessible to us, except fragmentarily and sporadically. Once more we must be watchful lest nomenclature, now so eminently reasonable and justified, induce us to think that we have discovered new facts and new truths, such as, for example, the birthdate of French.[6]

In the relatively rare cases where a language spreads over an area where no language had been spoken previously, where, in other words, no human beings had dwelled, its subsequent fate will owe nothing to any linguistic substratum but will be entirely due to the agency of time and possible superstratum influences. This may well have been the condition which the expanding dialects of IE met at times, in some places. While we are very inadequately informed on the density of population of neolithic and Iron Age Europe, there is at least no doubt that it was far below the present level and that there were vast stretches of unoccupied land. Also the extension of Spanish and Portuguese and English to the New World, while not filling a total linguistic vacuum, was subjected to minimal substratum interference because of the relatively small number of Indians, coupled with the cultural strangeness, incompatibility, and hostility between the natives and the conquerors, and the ultimate complete oppression, and in many instances extermination, of the former.

[6] When glottochronology establishes, by means of wordlists and by weighing and counting changes distinguishing two points on a continuum, the age and, by implication, the birthday of a language, it does no more than state hitherto possibly unstated criteria for 'sameness' and 'differentness' in linguistic nomenclature. If we are then told that a given language is of a certain age, that is to say, begins at a certain date, we are in fact told that on the basis of the criteria stated by himself the glottochronologist considers himself justified in, and solicits approval for, the application of a new name, at a determined moment, to something already existing (and which may or may not have had a name). The operation is, therefore, one of definition, and useful in that it proposes a certain formula for the criteria of a definition. But it does not essentially differ from fixing the beginning of something called the Middle Ages at 476 A.D., and it leads to no new insights on linguistic history. The belief that it does is, at best, naive. (Whether the method and its application as such are valid and produce acceptable results is another matter. I think not, for good reasons, such as stated, for example, by John A. Rea at the Summer Meeting of the Linguistic Society of America, at the University of Michigan, in August 1956.)

Thus Indian interference in North America is virtually restricted to local names, and even in South America, with its originally larger and more advanced and also more enduring Indian population, the influence of the native dialects upon Spanish and Portuguese, especially in what are considered the standard languages, is negligible. It is perceptible mainly, as one would expect according to the hierarchy of difficulty of borrowing, in the lexicon, and naturally quite high in domains, such as the native fauna and flora, where the European languages lacked appropriate terms. But a South American and a Spaniard are able to speak today quite the same language, at least to the extent that they did four centuries ago, with small differences in pronunciation and scarcely any in grammar and structure.

It is certain, on the other hand, that when Charlemagne came to Rome and was crowned by the pope in 800, his native Gallo-Frankish soldiers, though they spoke 'Latin', could not converse freely in their native speech with the Romans of Rome who spoke a quite different 'Latin'. Possibly both sides employed some lingua franca, maybe a Pidgin Latin, or Classical Latin – provided they knew it. But it is hardly likely that ordinary soldiers in Charlemagne's army or the populace of Rome were capable, at that date, of having recourse to the second.

It is almost equally certain, though proof is of necessity lacking, that the Italic and Keltic speaking natives of Italy and France of the seventh century B.C. could not have communicated with the contemporary inhabitants of their linguistic *Urheimat*, provided there were still IE-speaking people in that place, wherever it was. Time, distance, lack of communication, and last but certainly not least the substrata and possibly even some superstrata had by then thoroughly estranged from one another the various forms of IE. Today, the estrangement is such that the relationship among the IE languages is largely imperceptible to the ear and even to the eye; only the comparative linguist can tell that Hindi and Russian and English are akin to one another. Whether this centrifugal development of long standing is ever to be supplanted by a convergence, which may possibly extend itself also to non-IE tongues, depends on the historic and cultural events of the future.

V

In conclusion, I should list the following points. (1) A language can expand over a territory hitherto occupied by another language, in which case the latter is relegated to a substratum. This may be accomplished by migration or infiltration; I can, however, think of no case where diffusion alone sufficed to spread a whole language over a new area. Diffused linguistic items, I believe, constitute generally a superstratum. (2) The substratum modifies the gaining language through interference, thus causing the spreading language to differentiate itself from the language of the original linguistic homeland. While this is not the only cause of language diversification it is an important and discoverable one. (3) Interference varies in degree and kind chiefly in proportion to non-linguistic cultural receptivity or hostility, to a lesser extent also according to linguistic conditions, that is, the relationship between the losing substratum or superstratum and the gaining mainstratum. (4) Even where no linguistic interference takes place, where the expanding language occupies an empty or nearly empty area, the language of the new territoty follows together with other cultural features a path of historical development more or less divergent from that of the language of the homeland, depending in some measure also on the degree of continuance or severance of cultural ties between the motherland and the colony. (5) It is therefore at the least unnecessary to account for the diversity in the IE languages by postulating a corresponding diversity on a minor or embryonic scale in PIE. (6) We must therefore recognize that the term 'expansion' like the terms of descent and kinship which we customarily employ in linguistics, is to be understood figuratively and not literally; that every structure which we call language or dialect is peculiarly and uniquely a time-bound and locale-bound entity, a cultural phenomenon which in this form neither comes from somewhere nor can be transferred somewhere without either subtly or blatantly becoming something else. (7) Whether the 'new' language should or should not be called by the same name as the old is a problem that cannot be solved by appeal to verities but one that must be settled by agreeing on definitions and criteria. How alike must two idioms be to bear the same name, and how different may they be ? (Whether or not a true quantitative answer to this is possible is another matter. If there is one, it should be stated; if there is not, one should not act as if there were.) (8) As regards the history of languages and language families, it is therefore illicit to project freely and arbitrarily, without stating why and how and on what grounds one does so, the name of a language attested at a given time and in a given place into an earlier time and a different place, and to pretend that by this operation an equation of the *hic et nunc* with the *hac et tunc* has been 'discovered'. It has been, at best, hypothesized, at worst, invented. (9) As regards the description and classification of languages and dialects it is idle to argue whether Sardinian is a language or an Italian dialect; whether English has nine or ten vowel phonemes; and whether there do or do not exist Eastern and Western Romanic languages that are divided from one another by the La Spezia-Rimini dialect boundary of northern Italy. It seems to me that all these questions must be rephrased if they are to produce an unprejudiced answer; for as they stand they anticipate the answer at least in part. This is the manner in which I should propose to put the above questions: Shall we define, or have we defined, language and dialect in such a way that Sardinian is a language, or in such a way that it is a dialect of Italian? Shall we define English in such a way that the term includes dialects of both nine and ten vowel phonemes, or shall we renounce such an inclusive term 'English' in favor of two separate dialect groups of which one has nine and the other ten vowel phonemes? (If the latter, what shall we call them?) Shall we or shall we not consider the undoubtedly existing bundle of isoglosses that constitutes the La Spezia-Rimini line as significant enough to establish along it a major boundary separating two types of dialects which we call Eastern and Western Romanic?

Point (9) really leads beyond the scope of this article and, indeed, outside the domain of linguistics. In it I have made a case for asking questions which contain only previously defined and understood terms. In particular, a question must not contain terms on which another question ought first to have enlightened us; for if it does it is sure to entice us toward an ulterior answer, while the crucial point is glossed over. To a degree, we find ourselves in the position of the man who is requested to say Yes or No when asked: Have you stopped beating your wife? It is of course true that a mere rephrasing of questions, such as I have performed, is not productive of new facts or new knowledge: my revised questions teach us nothing new about Sardinian, or English, or Western and Eastern Romanic. But they have prevented us from giving answers of the kind solicited by the original questions, namely: Sardinian is (or is not) a language (or a dialect); English has (or has not) nine (or ten) vowel phonemes; there are (or are not) Western and Eastern Romanic languages – answers which give the appearance of contributing new factual knowledge but do not. They merely *imply* definitions of 'language' and 'dialect' and 'English' and 'Western and Eastern Romanic.' Thus discussions ensuing upon the first set of questions (and there has been no dearth of them) are, by being rephrased, removed from the spurious concern with truths and placed within the realm of definition and classification, where they belong.

UNIVERSITY OF MICHIGAN

ALF SOMMERFELT

ON SOME STRUCTURAL DIFFERENCES BETWEEN IRISH AND SCOTCH GAELIC

AMONG the special traits which characterize the Keltic phonemic systems the morphophonemic variation of word initials is the most striking. Initial consonants may change according to the preceding word or element and in certain cases independently of any preceding element. In the Goidelic group stops may alternate with spirants or nasals, and vocalic initial may be preceded by a consonant.

In Irish the voiced stops alternate with nasals and the unvoiced ones with voiced ones through the influence of a preceding nasal (a process called eclipsis in the traditional grammars). Thus in the Torr dialect of Donegal: *ə·mo*: 'their cow', from *bo*: 'cow' (*bo*); (*əN*) *dig'əN tuw*? 'do you understand' from *tig'əm* 'I understand' (*tuigim*); *ə-ŋræ*: 'in love', from *græ*: 'love' (*gradh*); *mər·ba:ʃt'i* 'your children' from *pa:ʃt'i* 'children' *(páisti)*; *ər·d'ax* 'our house' from *t'ax* 'house' (*teach*); *ə·g'art* 'right, all right' from *k'art* (*ceart*).

The alternation is found in Old Irish where in the case of the voiced stops it is usually represented by a prefixed nasal, e.g. *imbélre naill* 'in another language'; *indib ṅúarib deac* 'in twelve hours'. In the case of the voiceless stops the change is usually not marked, but there are some instances of the change $c > g$ and of $t > d$, e.g. *nach géin* 'for a long time' (acc. of *cían*); *condánicc* 'until he came' besides *contánic*. In later Old Irish we have examples which show that the pronunciation must have been that of Modern Irish: *atá debe mecnand* 'there is a little difference there' (from *bec* 'little') (Glosses of Milan, 9th century).[1]

We therefore have an Irish morphophonemic alternation:

b, b'	*d, d'*	*g, g'*	*p, p'*	*t, t'*	*k, k'*
m, m'	*N, N'*	*ŋ, ŋ'*	*b, b'*	*d, d'*	*g, g'*

[1] Cf. J. Vendryes, *Grammaire du vieil-irlandais* 86f. (Paris, 1908); R. Thurneysen, *A grammar of Old Irish* 147ff. (Dublin, 1946); H. Pedersen, *Vergl. Gramm. d. kelt. Sprachen* 1.389ff. (Göttingen, 1909).

In Scottish Gaelic, where the change is dependent upon the presence in the actual system of a nasal at the end of the proclitic element so that it occurs also after forms of the article, the alternation is from the phonemic point of view:

b	*d*	*d'*	*g*	*g'*
mb	*Nd*	*N'd'*	*Ng*	*N'g'*

and

p	*t*	*t'*	*k*	*k'*
mp	*Nt*	*N't'*	*Nk*	*N'k'*

as Oftedal has shown.[2] In Lewis the voiced stop is very short, e.g. [*m*^{b}*alə*], *mbalə*. In the case of the voiceless stops the phonetic realization is a voiced nasal consonant followed by aspiration, [*N'hahəð*], *Ntahəð* 'the father'. Sometimes the raising of the velum takes place before the release of the oral closure so that the impression is that of a voiced or voiceless stop, as in [*N*^{t}*hahəð*], [*N*^{d}*hahəð*].[3]

The same state of affairs is found in Bernera in Lewis. Borgstrøm writes: "The radical (initial) nasals are pure nasals followed directly by a vowel. The non-radical may occasionally give the same acoustic impression as the radical ones, but in principle they are different: at the end of the nasal one usually hears a very short and soft occlusive. After *ŋ*, *ŋ'* the stop is usually always heard."[4] The north-eastern and south-eastern dialects of Skye (Kilmuir, Portree and Sleat) have the same initial groups,[5] as have also the dialects of Tanera and Cóigeach.[6] In Barra, however, the nasal is weakly articulated and may be absent; Borgstrøm writes ^{m}*b*^{c}, ^{N}*ḍ*^{c}, ^{N}*ḍ'*^{cž}, ^{ŋ}*ġ*^{c}, ^{ŋ}*ġ'*^{c} opposed to *p*^{c}, *t*^{c}, *t*^{c}*'ʃ*, *k*^{c}, *k'*^{c} and ^{m}*ḅ*, ^{N}*ḍ*, ^{N}*ḍ'*^{ž}, *ġ*, *ġ'* opposed to *ḅ*, *ḍ*, *d'*^{ž}, *ġ*, *ġ'*.[7] This system is found also in Rosshire in the dialects of Red Point (Gairloch) and Aultbea, Kinlochewe, in Duirinish and Applecross.[8] In Argyllshire both the nasal and the stop may be fully pronounced, but the nasal may also be dropped. Holmer writes *naŋ-'gasən* 'of the feet' (*nan casan*), (*əm*)-*bju·ur* 'their sister' (*am piuthar*), (*ən*)-*di*: 'their tea' (*an tea*).[9] The Gaelic of Glengarry follows the same pattern[10] and so does that of Rathlin Island which is of the Scottish type, but here a certain number of cases are identical with the Irish usage.[11] Morphophonemically

[2] Magne Oftedal, *The Gaelic of Leurbost, Isle of Lewis* 166ff. (Oslo, 1956).
[3] Oftedal, *op. cit.* 101. The author uses [ ] to indicate phonetic forms.
[4] C. Hj. Borgstrøm, *The dialects of the Outer Hebrides* 22 (Oslo, 1940).
[5] C. Hj. Borgstrøm, *The dialects of Skye and Ross-shire* 13 (Oslo, 1941).
[6] *Ibid.* 124.
[7] Borgstrøm, *NTS* 8. 151ff. (1935).
[8] Borgstrøm, *Skye*, 102 and 132.
[9] N. Holmer, *Studies on Argyllshire Gaelic* 97ff. (Uppsala, 1938).
[10] H. C. Dieckhoff, *A pronouncing dictionary of Scottish Gaelic* xviff. (Edinburgh and London, 1932).
[11] N. Holmer, *The Irish language of Rathlin Island. Co. Antrim* (Dublin, 1942). On the adjoining mainland the usage must have been the usual Irish one; cf. Holmer, *On some relics of the Irish dialect spoken in the Glens of Antrim* 57 (Uppsala, 1940).

Scottish Gaelic, as far as it is known at present, follows the pattern Oftedal has established for Lewis. Radical:

b	*d, d'*	*g, g'*	*p*	*t, t'*	*k, k'*
mb	*Nd, N'd'*	*Ng, N'g'*	*mp*	*Nt, N't'*	*Nk, N'k'*

Phonetically in some dialects the stop is weakly articulated or disappears altogether; in other dialects the nasal is the weak part.

Manx must have had the Irish system; but the few who today are able to speak some Manx do not observe the old rules of nasalization. Jackson heard the fixed form *mə 'gi:t* = *my geayrt* 'about', Scottish *mu'n cuairt*.[12]

In its first period nasalization in Goidelic may have been different from what it is in Modern Irish. If the formula of assimilation in sandhi was the same in intervocalic position we may have had the following pattern

t, t'	*k, k'*	*b, b'*	*d, d'*	*g, g'*
d, d'	*g, g'*	*mb, m'b'*	*Nd, N'd'*	*Ng, N'g'*

Voiceless stops preceded by a nasal had already before the period of the Ogham inscriptions been voiced with the loss of the nasal (e.g. *dét*, Mod. Ir. *déad* 'tooth': Welsh *dant*; *éc*, Mod. Ir. *éag* 'death': Bret. *ankou* [nom. pl.]), whereas *mb*, *nd*, and *ng* did subsist until the late Old Irish period when they were assimilated to long or geminated consonants (*nn* [*N*], *mm* and *ŋ*). But even from the beginning the pattern may have been the same as later. Structurally the initial position with the morphophonemic rôle of the initial is different from the position between vowels or the word-end after a vowel. The development *-nt*, *-nk* > *-d*, *-g* may have commanded a similar treatment of the voiced stops. When *p* was introduced through Latin and Welsh loanwords – in the first period a foreign *p* was rendered by Irish *kʷ* (*q*), e.g. *clúm*:*pluma*, *cruimther* 'priest', Welsh *premter*, etc. – the corresponding nasalized form became *b*, a development not found in other cases.

The Scottish Gaelic pattern $\frac{b}{mb,}$ etc. does not continue a possible early Old Irish $\frac{b}{mb,}$ etc. It must be a comparatively recent development as there are in the dialects many remnants of the Irish pattern, e.g. Barra *hik'* 'will come', but with negation Barra *xa d'žik'*, O. Ir. *tic*[13]; Leurbost, *nax 'd'ig'*, *xa 'd'ig'*.[14] Another indication is the circumstance that the pattern $\frac{b}{mb}$ has been extended to cases where the initial

[12] J. Keen, *A grammar of the Manx language* 44 (London, 1931); K. Jackson, *Contributions to the study of Manx phonology* 66f. and 133 (Edinburgh, 1955).

[13] Borgstrøm, *NTS* 8.157 (1935); cf. also Borgstrøm, *Hebrides* 80.

[14] Oftedal, *op. cit.* 250; cf. also, for Rathlin Island, Holmer, *Rathlin Island* 66.

is vocalic. Borgstrøm writes: "I have heard pronounced *m*^{b}*ahəð̣'* 'my father', (ə)*m*^{b}*a:*^{h}*t*(ə) 'the boat', (ə)*N*^{d}*u̇l'* 'the blood',"[15] and Oftedal has in his phonemic notation: *mbahəð* 'my father', (ə)'*N 'd'εr*, dative of (ə) *fεr* 'the man'.[16]

Thomas O'Rahilly dates the development of the main traits of the Scottish usage to a period later than the years 1512 to 1526 when the Dean of Lismore wrote his manuscript. Since his time, O'Rahilly notes, the use of the nasal suffix in the eclipsing particles has been extended, the eclipsis of *f-* has for the most part been dropped, and the article *an* (when non-leniting) has come to be treated as an eclipsing word.[17] The pattern $\frac{b}{mb,}$ etc. may have existed in the Dean's time. According to O'Rahilly the Dean, as a general usage, eclipses, *p-*, *t-*, *c-*, *f-* and leaves *b-*, *d-*, *g-*, uneclipsed. He gives examples such as *ni glas* = Ir. *na gcleas*; *no ver*, *ni verr* = Ir. *na bhfear*; *nin draid* = Ir. *na dtréad*; but *ni geyll* = Ir. *na nGaoidheal*; *er a glenn* = Ir. *ar an ngleann*; *in der* = Ir. *i ndeireadh*; *ny ban finn* = Ir. *na mban bhfionn*; *da bea* = Ir. *dá mbeadh, dá mbeith*; *am bea* = Ir. *a mbí*. These examples may represent a phonemic pattern *k* : *Ng* (*Nk*), *f*: *mf*, *t*: *Nd* (*Nt*), *b*:*mb*, *g*:*Ng*, *d*:*Nd*. The usage differs from the present in so far as there seems to have existed an alternation *f*:*mv*. The irregular writing of a final nasal in the proclitic element may indicate a phonetic state corresponding to that described for Barra and some other dialects by Borgstrøm.

Another trait which characterized the Goidelic phonemic pattern was the systematic opposition between palatals and non-palatals, phonetically usually somewhat velarized consonants, which formed what the Prague phonologists have termed a correlative series. This system is in full existence in Irish whereas in Scottish Gaelic it has been much reduced. The labials (*b*, *p*, *m*, *f*,) do not know any such opposition and the same is true of the lenited forms of dental nasals and the *r-* and *l-* phonemes. In the southern dialects of Irish the labials are palatalized, the mid part of the tongue being raised to the *i*/*y* position; their articulation corresponds to that of the labials in Russian and Ukrainian.[18] In the northern and some of the western dialects this is not the case. As I have argued elsewhere,[19] this must be an archaic trait, the force of the system having brought about the palatalization of the labials in the southern dialects. In his interesting and valuable paper *Common Gaelic* Jackson is of the opinion that lack of palatalization in the northern Irish dialects is due to Scottish Gaelic influence. It is not clear what here is meant by Scottish Gaelic influence. There are changes in continuous dialect areas which spread from a center more or less like waves. Ireland and the Highlands of Scotland once constituted

[15] Borgstrøm, *Hebrides* 22.

[16] Oftedal, *op. cit.* 211 and 207. Cf. also Thomas F. O'Rahilly, *Irish dialects* 156–158 (Dublin, 1932).

[17] O'Rahilly, *Irish dialects* 157. Cf. also K. Jackson, *Common Gaelic* 90 (London, 1951).

[18] Cf. O. Broch, *Slavische Phonetik* 70ff. (Heidelberg, 1911).

[19] *Mélanges ... Pedersen* 267ff. (København, 1937).

such an area. If Jackson's theory refers to this period it is difficult to know whether the change started in Ireland or in Scotland. If the lack of palatalization in the labials in some Irish dialects were due to a change which had parted from Scotland, the change must be rather old and date from before the time when the single culture province of Ireland and the Highlands of Scotland was broken up, that is before the end of the sixteenth century.[20] That is not very probable since there exist many traces of an earlier system with palatalized labials in Scottish Gaelic, e.g. the numerous forms with initial *bj*, *pj*, *mj* going back to *be-*, *pe-*, *me-* before non-palatal consonant, such as *ḅi̯ahəχ* 'a pass between two hills': M.Ir. *belach*; *spi̯al* 'scythe': M.Ir. *spel*;[21] *mjal*: 'lump, a hill': M.Ir. *mell.*[22] Common Gaelic must have had a clear *a*, locally in certain cases *ε*, in such surroundings. This development of $e > a$ is very old as is seen by the Old Norse renderings of Irish names, e.g. *Kjallakr*: *Cellach*, *Myrkjartan*, *Kjartan*: Irish *Muirchertach*. Such cases as Scottish Gaelic *ḅi̯ahəx*, *mjal*: must therefore represent older $b'^{j}alax$, $m'^{j}all$. Palatalized labials still exist in the Scottish Gaelic dialect of Rathlin Island: *p'*, *b'*, *m'*, *f'*, *v'* are pronounced as in southern Irish.[23] On the adjoining mainland, in Antrim, however, the difference had disappeared if the speakers whom Holmer was able to find really represented the pronunciation when the language was actually spoken. Here too, however, there are many traces of ancient real palatal labials, e.g. *bjalax*, *bjεlax* 'road', *bjan* 'woman', *fjar* 'man', *nə pjaki* 'the sinners'.[24] Furthermore it is not correct to compare the state of the Scottish Gaelic labials to that of the Irish. In Scottish Gaelic the old difference between palatals and non-palatals has disappeared and we have a neutral labial. But in the northern and in some western Irish dialects there is a clear difference between the two series through the heavy velarization of the non-palatal labials; there seem to be traces of this in certain parts of Scotland, e.g. in Argyllshire.[25] Such a glide is very common in the dialect of Rathlin Island.[26]

A change of northern Irish b'^{j}, p'^{j}, m'^{j}, v'^{j} into *b*, *p*, *m*, *v* after the breaking up of the common area is not very probable. It would then be due to the influence of Highland settlers in Ulster or to the intercourse between Irish and Highland people in Scotland. That relations of this kind would lead to such a change in the phonemic system seems unlikely. The real palatal quality of the labials would, if it had existed, have been upheld through the influence of all the other palatals which, as distinct from Scottish Gaelic, have maintained themselves in Irish. It would also seem improbable that such a Scottish Gaelic influence should have extended itself as far as

[20] Cf. Jackson, *Common Gaelic* 77.
[21] Borgstrøm, *Hebrides* 62.
[22] Holmer, *Argyllshire Gaelic* 190.
[23] Holmer, *Rathlin Island* 30–31.
[24] Holmer, *Relics* 101ff.
[25] Holmer, *Argyllshire Gaelic* 82.
[26] Holmer, *Rathlin Island* 30–31.

Connacht. In the Gaelic of the Aran Islands the labials seem to be of the same type as in Donegal. Finck does not distinguish the two series.[27] Pedersen, who was also a great Slavic scholar thoroughly familiar with the Russian palatal labials, does not criticize Finck on that score.

The special character of the opposition between the labials, neutral as opposed to velarized consonants, found in part of Ireland, is therefore an archaic trait which corresponds well to the fact that the northern Irish dialects are the only ones which have maintained not only the system of palatals opposed to non-palatals, but also the phonemic distinction between short and long consonants as far as the *n*- and *l*- and partly the *r*- phonemes are concerned.

UNIVERSITY OF OSLO

[27] Finck, *Die Araner Mundart* 1.43ff. (Marburg, 1899). In Cois Fhairrge the palatal labials are of the Munster type; cf. Tomás de Bhaldraithe, *The Irish of Cois Fhairrge* 24ff. (Dublin, 1945).

ZEPH STEWART

LIQVIDI IGNIS (Virgil, *Buc.* 6.33)

MOST MODERN translators and commentators of Virgil's sixth *Eclogue* take the adjective in *liquidi... ignis* of line 33 to refer only to the fluidity of fire.[1] Here no more than elsewhere does majority opinion give assurance of accuracy. Little attention has been paid to Servius, 'Probus', and Macrobius, who all carefully pointed out that *liquidus* in this phrase was equivalent to *purus*, comparing Lucretius' *deuolet in terram liquidi color aureus ignis* (6.205), from which Virgil may be thought to have borrowed the expression for his 'Lucretian' passage.[2] The same translators who use 'liquid' or 'flowing' recognize well enough that in other places it must mean something else, as Mackail's 'crystal' (*Buc.* 2.59) and 'clear' (*Georg.* 2.200, 3.529, 4.18), to contrast untroubled with muddy waters (*fontes*). An examination of its 24 occurrences in Virgil's major works will show in fact that in most cases the meaning 'fluid', 'liquid' or 'watery' is possible, but in only two or three preferable, and in two actually excluded.[3] The related participle *liquens* is used with similar ambiguity, though in six occurrences the meaning 'clear' is nowhere required and twice excluded.[4]

[1] 'streaming' (Conington), 'fluid' (Mackail), 'flowing' (Williams), 'liquid' (Page), 'fluide' (de Saint-Denis), 'active' (Dryden), 'liquid... of heaven' (Trevelyan); but 'pure' (Davidson-Bailey), 'pur' (Goelzer), and even 'leuchtend' (Trendelenburg).

[2] Serv. 3(1).70 Thilo; 'Prob.' 3(2).333 Hagen, with interesting remarks; Macr. *Sat.* 6.5 *pro puro uel lucido, seu pro effuso et abundanti*. Lucr. uses the expression in still another passage, *foraminibus liquidus quia transuiat ignis* (6.349), where the meaning 'fluid' is superficially more appropriate. Ernout-Robin in their commentary on 4.168 note the comment of Serv. and on 3.40 discuss *liquidus=purus*, quoting Cic. *Fin.* 1.18.58 *liquidae uoluptatis et liberae* (for Greek ἀκέραιος). Bailey in his commentary on 6.205 refers to Serv., but disregards him: "'liquid fire', i.e., not concrete like a solid." Neither Bailey nor Ernout-Robin mention 'Prob.' or Macr.

[3] Preferable *Aen.* 5.525 (*nubibus*), 859 (*undas*), 7.699 (*nubila*). Excluded *Aen.* 10.272 (*nocte*) and, in spite of *nare*, *Georg.* 4.59 (*aestatem*).

[4] *Georg.* 4.442 (*fluuium*), *Aen.* 6.724 (*campos*).

Liquidus comes honestly by its two meanings. It is related to *liqueo* as, for example, *frigidus* to *frigeo* and *rigidus* to *rigeo.* But *liqueo,* except in its participial form, means 'be clear', and it appears not only in the common legal formula but in Plautus (*Pseud.* 760), for instance, figuratively as a synonym of *defaecatum est.*[5] Although Ernout is probably extreme in calling 'be liquid or fluid' a secondary meaning of *liqueo* and its relatives in Latin, Hofmann errs more in ignoring all other meanings.[6] There is sufficient evidence indeed that a root *$*leik^{u}$-* provides forms meaning 'pour', 'be fluid', perhaps 'wet'.[7] In Latin, however, a special aspect of a fluid, its clarity, is stressed in *liquo,* 'filter', in *liqueo* and in *liquidus.* As Ernout rightly implies, Latin writers tended in the course of time to stress the meaning 'liquid' in formations from this root.[8]

Greek offers an interesting and perhaps related parallel. From **lei-p-* (see below) come words relating to oil or grease, λίπος, 'fat', ἀλείφω, λιπαίνω, 'anoint', λίπα, 'unctiously'. One adjective form, however, λιπαρός, usually means 'shiny' or 'bright', stressing a particular characteristic in the same way as *liquidus.* Just as *liquidus* sometimes means 'watery', so λιπαρός sometimes means 'oily', but English 'oily' and 'greasy' are inappropriate for the other significance. It is more accurate to call λιπαρὴ γαλήνη (Theoc. 22. 19) a 'glassy calm' than an 'oily smoothness' (LSJ) or 'oily calm' (Gow), just as τοὺς ὀφθαλμοὺς λιπαίνειν (Plut. *Non posse suau. uiui sec. Epic.* 20 [1101A]) refers to the glister of eyes, not their oiliness, and λιπάω means as often 'be shiny' as 'be fat'.[9]

A few observations may help to clarify the historical situation, where the standard etymological dictionaries bring as much confusion as help. We are told, first of all, that Greek λίπος and its relatives represent enlargements with *-p-* of the root **lei-* found in Latin *lino,* 'smear, anoint', and that *lippus* shows the same enlargement of the root in Latin. But *lippus* means 'watery-eyed, runny', not 'oily-eyed or sticky-eyed', nor need one be led astray by the fact that in later times the affliction was treated with unguents.[10] It will then be a loanword from Osco-Umbrian formed from the same root as Latin *liqueo,* an origin far more satisfactory for the meaning and suitable as well to the expressive (colloquial) doubling of the *-p-*.[11] We are

[5] Also the participle without question in Gell. 18.5.11 *non turbidae fidei nec ambiguae, sed ut purae liquentisque.*

[6] *DEL,* s.v. *liquo* 1.644; *LEW* s.v. *liqueo* 1.812.

[7] I am inclined to accept the Keltic evidence rejected in *DEL* 645 as unsatisfactory for the sense, tentatively comparing *liquida nubila* and *liquidae nubes* (note 3 above). *WP* 2.397 find in the Keltic forms for 'wet' a basic meaning of the root.

[8] *DEL* 1.645.

[9] Gow himself abandons the metaphor at Theoc. 23.8, where he translates ὄσσων λιπαρὸν σέλας 'brightening of the eye'.

[10] For the sense Mart. 8.59.2 *lippa sub attrita fronte lacuna patet* seems decisive. For use of curative unguents see Hor. *Ep.* 1.1.29, *Serm.* 1.5.30.

[11] Ernout has more recently (*DEL* 1.640) almost abandoned his earlier suggestion (first in *Les éléments*

told, secondly, by implication that there are no formations in Greek from the otherwise widely represented root of Latin *liqueo*. There is more than sufficient evidence scattered under different words in *DEL* and in *LEW* (*lino*, *lippus*, *linquo*, *liqueo*, *liquo*) as well as in *DEG* (λίπος) to show confusion, demonstrable in Germanic and probable elsewhere, between the root **lei-* (often enlarged into **lei-p-* or **lei-n-*), 'smear, anoint, stick to, remain,' and **leik^u-* (often with nasal infix **lei-n-k^u-*), 'leave' (trans.).[12] It is difficult on the other hand to separate forms apparently derived from **leik^u-*, 'be fluid, in a state of leaving', from those derived from **leik^u-*, 'leave'.[13] Ernout and others have even concluded that there is a single root which "has had several developments with divergent sense."[14] In these circumstances it is hardly daring to suggest that in Greek, where **leik^u-* (*liqueo*) would often appear with a labial, contamination or confusion might well have occurred between formations from it and those from **lei-p-*, especially in view of the approximate meanings, 'that which is fluid' and 'that which is oily', and of the common confusion of 'clear' and 'shiny, bright'.[15]

Even though it is perhaps justified by the linguistic situation, it may come as a surprise to find a Latin writer equating *liquidus* with λιπαρός, as Lucan does when he translates Theocritus' λιπαρᾶς παλαίστρας (2.52) with *liquidae palaestrae* (9.661).[16] This would also suggest, as one might expect from the example of *clarus*, that *liquidus* could mean 'bright' as well as 'clear'. Though readers who prefer quaint translations may still be happier with 'liquid' fire, certainly a more accurate representation of what Virgil meant by *liquidi ignis* is expressed by some such compound adjective as 'clear-flowing' or 'bright-flowing', with considerable emphasis on the first element.

HARVARD UNIVERSITY

dialectaux du vocabulaire latin 191–192 [Paris 1909]) that *limpidus* is a borrowing of an Oscan-Umbrian form with nasal infix from the root of *liqueo*. It is strange that he did not note the clearer case of *lippus*. In connection with the doubling of the *-p-* it is an unusual coincidence that Lucretius sometimes treats the first syllable of *liquidus* as long (1.349, 2.452, 3.427, 4.1259).

12 *DEG* 583. The causative forms from **lei-p-* in the Germanic languages show "influence de la R. germ. **liƕ*: gr. λείπω lat. *linquo*." *LEW* 1.811: "Die Bed. infolge Aufsaugung der Wz. germ. **liƕ-*, s. *linquo*". Not very consistently the dictionaries put forms from **lei-p-* and from **lei-n-* under different words, thus separating, e.g., Epidaurian ἄλινσις from ἄλειψις.

13 Some of the evidence is summarized by Ernout in *DEL* 1.642-3 s.v. *linquo*, some s.v. *liquo* 644–5. Especially important are Old Prussian *po-linka*, intransitive though with nasal infix, and the intransitive uses of ἐκλείπω.

14 *DEL* 1.645. The disputed evidence is principally in Persian and Avestan. Suggested earlier by G. Curtius, *Grundzüge*[5] 463 and A. Fick, *Vergleichendes Wörterbuch* 1[4].121,533. Hofmann in *LEW* 1.812 s.v. *liqueo* finds the suggestion "unangängig".

15 Latin *clarus*, German *hell*, both transfers furthermore from sound to sight.

16 Perhaps similarly Virg. *liquidum odorem* (*Georg*. 4.415) and Hor. *liquidis odoribus* (*Carm*. 1.5.2): for λιπαρὰ ὀσμή see Aristotle *De Sensu* 443b10, *De Anima* 421a30. In this connection the other meanings given by Macr. (note 2 above) are significant. Obviously *liquidi oliui* (*Georg*. 2.466) also suggests a parallel.

PAUL THIEME

PĀṆINI AND THE PRONUNCIATION OF SANSKRIT

WHEN SPEAKING of Pāṇini's work, which has played such a decisive role in the development of linguistic studies in India and in the West,[1] as a 'grammar', we are actually committing a little inaccuracy. The more closely we study it, the more readily shall we agree with L. Bloomfield when he calls it 'one of the greatest monuments of human intelligence' (*Language* 11), but the more hesitant shall we feel, on the other hand, to look upon it as a 'perfect description of a language'. It is perfect in the consistency of its mechanistic approach and the precision of its observation, but it is imperfect as a full description of speech usage. Pāṇini's work is exclusively concerned with defining (*lakṣaya-*)[2] the procedures of regular word-formation (*saṃskāra*) – anything else does not fall within its scope; it is dealt with either sweepingly, as for example the unanalysable nominal stems (3.3.1 *uṇādayo bahulam*), or not at all. There are, for example, no rules concerning word order,[3] no rules concerning gender unless it is a function of a particular suffix.[4] There is no phonetic instruction.

1 The significance of Pāṇini's functional analysis of the word-forms of Sanskrit for the rise of comparative grammar has been defined best by Wilhelm Schulze, *Kleine Schriften* 5–6, 93–94. Cf. also L. Bloomfield, *Language* 11–12. With respect to linguistics, Filippo Sassetti's opinion (given in 1588) was fully justified: "... non è da farsi beffe della loro [= di questi Bragmeni] opinione, che le scienze siano uscite di qua [India]" (*Lettere di Filippo Sassetti* 416 [Firenze 1855]). (Bragmeni = brahmins.)

2 The work gives what is, in the words of Patanjali, *Mahābhāṣya* (ed. Kielhorn) I p. 6 l. 3 *sāmānya-viśeṣaval lakṣaṇam* 'a definition [that consists in] naming the generalia and the particularia'.

3 Cf. Patanjali, *op. cit.* I p. 39 l. 18 *saṃskṛtya saṃskṛtya padāny utsṛjyante. teṣāṃ yatheṣṭam abhisaṃbandho bhavati, tadyathā: āhara pātram, pātram āhareti* 'The finished words [of Sanskrit] are produced [in speech] after being formed [in the way defined by Pāṇini's rules] each individually. Their mutual connexion [by precedence and succession within a sentence] happens according to one's desire. For example: [one may say:] '*āhara pātram*' [or] '*pātram āhara*' [according to one's desire]."

4 Cf. Patanjali *op. cit.*, I p. 390 l. 18–9 (and elsewhere) *lingam aśiṣyaṃ lokāśrayatvāl lingasya* 'The gender [of a nominal stem] need not be taught, as the gender [of a nominal stem is not the function of a grammatical process, but] rests on [the usage of] the people [that constitute the speech community].'

In a special appendix, the Dhātupāṭha, Pāṇini enumerates all the verbal roots (*dhātu*) of his language. But he does not try to define their meanings.[5] His enumeration evidently has the sole purpose of making it possible for him to refer to certain groups of roots by short expressions (e.g. *divādi-* '[root] *div* etc.' = 'all the roots of the fourth class'). In another appendix, the *varṇopadeśa*, later also called Śiva-Sūtra (ŚS),[6] Pāṇini enumerates the sounds.

Already Kātyāyana (not later than at the beginning of the 3rd century BC) remarks that the assumption that this list of sounds is *iṣṭabuddhyartha* 'has the purpose to [make] recognize which sounds are desirable (correct) [in speaking Sanskrit]', cannot be correct (Introduction vārtt. 17, Mabhābhāṣya I p. 13), since the list is incomplete. It does not give all the sounds actually spoken, but only ideal types (*ākṛti*), abstractions like *a* for *a*, *ā*, *ā*3 etc. (vārtt. 18). The *varṇopadeśa* can only serve the purpose of making the procedure of the grammar possible: vārtt. 15 *vṛttisamavāyārtha upadeśaḥ* 'the teaching [of the sounds] has the purpose of [creating] an arrangement for the procedure [of the instruction]', vārtt. 16 *anubandhakaraṇārthaś ca* 'and it has the purpose [of making it possible] to attach symbolical sounds [to certain groups of sounds]'. Patanjali (2nd century BC) lucidly explains (I p. 13 l. 11): *vṛttisamavāyaś cānubandhakaraṇaṃ ca pratyāhārārtham.pratyāhāro vṛttyarthaḥ* 'The arranging of the sounds in a certain order[7] and the attaching of symbolical sounds [to certain groups] has the purpose of making possible [the formation of] short expressions (*pratyāhāra*). The formation of short expressions has the purpose of making the procedure of the instruction[8] possible.' This definition of the purpose of the ŚS.s has been accepted by the later Pāṇinīyas, e.g. by the Kāśikā (7th century AD): *atha kimartho varṇānām upadeśaḥ? – pratyāhārārthaḥ.pratyāhāro lāghavena śāstrapravṛttyarthaḥ*, and by the Siddhānta-Kaumudī (17th century AD): *māheśvarāṇi sūtrāṇy aṇādisaṃjnārthāni.*

We cannot but consider it correct. We must take it as established that the peculiar features of Pāṇini's *varṇopadeśa* are explainable only on the assumption that it is meant not as a table of sounds from which one is to learn, when it is recited by an

II p. 198 l. 15 Patanjali quotes the principle as taught by a particular 'teacher' (*paṭhiṣyati hy ācāryaḥ*), using an expression that might refer to Pāṇini or Kātyāyana, neither of whom actually teaches it in this form. Attention must be drawn, in this connection, to the discussion Pāṇ. 1.2.53-57, which, however, would call for a detailed technical analysis I cannot give on this occasion.

[5] The Dhātupāṭha in the form we have it contains 'meanings'. They can be proved to be an addition, later than Patanjali. Cf. B. Liebich, *Kṣīrataranginī* 244–5 (1930).

[6] The legend that they are inspired by God Śiva (Maheśvara) is unknown to Patanjali. His discussion on ŚS 6, in particular his expression I p. 35 l. 15–8, shows that he held Pāṇini himself responsible for the peculiar formulation of the ŚS.s.

[7] Patanjali's explanation of *samavāya*: I p. 13 l. 6 *atha kaḥ samavāyaḥ?* — *varṇānām ānupūrvyeṇa saṃniveśaḥ* 'And a *samavāya* is what? — An arranging of the sounds in a certain order.'

[8] Patanjali's explanation of *vṛtti*: l. 5 *kā punar vṛttiḥ?* — *śāstrapravṛttiḥ* 'But *vṛtti* is what? — The procedure of the instruction.'

authoritative teacher, what are the correct sounds of the Sanskrit language, but only as a contrivance by which it becomes possible to refer to certain sound groups by short expressions (like *ac* 'all the vowels', *hal* 'all the consonants', *aṭ* 'all vowels and semivowels except *l*', *śar* 'all sibilants', *al* 'all sounds').

Certain sounds are neither specially taught in the ŚS.s, nor capable of being included in any short expression with the help of Pāṇ. 1.1.69, for example the *anusvāra* (*ṃ*) and the *visarjanīya* (*ḥ*). Two reasons are responsible for their not being enumerated in the ŚS.s. They are, firstly, only occurring as substitutes for other sounds according to special rules – they are no main phonemes but 'variants'. Secondly, it is not necessary to refer to them, in the body of the work, either in bulk or together with other sounds. It is true that, according to Kātyāyana vārtt. 6–8 on ŚS5 and Patanjali on these vārttikas, various reasons would make it desirable to have them included in certain short expressions (*aṭ*: vārtt. 6, *śar*: vārtt. 7) or generally in *al* 'sound' (vārtt. 8). Yet, these reasons are so subtle, they rest on the application of such strict principles of interpretation as to make it obvious that we shall do no injustice to Pāṇini when submitting that he did not consider them.

2

Only on two places in Pāṇini's work have I come across a rule that is understood best on the assumption that it is supposed to teach a pronunciation:

Pāṇ. 1.1.8 *mukhanāsikāvacano 'nunāsikaḥ* 'an anunāsika is [a sound] which is produced by mouth and nose'.

Pāṇ. 1.2.32 *tasyādita udāttam ardhahrasvam* '[a measure of the length of] half a short vowel in the beginning of this [= a *svarita*-vowel] is high-pitched [and the rest low-pitched]'.

We may ask why Pāṇini defines the pronunciation of an *anunāsika* (nasal sound) when he does not define, for example, the pronunciation of an *anusvāra* or a *visarjanīya*. The reason cannot be that the term *anunāsika* is less clear than the two other terms. Its linguistic analysis is rather obvious: '[a sound that is spoken] along the nose (*anu nāsikām*)'. It can only be a *bahuvrīhi* with a *karmapravacanīya* (Pāṇ. 1.4.83ff.) as first member governing the second one: Wackernagel, *Altindische Grammatik* II 1 § 119 bα. Avestic *anu.zafan-* '[going] along the mouth' offers a precise correspondence.

As an answer to our question I suggest that Pāṇini defines the pronunciation of a nasal sound (*anunāsika*), because it can be looked upon as *saṃskṛta* in a specific sense: it is 'made up' of two different, independently occurring sounds, 'main phonemes': a vowel or half-vowel (*y*, *v*, *l*) + nasality (*ānunāsikya*, as observable in a pure form in the *anusvāra*).

Pāṇini knows of course, as all Indian phoneticians do, that other sounds, too, are complex units. His formulation in 1.1.9 shows that he was able to distinguish the '[articulatory] effort of the mouth' (*āsyaprayatna*) from other features of pronunciation such as voice (*nāda*), pitch (*svara*), aspiration (*śvāsa*). The difference is that an *anunāsika* often appears as a substitute for a simpler entity: *ā̐* for *ā*, *y̐* for *m* before *y*, etc.

There are, then, two qualities in the *anunāsika* that, in their union, call for a special treatment in Pāṇini's work: its being a substitute, a 'variant' – in contradistinction to *ā*, *y* etc., and its being complex, 'made up' – in contradistinction to other substitute sounds as *visarjanīya* and *anusvāra*.

This explanation is borne out as correct by Pāṇini's description of a *svarita*-vowel (1.2.32). A *svarita*-vowel is also a substitute for another sound, a vowel either with or without high pitch, and a *svarita*-vowel can also be considered as *saṃskṛta* 'made up [of two different units]'.

To understand Pāṇ. 1.2.32 properly, we have to look at the context. Immediately before, Pāṇini has given the definitions: 1.2.29 [*ac*: 1.2.27] *uccair udāttaḥ*, 1.2.30 [*ac*] *nīcair anudāttaḥ*, and 1.2.31 [*ac*] *samāhāraḥ svaritaḥ*, which should be paraphrased: 'By the term "*udātta*" [when used in this work] is meant a vowel (*ac*) that is high-pitched, by "*anudātta*" a vowel that is low-pitched, by "*svarita*" a vowel that is a mixture [of both].'

It is of vital importance to realize that Pāṇini does not explain here the differently pitched vowels, but the technical terms *udātta* etc., just as he explains the terms 'short', 'long' and 'overlong' (*hrasva*, *dīrgha*, *pluta*) in 1.2.27, or the terms 'light' and 'heavy' (*laghu*, *guru*) in 1.4.10–12, or, for example, the terms *guṇa* and *vṛddhi* in 1.1.1–2.[9]

Quite different is the case of the rule Pāṇ. 1.2.32 *tasyādita udāttam ardhahrasvam*. It does not serve to define the term '*svarita*', which was done by 1.2.31, but it volunteers an information on the actual pronunciation of a *svarita*-vowel itself. The peculiar nature of the rule has been clearly understood by Patanjali.

kimartham idam ucyate 'For what purpose is this [rule: 1.2.32] being taught?' he asks (I p. 208 l. 12), intimating that 1.2.31 would be quite sufficient as a definition of the term *svarita*. His answer: ... *ācāryaḥ suhṛdbhūtvānvācaṣṭe* ... 'Having become friendly the teacher [Pāṇini] gives an explanation [of the pronunciation of a *svarita* vowel]' (l. 16), which strictly speaking would be unnecessary: *yady ayam evaṃ suhṛt kim anyāny apy evaṃjātīyakāni nopadiśati? – kāni punas tāni? – sthāna-karaṇānupradānāni* 'If this [teacher, Pāṇini] is thus friendly, why does he not teach also other things of the same kind? – Which [would] these be? – The places of articulation (*sthāna*), the organs of articulation (*karaṇa*) and the modes of production (*anupradāna*)' (l. 17–8).[10] It is obvious that, in general, Pāṇini presupposes a know-

[9] Cf. Thieme, *Pāṇini and the Veda* 111 (Allahabad 1935).

[10] It is with these items that treatises deal that do contain phonetic instruction (the Prātiśākhyas, later the Śikṣās). Already Filippo Sassetti (*Lettere* 283) reports of the (phonetic) elements (*elementi*) of

ledge of the pronunciation of Sanskrit in a student of his work: *vyākaraṇaṃ nāmeyam uttarā vidyā. so 'sau chandaḥśāstreṣv abhivinīta upalabdhyāvagantum utsahate. – yady evam nārtho 'nena. idam apy upalabdhyā gamiṣyati* 'What is called "[word-]formation"[11] [taught in Pāṇini's work] is a science that follows [upon other instruction]. Having been trained in the Veda and the *śāstras* a man [a student of Pāṇini] is capable of understanding [those other things: *sthāna, karaṇa* and *anupradāna*] through observation. – If that is so, there is no purpose [served] by this [rule: 1.2.32]. Also this [the distribution of the high-pitched and the low-pitched part within a *svarita* vowel] a man will get [by himself] through observation.'

After trying unsuccessfully to find a specific purpose consistent with the rest of Pāṇini's purposes in the rule 1.2.32, Patanjali gives as his final view (*siddhānta*): *anvākhyānam eva tarhīdaṃ mandabuddheḥ* 'This rule [1.2.32] is, then, nothing but an explanation [of a pronunciation] for one of slow intelligence'. It is only on this point that I dare to disagree with him: Pāṇini teaches the pronunciation of a *svarita*, I claim, because a *svarita*-vowel can be shown to be *saṃskṛta* in the same sense as an *anunāsika*.

While disagreeing on a particular detail, I am in full accord with Patanjali's general principle, III p. 54 l. 4:

sāmarthyayogān na hi kiṃcid asmin
paśyāmi śāstre yad anarthakaṃ syāt

'For, since it is fitting [*yukta*; *-yogāt* short for *yuktatvāt*] that it [Pāṇini's teaching] be purposeful (*samartha*), I do not see (recognize) anything in this instruction [of Pāṇini's] that would be without [specific] purpose.'

Patanjali I p. 39 l. 11f. : *aśakyaṃ varṇenāpy anarthakena bhavitum, kiṃ punar iyatā sūtreṇa* 'It is impossible that [in Pāṇini's work] even a [single] sound should be without purpose, how much more such a big rule.'

Sanskrit: "de' quali tutti rendono raggione facendoli nascere tutti dai diversi movimenti della bocca e della lingua," 'for all of which they account by showing that they originate from the various movements of the mouth and of the tongue'. This was, to him, a new and remarkable way of looking at things. He deserves praise for not confounding, as it was customary in Europe up to the times of Jacob Grimm, the (phonetic) '*elementi*' with the letters; unfortunately, but quite understandably, he confounds them in the following remarks with the grammatical elements (roots, suffixes, endings) of which his informants must have been speaking when leading him to the opinion: "Traducono nella loro [lingua: 'Sanscruta'] facilmente tutti i concetti nostri, e stiman che noi non possiamo fare il medesimo de' loro nella lingua nostra, per mancare della metà degli elementi, o più," 'They translate easily into their language all our concepts, and they reckon that we cannot do the same with theirs into our language for want of half, or more, of the elements'. Interesting as a curiosity is Sassetti's theory (*l.c.*), that the great number of their (phonetic) elements is largely due to the different 'temperature' of their tongues, caused by their continuously chewing betel leaves and areca nuts.

11 I analyze *vyākaraṇa* as: *vividhena prakāreṇa* (or *viśeṣeṇa*) *ākṛtayaḥ kriyante yena*.

3

The two exceptions to the rule that Pāṇini does not teach pronunciations not only confirm it but make clear its rationale: Pāṇini's grammar is not concerned with describing features of speech usage, but with defining abstract procedures of 'formation'; it is not a description of Sanskrit speech, but an argument that is meant to show that most of the speech units (*śabda*) of the sacred language are 'built up' (*saṃskṛta*) from simpler elements in a peculiar way that can be stated by definitions. Anything that may be looked upon as 'complex' is of interest to him, anything 'simple' – the pronunciation of the primary phonemes, the roots, the simple prepositions *pra* etc. (1.4.58, contrast Yāska's treatment, Nir. 1.3), and many other things – is not. He teaches these items only *vṛttisamavāyārtha* and *anubandhakaraṇārtha*, that is, in order to be able to refer to them by short expressions.

Originally, *saṃskṛta* 'prepared' was applied to the language of the educated (*śiṣṭa*) brahmins of the North in the derived sense of 'ornate', hence 'fit for ritual use' = 'ritually pure'. To a linguistically naive thinking, its distinction lay in its clear pronunciation: Kauṣ. Br. 7.6. ... *udīcyāṃ diśi prajnātatarā* ('particularly clear') *vāg udyata udanca u eva yanti vācaṃ śikṣitum.yo vā tata āgacchati tasya vā śuśrūṣante.* Brahmins who recite the Veda speak *śabdasaṃskārasaṃyuktam* 'with ornateness of sound' (Mahābhār. ed. Sukthankar I 64.34); on a special occasion, there comes from the 'moonlike face/mouth' of a woman a *vāṇī saṃskārabhūṣaṇā* 'a [solemn] speech ornamented by *saṃskāra* ('pure pronunciation')' (Mahābhār. Bombay 13.41.14, 15): compare Rām. 7.4.8 *vacaḥ saṃskārālaṃkṛtam*, Mahābhār. (Bombay) 14.43.23 *svaravyanjanasaṃskārā bhāratī* '[sacred] speech characterised by *saṃskāra* ('pure pronunciation') of vowels and consonants'; in Rām. 5.30.18 *vāk saṃskṛtā* 'ornate speech' is contrasted with *vākyam arthavat* 'speech characterised by purpose [only]'.[12]

Not explicitly, but by distinct implication, Pāṇini restores the etymological meaning of *saṃskṛ* 'build up'. The 'ornate, ritually pure' (*saṃskṛta*) speech is shown by his 'formation' (*vyākaraṇa*) to be *saṃskṛta* in the word's boldest sense: 'built up [from elements through definable procedures]'. In this sense *saṃskṛ* is used by Yāska, Nir. 2.1, when he demands of the etymologist (*nairuktika*), in contradistinction to the grammarian (*vaiyākaraṇa*), that, in explaining difficult, doubtful words 'he

[12] That is, a form of speech in which it is essential only that it be understood; it need not possess beauty or purity. According to Vāj. Prāt. 1.2 the words of daily speech (*laukika*), in contradistinction to Vedic words, are *arthapūrvaka* 'following purpose [only]'; Kātyāyana, Introduction värtt. 1 (I p. 8) formulates... *lokato 'rthaprayukte śabdaprayoge śāstreṇa dharmaniyamaḥ* 'while the use of the speech-forms on the part of [everyday] people is motivated by purpose [only], there is a restriction for the sake of religious duty (*dharma*) [to be taught] by the instruction [contained in Pāṇini's grammar]'. — In *Zeitschrift für Indologie und Iranistic* 8.26ff., I have tried to analyze the full implications of these ideas and their theoretical background.

should not heed the [correct word-]formation [as taught by Pāṇini]': *na saṃskāram ādriyeta*, or when he refers (Nir. 4.1) to certain Vedic words (*nigama*) as *anavagatasaṃskāra* 'of ununderstandable formation'; by Kātyāyana, Vājasaneyi-Prātiśākhya 1.1 *svarasaṃskārau* 'accent and [word-]formation'; and, finally and most clearly, by Patanjali (I p. 39 l. 18): *saṃskṛtya saṃskṛtya padāny utsṛjyante* 'the [finished] words [of Sanskrit] are produced [in speech] after being formed [in the way defined by Pāṇini's rules] each individually'.

Later, *saṃskṛta* may be meant or understood in both ways, in the more technical and in the more popular sense. When commenting on Kālidāsa's expression *kṛtasaṃskārā ... bhāratī* (Raghuv. 10.36), Mallinātha explains *saṃskāra* as: *sādhutvaspaṣṭatādiprayatnaḥ* 'the effort leading to correctness [of word formation](as taught by Pāṇini)[13] and clearness [of pronunciation][14] (as characteristic for Sanskrit according to Kauṣ. Br. and the epics)'. *saṃskṛta* and *saṃskāra*, when used with reference to the sacred language, retain, of course, certain connotations that accrue from various contexts in which the words are characteristically used. There is the connotation of 'good quality': Patanjali II p. 367 l. 7 *saṃskṛtam annam guṇavad ity ucyate* 'a prepared meal is called "of good quality"'; there is the connotation of 'fitness for sacred purposes': Patanjali III p. 57 l. 27 *upanayanaṃ saṃskārārtham* ... p. 58 l. 1 *upanītaḥ saṃskṛto bhavati* 'the investiture with the sacred thread has the purpose of preparing [for the study of the Veda], ... invested with the sacred thread he becomes prepared [for the study of the Veda]'; and there is the connotation of 'bestowing purity': Patanjali I 475.9 *pātraṃ saṃskāreṇa śudhyati* 'through [special] preparation a vessel [that was used by certain low-castes] is purified'.

Kālidāsa (Kum. Saṃbh. 7.90) lets Sarasvatī, the goddess of speech, herself bestow her blessings at the wedding of Śiva and Pārvatī, in Sanskrit on the bridegroom, in vernacular on the bride – *vāgmayena ... saṃskārapūtena* 'by a speech purified by *saṃskāra*' (= Sanskrit), *sukhagrāhyanibandhanena* 'by a speech whose formulation is easy to grasp' (= vernacular) respectively. The explanation of *saṃskārapūtena*, as it would result from my above remarks, I can give in the words of Mallinātha: *saṃskāreṇa śāstravyutpattyā pūtena, prakṛtipratyayavibhāgaśuddhena, saṃskṛtenety arthaḥ* '[by speech] purified by *saṃskāra*, [that is,] derivation [as taught] by the instruction [of Pāṇini]; [that is,] pure through the separation of roots and suffixes; the meaning is: by Sanskrit'.

To a Vedologist, Kālidāsa's expression *saṃskārapūta* conjures up yet more complicated associations. It sounds like a distant echo of a verse of the Rigveda, older perhaps by two millennia:

[13] Cf. his remark on Kālidāsa, Kum. Saṃbh. 7.90, quoted below; also on Kum. Saṃbh. 1.18 *saṃskāro :vyākaraṇajanyā śuddhiḥ*.

[14] Cf. the first explanation of 'Sanskrit', given by a European according to what he was told by an Indian scholar: "Sanscruta, che vuol dire bene articulata," '*Sanscruta*, which means well articulated' (Filippo Sassetti, *Lettere* 415).

10.71.2 a, b, d *sáktum iva títaünā punánto*
yátra dhī́rā mánasā vā́cam ákrata ...
bhadraíṣāṃ lakṣmī́r níhitā́dhi vācí

'Where (on which occasion) the wise ones have created speech, purifying it through their thinking like barley grits through a sieve ..., [on that occasion] an auspicious beauty is contained in their speech.'

Purity is the abiding quality of Sanskrit. But the ideas as to the *saṃskāra* that produces it, change: in the Rigveda, it is the poetic formulation; later, it is the correct pronunciation in recitation and everyday usage; finally, it is the regular formation of the words as taught by 'the son of Dākṣī, Pāṇini'.

YALE UNIVERSITY

EMIL VETTER

EIN GALLISCHER HEILSPRUCH BEI MARCELLUS EMPIRICUS

IM ANFANG des V. Jahrhunderts n. Chr. verfaßte ein gewisser *Marcellus* aus *Burdigala* (Bordeaux), der als *magister officiorum* im Codex Theodosianus erscheint (6.29.8 und 16.5.29), als *ex mag. off.* eine Sammlung von Beschreibungen einfacher und volkstümlicher Heilmittel unter dem Titel: *De medicamentis.* Sie ist in erster Reihe für Reisende und arme Leute bestimmt, die ärztliche Hilfe nicht zur Verfügung haben oder sich solche nicht leisten können. Der Verfasser war Laie und schöpft seine Kenntnisse hauptsächlich aus Scribonius Largus und der aus dem älteren Plinius etwa hundert Jahre vor Marcellus von einem unbekannten Verfasser kompilierten sogenannten *Medicina Plinii.* Obwohl er Christ war (in den beiden Stellen des Cod. Theod. erhält er den Auftrag, gegen Heiden einzuschreiten, die im Hofdienst stehen) und z.B. 25.13 beim Einsammeln einer Heilpflanze den Namen Christi anruft, ist er doch ganz im Banne des volkstümlichen Aberglaubens; diesem Umstande verdanken wir es, daß er auch Beschwörungsformeln in gallischer Sprache mitteilt. Auf diese Weise hat er uns, was für den Sprachforscher bei der Spärlichkeit des überlieferten festlandkeltischen Sprachmaterials höchst wichtig ist, zwei gallische Sätze erhalten. Er gibt auch bei manchen Pflanzennamen die gallische Bezeichnung an, z.B. 7.13 *herba, quae Graece acte, Latine ebulum, Gallice odocos dicitur.* Gelegentlich streut er in sein im allgemeinen fehlerloses Latein aus dem Gallischen entlehnte Wörter ein.

Soviel dürfte genügen, dem Leser die Eigenart des Marcellus verständlich zu machen. Es ist aus dem 3. Band der von Kroll und Skutsch besorgten Auflage von Teuffels *Geschichte der Lateinischen Literatur* (§ 446, 1–4 der 6. Auflage) entnommen.

Der Text der beiden Zauberformeln (ed. Niedermann, Teubner 1916, S. 121; Dottin, *Langue Gauloise*, Formel Nr. 9 und 10) lautet:

Omnia quae haeserint faucibus, hoc carmen expellet: heilen prosaggeri vome si polla nabuliet onodieni iden eliton. Hoc ter dices et ad singula exspues. Item fauces, quibus aliquid inhaeserit, confricans dices: xi exucricone xu criglionaisus scrisu miovelor exugri conexu grilau.

Man muß natürlich darauf gefaßt sein, daß die Abschreiber, die ja nicht Keltisch verstanden, ebenso wie etwa die Abschreiber der griechischen Wörter und Sätze in den Cicero-Briefen die keltischen Wörter entstellten. Dabei folgten sie, bewußt oder unbewußt, einer in solchen Fällen sich einstellenden Tendenz, ihnen bekannt erscheinende Wörter auszusondern, auch über die ihnen etwa in der Vorlage überlieferten Wortgrenzen hinweg. Überall also, wo im keltischen Text lateinische oder griechische Wörter erscheinen, besteht von vornherein der Verdacht, daß scriptura continua falsch aufgelöst ist oder die Wortgrenzen der Vorlage geändert sind.

Dies gilt im ersten Spruch, der übrigens hier weiter nicht behandelt werden soll, z.B. von den Buchstabengruppen *vome,*[1] *si*, *polla*; im zweiten Spruche von *conexu.* Für uns kann als Kriterion der richtigen Worttrennung nur die Beobachtung etwa zu erkennender gleicher Endungen in parallelen Satzteilen in Betracht kommen. Von der Worttrennung unseres handschriftlichen Textes müssen wir uns bei Deutungsversuchen ganz unabhängig machen.

Nun hat Otto Haas in der Zeitschrift *Sprache* 1 (Festschrift für Prof. Havers) 50 ff. (1949) den zweiten Spruch teilweise zu deuten versucht und drei der darin erscheinenden gallischen Wörter außerordentlich scharfsinnig, ja meiner Ansicht nach überzeugend und entscheidend erklärt. Bei der Deutung eines vierten Wortes ist er, wie ich glaube, in die Irre gegangen und gerade diese Fehldeutung hat ihn auch zu der resignierten Erklärung veranlaßt, die ganze Formel sei nicht zu deuten. Ich meine im Gegenteil, daß die drei glänzenden Worterklärungen von Haas auch den Weg zur Deutung der ganzen Formel gewiesen haben und damit ihrerseits stark an Sicherheit gewinnen. Denn es ist immer zu beobachten, daß richtige Erkenntnisse zu weiteren richtigen Erkenntnissen führen.

Übrigens muß man auch den Abschreibern unseres Textes dankbar sein; es wird sich nämlich zeigen, daß die zu befürchtende Textverderbnis gar nicht schlimm ausgefallen ist, ja sich eigentlich wahrscheinlich auf das erwähnte falsche Zusammenziehen von Buchstabengruppen zu einem vermeintlich bekannten lateinischen Worte beschränkt: *exugri conexu* statt des richtigen *exu gricon exu.* Dazu kommt nur noch Vertauschung von *g* und *c* in *criglion* (statt *gr-*) und *gricon* an zweiter Stelle statt (*cr-*).

Haas vergleicht *cricon-* mit tschech. *krk* 'Hals', *criglion-* mit lat. *gurgulio*, und *grilau* mit tschech. *hrdlo* 'Kehle'. Sowohl der im lateinischen Text klar angegebene Zweck

[1] Schon deswegen sollte man sich nicht auf dieses *vome* berufen, das Haas, *Sprache* 1.51 (1949) für seine Deutung von *xu* und *xi* 'speie' benützt und das gar nicht 'speie aus', sondern 'erbrich' bedeutet; Haas läßt sich hier durch den nhd. Sprachgebrauch irreleiten, der 'speien' statt des unfeinen 'kotzen' verwendet. Dem Lateinischen ist diese Übertragung fremd.

der Besprechung, Fremdkörper aus dem Schlund zu entfernen, wie die Lautverhältnisse gegenüber den verwandten slawischen[2] und lateinischen Wörtern scheinen mir diese drei Wortdeutungen völlig zu sichern.

Dagegen ist die vierte Deutung – *xu* gleich lat. *exspue* und *xi* damit gleichbedeutend mit dem *i*-Vokal von nhd. *speien*, got. *speiwan* – schon aus dem Zusammenhang des lateinischen Textes als unrichtig zu erweisen. Dreimal ausgespuckt wird beim *ersten* Spruch, wie Haas selbst richtig versteht, nicht beim zweiten, und das vermeintliche keltische *xu* kommt in der zweiten Formel nicht dreimal, sondern *viermal*[3] vor; auch hebt sich deutlich *exu*, nicht *xu* als Wort aus dem Text heraus; es wäre gegen alle Wahrscheinlichkeit, daß zufällig *viermal* vor *xu* ein nicht zugehöriges *e* erscheinen sollte. Damit fällt auch die Annahme von Haas, daß die drei von ihm richtig gedeuteten Wörter im *Dativ* erscheinen; dies ist schon deshalb unwahrscheinlich, weil die Fremdkörper ja aus dem Schlund *hinaus* gebetet werden müssen, während doch der Dativ eher die Richtung auf den Schlund zu bedeuten müßte. Vielmehr ist nicht mit Haas (wie es oben nach Haas durch die Schreibung *cricon-* und *criglion-* mit Bezeichnung vermeintlicher Unvollständigkeit der Wortform angedeutet wurde) Dativ, sondern Akkusativ auf *-on* anzunehmen. Dieser Akkusativ ist zu verbinden mit dem viermal wiederholten *exu*: ... *exu cricon, exu criglion* (zu verbessern zu *griglion*) ... *exu gricon* (zu verbessern zu *cricon*), *exu grilau*. Da der Zweck des Zauberspruches die *Entfernung* eines Fremdkörpers aus dem Schlunde ist, drängt sich für kelt. *exu* der Zusammenhang mit gr. ἔξω unwiderstehlich auf. Das Adverbium, ursprünglich in der Bedeutung von lat. *foris*, hat wie italien. *fuori* (und *ove*, *dove*) auch die Bedeutung des Zielkasus übernommen; auch neugr. ist ἔξω ebenso 'draußen' wie 'hinaus' (und μέσα 'drinnen' und 'hinein'). Die weitere Entwickelung vom Adverbium zur Präposition ist so allgemein, daß sie näherer Begründung nicht bedarf; verwiesen sei nur auf das moderne englische '*out the window*' für älteres '*out of the window*'.

Das erste Wort der Formel *xi* muß dann das Verbum sein: lat. *exi*, aber doch wohl nicht aus dem Lateinischen entlehnt, sondern als keltisch anzusehen. Ob im Gallischen wirklich *exi* zu *xi* verkürzt wurde, was wohl möglich wäre, oder ein Schreibfehler

[2] Die engen Beziehungen des keltischen Wortschatzes zum Baltisch-Slawischen, zeitweise verdunkelt durch die lange Zeit herrschende Annahme einer vermeintlichen 'italokeltischen Spracheinheit', blieben Kennern des Keltischen nicht verborgen. Vor mir liegt ein Brief (Hongkong, 12. Dezember 1956) des nach mehr als zweijähriger chinesischer Gefangenschaft zurückkehrenden, mir durch gemeinsames Interesse am Etruskischen verbundenen Wilhelm Liedtke, aus dem ich anführe: "Bisweilen ist eine ganze Wortfamilie im Keltischen und im Baltoslawischen reich belegt und zeigt Übereinstimmung in Suffixen, Bedeutungen usw. bis ins Kleinste; das Lateinische aber schweigt." Die beiden von Haas erkannten Wortgleichungen gall. *crico-*, tschech. *krk* und gall. *grilau*, tschech. *hrdlo* werden für Liedtke eine willkommene Bereicherung seiner Sammlungen liefern.

[3] Haas tut diesen Umstand mit der Bemerkung ab (S. 51): "Da eine Zeile wiederholt ist [er meint die Wörter *xu cricone* oder *gricone*], soll wohl nur dreimal gespuckt werden". Dies ist nicht recht klar: meint er etwa irrig wiederholt vom Abschreiber, also Dittographie, oder Erweiterung der Formel über den ursprünglichen Bestand hinaus? Beides ist mir nicht wahrscheinlich.

vorliegt, muß dahingestellt bleiben. Als keltisch wird *ex* erwiesen durch die keltischen Namen *Excingilla*, *Excincomarus*, *Exobnus*; auch das *Glotta* 30. 72f. (1943) besprochene *ekstaluš* (Gefäßinschrift aus Val Trebba bei Comacchio, jetzt im Museum in Ferrara) ist das deutliche Gegenstück zu dem keltischen Personennamen, der zu *Eni-stalus*, *Eni-stalius*, *En-stalius*, *Ene-stal-*, *Ena-stellio* latinisiert wurde. Keltische Herkunft für den von manchen für etruskisch gehaltenen Namen, der aber keine Anknüpfung an etruskische Namen hat, wurde schon an der erwähnten Glottastelle vermutet. Mit diesem Adverb *exu* 'hinaus' ist dann der Akkusativ verbunden: der passendere Ablativ war also damals schon verloren.

Für die Worttrennung *cricon*, nicht *cricone* (so Haas) spricht erstens das *eliton* am Ende der ersten Formel, zweitens das *criglionaisus* der zweiten, das Haas in *criglionai sus* zerlegt, indem er *criglionai* als Dativ auffaßt (a.a.O. S. 53). Erhaltenen Zwielaut *-ai* in der Endsilbe im Beginn des 5. Jahrhunderts nach Chr. im Gallischen anzunehmen wird man sich kaum entschließen. Auch Schwanken der Schreibung zwischen *-ai* und *-e* (im vermeintlichen *cricone*) in einem so kurzen Spruche ist nicht recht glaublich. Einfacher und glaublicher ist die Annahme der Worttrennung *criglion aisus* (oder *ai usus*, wie weiter unten vermutet werden wird).

Zu dem Befehl 'komm heraus' oder 'geh hinaus' sei ein scheinbar weit abliegendes Beispiel angeführt. In der hurrischen, in hethitischer Sprache überlieferten Theogonie, jetzt am bequemsten bei P. Meriggi, *Athenaeum* 31. 110ff. (1953), lautet eine Beschwörung in M.s Übersetzung: 'per la gola ... *vieni fuori*' (S. 115) und 'per la bocca *vieni fuori*!' (S. 117), im Urtext *pa-ra-a ehu*, also mit derselben idg. Verbalwurzel *ei-* ausgedrückt. Wenn auch ganz verschieden nach Zeit und Ort kann dieses Beispiel doch zeigen, wie leicht ein solcher Befehl bei einer Beschwörung sich einstellt. Die hurrische Beschwörung scheint mir für die Erklärung des gallischen (*e*)*xi exu* als 'geh hinaus, komm heraus' immerhin eine gewisse Stütze zu sein.

Dasselbe *i* 'geh' wie in (*e*)*xi* finde ich auch in *ai*, das hinter *criglion* überliefert ist: 'geh ab'. Es ist mit dem folgenden *sus* zu verbinden wie (*e*)*xi* mit *exu* und weiter *scri* mit *su*. Ein Fremdkörper kann entweder durch die Speiseröhre 'abgehen' oder aus der Luftröhre durch den Mund herausgestoßen werden, kann durch Würgen oder Husten heraus*springen*.

Dieser Überlegung folgend deute ich *ai sus* als 'geh ab hinunter' und *scri su* als 'spring herauf'. Darin sind *sus* und *su* wohl romanisch; *scri* stimmt gut zu gr. homer. σκαίρω 'hüpfe'.[4]

Das auf *scrisu* folgende *miovelor* ist wohl in zwei Wörter zu zerlegen: *mio velor*.

[4] Haas (S. 53) legt seiner Deutung nicht *scri*, sondern *cri* zu Grunde und erklärt mit Berufung auf eine andere mit *crisi* beginnende Zauberformel (Dottin 8) gegen Schmerzen am Zäpfchen *crisu* als 'Zäpfchen'. Doch wird man die Gruppen *aisus scrisu* nicht als *aisuss crisu* trennen wollen und erwartet kaum eine Erwähnung des Zäpfchens in einem Spruch zur Entfernung eines Fremdkörpers aus dem Schlunde.

Als Bedeutung läßt sich vermuten 'nach meinem Willen'. Vor dem *e-* des nächsten Wortes *exu* könnte die Kasusendung von *velor* ausgefallen sein, so daß zu verstehen wäre *velor(e)*. Die für lat. *meus* zu erschließende ältere Stufe **mei̯os* kann auch für gall. *mio* angenommen werden. Wie das Suffix in *velor* zu beurteilen ist, läßt sich bei dem Stand des Materials für das Gallische nicht sagen. Wenn im Griechischen gerade dieselbe Wurzel, allerdings von einem mit Delta erweiterten Verbal-Stamme, in ἐέλδωρ *r*-Suffix zeigt, liegt sicher nur parallele Entwicklung vor. War gall. *velor* auf der ersten Silbe betont, was wohl anzunehmen ist, dann war das *o* kurz. Langes *ō* in unbetonter Silbe ist im Gallischen zu *u* geworden, wie man aus gall. *exu*, gr. ἔξω ersehen kann. Welcher idg. Kasus für *mio velor* oder vielleicht für *mio velor(e)* anzunehmen ist, muß dahingestellt bleiben. Der Bedeutung nach entspricht der Ausdruck einem Instrumental.

Zu *grilau*, das Haas sicher richtig mit tschech. *hrdlo* 'Kehle, Hals' vergleicht, möchte ich daran erinnern, daß im Griechischen Bezeichnungen einer großen Zahl von Körperteilen *u*-Stämme sind: γόνυ, γένυς, δελφύς, ἰγνύς, ἰξύς, νηδύς, ὀφρύς, πῆχυς (auch νέκυς kann man dazu rechnen). So könnte auch dieses Wort ursprünglich *u*-Stamm gewesen sein und im Slawischen wie viele andere *u*-Stämme (vgl. *drěvo*, gr. δόρυ) in die *o*-Deklination übergegangen sein. Der *u*-Zwielaut in *grilau* wäre bei einem *u*-Stamm immerhin verständlich; er könnte aus den obliquen Kasus eingedrungen sein. Jedenfalls liegt in *grilau* wie in *cricon* und *griglion* nicht Dativ vor(so Haas S. 53), sondern Akkusativ. Bewahrung eines *u*-Stammes würde zu dem altertümlichen Gesamtcharakter des Gallischen gut stimmen.

WIEN

CALVERT WATKINS

LATIN *MARITUS*

WHILE the general lines of the etymology of Lat. *marītus* have been known for some time, no satisfactory analysis of the derivational process or of the presumed noun base has been made to date. It is the purpose of this paper to show that a relatively simple solution to the problem of this form may be achieved by considering it in the proper morphological and semantic context.

Marītus is attested in Latin since Plautus, both as adjective and as a substantivized masculine. The adjectival use is clearly the earlier, and the noun derives from the fact that the adjective is applied only to the male member of a couple in the earlier language, e.g. *senex hic maritus habitat* (Plaut. *Cas.* 35). The adjective is also found in the language of agriculture, referring to the 'marriage' of tree and vine: *arbores facito uti bene maritae sint* (Cato, *Agr.* 32.2). In Plautus the use as noun is almost always either predicative, where it may frequently be taken simply as the adjective 'married', or in opposition to another term, especially *caelebs* or *nupta* (*-us*). The sense as noun in the earlier language is 'married man', not 'husband', for which Plautus uses *uir*. Compare, as predicate: *continuo ut maritus fiat* (Plaut. *Epid.* 190); *amabo, an maritust* (Plaut. *Merc.* 538); for the antithetical usage: *caelibem te esse mauis liberum / an maritum seruom* (Plaut. *Cas.* 290–1, cf. *Merc.* 1018); *nouom maritum et nouam nuptam* (Plaut. *Cas.* 782, cf. 859). The acceptation 'husband' is later, as well as the feminine noun *marīta*, which is a creation of the imperial age. From the masculine a denominative transitive verb *marītare* was formed, which takes the female as object; this was probably in origin an agricultural term '*feminam mari sociare*' (*TLL* s.v.): *tum enim dicuntur catulire, id est ostendere uelle se maritari* (Varro, R.R. 2.9.11).

There is no extant nominal base in Latin from which *marītus* could have been formed. The usual analysis (e.g. *LEW*) has been **marī-tos* 'furnished with a young woman or wife', with **-tos* the secondary derivative familiar in Latin as the type *barbātus*, and **marī-* a feminine of the *devī́* or *vṛkī́ḥ* type.[1] This explanation is qualified in *DEL* as an "hypothèse arbitraire" in view of the absence of a form **marī-* in any of the Indo-European languages. However, a morphological analysis of the roster of cognates, which show surprising diversity in form, would indicate that a superficially similar base is quite plausible. We have the following: Lith. *mergà*, OPrus. *mergo* 'girl' < **mer-g^w-ā*; W. *merch* 'daughter, girl' < **mer-k-ā*;[2] Lith. *martì* 'bride' < **mor-t-ī/yā*; Crimean Goth. *marzus* 'wedding' (Goth. *-*þus*); W. *morwyn* 'maiden' < **mori-gnā*; Alb. *shemërë* 'second wife' (in polygamy) < *$s_o m$-$m_o r$(*i*?)-; Vedic *márya-* 'young man, groom, suitor', *maryaká-* 'little man', Iran. **maryaka-* 'id.' in MPers. *mērak*; Gk. μεῖραξ 'young girl', dimin. μειράκιον 'lad'.

Certain of these forms require special comment. Martinet[3] has recently analyzed the velar element in μεῖραξ and *maryaka-* as the phonetic reflex of a 'laryngeal' with velar fricative allophones, regular before *-s*(-) and analogically generalized through the rest of the paradigm, with a further addition of the thematic vowel in the Sanskrit form. The Greek form would thus go back to a *$mery$-eH_2-s. While accepting this derivation of μεῖραξ, I must point out that the likelihood of such an analysis of *maryaká-* is by no means so great. For both the semantic acceptation (see RV 5.2.5) and the oxytone accentuation show that *maryaká-*, in opposition to the simplex *márya-*, belongs to the secondary, late, and productive category of diminutives in *-ká-*;[4] one should not make too much of the simple coïncidence of velar formants in the two languages.

LEW attempts to support the separation **marī-tos* by adducing Alb. *shemërë*, derived from *$s\d{m}$-$m_o r\bar{\imath}$ by Norbert Jokl.[5] The argument is circular; Jokl himself postulates a final *-*ī* only on the evidence of Lat. *marītus*, and not on any internal Albanian evidence (p. 6). As he admits, IE **ĭ* and **ī* fell together in Albanian generally, and were lost in final position. The final *-ë* in *shemërë* is on the analogy of the accusative (Jokl, p. 8).

To term Lith. *martì* a stem in *-*tī*, as does Pokorny, is to beg the question; there is no Lithuanian suffix *-tī/tyā-*. The only other common form in Lithuanian with nom. sg. fem. *-ì* is *patì* 'wife', remade from *patni* (Skt. *pátnī*, Gk. πότνια) on the analogy of the masc. *patìs*, cf. OLith. *wieschpatni*. A *viešnì* 'female guest' beside regular (remade) *viešnẽ* is also attested,[6] which would be another archaic feminine in *-*nī*-, cf. masc.

[1] Pokorny, *IEW*, 739, suggests *$m_e r\breve{\bar{\imath}}$-, and Specht, *KZ* 62.217 (1935) prefers a base **marĭ-*, but with little formal justification offered.

[2] Similar forms exist in Cornish and Breton. It is unnecessary to assume a **merkkā* with expressive gemination (Pokorny), as *-rx-*, W. *-rch-*, is the normal Brittonic reflex of the group *-*rk*-.

[3] "Le couple *senex-senātus* et le 'suffixe' *-k-*," *BSL* 51.42–56 (1955); cf. also "Some cases of *-k-/-w-* alternation in Indo-European," *Word* 12.1–6 (1956).

[4] See Kuryłowicz, *L'Accentuation des langues indo-européennes* 45–6 (Kraków, 1952).

[5] *Linguistisch-kulturhistorische Untersuchungen aus dem Bereiche des Albanischen* 4–6 (Berlin and Leipzig, 1923).

[6] Leskien, *Litauisches Lesebuch* 158 (Leipzig, 1919) and Fraenkel, *KZ* 50.214 (1922).

viešis 'guest'. It is conceivable that *marti* itself was remade from an earlier **mort-nī-*, with the base a root noun of the shape **mórt-*, **mr̥t-é/ós*,[7] but this cannot be demonstrated.

The confrontation of this series of cognates of *marītus* shows clearly that that we have to deal with a radical **mer-(mor-)* with several extensions (Benveniste's 'élargissements'): **mer-gʷ-*, **mer-k-*, **mer-t-*, and **mer-y-*. The absence of characteristic alternations in form, *-ek-/-k- -et-/-t-* etc., shows that these elements are not suffixes but 'élargissements' (*Origines* 148 et passim). In these terms we may either assume an unsuffixed root **mer-* with various extensions, or perhaps more likely a root **Hem-* suffixed by *-er-/-r-*, in state II **Hmer-* before extension. There is unfortunately no evidence either for the radical **Hem-* or for the state I **Hemr-*, which may be attributed in the one case to the great number of quasi-homophones in *H_x*em-*, and in the other to the unusual root-final cluster *-mr-*.[8]

The form **mer-y-* is of particular interest for the purposes of this paper, since it underlies Lat. *marītus*. For the formal structure, as well as the fluctuation in gender and sex among the historical forms, indicates that originally **me/ory-* was a radical neuter in *-y-* extension (nom. sg. n. **mori*), the type *H_2*ewy-* 'sheep', *H_3*ewy-* 'bird', the existence of which has been convincingly demonstrated by Benveniste.[9] The original neuter denoted in all likelihood a young person of marriageable age of either sex;[10] the association with marriage is quite prominent among the cognate forms, sometimes even where the lexical meaning does not involve this, as in the case of Lith. *mergà* 'girl' beside the compound *mer̃gvakaris* 'der Hochzeitsabend, an dem die Gespielinnen und Freundinnen der Braut zusammenkommen, die Braut schmücken mit dem Rautenkranz, und dabei bestimmte Lieder singen' (Leskien). In Indo-Iranian this neuter was thematized to a masculine; in the European languages the transference was to the feminine. I postulate an Italic or Proto-Latin feminine **maris*,[11] Brit. Kelt. **moris*, with the same addition of *-s* as in **awi* > Lat. *auis* f. 'bird' and **owi* > OIr. *ói* (f.) 'ewe'. One may note the striking parallelism in the following three radical and thematized bases illustrating the formation:

[7] Compare the discussion in Kuryłowicz, *L'Apophonie en indo-européen* 48–58 (Wrocław, 1956). The *-t-* of **mort-/mr̥t-* might also be analysed as an enlargement to a light base in final resonant, the Sanskrit type *-kr̥-t-*, provided this is to be viewed as inherited.

[8] Compare the parallel extended state II *H_2*mel-g-* (Gk. ἀμέλγω), where no state I *H_2*eml-* is found.

[9] *Origines de la formation des noms en indo-européen* 60–1, 72ff., and 155 (Paris 1935).

[10] The neuter gender in this lexeme is perhaps to be correlated with the neuter gender characteristic of the word for 'child' in many Indo-European languages, e.g. Gk. τέκνον, ORuss. *dětja*, OE *cild*, OHG *kind*. It should be remembered that we do not know exactly what constituted marriageable age among the primitive Indo-European speaking peoples.

[11] The appearance of the vowel *a* before resonant under certain conditions is an analogical generalization, characteristic of the southern group of European languages, and particularly frequent in Italic. For the general theory and detailed illustrations see Kuryłowicz, *L'Apophonie en i.-e.* 171ff.

móry*- n. 'young person' (moris* f.)	*H_3*ówy*- n. 'sheep' (**owis* f.)	**móry*- n. 'sea'
Lat. **maris*, Brit. **moris*	OIr. *ói*	Lat. *mare* n., OIr. *muir*
**móry-o-*	*H_3*ówy-o-*	**móry-o-*
Skt. *márya-*	Skt. *ávya-*	OCS *morje*

The remaining question is that of the suffix by which *marītus* was formed from **maris*. As has long been recognized, both the form and the semantic parallels (on which see further below) indicate that this is the secondary suffix *-*tó*- to nominal stems with the sense 'provided with, furnished with' or the like.[12] The difference between my own and earlier analyses hinges upon a morphophonemic fact about this suffix which has been insufficiently appreciated until quite recently. For in all the instances of this suffix in all the cognate languages exhibiting it, the stem vowel of a nominal vocalic base appears as lengthened before the *-*tó*-.[13] Thus an *o*-stem gives -*óto*-, a *u*-stem -*ūto*-, and an *i*-stem -*īto*-. Compare the following: *o*-stems Gk. ἀπύργωτος < πύργος, 'tower', Lith. *ragúotas* < *rãgas* 'horn', OCS *krilatŭ* < *krilo* 'wing'; *u*-stems Gk. ἀδάκρῡτος < δάκρυ 'tear', Lat. *uerūtus* < *uerŭ*'spit'; *i*-stems Gk. ἀδήριτος < δῆρις 'strife', Lith. *akýtas* < *akìs* 'eye', OCS *mastitŭ* < *mastĭ* 'fat', and the whole Latin series *aurītus* < *auris*, *pellītus* < *pellis*, *crīnītus* < *crīnis*, *turrītus* < *turris*, *ratītus* < *ratis*, *pēnītus* < *pēnis*,[14] and *corbīta* < *corbis*. It is thus absolutely regular for the form **maris* suffixed by *-*tó*- to appear as *marītus*. The heretofore postulated base **marī*- is a purely gratuitous and ad hoc assumption to account for the long vowel in *marītus*; this long vowel may be better explained on functional and morphological grounds, and the **marī*- for which there is not a scrap of evidence may be discarded.

By this analysis of its formation *marītus* enters into a clear semantic pattern in the Indo-European languages. In OCS *ženatŭ*, Goth. *unqeniþs*, and OIcel. *ūkvǣndr*, '(un-)married' (of a man!) is expressed by the suffixation of *-*tó*- to a noun meaning 'woman' or 'wife'. It is not of importance whether the Germanic forms are taken as participles (cf. OIcel. *kvǣna* 'marry'), since the primary and secondary *-*tó*- adjectives are not to be differentiated in Germanic. Germ. *unbeweibt*, though clearly deverbative, illustrates the formation equally well from the semantic point of view. Lat. *marītus* is precisely '(he) who has a young woman'. One may compare the converse in the Aeschylean ἀταύρωτος 'unwedded (of a woman)', formed from ταῦρος 'bull' by the same

[12] The value of this suffix in general, both as primary and as secondary, has been defined by Benveniste as "l'accomplissement de la notion dans l'objet". See his *Noms d'agent et noms d'action en indo-européen* 167–8 (Paris, 1948).

[13] A convincing explanation of this phenomenon of antesuffixal lengthening in certain morphological categories in Indo-European (including secondary *-*tó*-) has been given by Kuryłowicz in *L'Apophonie en i.-e.* 125ff.

[14] Penita offa: absegmen carnis cum coda (Naevius ap. Fest.)

morphological means. This characteristic pattern was evidently not considered by Ernout-Meillet, *DEL*, who state: "La spécialisation dans le sens de 'mari' semble indiquer une influence secondaire de *mās*", for in fact the development in Latin was in the opposite direction; *marītus* originally applied only to the male, and the feminine *marīta* is a much later creation. There is furthermore in earlier Latin no discernible association of *mās* and *marītus*. The situation in Latin where *marītus* was restricted to the male (which can alone explain its substantivation, for the *marītus* par excellence), recurs exactly in Russian, where *ženatij* is said of a man, as well as *ženit'sja* 'marry', while for a woman the adjective is *zamužnjaja* (more commonly *byt' zamužem*), and the verb 'marry' *vyjti zamuž*, all derivatives of *muž* 'husband'.

It is relatively easy to see why the Proto-Latin **maris* should have disappeared with only a secondary derivative as trace. It is probable that **maris* 'young woman' and **mari* 'sea', even though homophonous except in nominative and accusative,[15] could have coexisted with little opportunity for confusion. Their semantic areas are quite disparate, and an obvious parallel in Latin is the pair *mare* 'sea' and *mās* 'male' in the classical period (with the additional difference of the ablatives singular), as well as Fr. *mère* and *mer*. But after the working of rhotacism the stem of *mās* became *mar-*, and the almost complete homophony ensuing between 'male' and 'young woman', where contexts could be identical, would have created a serious embarrassment in the language. It seems not implausible to suggest that **maris* was for this reason simply dropped from usage in favor of such terms as *uirgō* and *mulier*,[16] which imply as well a somewhat differing conceptualization of the categories of female society.[17]

HARVARD UNIVERSITY

[15] One may note, however, that in Brittonic where the same pair had the stem **mori-*, 'young woman' was differentiated from 'sea' by the addition of the suffix *-gnā*.

[16] Both of these are peculiar to Latin, and without satisfactory etymology. As pointed out in *DEL* s.v. *uirgō*, there is no Indo-European word for 'virgin'.

[17] It is perhaps legitimate to see in certain acceptations of *puella* and especially of the borrowing *nympha* in the lyric and elegiac poets, a recreating of the old Proto-Latin concept of the **maris*.